LAW FOR HOUSING MANAGERS

LAW FOR HOUSING MANAGERS

TOM HARRISON B.A. (Law) Grad. Cert. Ed.
Senior Lecturer in Law

Faculty of Administrative and
Business Studies
New College, Durham

BUSINESS EDUCATION PUBLISHERS

Published in Great Britain by
Business Education Publishers
Leighton House, 17 Vine Place
Sunderland, Tyne and Wear

First published August 1982

ISBN 0-907679-12-9

Printed in Great Britain by
City Printers, Chester-le-Street, County Durham.

To my wife Glyn
with all my love

Preface

This book represents an attempt to examine in straightforward language the main areas of law relevant to housing management. I must stress from the outset that the book is intended as an introductory text only and contains a condensed version of the law.

The fundamental aim of the book is to achieve a comprehensive coverage of the syllabus specified by the Institute of Housing for Legal Studies I II and II of their professional examinations. It is also intended to be of use to students of professional bodies such as Chartered Surveyors, Chartered Auctioneers, Chartered Land agents, Architects and also those studying for Housing Diplomas. In addition I hope the book will provide a practical guide for housing administrators to relevant aspects of contract, land, landlord and tenant, housing and employment law. If I have succeeded in rendering intelligible some of the intricacies of the workings of the English legal system and the areas of substantive law covered, then the book will have achieved one of its basic objectives.

Acknowledgements

I should like to express my gratitude to all those who have been concerned in the writing and publication of this book, in particular Paul Callaghan, Senior Lecturer in Economics at New College Durham, whose careful and perceptive editing has hopefully rid the book of its grosser obscurities. Also Jim Underwood, Director of the Two Castles Housing Society, a man of wide public sector housing experience who read the manuscript and gave me valuable help and encouragement. My sincere thanks go out to others who have given assistance including Bernard Callaghan, Mike Williams, John Ellison, John Hall, Glenn Robison, Allen, Don, Mac and Len and all at City Printers, Chester-le-Street and Janet McKibbin who produced an immaculate typescript from my messy handwriting. Also may I express my gratitude to Durham City Council and North Tyneside Metropolitan Borough Council who kindly gave me permission to reproduce some of the documentation included in the appendices. The responsibility for any errors that appear is entirely my own.

Durham   Tom Harrison
August, 1982.

CONTENTS

Part 3 Landholding

Part 4 Liability

Part 5   Statutory Protection

Part 6 Housing Control and Management

Part 7 Employment Law

Chapter 18 The Creation of the Contract of Employment

Chapter 19 Termination of Employment

Chapter 20 Discrimination

Table of Statutes

xi

Table of Cases

Honeywill v. Larkin Brothers *(1934)* 1 K.B. 191., **155**
Hopwood v. Cannock Chase District Council *(1975)* 1 W.L.R. 373; *(1975)* 1 All. E.R. 796., **161**
Horner v. Horner *(1982)* 2 W.L.R. 914., **123**
Household Fire Insurance Co. v. Grant (1879), 4 Ex.D. 216., **54**
Hughes v. Metropolitan Railway Co. (1877) 2 App. Cas. 439., **74**
Hyde's Case 1886, **111**
Hyde v. Wrench (1840), 3 Beav. 334., **52**

Inland Revenue Commissioners v. Hinchy *(1960)* A.C. 748; *(1960)* 2 W.L.R. 448; *(1960)* 1 All. E.R. 505., **17**
Innes v. Wylie (1844) 1 Car. & Kir. 257., **150**
Isle of Wight Tourist Board v. Coombes *(1976)* I.R.L.R. 413., **317**

Joel v. Swaddle *(1957)* 1 W.L.R. 1094; *(1957)* 3 All. E.R. 325., **196**
Jones v. Vernon's Pools Ltd. *(1938)* 2 All. E.R. 626., **46**

Kelsen v. Imperial Tobacco Co. Ltd. *(1957)* 2 Q.B. 334; *(1957)* 2 W.L.R. 1007; *(1957)* 2 All. E.R. 343., **151**
Kennaway v. Thompson and Another *(1980)* 3 W.L.R. 361 *(1980)* 3 All. E.R. 329., **175, 178**
Krell v. Henry *(1903)* 2 K.B. 740., **77**

Ex-parte Ladbroke Group (1969) 119 New L.J. 225., **36**
Lally v. Kensington & Chelsea Royal Borough, The Times March 27 1980., **255**
Lambeth BC v. Stubbs 1980 J.P.L. 517., **170**
Latimer v. AEC *(1952)* 2 Q.B. 701; *(1953)* A.C. 643; *(1953)* 3 W.L.R. 259; *(1953)* 2 All. E.R. 449., **147, 307**
Lee v. K. Cater Ltd. *(1949)* 1 K.G. 85; *(1948)* 2 All. E.R. 690., **130**
Lee-Parker v. Izzet *(1971)* 3 All. E.R. 1099., **159**
Lewis v. North Devon DC *(1981)* 1 All. E.R. 27., **254**
Lewis v. Weldcrest Ltd. *(1978)* 1 W.L.R. 1107; *(1978)* 3 All. E.R. 1226., **187**
Lightcliffe & District Cricket and Lawn Tennis Club v. Walton (1978) 245 E.G.E. 93., **197**
Liverpool City Council v. Irwin *(1977)* A.C. 239., **160**
Lloyd v. Sadler *(1978)* 2 All. E.R. 529; *(1978)* Q.B. 774; *(1978)* 2 W.L.R. 721., **104**
Lurcott v. Wakely *(1911)* 1 K.B. 905., **158**

Re McArdle *(1951)* Ch. 669., **57**
McCaffrey v. A. E. Jeavons & Co. Ltd. (1967) I.T.R. 636., **300, 324**
McCall v. Abelesz *(1976)* Q.B. 585; *(1976)* 2 W.L.R. 151; *(1976)* 1 All. E.R. 727., **126**
Macdonnel v. Daly *(1969)* 3 All. E.R. 851; *(1969)* 1 W.L.R. 1482., **212**
Maddison v. Alderson (1883) 8 A.C. 467., **99**
Marchant v. Charters *(1977)* 1 W.L.R. 1181; *(1977)* 3 All. E.R. 918., **104**
Marriott v. Oxford & District Co-op. Soc. Ltd. *(1970)* 1 Q.B. 186; *(1969)* 3 W.L.R. 984; *(1969)* 3 All. E.R. 1126., **301**

Meering v. Graham White (Aviation) (1919) 122 L.T. 44., **150**
Miller v. Jackson *(1977)* Q.B. 966; *(1977)* 3 W.L.R. 20; *(1977)* 3 All. E.R. 338., **176, 178**
Ministry of Defence v. Jeremiah *(1980)* Q.B. 87; *(1979)* 3 W.L.R. 857; *(1979)* 3 All. E.R. 833., **334**
Morrison v. Jacobs *(1945)* K.B. 577., **107**
Morrison Holdings Ltd. v. Manders Property (Wolverhampton) Ltd. *(1976)* 1 W.L.R. 533; *(1976)* 2 All. E.R. 205., **186**
Morton Sundour Fabrics v. Shaw (1967) 2. K.I.R.1., **324**
E. Moss Ltd. v. Brown *(1946)* 2 All. E.R. 557., **104**
Murrayfield Real Estate Co. v. Edinburgh Magistrates SLR XLIX 148., **18**
Mykolyshyn v. Noah *(1971)* 1 All. E.R. 48; *(1970)* 1 W.L.R. 1271., **213**

Nash v. Finlay (1901) 85 L.T. 682., **15**
Nash v. Inman *(1908)* 2 K.B. 1., **58**
Nash v. Sheen, The Times, March 13 1953., **150**
NCB v. Thorne *(1976)* 1 W.L.R. 543., **170**
New Windsor Corporation v. Mellor *(1975)* 3 All. E.R. 44; (1975) 3 W.L.R. 25., **8**
Nolan v. Dental Manufacturing Co. *(1958)* 1 W.L.R. 936; *(1958)* 2 All. E.R. 449., **309**
Northland Airliners Ltd. v. Ferranti Meters Ltd. (1970) 114 S.J. 845., **54**

Ocedar v. Slough Trading Co. *(1927)* 2 K.B. 123., **126**
O'Connor v. Swan & Edgar (1963) 107 S.J. 215., **180**
Olley v. Marlborough Court Ltd. *(1949)* 1 K.B. 532; *(1949)* 1 All. E.R. 127., **63**

Panesar v. Nestle *(1980)* I.C.R. 144., **332**
Pannett v. McGuinness Ltd. *(1972)* 2 Q.B. 599; *(1972)* 3 W.L.R. 386; *(1972)* 3 All. E.R. 137., **181**
Paradine v. Jane (1647) *(1558-1774)* All. E.R. Rep. 172., **76**
Paris v. Stephney BC *(1951)* A.C. 367; *(1951)* 1 All. E.R. 42., **146, 309**
Parker v. Clark *(1960)* 1 W.L.R. 286; *(1960)* 1 All. E.R. 93., **46**
Partridge v. Crittenden *(1968)* 1 W.L.R. 1204; *(1968)* 2 All. E.R. 421., **50**
Peake v. Automotive Products Ltd. *(1978)* Q.B. 233; *(1977)* 3 W.L.R. 853; *(1978)* 1 All. E.R. 106., **333**
Pearce v. Gardner *(1897)* 1 Q.B. 688., **98**
Performing Right Society Ltd. v. Mitchell and Booker *(1924)* 1 K.B. 762, **297**
Pembery v. Lamdin *(1940)* 2 All. E.R. 434., **158**
Pepper v. Webb *(1969)* 1 W.L.R. 514; *(1969)* 2 All. E.R. 216., **312, 314**
Pharmaceutical Society v. Boots Chemists Ltd. *(1953)* 1 Q.B. 401; *(1953)* 2 W.L.R. 427; *(1953)* 1 All. E.R. 482., **50**
Pinnels Case (1602) 5 Co. Rep. 117a., **73**
Powell v. Kempton Park Racecourse *(1899)* A.C. 143., **19**
Powell v. May *(1946)* K.B. 330, 1 All. E.R. 444., **15**
Prescott v. Birmingham Corporation *(1954)* 3 W.L.R. 990; *(1954)* 3 All. E.R. 698., **37**
Price v. Gourley Bros. *(1973)* I.R.L.R. 11., **319**
Printers & Finishers Ltd. v. Holloway *(1965)* 1 W.L.R. 1; *(1964)* 3 All. E.R. 54n., **312**

R v. Barnsley Metropolitan Borough Council Ex-parte Hook *(1976)* 1 W.L.R. 1052; *(1976)* 3 All. E.R. 452., **36**
R v. Bristol City Council Ex-parte Brown *(1979)* 3 All. E.R. 344; *(1979)* 1 W.L.R. 1437., **256**
R v. Electricity Commissioners *(1924)* 1 K.B. 171., **35**
R v. Epping (Waltham Abbey) J. J. Ex-parte Burlinson *(1948)* 1 K.B. 79., **172**
R v. Hereford Corporation Ex-parte Harrower *(1970)* 1 W.L.R. 1424; *(1970)* 3 All. E.R. 460., **67-68**
R v. London County Council, Ex-parte Corrie (1918) I.K.B. 68., **33**
R v. Northumberland Compensation Appeal Tribunal, Ex-parte Shaw *(1952)* 1 K.B. 338; *(1952)* 1 All. E.R. 122., **35**
R v. Secretary of State for the Environment Ex-parte Norwich City Council *(1982)* 2 W.L.R. 580., **248-249**
R v. Tameside Metropolitan Borough Council, Ex-parte Secretary of State for Education and Science *(1976)* 3 W.L.R. 641; *(1976)* 3 All. E.R. 665., **34**
R v. Wood (1855) 5E & B.49., **15**
Race Relations Board v. Mecca *(1976)* I.R.L.R. 15., **332**
Ramsgate Victoria Hotel v. Montefiore (1866) L.R. 1 Exch. 109., **53**
Rands v. Oldroyd *(1959)* 1 Q.B. 204; *(1958)* 3 W.L.R. 583; *(1958)* 3 All. E.R. 344., **18**
Ravenseft Properties Ltd. v. Davstone (Holdings) Ltd. *(1979)* 1 All. E.R. 929., **158**
Rawlinson v. Ames 1925 Ch. 96., **99**
Ready Mixed Concrete Ltd. v. Ministry of Pensions *(1968)* 2 Q.B. 497; *(1968)* 2 W.L.R. 775., **297**
Rhyl Urban District Council v. Rhyl Amusements Ltd. *(1959)* 1 All. E.R. 257., **61**
Robinson v. Kilvert 1889 41 Ch. D. 88., **175**
Roles v. Nathan *(1963)* 1 W.L.R. 1117; *(1963)* All. E.R. 908., **179**
Rondel v. Worsley *(1969)* 1 A.C. 191; *(1967)* 3 W.L.R. 1666; *(1967)* 3 All. E.R. 993. **40, 146**
Rose v. Plenty *(1976)* 1 W.L.R. 141; *(1976)* 1 All. E.R. 97., **154**
Rose and Frank Co. v. Crompton Bros. *(1923)* 2 K.B. 261., **47**
Routledge v. Grant (1828) 4 Bing. 653., **53**
Royal Life Saving Society v. Page 1978, The Times 2 June., **187**

Safeway Foodstores v. Morris (1980) 254 E.G. 1091., **192**
Sagar v. Ridehalgh *(1931)* 1 Ch. 310., **302**
Saif Ali v. Sydney Mitchel *(1977)* 3 W.L.R. 421., **40**
Salford City Council v. McNally *(1976)* A.C. 379., **169**
Scammell v. Ouston *(1941)* A.C. 251., **49**
Scala House v. Forbes *(1974)* Q.B. 575., **136**
Scott v. London & St. Katherine Dock Co. (1865) 3 H & C. 596., **147**
Secretary of State for Employment v. Associated Society of Locomotive Engineers and Firemen *(1972)* 2 Q.B. 455; *(1972)* 2 W.L.R. 1370; *(1972)* All. E.R. 949., **302, 311**
Re Sigsworth *(1935)* Ch. 89., **17**
Simmons v. Pizzey *(1979)* A.C. 37; *(1977)* 3 W.L.R. 1; *(1977)* 2 All. E.R. 432., **262**
Simpson v. Wells (1872) 7 Q.B. 214., **7**
Sinclair v. Neighbour *(1967)* 2 Q.B. 279; *(1967)* 2 W.L.R. 1; *(1966)* 3 All. E.R. 988., **314**
Singh v. London County Bus Services Ltd. (1976) 11 I.T.R. 131; *(1976)* I.R.L.R.176., **319**
Sirres v. Moore *(1976)* Q.B. 118; *(1974)* 3 W.L.R. 459; *(1974)* 3 All. E.R. 776., **42**
Smith v. AEK Purdy Trawlers Ltd. *(1966)* I.T.R. 508., **325**

Part 1 - The Legal System

CHAPTER 1　The Nature of Law and the Law Making Process

1.1 The Nature and Purpose of Law

The nature and purpose of law are two questions which have provided legal academics with worthy debating material throughout the development of the English legal system. While this debate is of great interest to lawyers it may not be so to those involved in housing management. The content of this section has been limited therefore to a brief examination of the traditional view of law and its purpose.

The underlying role of law is to provide the means by which conflicts in society can be resolved within the existing social, economic and political environment. The law may be described simply as a body of rules by which society functions. A more formal definition is **'the body of rules recognised and applied by the State in the administration of justice'**. In the development of civilisation, sophisticated societies have found rules of law and a legal system to administer them, necessary to achieve the following purposes:

a.　**Provide order in society.**

b.　**Provide remedies to victims of wrongful acts and the abuse of power.**

c.　**Provide the means by which organisations or individuals can enter into agreements which are enforceable under the law.**

a.　**Provide order in society** Certain acts are regarded as so serious that they offend society as a whole. They are called **criminal offences.** The criminal law has the effect of restricting an individual's total freedom in return for protecting him from the criminal acts of another. These acts range from offences against the person (such as murder or manslaughter) and offences against property (such as theft or arson). An individual who breaks the criminal law commits a wrong against the State for which he may be prosecuted in the name of the

Crown in a criminal court. If convicted of the crime he may be sentenced to some form of punishment, e.g. fines, imprisonment, community service, probation.

As far as local authorities are concerned, they are more likely to come into contact with that section of the criminal law which contains **regulatory offences.** Such offences are usually created by **Acts of Parliament (Statutes)** and often impose duties on local authorities in relation to enforcement.

Consumer Protection departments or Trading Standards departments within county councils employ trading standards officers whose function is to enforce much of the consumer legislation including:-

1. Any legislation recommended by the Director General of Fair Trading under the **Fair Trading Act 1973;**

2. Regulations made under the **Consumer Safety Act 1978;**

3. The investigation of complaints under the **Trade Descriptions Acts 1968** and **1972;**

4. The duties imposed under the **Food and Drugs Act 1955** involving the sampling of food for analysis and the investigation of direct complaints;

5. Many offences created by the **Consumer Credit Act 1974** and the **Unsolicited Goods and Services Act 1971.**

Also Environmental Health Departments and Housing Departments within local authorities have a role to play in the enforcement of the criminal law applicable to housing and the environment including:-

1. Offences created under housing legislation such as overcrowding, harassment, the payment of unlawful premiums;

2. Offences created under public health legislation such as statutory nuisances, and legislation relating to creating a clean environment such as the **Control of Pollution Act 1974.**

It should be emphasised that for many of the statutory offences, including some already mentioned, liability is said to be **strict.** This means that an offence could be committed by an individual who has not shown any guilty intention. For the more serious criminal offences it is necessary to prove the existence of:-

an actus reus (a guilty act), i.e. the accused committed the act which constitutes the offence;

a mens rea (a guilty mind), i.e. the accused committed the act intentionally, recklessly or even negligently for some crimes.

Thus to commit the crime of theft it would be necessary to prove:-

that the accused took the owner's property away; and
that the accused did so dishonestly with the intention of permanently depriving the owner of it.

For many of the regulatory offences however liability is strict and there is no need to prove that the accused had mens rea when he committed the act which constitutes the offence, e.g. the butcher who sells bad meat; the licensee who sells alcohol to the underage drinker; the employer who fails to securely fence the dangerous machine; the car owner who fails to display a tax disc; the occupier of a house in multiple occupation who fails to reply to a local authority request for information; the occupier of a house who permits it to be overcrowded.

b. **Provide remedies to victims of wrongful acts and abuse of power**
All law other than criminal law is classified as **civil law** of which there are numerous branches. The majority of rules governing the relationships which exist between individuals and also between individuals and organisations in society come within the realm of civil law. Civil law contains therefore the rules relating to:

1. the relationship between an individual and government (both central and local);

2. the acquisition and disposal of property (including land);

3. the creation of unincorporated and corporate bodies;

4.   the rights and duties of the parties to a contract and a trust;

5.   the rights and duties of the parties where an alleged civil wrong has been committed.

If a dispute arises under the civil law an individual who alleges that he has been harmed (the **plaintiff**) may sue the alleged wrongdoer (the **defendant**) in the civil courts in order to obtain a remedy (**damages**) which is in the form of monetary compensation. Under the civil law there are clearly defined acts which constitute civil wrongs. These are termed **torts**, examples of which would include where a defendant causes harm to a plaintiff by trespassing on his land; damaging his goods; negligent workmanship; interfering with the use or enjoyment of his land; giving negligent advice. The difficulty is that the same conduct which amounts to a tort may also be criminal in nature and punishable by a criminal prosecution. Thus the negligent driver who injures the pedestrian could find himself:

1.   prosecuted in the criminal courts for the crime of dangerous driving and if convicted sentenced to some form of punishment;

2.   sued in the civil courts under the tort of negligence and if found liable ordered to pay damages as compensation to the plaintiff.

c.   **Provide the means by which organisations and/or individuals can enter into agreements enforceable under the law** The third major purpose of law could be said to be to provide the means by which agreements imposing rights and duties on the parties to them, may be enforced under the law. Organisations and individuals require that, if they make agreements, they may turn to the law to require that the obligations under them will be fulfilled. This requirement is met by the law of contract, which contains the rules which are fundamental to the determination of the rights and duties of the parties in areas such as:

1.   transacting for goods;

2.   transacting for land;

3.   entering into employment;

4.   entering into marriage.

The rules relating to the formation of a contractual bargain are considered in Chapter 3. particular emphasis is gven in this book to those contracts which are of importance to those engaged in the provision and management of housing e.g. the contract for a lease, the building contract and the contract of employment.

1.2 Sources of English Law

There are two major sources of English law, the **Common Law** (case-law) and **Statute** (Acts of Parliament and delegated legislation). The rules relating to different areas of law are found by examining both statutory provisions and the judgements of cases. Some areas of law are essentially common law in nature, e.g. the law of tort and the law of contract, while others are mainly embodied in statute, e.g. housing law and criminal law. We shall see later however that if a dispute arises as to the meaning of a statutory provision it may be interpreted by the courts who may in their judgement create a **precedent** (a rule of law) as to the provision's meaning. Before considering the operation of statute and case law (precedent) it is useful first to briefly outline the contribution and origin of earlier sources of English law.

The Contribution of Custom

Custom is the oldest source of English law and in its **general form** as applicable to the whole country has been embodied within the common law of England. Any reference to custom as a source of law today means custom in its **local form,** that is when it applies to a particular area or set of individuals. It is possible however for a local custom to be upheld as part of the law if it satisfies certain criteria. These are that the custom is reasonable, certain, has continued without interruption and has existed since time immemorial. To satisfy the time immemorial criteria the custom must date back to 1189 but provided it can be shown to have existed within living memory then a presumption is raised that it has existed since 1189. This presumption can of course be **rebutted** (shown to be false).

> In *Simpson v. Wells 1872,* the customary right of running a stall which blocked the highway at an annual meeting was held not to have the force of law. Although it was shown to have been carried on since the time of Elizabeth I, the right to hold the meeting was authorised by the **Statute of Labourers of Edward III** and could not have existed before then. The presumption

of antiquity was therefore rebutted and the claim of a customary right having the force of law was held to fail.

Alternatively a successful claim was made in *New Windsor Corporation v. Mellor 1975* Here an old resident raised objection to the action of the local authority which had turned part of a village green into a car park and school playground. The Court of Appeal held that the green should not have been converted in this way as the inhabitants had a customary right which had the force of law to use the green for sports and pastimes.

The Common Law and Equity

In its modern day usage the expression 'common law' means all law other than statutory provisions. Thus common law in this sense means judge made law embodied in case decisions. The expression 'common law system' however is a reference to the type of legal system that operates in England and Wales and indeed has been adopted by countries all over the world and particularly the Commonwealth. The common law of England dates back as far as the Norman conquest and has its origins in the decisions of the royal judges who attempted to apply law which was 'common' to the whole of the country. This they did by modifying and adapting rules of Norman law, and rules contained in Saxon local custom. The development of the common law was a long process evolving over hundreds of years. This process was assisted by the practice of conferring wide powers on itinerant justices to dispense law throughout England and Wales and also the creation of specialist common law courts each with its own distinct jurisdiction, e.g. the Court of Exchequer having jurisdiction over revenue disputes, the Court of Common Pleas having jurisdiction over civil disputes, and the Court of King's Bench having jurisdiction over civil and criminal disputes.

Unfortunately the early common law suffered from a number of defects. A court action brought at common law would fail if the correct procedure was not strictly adhered to, e.g. there was some imperfection in the **writ,** the document commencing the action. This rigidity was also demonstrated by the reluctance of the common law judges to recognise certain wrongs by creating new writs or to provide alternative remedies. A prospective **litigant** could suffer injustice therefore in a number of ways. He may adopt the wrong writ, there may be no writ to cover his cause of action, or, having succeeded in his action the common law remedy of damages may prove to be unsuitable.

To overcome these problems in the thirteenth and fourteenth centuries, the practice grew up of seeking justice elsewhere. Persons with a grievance would petition the King who as the 'fountain of justice' had authority to provide a remedy. Eventually this function of hearing petitions passed to the **Lord Chancellor** who as 'the Keeper of the King's Conscience' granted relief from injustice at common law. In dispensing justice, the Lord Chancellor was not concerned with matters of form and procedure but rather truth and conscience. The popularity of this alternative source of justice led to the creation of the **Court of Chancery** headed by the Lord Chancellor and dispensing justice which became known as **Equity**. Originally equity acted as merely a supplement to the common law but conflict was inevitable. Over the centuries, there grew up in England and Wales a legal system, in which two sets of courts existed side by side, one dispensing common law and the other equity. Finally, the **Judicature Acts 1873-75** created a single system of courts with power to administer both common law and equity. The supremacy of equity was maintained by the provision that in any conflict between a rule of common law and a rule of equity the rule of equity should prevail. It would be wrong to say however that as a result of the creation of a single court system the principles of common law and equity have become merged. Rather it is the administration of the forms of law that has merged. Today common law and equity are still regarded as separate forms of law and reference is made throughout this book to legal (common law) rights and equitable rights, legal remedies and equitable remedies. We shall see that some areas of law, particularly land law, owe much of their development to the intervention of equity.

Judicial Precedent

While it is still true to say that English law has the common law as its base, over the centuries common law rules have become embodied in precedent (case decisions) and so today the expression common law and case-law are virtually synonymous and may be referred to as 'judge made' law.

'Judge made' law is found in the law reports (reports of all important cases) and, when you consider that there are well over half a million reported cases, it is not difficult to appreciate that the rules relating to many areas of law are contained in precedents. Under the **doctrine of judicial precedent,** judges when deciding cases must take into account previous past precedents in the same area of law. The superior courts form

CIVIL COURTS

Possible routes of
appeal are show
by – – – – –➤

Reference may be made
from any court to the
European court for a
ruling on European law

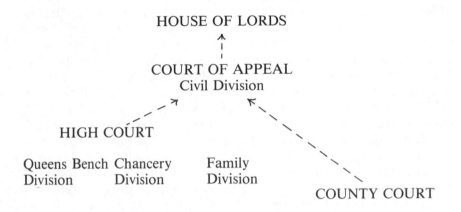

EUROPEAN COURT

HOUSE OF LORDS

COURT OF APPEAL
Civil Division

HIGH COURT

Queens Bench Chancery
Division   Division

Family
Division

COUNTY COURT

CRIMINAL COURTS

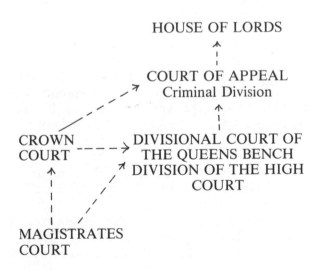

HOUSE OF LORDS

COURT OF APPEAL
Criminal Division

CROWN
COURT

DIVISIONAL COURT OF
THE QUEENS BENCH
DIVISION OF THE HIGH
COURT

MAGISTRATES
COURT

a hierarchy and, as a general rule, decisions of higher courts will bind lower courts in the hierarchy.

The binding element of a judgement When a decision is reached on a dispute before a superior court, the judges will make their decision known by making speeches (the judgement). Within a judgement, the judges will refer to numerous matters such as the relevant legal principles (from cases or statutes), a review of the facts of the case, their opinion on the relevant law, the actual decision, and the reasons for it. As far as the parties to a dispute are concerned the matter they are most concerned with is the actual decision, i.e. who has won the case. The main matter of relevance to the law, however, is the reasons for the decision. This is known under the law as the **'ratio decidendi'** (the reason for deciding). The 'ratio' forms the underlying legal principle relied on in reaching the decision and it is this that constitutes the **binding precedent.** All this means is that if a lower court in a later case is faced with a similar dispute they would be bound to apply the earlier 'ratio decidendi'.

The persuasive element of a judgement All other matters referred to in a judgement are called **'obiter dicta'** (things said by the way). The 'obiter' forms **persuasive precedent** and should be taken into account by a lower court in a later similar case but it is not bound to follow it.

Higher courts, as well as having the power to bind lower courts by their decisions, have also the power to **overrule** the past decisions of lower courts and effectively change the law. In overruling, of course, it is the legal principle, i.e. the 'ratio decidendi' that is changed, the previous decision of the lower court remains unaltered. Court decisions may only be altered by an appeal process. A party who has lost a case in the High Court may, if there are sufficient grounds, request the Court of Appeal to review the decision. If the Court of Appeal disagrees with the lower court's decision it has power to **reverse** it.

In 1966, the highest court of appeal, the House of Lords, announced that in future, as well as having the power to overrule the past precedents of lower courts, it intended to overrule its own past decisions where it thought right and proper. An example of this occurring is the House of Lords' decision in *British Railways Board v. Herrington 1972.* The case concerned the possible liability of an occupier of land to a child trespasser injured on the land. The House of Lords had previously laid down in *Addie v. Dumbreck 1929* the legal principle that an occupier was not responsible

11

under the law for injuries caused to a mere trespasser on his land. In attempting to reflect society's present-day attitude to the question, the court in 1972 decided to overrule the legal principle in *Addie v. Dumbreck* and conclude that an occupier may be responsible under the law in some cases for injuries caused to a trespasser on his land.

Statute and Delegated Legislation

Today, the primary source of law is that passed by Parliament in the form of Statutes. This means that a new statute will have the effect of overruling any existing custom, judicial precedent or earlier Act of Parliament with which it is in conflict. Although individual members of Parliament occasionally attempt to initiate legislation through **private members bills,** most legislation that is passed by Parliament is government sponsored through **government bills.** As well as having different sponsors, bills may be of two types:-

1. **Public Bills** which relate to the government's public policy and are of general application, e.g. **The Employment Act 1980, The Housing Act 1980;**

2. **Private Bills** which are only of application to the specific individual or organisation referred to and usually involve conferring legal powers, e.g. **The British Railways Act 1968, The Glamorgan Act 1976.**

To be enacted and become part of the law, a bill must pass through both Houses of Parliament and receive the Royal Assent. Basically, the procedure in both Houses is similar and involves the following stages which are briefly:-

Introduction of the Bill - by presentation of the bill in either House;
First Reading - the clerk of the house reads out the short title of the bill;
Second Reading - an important stage where the major proposals of the bill are debated followed by a vote;
Committee Stage - here the bill's proposals are examined in more detail by a Standing Committee or, for an important bill, a committee of the whole House. Amendments to the bill are suggested, debated and voted upon;

Report Stage - the committee reports back to the House and the amended bill is reconsidered;

Third Reading - following a final debate on the major proposals of the bill a further vote is taken.

Having passed through these stages in one House, the bill is transferred to the other House where it will go through a similar procedure, and then receive the **Royal Assent** (a formality) and so become an Act of Parliament.

The expression **'Consolidating Act'** is used to describe a statute which gathers together several Acts on one topic and re-enacts them in the same Act, e.g. **The Rent Act 1977.** A **Codifying Statute** is one which has the effect of enacting the whole law on a particular subject including law that was previously embodied in precedent, e.g. **The Sale of Goods Act 1979.**

Delegated Legislation

You would have the wrong impression if you thought that Parliament itself had sufficient machinery to enact all the statutory provisions necessary to keep pace with the changing society in which we live. Today, Acts of Parliament often only contain the framework of rules, and within the Statute power is delegated to other bodies (e.g. Ministers, statutory bodies) to fill in the detail by making regulations. Such regulations made by Ministers are called **Statutory Instruments** and must be submitted to Parliament for approval. In addition, there is a Select Committee on Statutory Instruments with the function of reviewing all statutory instruments to ensure that there is no abuse of power. In some cases, the public statute itself will create the body to which it delegates law making power. Thus, under the **Health and Safety at Work Act 1974,** the Health and Safety Commission was created with power delegated to it to make detailed regulations. Unlike public legislation, delegated legislation is also subject to the scrutiny of the courts who may determine its validity. It is proposed to examine one form of delegated law making power in some detail. It is the widespread use by local authorities of by-law making powers.

By-laws

General power is conferred on district councils and London boroughs to make by-laws for good rule and government and the suppression of nuisances under **s.235 Local Government Act 1972.** This general power gives local authorities a wide choice of the number of local offences they can create relating to such matters as:-

    i.   Music near churches or hospitals;
    ii.   Dangerous games in the streets;
    iii. The fouling of footpaths by dogs;
    iv. Cycling on the footpaths;
    v.   Indecent language;
    vi. Nuisances contrary to public decency.

Specific by-law making powers are conferred on local authorities by numerous statutes for instance the **Public Health Act 1936** in relation to common lodging houses, the **Housing Act 1957** in relation to the management, use and regulation of houses provided by local authorities and also relating to underground rooms and the **Small Holdings and Allotments Act 1908** in relation to letting.

There are two main limitations on the by-law making powers of local authorities:

    1.   All by-laws require confirmation by the confirming authority who is the Secretary of State; and
    2.   If challenged as invalid, a by-law must satisfy the court's scrutiny.

1.   **Confirming Authority** (Secretary of State) There is a strict procedure that a local authority must adhere to in exercising its by-law making powers. Notice of intention to submit the by-law for confirmation must be published, after which it is submitted to the confirming authority who will both determine whether the by-law is necessary and also decide whether the by-law is likely to satisfy judicial scrutiny. In practice an authority may adopt model by-laws issued by central government. An authority wishing to make by-laws in relation to common lodging houses under **s.240 Public Health Act 1936** may therefore adopt model by-laws issued by the Department of Health and Social Security and contained in **The Model By-law Series III (1938).**

2.   **Judicial Scrutiny** In the case of public statutes we have already stated that the courts have no power to question their validity and the courts' only role is to discover the meaning of the Act's provisions through

the process of statutory interpretation. As far as by-laws are concerned, however, as a form of delegated legislation, the courts have developed a number of rules so that their validity may be tested. To be valid therefore all by-laws must not be any of the following:

i.   **Ultra Vires** (beyond the powers) In exercising by-law making powers a local authority must ensure that the strict limits of the power given by the statute are not exceeded.

In *R v. Wood 1855,* the **Public Health Act 1848** conferred power on boards of health to make by-laws relating to the removal by an occupier of dust, ashes, rubbish, and soil. A by-law made by a board requiring the occupier to remove snow was held to be invalid as ultra vires the enabling power.

ii. **Inconsistent with the General Law** If a by-law attempts to permit what a public statute forbids or forbid what a public statute permits, it may be declared invalid as contrary to the general law.

In *Powell v. May 1946* a local authority made a by-law to prohibit betting in a public place despite the **Betting and Lotteries Act 1934** allowing such betting in certain circumstances. The by-law was held to be invalid as contrary to the general law.

iii. **Uncertain** To be valid, a by-law must be positive and unambiguous in its terms. In *Nash v. Finlay, 1901,* a by-law provided that "no persons shall wilfully annoy passengers in the street". It was held to be void on the grounds of uncertainty.

iv. **Unreasonable** While the attitude of the courts is that a by-law should be supported if possible, they will nevertheless declare one invalid if it is obviously unjust in its operation, demonstrates bad faith, or was shown to involve an oppressive interference with individual rights. The ground of unreasonableness was relied on in the following case.

Burnley Borough Council v. England and others 1977. Here the local authority had infuriated dog owners by introducing a by-law to prohibit the entry of dogs (except guide dogs) into its public parks and pleasure grounds. The validity of the by-law was challenged on the ground of unreasonableness in its operation. This challenge was rejected by the court who felt that the by-law was not discriminatory in nature.

The relevance of the above judicial tests to contemporary by-laws was questioned by Ld. Denning, M.R. in the recent case of *Cinnamond v. British Airports Authority 1980.* In determining the validity of modern by-laws he said that a different approach should be adopted. "If the by-law is of such a nature that something of this kind is necessary or desirable ...then the courts should endeavour to interpret the by-law so as to render it valid rather than invalid. If it is drafted in words which on a strict interpretation may be said to be too wide or too uncertain or to be unreasonable then the court - so long as the words permit it - should discard the strict interpretation and interpret them with any reasonable implications or qualifications which may be necessary so as to produce a just and proper result."

1.3 Statutory Interpretation

The role of the courts in relation to Statute is an interpretative one. This task may be simply defined as one of giving a meaning to statutory provisions which is in accord with Parliament's intention when the statute was given the force of law. The enormity of the task may be appreciated when you consider that the courts are restricted under the law to a consideration of the language of the statute in isolation in deciding its effect. Statutory rules are designed to apply to factual situations and it is the role of the courts to decide whether the factual situation before them is one envisaged by Parliament when it made the rule. Problems also arise when the courts are faced with ambiguous statutory rules arising from poor or unclear wording or insufficient examination in Parliament. In carrying out their function as interpreters of rules, the courts may adopt various approaches to give them guidance:

The Literal Rule approach In adopting this approach the courts would say that Parliament's intention is to be found in the everyday literal meaning of the language of the Statute. Thus, if the words of a rule have one clear meaning, that is the meaning to be adopted. Of course, the difficulty arises where words have more than one clear meaning. If the courts adopt a purely literal interpretation of an ambiguous rule, they may fail to achieve Parliament's intention and it could lead to injustice.

In *Inland Revenue Commissioners v. Hinchy 1960,* the House of Lords was called on to interpret a provision of the **Income Taxes Act 1952** which stated that if a taxpayer submitted a false return, a fine of treble the tax payable under the Act plus a fixed sum of £20 should be imposed. The defendant having submitted a false return under the Act was liable to pay the fine. The difficulty facing the court was in determining whether the fine should be treble the defendant's total tax bill for the year or treble the undisclosed amount. The court held that the provision, although obviously wrongly drafted, had one unambiguous meaning and fined the defendant treble his total tax bill. In fact of course, Parliament's intention was to impose a fine of three times the undisclosed amount and because of this decision Parliament was moved to amend this Statute by a Repealing Act.

The Golden Rule approach Basically, adopting this approach, if the language of the statute is capable of more than one literal meaning, the most reasonable should be interpreted which is thought most in line with Parliament's intention. Under the golden rule, an Act therefore should be interpreted so as to avoid any absurdity.

In *Re Sigsworth 1935,* the court adopted the golden rule to avoid a possible absurdity. Here a son, having murdered his mother, claimed to be entitled to her property as her sole surviving child under the **Administration of Estates Act 1925.** The court held that he could not inherit, applying the general principle that no one should profit from their own crimes. This was to limit the effect of the Act in this case.

The Mischief Rule approach Here the courts discover the meaning of a statutory provision by considering the 'mischief' that the rule was designed to remedy. This involves looking beyond the statute at the state of affairs that preceeded it.

A good example of this approach being adopted was the case of *Smith v. Hughes 1960.* Here the court was called on to interpret the **Street Offences Act 1959** which had created the offence of soliciting in a street or public place. The court had to decide whether the Act applied to two ladies of questionable virtue who had been soliciting by gesturing from a window of a private flat. The court held, after deciding that the object of the Act was to prevent passers-by in the street being molested or solicited, that an offence had been committed.

A recent example of the application of the mischief rule occured in *Chorley BC v. Barrat Development (North Western) Ltd. 1979.* The case arose out of an interpretation of **s.5 Housing Act 1957.** Under this section, back to back houses intended to be used as dwellings for the working classes are deemed to be unfit for human habitation. An attempt at defining back to back houses had been made by Ld. Guthrie in *Murrayfield Real Estate Co. v. Edinburgh Magistrates 1949* when he said that "Back to back houses are houses facing opposite ways and with one common back wall".

In *Chorley BC v. Barrat Development (North Western) Ltd. 1979,* the High Court was called on to consider whether four new semi-detached houses sharing a common back wall built in a block with two front doors at the front and two at the rear were covered by s.5. The court concluded that they were not, holding that:-

1. s.5 was intended to apply to a terrace of houses rather than a block of four semi-detached properties.

2. The properties in question were not reserved for the working classes which in this context should be interpreted as being linked with disadvantaged groups.

3. Considering the mischief that s.5 was intended to remedy, that of back to back terraced houses with no through ventilation, as there was no lack of ventilation here the section was held to be inapplicable.

The three above rules are examples of the major approaches which may be adopted by the judges when faced with the task of interpreting statutory provisions. In addition, there are a number of minor rules and statutory presumptions which may be adopted. One such rule is referred to as the **"ejusdem generis"** (of the same kind) rule. This is used where general words are used in a statutory provision and immediately preceded by specific words. The rule is that in such a case the general words are to be confined to a meaning (ejusdem generis) of the same kind as the specific words.

18

In *Powell v. Kempton Park Racecourse 1899,* the question arose as to whether Tattersall's ring at Kempton Park Racecourse was an "other place" for the purposes of the **Betting Act 1853.** The relevant statutory provision prohibited the keeping of a 'house, room, office or other place' for betting with persons resorting thereto. The court applied the ejusdem generis rule deciding that 'or other place' referred to a building or at least covered accommodation and did not therefore include Tattersall's ring.

To sum up a good example of the discretionary nature of this interpretative role of the courts is provided by the case of *Rands v. Oldroyd 1959.* Here the court was called in to consider **s.76 Local Government Act 1933** (now included as **s.94 Local Government Act 1972)** which states that if a council member has a pecuniary interest, direct or indirect, in any contract or proposed contract or other matter and is present at the meeting when it is discussed, he must disclose the fact and refrain from discussion and voting.   The case concerned R, a building contractor and local authority member, who had resolved not to tender in future for council building contracts. Subsequently a motion came before the council that in cases where public tenders were invited for work, the borough engineer should tender on behalf of his department and where necessary the direct labour force should be increased. An amendment to delete that part of the motion dealing with an increase in the labour force succeeded, R voting for the amendment. The question before the court was whether R had an interest which he should have declared and therefore not voted. In support of R it was argued that the words 'or other matter' in the section should be interpreted 'ejusdem generis' with 'contract or proposed contract' and confined to meaning a specified transaction under discussion. Surprisingly this argument was rejected, the court deciding that bearing in mind the mischief aimed at by this section (the possibility of corruption) the words 'or other matter' should be read in a very general way and included the matter under discussion. Interestingly, the fact that this section of the **Local Government Act 1933** was inserted unaltered in the **Local Government Act 1972** demonstrates that Parliament's intention had been found in this case.

CHAPTER 2 The Machinery for Resolving Disputes

In this Chapter it is proposed to examine the machinery that exists for resolving disputes in the English legal system. Three distinct areas will be considered all of which have relevance for those involved in housing management. These are civil disputes, criminal disputes and those termed as administrative disputes.

2.1 Civil Disputes

It should be stressed from the outset that the majority of civil disputes between organisations and/or individuals are settled by the parties involved without resorting to an independent agency such as the courts or a tribunal. The parties to a dispute may be able to reach an amicable settlement themselves or with the aid of the solicitors who represent them. It is the duty of the legal profession to advise their clients as to the benefit of an 'out of court' settlement even with compromise rather than face the prospect of litigation. The reason for this is time and risk of high cost in pursuing a legal action and unfortunately it is this prospect which may deter even an individual with a just cause. As a general rule the legal costs of suing are met by the party who loses the action but the court has a discretion on this matter. However where one party to an action is claiming a sum of less than £500 the matter is automatically referred to arbitration by the court registrar except in certain circumstances. In such cases where a referall is made, both parties are required to bear their own costs although a successful plaintiff can recover the court fee and a nominal amount in respect of solicitor's costs.

Legal Aid and Advice

With the aim of promoting a fairer system of legal redress depending upon a just cause rather than financial backing, a legal aid scheme exists to give assistance to the poorer members of society. The present scheme is regulated by the **Legal Aid Act 1974** and covers both criminal and civil cases. Under it, legal costs are payable out of public funds if the applicant's financial position is such that he cannot reasonably be expected to pay for it himself. To determine an applicant's financial status involves

21

inevitable form filling to calculate his disposable income (e.g. income less income tax, rates, rent, National Insurance contributions) and his disposable capital (e.g. savings). Having calculated these figures it is then possible to determine whether the applicant qualifies for having all or a proportion of his legal costs paid out of public funds. The financial limits are not included here as they are constantly changing to keep pace with inflation but a major criticism of them is that they are set at too low a level so that only the very poor are given assistance rather than the average earners who may still find it difficult to meet the costs of legal action.

In relation to civil cases most solicitors take part in the legal advice and assistance scheme. An applicant has to make written application showing his financial position, etc., known as the green form scheme. If the applicant appears to be within the financial limits then the solicitor may do preliminary work up to the value of £40. This could involve giving advice, writing letters, etc. but certainly not representing his client in a court or tribunal. Giving immediate advice under this scheme is of immense value to a client, particularly in housing matters where there is often a need simply to confirm an individual's position under the law, e.g. in relation to security of tenure or rent control. If the client requires more than £40 worth of work or the solicitor to commence proceedings or represent him in court, authority from the Legal Aid Committee of the Law Society must be obtained. To decide this matter the committee will concern itself with two questions. Firstly, are the applicant's means within the financial limits and secondly, what are his chances of success. The committee is very concerned that public money should not be used on risky undertakings and for this reason they may grant legal aid but this may be subject to certain conditions. These conditions could include the applicant paying part of the costs, or the legal aid being limited to cover taking counsel's opinion only. There are certain matters for which legal aid will not be granted including cases of alleged libel and more recently for undefended divorces. A major shortcoming of the system of legal aid is that it is not available to a prospective litigant in a dispute before a tribunal. The increasing importance of industrial tribunals as bodies dealing with a large number of industrial disputes means that a relatively less affluent litigant will suffer under an unfair disadvantage in a case against an affluent employer who can afford skilled representation.

It is convenient at this point to also mention briefly the provisions for legal aid in criminal cases. Once again the applicant fills in a form stating his means and responsibilities. In criminal disputes, however, the criminal courts (Crown Court and Magistrates Court) have authority to grant legal aid "where it appears to the courts desirable to do so in the interests of justice". If granted it consists of "representation by a solicitor and counsel assigned by the court including advice on the presentation of that person's case for those proceedings". Even where legal aid is granted the court still has an overall discretion to require the defendant to contribute towards the costs of the case (even if acquitted) if it is just and equitable in the circumstances.

Arbitration

It is becoming an increasing practice for the parties to a transaction to provide by the terms of their contract that any dispute relating to the transaction should be referred to an independent **arbitrator** rather than the ordinary courts. This practice has obvious advantages of speed, less cost, and no publicity and also enables the dispute to be resolved by specialists skilled in the area of the dispute. An arbitrator may be specifically named in the contract or alternatively the machinery by which he may be appointed may be set out. Arbitration clauses are usually found in standard form contracts (i.e. contracts set out in writing in standard form) such as building contracts (see Chapter 4) or they may be expressly inserted into a contract voluntarily by agreement between the parties. In some cases the parties have no choice but to submit a dispute to arbitration. **The Agricultural Holdings Act 1948** (see Chapter 11) requires certain disputes concerning agricultural tenancies to be submitted to arbitration. The reason for this is that such disputes may involve complex points of law where the services of a legally qualified arbitrator are required who is often also a qualified surveyor.

The law relating to arbitration agreements is contained in the common law and the **Arbitration Act 1950** as amended by the **Arbitration Act 1979.** To be legally valid they must be in writing and stamped in accordance with the **Stamp Act 1891.** They are also subject to the courts supervision in relation to the conduct of the arbitration. If a dispute arises it is the duty of the appointed arbitrator to fix a hearing which he will do after defining the dispute. The procedure adopted is usually similar to a civil trial but it is held in private. The rules of evidence and incidentally the rules of natural justice, (which will be considered later in this chapter) are applicable to the hearing and difficult points of law may be referred to the High Court for determination. After hearing the evidence the arbitrator will make an award and also decide how the costs are to be paid. The **Arbitration Act 1979** confers a right of appeal to the High Court on a question of law arising from the award and the court may vary, confirm or set aside the award.

The Civil Courts

The court system in England and Wales is organised in a hierarchy so that the minor disputes are dealt with by the courts at the lowest level of the the hierarchy whereas more serious matters are dealt with in higher courts. In civil matters the seriousness of a dispute is generally related to the sum of money or claimed damages, or the value of property involved, and the jurisdiction of the courts is determined accordingly.

The County Court

The majority of civil disputes are dealt with by the county courts created by the **Courts Act 1846.** Their main function is to act as local courts dealing with civil disputes relating to small claims. At the present time the country is divided into districts which are arranged into fifty-four circuits. Each circuit has one or more circuit judges assigned to it and the number of courts throughout England and Wales is in excess of four-hundred. Circuit judges are a creation of the **Courts Act 1971** and are appointed from barristers of at least ten years standing. The administrative work of County Courts is carried on by a **Registrar** who is a civil servant and must be a solicitor of seven years standing. Registrars also have jurisdiction to try cases where the amount claimed is less than £500. The majority of civil disputes which lead to court action are now heard in the County Courts as their jurisdiction has been extended to cover such matters as cases in contract and tort up to a limit of £5,000, housing and landlord and tenant disputes, hire purchase, undefended divorces, many employment disputes, bankruptcy and the winding up of small companies.

As County Courts fulfil such an important role in the settling of housing, landlord and tenant disputes and matrimonial disputes it is proposed to set out their precise jurisdiction in some depth. The most important matters they deal with are:-

1.   Actions in contract and tort where the sum claimed does not exceed £5,000 (no limit if both parties agree);

2. Matters which are equitable in nature where the amount involved does not exceed £30,000, e.g. trusts, mortgages and dissolution of partnerships;

3. Petitions in relation to bankruptcy and the winding up of companies with a paid up share capital not exceeding £120,000 (limited to certain county courts outside London);

4. Under the **Matrimonial Causes Act 1967** every matrimonial cause, e.g. divorce, nullity of marriage, must be commenced in the County Court and if not contested, heard there. Otherwise it must be transferred to the High Court;

5. Actions arising from disputes regarding the grant of probate or letters of administration where the estate of the deceased is less than £15,000;

6. Actions concerning title to land and actions for the recovery of possession of land where the net annual value for rating does not exceed £2,000. Also the **Rent Act 1977,** the **Landlord and Tenant Act 1954** and the **Housing Act 1980** all confer jurisdiction on the County Courts to determine applications for possession orders on the grounds specified in the legislation;

7. The County Court is referred to throughout this book as the court to which an aggrieved person has statutory right of appeal in all manner of housing matters including:-

   i. the exercise by a housing authority of powers under the **Housing Acts 1957, 1969, 1974 and 1980** in relation to unfitness and disrepair and the compulsory improvement of property;

   ii. the exercise by a housing authority of powers under the **Housing Acts 1961, 1969, 1974 and 1980** in relation to the control and supervision of multi-occupied property.

The jurisdiction of County Courts is also limited to their locality so that actions must normally be commenced in the court for the district in which the defendant resides or carries on business, or in the court for the district in which the cause of action arises. The importance of the County Court can be seen by the fact that there are over three times as many proceedings commenced in the County Court than in all the divisions of the High Court, which deals with all other civil disputes. It should be stressed however, that only a small percentage of the numerous County Court cases that are begun ever go to full trial. This is often because when proceedings are commenced against individuals or organisations, they are more likely to back down and fulfil their obligations by repaying a debt.

In considering County Courts, some mention should also be made of the **small claims arbitration procedure** introduced by the **Administration of Justice Act 1973.** As previously stated where one party to an action is claiming a sum of less than £500, the case is automatically referred to arbitration by the court registrar. Usually the arbitrator will be the Registrar himself and he will hear the case in private and decide the dispute on the basis of statements and documents submitted by the parties without the need for legal representation. This procedure, with the minimal cost attached to it, has proved of great value to the individual, particularly in consumer disputes.

The High Court

The High Court of Justice was created by the **Judicature Acts 1873-5** and is based at the Royal Courts of Justice in London but may sit anywhere in England and Wales. It has a wide jurisdiction over civil disputes and, as a matter of convenience, is split into three divisions - **Queen's Bench, Chancery** and **Family.** Judges of the High Court are called **puisne (younger) judges,** and they are allocated to each division by the head of the English legal system, the **Lord Chancellor.**

The Queen's Bench Division This is the largest and most important division of the High Court and has jurisdiction over any civil matter not specifically allocated to the other divisions. In particular, the Queen's Bench hears contract and tort cases and has a separate Commercial court and Admiralty court within the division. The head of the division is the Lord Chief Justice and Queen's bench judges also sit in Crown courts where they hear criminal and civil cases. The court also hears appeals on matters of law from the Magistrates court and for this purpose the judges sit as Divisional courts. The Queen's Bench has supervisory control over all inferior courts and tribunals and acts as a check on the abuse of power.

The Chancery Division This division is in practice headed by the Vice Chancellor and is the smallest of the three. Its jurisdiction is related to specialist matters including company and partnership law, bankruptcy, mortgages, taxation, land and probate (disputes over wills).

The Family Division The Family Division is the most recently established part of the High Court created by the **Administration of Justice Act 1970** and is headed by the President. As its name suggests, the court is concerned with civil disputes relating to family law including divorce, nullity, legitimacy, wardship and marriage property disputes.

The Civil Appeals Courts

The majority of cases that are referred to in this book are decisions which have involved important points of law and have in some cases created precedents. In the main, these have been cases which have gone on appeal to the Court of Appeal or the House of Lords.

The Court of Appeal (Civil Division) This court is headed by the Master of the Rolls and sixteen Lords Justices of Appeal. As an individual appeal court three judges preside, hearing appeals involving questions of fact and/or law. In practice, the evidence is not reheard but rather reliance is placed on the record of the previous trial. The majority of appeals come from the High Court, County Courts and the Restrictive Practices Court. The court has power to reverse, affirm or amend the previous decision and in some cases order a retrial.

The House of Lords (Judicial Committee) As an appeal court (rather than a legislative body), the House of Lords is composed of the Lord Chancellor, who is head of the English legal system and a member of the government of the day and also the Lords of Appeal in Ordinary (Law Lords). It is the highest court of appeal for England, Wales, Scotland and Northern Ireland in civil disputes, and similarly in criminal cases (except for Scotland). Usually, five judges will form a court and the relatively small number of cases which go to it come mainly from the Court of Appeal. In cases involving a point of law of general public importance, an appeal may go direct to the House of Lords from the High Court. This is known as the "leap-frog" procedure and it was introduced by the **Administration of Justice Act 1969.**

2.2 Criminal Disputes

The machinery that exists to deal with individuals or organisations that infringe the criminal law is the system of criminal courts. The nature of a crime was examined earlier in chapter 1 where it was shown that in addition to the many traditional criminal offences such as murder, theft, manslaughter, etc. there are thousands of statutory offences which are regulatory in nature and are often of strict liability. Among the many statutory crimes of concern to a housing authority include the offences of statutory nuisance, harassment, and overcrowding for which prosecutions may be brought in the lower of the criminal courts, the Magistrates Court.

The Magistrates Court

Although it is the lower of the criminal courts it nevertheless deals with the majority of criminal cases and indeed all criminal trials will start in the Magistrates Court. Judges in the majority of Magistrates courts are laymen who have no legal training. They are Lay Magistrates, also known as Justices of the Peace. Their role in a criminal trial is to determine guilt or innocence and then pass sentence. As far as matters of law and procedure are concerned, they rely on the advice of the Clerk to the Court who is usually a barrister or a solicitor. The court's jurisdiction extends to dealing with **summary offences** (i.e. less serious offences), however Magistrates may also try more serious crimes known as **hybrid offences** (e.g. Theft), if the prosecution and accused agree. Otherwise they are triable in the Crown Court. As far as imposing sentences is concerned, the Magistrates are restricted to a fine of up to £1,000 and/or six months imprisonment. Alternatively they may commit the accused for sentence to the Crown Court.

In addition, it is their role to act as Examining Magistrates determining whether there is sufficient evidence against the accused for there to be a case to answer in an indictable offence e.g. an offence triable in the Crown Court with a judge and jury such as murder. This is called a committal proceeding and if the Examining Magistrates decide that a **'prima facie'** case has been established, then they must commit the accused for trial to the Crown Court and also decide whether he should be remanded in custody awaiting trial or allowed **bail** (i.e. set free until the trial date subject to conditions).

Finally, some mention should be made of the civil jurisdiction of Magistrates. This extends to hearing licensing applications and also sitting as a domestic court exercising jurisdiction conferred by the **Domestic Proceedings and Magistrates Courts Act 1978** (see Chapter 7).

The Crown Court

Crown Courts were introduced by the **Courts Act 1971** as a replacement for the ancient Assize Courts and Quarter Sessions. They are situated in all major towns and cities in England and Wales and are responsible for trying all serious criminal cases (i.e. **indictable offences**). For this purpose, the offences dealt with are classified into four groups ranging from the very serious (e.g. murder or treason) to the less serious (e.g. hybrid offences such as theft). There are also three types of judge who will preside over a Crown Court ranking in order of importance and the offences they deal with will reflect this, e.g.

    i.   **High Court judges**
    ii.   **Circuit judges**
    iii. **Recorders** (barristers or solicitors of at least ten years standing who sit as part-time judges).

The role of the judge is to determine questions of law and evidence and generally ensure a fair trial. It is the jury, however, who will decide the accused's guilt or innocence and, if the accused is found guilty, the judge will fix the sentence. Juries are selected at random from the electors of the particular area. The **Central Criminal Court** (i.e. the Old Bailey) is the Crown Court with jurisdiction over the London area.

Criminal Appeal Courts

We have already mentioned that the Queen's Bench Division of the High Court fulfils the role of criminal appeal court when appeals are made on questions of law from the Magistrates Court. The Crown Court also sits as an appeal court when appeals are made on questions of fact from the Magistrates. Appeals in serious cases tried in the Crown Court however, are made to the Court of Appeal (criminal division) and in rare cases may go further to the House of Lords.

Court of Appeal (criminal division) For the purposes of hearing criminal appeals, the court is presided over by Lord Justices of Appeal and puisne judges of the Queen's Bench Division, three of whom will constitute a court. Appeals may be made **as of right** if a question of law is involved, (e.g. the interpretation of the wording of an offence), but only **with leave,** (e.g. permission of the court or a High Court judge), if it is made on a question of fact (e.g. insufficient evidence to convict). The court may allow

29

the appeal and quash the conviction, substitute a conviction for a lesser offence, alter the sentence but not increase it, or in some cases order a re-trial.

The House of Lords In rare cases, appeal may be made to the House of Lords from the Court of Appeal or also from a Divisional court of the Queen's Bench Division. Appeals are only heard where the court below certifies that a point of law of general public importance is involved and either the court below or the House of Lords grants leave to appeal.

2.3 Administrative Disputes

Since the Second World War, there has been a dramatic increase in the exercise of government functions involving:-

1.   an increase in social legislation (pensions, industrial injuries, sickness and unemployment benefits);

2.   an increase in powers to acquire land by compulsory purchase;

3.   increasing intervention in the private rented sector by establishing a system whereby rents of dwellings may be controlled.

In addition, there is a growing amount of statute law in relation to employment, covering such matters as redundancy, unfair dismissal, equal pay, sex and race discrimination.

To resolve disputes arising in these areas machinery has been set up in the form of administrative tribunals. Tribunals are thought to be better equipped to deal with administrative disputes rather than the overloaded courts because:-

1.   They will include a specialist expert in the area concerned to help resolve the dispute;

2.   They are speedier and less costly than the ordinary courts;

3.   They have wide discretionary powers which are necessary to enable them to resolve administrative disputes.

Administrative Tribunals

Administrative tribunals are set up by statutes which will also define the extent of their power. Different tribunals have been created to deal with the various types of administrative disputes, including:-

Social Security Tribunals These tribunals hear disputes arising from individual claims for welfare benefits, e.g. supplementary benefit. For this purpose, the tribunal will consist of a chairman appointed by the Secretary of State and one representative of employers and one of employees. Similar local tribunals have been set up to deal with disputes arising from claims for industrial injuries benefit.

Lands Tribunal This is a highly professional body whose main function is to decide questions surrounding the value of land particularly when land has been compulsorily acquired (see Chapter 17).

Rent Tribunals These are bodies which were created under the Rent Acts to determine the rents of certain types of private rented accommodation and also grant limited security of tenure to a tenant. Under the **Housing Act 1980** the functions of Rent Tribunals have been transferred to **Rent Assessment Committees** but when dealing with a Rent Tribunal function, the **Housing Act 1980** provides that they are to be known as **Rent Tribunals.** The functions and workings of Rent Assessment Committees are considered in detail in Chapter 12.

Special Tribunals

Industrial Tribunals These are bodies created under employment legislation and are not concerned with administrative matters but rather with disputes relating to employment, e.g. unfair dismissal and redundancy. The functions and workings of Industrial Tribunals are considered in detail in Chapter 18.

Domestic Tribunals Domestic tribunals are simply disciplinary committees of particular professions, e.g. doctors, lawyers, dentists, with power to discipline members of the various professions for professional misconduct.

Administrative Enquiries

Some areas of administrative action by government or local authorities, e.g. housing and planning, provide no appeal route to tribunals from the process of decision making. Rather, provision is made under statute for an aggrieved individual to argue his case at a **public local enquiry.** The majority of such enquiries arise out of the compulsory acquisition of land by housing authorities. They are conducted before a Minister's inspector who, after hearing the evidence, will report to the Minister concerned. The final decision is made by the Minister himself. The powers and functions of local enquiries are considered in detail in Chapter 17.

The Tribunals and Inquiries Act 1971 Following a great deal of criticism of the workings of Tribunals in the late 1950's, the Franks Committee was given the task of inquiring into the criticism and, following its recommendations, the **Tribunals and Inquiries Act 1958** was passed. Most of the law is now embodied in the **Tribunals and Inquiries Act 1971.** This statute provided for the setting up of a review body, the **Council on Tribunals,** which is given the task of reviewing the working of tribunals and reporting annually to Parliament. In addition, it is now a requirement that in most cases, if the parties request it, reasons for decisions must be given. This provision, of course, enables an individual who is aggrieved at a decision to more easily challenge it in the ordinary courts. The ordinary courts have power to supervise the decision making of Tribunals and administrators (e.g. the Executive) generally.

Judicial Control of the Action of Public Bodies

The Queen's Bench Division of the High Court has a supervisory jurisdiction over the acts of any executive agency (e.g. nationalised industries, local authorities, government departments and ministers) and inferior courts and tribunals. This jurisdiction covers matters such as granting various orders, (e.g. mandamus, prohibition and certiorari) issuing declarations and injunctions, and hearing statutory appeals.

Mandamus The order of mandamus may be issued by the Queen's Bench Division of the High Court to compel the performance of a public duty imposed by the law on some person or body. It should be stressed however that this order is only available where:-

1. There is no other remedy provided by statute or the common law to redress the grievance;

2. The applicant for the remedy has a substantial personal interest in the matter;

3. The complaint relates to the non performance of a public duty rather than the exercise of a discretionary power, i.e. mandamus would not be granted to require the making of a particular by-law by a local authority.

Therefore wherever statutory duties are imposed on public bodies, for instance duties on local authorities in relation to education, housing, public health and highways and these are not fulfilled, then mandamus may be issued from the High Court to require performance. Thus if a housing authority failed to fulfil a statutory duty under the **Housing (Homeless Persons) Act 1977** then an aggrieved person could apply to the High Court to grant an order of mandamus to compel the authority to carry out its duty.

The use of Mandamus in Administrative Supervision Mandamus will not lie as a remedy to compel the exercise of a discretionary power conferred on administrators. However if a power is conferred by statute, mandamus may be issued to compel its exercise one way or the other and ensure at least that an individual case is dealt with fairly.

> In *R v. London County Council, Ex-parte Corrie 1918* a by-law was made by the defendants, prohibiting the sale of articles in the parks under their control without their consent. The defendants resolved to revoke existing permissions to sell already granted, and not to grant new permissions. The court held that as the defendants had a power to grant permission they had a corresponding duty to hear applications and decide them on their merits. Mandamus was granted to require the defendants to hear applications. Of course, if the council did not want the power it could amend or repeal the by-law.

It is not uncommon for a particular statute to include mandamus as a remedy to require compliance with its provisions, e.g. under **s.68 The Education Act 1944,** the Secretary of State for Education has power to issue directions to local education authorities which in his opinion are proposing to act unreasonably in the exercise of their powers and the performance of duties conferred on them by the Act. The extent of this wide ministerial discretion was examined in the Tameside case 1977.

> *R v. Tameside Metropolitan Borough Council, Ex-parte Secretary of State for Education and Science 1977.* The case concerned a decision by the newly elected Conservative Council at Tameside to postpone a half completed scheme to convert five grammar schools into three comprehensives and two sixth form colleges. This scheme had been introduced by the then Labour Council and approved by the Minister in 1975. The Secretary of State, believing that the scheme had progressed too far to be stopped by the Conservative Council, directed them to carry out the changeover (i.e. under **s.68 Education Act 1944**). When the Council ignored this direction, the Secretary of State applied successfully to the High Court for an order of mandamus to require the council to fulfil their duty and carry out the changeover. On an appeal by the Tameside Council to the Court of Appeal, the court acknowledged that a postponement of the changeover to comprehensive schools would cause disruption. Nevertheless, the power of the Minister to intervene depended on whether the newly elected Council at Tameside were acting unreasonably in taking the course they proposed to take. Ld. Denning, M.R. put forward the view that a 'body' could not be labelled as unreasonable unless they were not only wrong but unreasonably wrong - so wrong that no reasonable person could take that view. Thus, for the Council to be acting unreasonably it must have been following a course which it did not feel was in the best interests of the community and would not work. This was not the case here, so therefore the Council were not acting unreasonably and the Minister was not entitled to mandamus. On a further appeal to the House of Lords this decision was upheld.

The above case is an outstanding example of the principle that even where wide discretions are conferred on administrators in central and local government in this country, the courts are nevertheless willing to intervene and supervise the exercise of their powers if they feel that there has been an abuse.

Prohibition and Certiorari These orders may be issued from the Queen's Bench Division of the High Court in cases where a judicial body (such as an inferior court, tribunal or even a local authority) has acted or is proposing to act unlawfully or has otherwise exceeded its powers and acted ultra vires. The order of certiorari has the effect of quashing such a decision already made and the order of prohibition will restrain a body from completing an act already begun. Today, the orders are most frequently used when a body in reaching a decision ignores what are called the principles of **natural justice**. These principles are not easily defined but generally require the body reaching the decision to:

1. Act fairly without bias and in good faith;

2. Give both sides to a dispute an opportunity to put their case;

3. Ensure that no party to the decision making has an interest in the matter before them.

In deciding to which bodies these orders apply, it is possible to consider the words of Atkin, L.J. in *R v. Electricity Commissioners 1924* where he said that they will apply "whenever any body of persons having legal authority to determine questions affecting the rights of subjects, and having a duty to act judicially, act in excess of their legal authority".

The orders extend therefore, not only to the actions of inferior courts but also to administrative tribunals.

> In *R v. Northumberland Compensation Appeal Tribunal, Ex-parte Shaw 1952* the tribunal's decision contained the reasons for it, and from these reasons it was clear that the tribunal had made an error of law. The court of appeal granted certiorari to quash the decision and stressed that the supervisory control of the courts extended not only to seeing that inferior tribunals keep within their jurisdiction but also to seeing that they observe the law.

The importance of these orders as far as local government administration is concerned is that there are many occasions where administrators decide questions affecting the rights of individuals and act in a judicial manner. It is now recognised that if such decision-making discloses any abuse of power then the courts will intervene.

In *Ex-parte Ladbroke Group 1969* the proceedings of a licensing committee appointed under the **Gaming and Lotteries Act 1963** were put under the scrutiny of the Queen's Bench Division of the High Court. The complaint related to the decision of the committee as to whether a licence should be granted and the statutory requirement that objectors should be heard. The evidence showed that the committee's decision was not a corporate one but rather that of the dominant chairman, who sat so far from the rest of the committee that it was impossible to confer with them. The chairman also had made it plain that he was willing to make a decision before hearing all the evidence. These the court held, were sufficient grounds to issue certiorari to quash the eventual decision made.

It is also clear that the orders will now lie in relation to purely administrative decisions.

In *R v. Barnsley Metropolitan Borough Council, Ex-parte Hook 1976* a licensed street trader, in breach of local authority by-laws, urinated in a side street after the market had closed. When spotted by a security officer and rebuked by him for his conduct, the trader exchanged words of abuse. Of course the matter then escalated, the market manager was informed, he reported the incident to the relevant local authority committee and they decided to ban the trader for life from the market. In a subsequent appeal to the local authority sub-committee against this decision, the trader's representatives were given the opportunity to put his case. The problem was that during the committee's deliberations, the other side to the dispute (the market manager) was present throughout, and the committee decided to confirm the ban. Failing to obtain a remedy from the High Court who decided that the committee's decision was a purely administrative one, the trader appealed to the Court of Appeal. The court unanimously held that certiorari would lie to quash the committee's decision on the grounds that the rules of natural justice had not been complied with. The presence of the market manager throughout the decision making was a violation of the rule against bias. On the question as to whether certiorari would lie to quash an administrative decision, the court held that the order was relevant as the local authority was determining questions affecting the rights of subjects. Ld.

Denning M.R. emphasised the point when he said "certiorari will lie to quash not only judicial decisions but also administrative decisions". The fact that the prerogative orders will now extend to purely administrative proceeding has far reaching effects for administrators particularly in relation to the rules of "fair play" in decision making.

Declarations and Injunctions As an alternative to seeking a prerogative remedy, an aggrieved individual may question the legality of the action of a public body by requesting the High Court to declare the law and/or grant an injuction to refrain from action.

> In *Prescott v. Birmingham Corporation 1955* a ratepayer requested the High Court for a declaration that the granting of free bus travel to old age pensioners was ultra vires. The court declared that the practice was illegal in the absence of clear authority under statute. Such authority had not been granted although now the practice would probably be justified under the **Local Government Act 1972.**

It should be noted however, that where it is a public grievance that is complained of, e.g. a public nuisance or non compliance with an Act of Parliament, then an action must be brought in the name of the Attorney-General (the protector of public rights), unless an individual can show that he has suffered special damage. Normally, the Attorney-General will permit his name to be used, the Attorney-General suing 'at the relation of' the aggrieved individual. This is called a **relator action.**

Statutory Appeals Finally, some mention must be made of the multitude of statutes that give a right of appeal to an individual who is aggrieved at non compliance or supposed compliance with their provisions. Thus a local authority may under the **Public Health Act 1936,** by the service of an abatement notice, require an owner of a ruinous building to repair it. Appeal lies to the Magistrates Court for an individual owner against a local authority decision in this respect. Similarly, the **Highways Act 1959** places duties on local authorities in relation to highway repair and provides that an individual may ask the Crown Court to order the local authority to act in this respect. Finally, the many Housing Acts provide for rights of appeal to the County Court by individuals who are aggrieved at action taken by housing authorities under their provisions. Rather than an appeal to a court a statute may provide for an alternative means of seeking redress.

The **Housing Act 1980** confers wide default powers on the Secretary of State for the Environment in relation to the right to buy provision. This default power is examined in detail in Chapter 13.

The Role of the Parliamentary Commissioner for Administration

Another body which has been created in order to resolve administrative disputes is the **Parliamentary Commissioner Act 1967.** His functions in anticipation of the **Parliamentary Commissioner Act 1967.** His functions under the Act include the investigation of complaints in relation to actions by various government departments and authorities in the exercise of administrative functions. The power of the Commissioner to investigate is limited to complaints referred to him by a Member of Parliament. An individual who claims to have sustained injustice in consequence of maladministration must therefore make a written complaint to a member of the House of Commons who will refer it to the Commissioner. There are still a large number of complaints referred to the Commissioner which are outside his jurisdiction for he has no right to investigate cases where there is a possible right of appeal to a tribunal or a remedy exists through legal action in the courts. Having investigated a complaint, the Commissioner will send a report to the Member of Parliament who referred the matter to him and also the Department concerned. However, the Commissioner has no power to require action to be taken but can only make recommendations. He also makes an annual report to Parliament which is subject to review by a Select Committee. In Britain, where there is no free access to information (as there is in the United States of America) the investigatory powers of the Commissioner, which include the right to obtain documentary and other evidence from departments, may provide a useful tool for the private individual who has suffered at the hands of a large government department.

Local Commissioners for Administration

Under the **Local Government Act 1974** machinery was established for the investigation of complaints by individuals who have suffered as a result of maladministration by local and other authorities. The Act provides for the appointment of **Local Commissioners for Administration (Local Ombudsmen),** who are given responsibility for particular areas. Their jurisdiction is limited in the same way as the Parliamentary Commissioner in that they will only hear complaints referred to them by a councillor of the authority concerned, unless there is evidence to show that a councillor had failed to pass a complaint on. Thus the local authority has an opportunity to put the matter right before a referral is made. Local ombudsmen have no power to investigate matters where there is a right of appeal to a tribunal or to a Minister or a possible legal remedy exists. In addition, recent case law suggests that the investigatory power of the local ombudsman in relation to obtaining documentary evidence is much more restricted than that of the Parliamentary Commissioner. Finally, it should be mentioned that even where a conclusion of maladministration is reached, by either the Parliamentary or Local Ombudsman, they have no power to require remedial action but can only make recommendations. As far as local ombudsmen are concerned however, where local authorities are found to be guilty of maladministration, remedial action is taken by over ninety per cent of the authorities concerned. It should be mentioned that complaints in relation to housing matters constitute the largest category of referalls to the Local Ombudsman.

The Legal Profession

The legal profession in England and Wales is divided into two branches, solicitors and barristers, the term 'lawyer' referring to either branch.

a. **Solicitors** The full title of a solicitor is **'Solicitor of the Supreme Court'** and as such he is an officer of the court and owes it a duty. It is the solicitor who deals directly with the public advising them of legal problems and carrying out legal transactions, e.g. drafting contracts, wills and deeds. They have the right to act as an advocate for a prospective litigant in the County Court, Magistrates Court and certain tribunals. For more important cases dealt with in the higher courts a solicitor must 'brief' a barrister (instructing a barrister to appear in court on the client's behalf). As barristers often specialise in different areas of law, a solicitor may also 'take counsel's opinion' which is simply obtaining a barrister's view of the law which applies to the client's problem. The body responsible for the training and conduct of solicitors is the Law Society which maintains a register of those entitled to practice as solicitors. To qualify as a solicitor it is now usual to obtain a degree and then pass the Law Society's qualifying examinations. Full-time study is now a requirement for the final examinations. In addition, a prospective solicitor must serve for a number of years as an articled clerk for what may be termed apprenticeship. Having been admitted as a solicitor the choice is then of salaried employment in industry, the civil service or local government or alternatively, private practice which usually involves joining a firm of solicitors and eventually becoming a partner. One of the most fundamental privileges of a solicitor is that he cannot be made to disclose matters revealed to him while giving advice but in return a solicitor must act competently and honourably in carrying out his client's affairs.

There are numerous occasions where it will be necessary for those engaged in housing management to seek legal advice from a solicitor or require him to commence legal proceedings. In such circumstances, the golden rule is that to adequately advise or take action, the solicitor must be presented with all the available facts. Assertions of fact made by a solicitor in a court case must be supported by evidence. It is of great benefit therefore to enable prompt action to be taken, to supply the solicitor with such evidence at the earliest opportunity e.g. in an action for possession on the grounds of the breach of a repairing covenant it is advisable to provide the solicitor with a full inventory of the items of disrepair. It would also be useful where possible to provide photographic evidence of the disrepair. One of the fundamental aims of this book is to enable those engaged in housing management and faced with legal problems to anticipate the necessary information required by a professional lawyer to competently advise and if necessary commence legal proceedings.

b. **Barristers** Barristers are regarded as the senior branch of the legal profession. They are engaged by solicitors rather than directly by the public to give advice on complex points of law (called **paperwork**) and to represent clients in court (**advocacy**). Barristers work independently but groups will share offices (chambers) and usually a barrister's clerk. Within their chambers individual barristers will specialise in certain areas of law. Their main role is to act as advocates in the superior courts specialising in different areas of law. When engaged by a solicitor to represent a client they are sent a 'brief' (i.e. the necessary documents) with a fee for the work negotiated between the barrister's clerk and the solicitor. However, there is no contractual relationship between a barrister and a solicitor. Neither does a barrister owe a duty of care under the tort of negligence to a client for his conduct in presenting a case. This immunity was confirmed by the House of Lords in *Rondel v. Worsley 1969* as being in the public interest. In *Saif Ali v. Sydney Mitchel 1977* the Court of Appeal held that this immunity also extended to paperwork. To qualify as a barrister involves acquiring a degree, joining one of the Inns of

Court as a student and passing their examinations. A law student who is 'reading for the bar' is also required to attend and dine at his Inn on a specified number of occasions before presenting himself for examinations and also admission as a barrister ('called to the bar'). An ordinary barrister is referred to as a 'junior' and after a number of years practice he may apply to the Lord Chancellor to be appointed as a Queen's Counsel ('taking silk'). It is the senior branch of the legal profession which provides the individuals who are candidates for elevation to the higher levels of the judiciary.

The Judiciary

No account of the machinery that exists for resolving disputes would be complete without special mention of the role of the judges in this process. The most fundamental feature of the English judiciary is that it is independent. This means that judges decide cases without fear of external pressure and certainly no government in Britain would put pressure on a judge to decide a case in a particular way. This is despite the fact that the method of judicial selection is executive appointment, (judges being appointed by the Crown, chosen by the Lord Chancellor and Prime Minister who are members of the Government). Although solicitors may become Recorders (part-time judges) and become Circuit judges on further promotion, judicial appointments are made basically from the ranks of successful barristers. Generally therefore, political considerations do not play a part in the appointment of judges, the only exception being Lay Magistrates. Here appointments are made by the Lord Chancellor on the advice of local advisory committees. These committees, whose membership is secret, on making a recommendation, take into account the political leanings of the candidate in an attempt to keep a fair balance between the supporters of the various political parties when making appointments. One major criticism of the appointment of judges from the ranks of barristers is that barristers themselves do not represent a fair reflection of balanced political view and come from a narrow section of society. This is despite the fact that eminent judges (Lord Denning, M.R. included) may try to persuade us otherwise. A major feature of judicial office that ensures their independence is that they are not easily removed and judges of the High Court, Court of Appeal and House of Lords by virtue of the **Act of Settlement 1701** enjoy their offices "during good behaviour". They may only be removed from office by the Queen on an address presented to her by both Houses of Parliament. Circuit judges and Recorders however, may be removed from office by the Lord Chancellor for inability or misbehaviour under the **Courts Act 1971.** Also in their official capacity judges enjoy immunity from any legal proceedings arising from what they say and do.

> In *Sirros v. Moore 1974* the plaintiff failed in his action to sue a circuit judge for false imprisonment. Ld. Denning stated that "The orders that a judge gives, and the sentences which he imposes, cannot be made the subject of civil proceedings against him. No matter that the judge was under some gross error or ignorance, or was actuated by envy, hatred or malice and all uncharitableness, he is not liable to an action ... The reason is not because the judge has any privilege to make mistakes or to do wrong. It is so that he should be able to do his duty with complete independence and free from fear".

Contempt of Court Finally some mention should be made of the wider common law power of the judiciary to punish people who are in contempt of court by imprisonment or a fine. The two kinds of contempt are:

a. **Civil contempt.** This occurs where an individual refuses to obey an order of a court, e.g. an order of damages, injuction or mandamus.

b. **Criminal contempt.** This may be committed by an individual who does anything which interferes with the administration of justice or brings the judiciary into disrepute. One important type of criminal contempt is a breach of the **sub judice rule,** i.e. if legal proceedings are imminent and any public comment is made (in newspapers or television) which might prejudice their outcome. The Attorney-General has power to initiate proceedings in such a case to bring the matter before the Queen's Bench Division of the High Court.

> A recent example of criminal contempt arising from a wilful attempt to interrupt court proceedings occurred in *Balogh v. Crown Court at St. Albans 1974.* Here a solicitor's clerk, who became increasingly bored at a pornography trial, stole a cylinder of nitrous oxide (laughing gas) from a nearby hospital with the intention of introducing it into the air conditioning of the court. When his scheme came to light, he was brought before the judge who sentenced him to six months imprisonment for contempt. The Court of Appeal, while confirming that such an act could have amounted to criminal contempt, thought the punishment a little harsh and released the clerk from prison.

Part 2 - **Contract**

CHAPTER 3   The Formation of Contract

An understanding of the general principles of the law of contract is a fundamental prerequisite to obtaining an appreciation of the various legal relationships that exist in housing management, e.g. the relationship of landlord and tenant, employer and employee, employer and building contractor. It is proposed therefore in this chapter to examine the essential elements in the formation of a valid simple contract. The contents of the building contract, the contract of employment and the contract for a lease are considered later in the book.

3.1 The Essentials of a Contract

A contract is simply an agreement that is enforceable by the law. It may be defined as an agreement intended by the parties to it to have legal consequences and to be legally enforceable. The contract is the instrument by which people and organisations transact both in the short and long term, e.g.

> A retailer agrees to sell goods to a customer.
> A builder agrees to repair a roof for a householder.
> An investor agrees to lend money to a company.
> A garage owner agrees to sell a car on hire purchase to a hirer.
> An employee agrees for wages to work for an organisation.
> A taxidriver agrees to take a hirer to the station.
> A landlord agrees to let property to a tenant.

The above are all everyday examples where the parties to an agreement achieve their objectives by virtue of a contract. The fact that the parties have respective rights and duties which are contractual in nature simply means that if one party to the contract fails to perform his obligations, or performs his obligations in a defective manner, then the other party may sue for **breach of contract** and obtain a court remedy such as damages (compensation) and for serious breaches terminate the contract.

It is possible at this stage to distinguish contracts from mere agreements, which do not have legal consequences. The deciding factor is often that in a mere agreement the parties do not intend to create a legal relationship.

Of course, if the parties to an agreement have not expressed their intentions clearly, then it is often left to courts to determine whether the parties **intended to create a contract.** To decide this question the courts will firstly look to the relationship of the parties and decide whether it may be classified as either a social or domestic agreement, or a business agreement.

a.   **Social or Domestic Agreements** Having classified the agreement as a social or domestic one, it is then presumed that the parties to such an agreement do not intend legal consequences unless there is clear evidence to the contrary.

> In *Balfour v. Balfour 1919* a family agreement where a husband agreed to pay his wife an allowance of £30 per month was held not to be intended to be legally binding and did not give rise to a contract.

> Alternatively, in *Parker v. Clark 1960* the defendants, an elderly couple invited their niece and her husband (the plaintiffs) to come and live with them, and in return for domestic help promised to leave the plaintiffs their property in their will. The plaintiffs accepted the offer, sold their home, and moved in with the defendants. Unfortunately, differences between the parties arose and after much unpleasantness, the plaintiffs were asked to leave. In an action to recover damages for breach of contract, the court held that the evidence was sufficient to show that the parties intended the agreement to have legal consequences, particularly when considering that the plaintiffs had sold their home. Accordingly, a contract had been concluded and damages were payable for its breach.

b.   **Business Agreements** As far as business or commercial agreements are concerned, the courts apply the presumption that the parties intend to create legal consequences unless there is clear evidence to the contrary.

> The inclusion of the phrase 'binding in honour only' on a football coupon was held by the court in *Jones v. Vernons Pools Ltd 1938* to amount to clear evidence that there was no intention to create a contract.

Similarly, in *Rose and Frank Co. v. Crompton Bros. 1925,* a written agreement entered into by two commercial organisations included the following clause:-

"This arrangement is not entered into, nor is this memorandum written, as a formal or legal agreement ... but ... is only a definite expression and record of the purpose and intention of the ... parties concerned, to which they each honourably pledge themselves". This clause, the court held, was sufficient evidence to overturn the presumption that commercial agreements are intended to be legally binding.

An everyday example of the use of such an exclusion is the common practice in the sale of property to agree to contract in the future by selling **'subject to contract'.** Such an agreement is not legally binding and at this point both parties are still free to withdraw from the sale.

Types of Contract

There are three types of contract:-

a. **Specialty Contracts** These are formal contracts also referred to as contracts under seal or deeds. The terms of such contracts must be in writing, signed, sealed, delivered and witnessed. As a general rule, specialty contracts are required if a legal lease of more than three years is to be entered into and also if a legal estate of property is to be transferred, e.g. a conveyance for the sale of freehold land.

b. **Contracts of Record** These require little explanation and refer to obligations imposed upon a person by a court, e.g. a judgement.

c. **Simple Contracts** These form the majority of contracts entered into by individuals and organisations and it is proposed to consider their formation in some detail. Such contracts are created when the parties reach an agreement which is intended to be legally enforceable. The general rule is that there are **no** legal formalities attaching to such contracts, so that they may be purely oral, e.g. the majority of contracts for the sale of goods. Of course, the existence and content of an oral contract is often more difficult to prove than a written contract, but they are nonetheless legally enforceable. In addition however, the law provides that writing is a requirement for certain types of simple contract which are as follows:-

47

1. **certain contracts are void** (i.e. of no legal effect) **unless in writing,** e.g. contracts of marine insurance, acknowledgements of debts where the statutory period for suing for repayment has expired (6 years for simple contracts), cheques.

2. **certain contracts are unenforceable** (i.e. unenforceable by the courts) **unless in writing,** e.g. consumer credit transactions (hire purchase or money lending).

3. **certain contracts are unenforceable unless evidenced in writing,** e.g. a contract to guarantee a debt or a contract for the sale or other disposition of any interest in land. Contracts concerning land are regulated by **s.40(1) Law of Property Act 1925.** This requirement is considered in more depth later in chapter 6.

3.2 Formation of Simple Contracts

As previously stated, the substance of any contract is an agreement intended by the parties to it to have legal consequences. Having considered the contractual rules relating to intention to create legal relations, it is now possible to examine the rules relating to the formation of a contractual agreement. The agreement is said to come into existence when one party declares he is willing to be bound by certain terms and makes an offer (he is called the **offeror**) **AND** the other party declares he is willing to be bound by the same terms and accepts (he is called the **offeree**).

For instance where X offers to sell his car to Y for £1,000 **AND**
Y agrees to pay £1,000 for the car.

Often, it is necessary to analyse all the stages in the contractual negotiations to determine whether a valid offer has been made and also if there is a valid acceptance. It is then possible to discover whether a contractual agreement has come into existence.

3.3. The Contractual Offer

In relation to a valid contractual offer the following points may be made:-

a. **An Offer must be Certain** The details of the offer must be certain or capable of being made certain otherwise the offer is not capable of acceptance.

In *Scammel v. Ouston 1941* an agreement was reached for the sale of a van in which balance of the purchase price was expressed to be payable "on hire purchase terms over a period of two years". In deciding whether a valid contract had been entered into the court held that the words 'on hire purchase terms' in the offer were too vague and therefore not capable of acceptance. The court would have been prepared to enforce the contract had there been a previous course of dealing between the parties from which it was possible to interpret the vague parts of the agreement, i.e. the parties had contracted on hire purchase terms in the past.

Similarly, a vague term may be included in a binding contract if the parties agree the machinery to make such a term certain.

In *Sykes (Wessex) v. Fine Fare 1966* a producer of chickens agreed to supply between 30,000 and 80,000 chickens a week to certain retailers for one year and for a further four years, "such other figures as might be agreed". The contract provided that any differences should be referred to arbitration. In deciding a claim whether the agreement was void for uncertainty, the Court of Appeal held that as the parties had laid down an agreed procedure of arbitration to settle disagreements, the agreement was certain and legally binding.

b. **An Offer must be Distinguished from a Mere Invitation to Treat,** i.e. an invitation to make an offer. A contractual offer may be made to an individual, a specific group, or in some cases to the world at large.

The famous case of *Carlill v. Carbolic Smokeball Co. 1893* laid down the principle that a contractual offer could be made to the world at large. The defendant company had inserted an advertisement in various newspapers offering to pay £100 to any person who, having used their medicinal product, the carbolic smokeball, for a specified period, contracted influenza. It was also claimed in the advertisement that £1,000 had been placed on bank deposit "to show our sincerity in the matter". The plaintiff used the ball as advertised, contracted the 'flu, and claimed the reward. Having been refused payment, the plaintiff sued the company alleging that a contract had been

49

entered into. The court agreed, deciding that, in the advertisement, the company had communicated an offer of reward to the whole world and such an offer was capable of acceptance by any person who complied with its terms, i.e. used the smokeball in the prescribed manner.

Invitation to treat. It is important to distinguish a contractual offer from various situations which are no more than an invitation to make an offer, e.g.

1. **Advertisements** Apart from the exceptional 'offer of reward' as in *Carlill v. Carbolic Smokeball Co.,* advertisements of goods or services for sale contained in newspapers, magazines or trade catalogues are merely invitations to the reader to make a contractual offer. The individual or organisation who placed the advertisement is therefore in a position to reject an offer made for the goods or services.

   This principle was upheld in *Partridge v. Crittenden 1968* where an advertisement had been placed in a magazine stating "Bramblefinch cocks, and hens 25sh each". The party who placed the advertisement was prosecuted under the criminal law for unlawfully 'offering for sale' a wild bird contrary to the **Protection of Birds Act 1954.** The court held that no offence had been committed as the advertisement did not constitute an 'offer for sale' but merely an invitation to treat.

2. **Display of Goods** The same principle applies to the display of goods for sale by a shopkeeper.

   In *Fisher v. Bell 1961* the display by a shopkeeper of a flick knife for sale did not constitute the offence of offering for sale an offensive weapon contrary to the **Restriction of Offensive Weapons Act 1959.**

   As far as self-service stores are concerned, the court in *Pharmaceutical Society v. Boots Cash Chemists Ltd. 1953* confirmed the principle that the display of goods on shelves is merely an invitation to treat and the contractual offer is not made until the shopper presents the goods at the cash till and communicates his intention to purchase.

3. **Tenders** Tenders are examined in more depth in chapter 4 particularly in relation to building contracts. At this stage it is sufficient to point out that a tender must be distinguished from an invitation to tender which does not constitute a contractural offer. It is merely an invitation by an individual or organisation wishing to purchase goods or services to requiest suppliers to submit a contractural offer in the form of a tender. If the invitation to tender stipulates expressly or impliedly that the goods or services will be required, then an acceptance of the tender will create a binding contract. Alternatively, the invitation may stipulate that the goods or services may be required, in which case an acceptance of the tender results in a standing offer to supply as and when required. A failure to order by the buyer in those circumstances will not result in a breach of contract.

4. **Auction Sales** As far as auction sales are concerned, the law is largely settled. The bidders at an auction make the offers, the acceptance of which is signalled by the fall of the auctioneer's hammer. As we shall see later an offer may be withdrawn at any time prior to acceptance so, surprisingly, it is possible for a bidder at an auction sale to withdraw his bid prior to the fall of the hammer.

    Reluctantly, upholding the principle that an auctioneer makes an invitation to treat, the court in *British Car Auctions v. Wright 1972* held that an auctioneer could not be convicted of 'offering for sale' a motor vehicle in an unroadworthy condition contrary to the **Road Traffic Act 1972.**

    The recent Court of Appeal decision in *Gibson v. Manchester City Council 1978* has cast some doubt on the traditional legal approach of distinguishing between an offer and an invitation to treat where protracted correspondence has taken place. The case involved the prospective sale of a council house. The plaintiff council tenant, having completed a request for information, received a letter from the council saying it might be prepared to sell the house to him for £2,180 freehold and that if he wished to make a formal application to purchase he should return an application form. This the tenant did. Unfortunately he left the purchase price blank requesting that the price should take into account defects in the path of the property. A further letter from the council stated that defects in the path had been taken into account in fixing the price. In interpreting the above correspondence a majority of the Court of Appeal held that a contract of sale had indeed been entered into. Lord Denning, M.R. put forward the view that in such circumstances there was no need to look for a strict offer and acceptance rather, "you should look at the correspondence as a whole and at the conduct of the parties and see therefrom whether the parties have come to an agreement on everything that was material". This decision was later reversed following a further appeal to the House of Lords in 1979. The Law Lords adopted the more traditional approach by analysing each piece of correspondence and held that no firm offer had been made or accepted by the council. The words the council "may be prepared to sell" only amounted to an invitation to treat and thus no contract of sale had resulted.

c. **An Offer will Terminate or may be Terminated**

1. **By Rejection** A contractual offer will terminate if it is expressly rejected, (i.e. the offeree communicates his rejection) or impliedly rejected, (i.e. the offeree ignores the offer). In addition, if the offeree makes a 'counter offer' this will have the effect of terminating the original offer.

    In *Hyde v. Wrench 1840* an offer to sell land for £1,000 was met by a counter offer to purchase the land for £950. The court held that the counter offer destroyed the original offer which could not then be accepted unless revived by the original offeror.

    It is important, however, to distinguish a counter offer from a mere request for further information which will not destroy the original offer.

    In *Stevenson v. McLean 1880* having received an offer to purchase iron at 40s a ton the plaintiffs asked the offeror whether payment could be made over two months. Receiving no reply the plaintiffs nevertheless communicated their acceptance. The court held that a binding contract had been entered into as the enquiry relating to payment was a mere request for further information and not a counter offer which would have extinguished the original offer.

2. **By Lapse** A contractual offer will lapse if expressed to be open for a particular time when that time has expired, or, if no time period is expressed, after a reasonable length of time. For this purpose, what amounts to a reasonable length of time will depend upon the circumstances of the case, in particular the subject-matter. Obviously, an offer to purchase perishable goods or goods subject to a fluctuating market value must be taken up reasonably promptly.

    In *Ramsgate Victoria Hotel v. Montefiore 1866* the court held that an offer to purchase shares had lapsed prior to acceptance six months later. Such a period was regarded as unreasonable, particularly when you consider that the value of the shares was fluctuating daily.

3. **By Withdrawal of the Offer** An offer may be revoked (withdrawn) at any time prior to acceptance provided that the offeror communicates his revocation to the offeree. For example, a bidder at an auction may withdraw his bid prior to acceptance or a shopper in a supermarket having offered to buy goods at the cash till may revoke the offer by replacing the goods chosen.

    In *Routledge v. Grant 1828* the defendant, having offered to purchase the plaintiff's house and given the plaintiff six weeks to think it over, decided to withdraw the offer before the six weeks expired. In determining whether the revocation was effective, the court held that an offer can be withdrawn at any time before acceptance and there was no obligation on the offeror to keep the offer open. Such an obligation would of course be imposed on an offeror who contracted to keep an offer open for a specific period.

Having stated that a revocation must be communicated, there is no requirement that it must be communicated by the offeror.

    In *Dickinson v. Dodds 1876* the plaintiff having received an offer to purchase some property, discovered from a third party that the offeror had then sold the property to someone else. The court held that once the offeree was aware that the property had been sold to someone else the offer was impliedly revoked and not capable of acceptance.

3.4 The Acceptance of an Offer

An unconditional acceptance of the terms of the offer by the offeree will result in a contract and thus terminate the offer.

As previously stated, a conditional acceptance is no acceptance.

> Therefore in *Northland Airlines Ltd. v. Kerranti Meters Ltd. 1970* an offer for the sale of an aircraft to the offeree was held not to have been accepted when the offeree agreed to the offer subject to different terms relating to delivery and payment.

Communication Of course an offer must be communicated and it is not possible to accept an offer of which you are unaware, e.g. if a person finds and returns a lost dog without being aware that the owner had offered a reward for its return, he has no right to claim the reward. Similarly an acceptance must be communicated to the offeror and it is not possible to require that the offeree is to accept by remaining silent.

> In *Felthouse v. Bindley 1862* the plaintiff wrote to the defendant offering to buy a horse stating, "If I hear no more about him, I consider the horse mine at £30.15s". When the defendant made no reply the plaintiff claimed a contract. The court held that no contract had been concluded as it is not possible to stipulate that silence of the offeree will constitute acceptance.

At this point, some mention may be made of the rules that apply when the offeree relies on the post to effect an acceptance. The general rule is that if the use of the post as a means of acceptance is expected by the parties because either:-
  i.   the offer was made by post: or
  ii.   the offeror stipulates that post may be used to accept,
then the acceptance is complete, and therefore the contract, on the posting of a properly addressed and stamped letter of acceptance.

> In *Household Fire Insurance Co. v. Grant 1897* the defendant had offered to buy shares in the plaintiff company, and a letter of acceptance was subsequently posted to him. Despite the defendant having never received the letter of acceptance, the court concluded that the contract had been entered into when it was posted.

An illustration of this rule and the rule relating to revocation of offer can be seen from the case of *Byrne v. Van Tienhoven 1880.* Here, the defendants offered, by post, to sell goods to the plaintiffs on 1st October. Having received the offer on 11th October, the plaintiffs accepted by telegraph the same day. Three days earlier the defendants had posted a letter revoking the offer and this letter was not received until 20th October. In deciding that a contract had been entered into the court confirmed the basic rules that:-

i.   The revocation of an offer is not effective until actually communicated to the offeree; and

ii.   Following an offer by post an acceptance is complete on posting.

Of course, the rule relating to postal acceptance may be expressly excluded by agreement.

In *Holwell Securities Ltd. v. Hughes 1974* an option (offer) provided that it should be exercisable 'by notice in writing'. The court held that this requirement effectively excluded the postal rule and that actual receipt of the letter of acceptance was necessary to conclude a contract.

3.5 Consideration

Under English law a further requirement for the formation of a simple contract is that the parties must have furnished **'consideration'**. Consideration may be described as the value that is transferred by the parties and has been defined as "Some right, interest, profit or benefit accruing to one party, or some forebearance, detriment, loss or responsibility given, suffered or undertaken by the other". It is most easily recognisable in a contract for the sale of goods where the consideration takes a tangible form of the price paid in return for the goods, e.g. 50p for a packet of biscuits. However, many commercial sales of goods or services are usually agreements to sell, and the performance of the contractual obligations is delayed until some future date, e.g. an agreement to sell on credit a consignment of biscuits for £1,000. Here the consideration transferred under the contract is said to be **'executory'** the parties having exchanged promises to act in the future. Finally, if a promise is given in return for the performance of an act, e.g. £10 reward for the return of a lost dog, the consideration is said to be **'executed'** since in order to accept the offer the offeree is required to perform an act, i.e. find and return the dog.

The following points may be made relating to the consideration necessary to support a simple contract:-

a. **Consideration must be valuable but need not be adequate** All this means is that the consideration transferred must have some value but it need not be adequate to support the bargain, e.g. £5 in exchange for a new car. Generally, the courts leave the parties free to make their own bargains and provided there is no fraud, misrepresentation, duress or undue influence the courts will not grant a remedy to a party who has simply made a 'bad deal'.

b. **Consideration must be sufficient** Consideration is said to be insufficient when a party attempts to use an existing contractual or public duty as consideration to support a contract.

> In *Stilk v. Myrick 1809* the existing contractual duty was to sail a ship on a round trip from London to the Baltic. When two sailors deserted, the Captain promised to divide their wages between the rest of the crew if they would work short-handed. The court held that such a promise was unenforceable as it was not supported by sufficient consideration as the sailors were under an existing contractual duty.

Of course, if the promise of additional payment is given in exchange for something extra in return, e.g. performing more hazardous work, then it will be legally binding.

> An example of an existing public duty imposed under the law is the case of *Collins v. Godefroy 1831*. Here the plaintiff had received a subpoena (a court order) to give evidence in court. He then agreed with the defendant to give the evidence in return for his expenses. The court held that there was no contract for the payment of expenses, as the promise of payment was not supported by sufficient consideration. The plaintiff was under an existing public duty to give evidence.

c. **Consideration must not be past** All that is meant here is that a party to a contract cannot use a past act as a basis for consideration. Therefore, if one party performs an act for another, and only receives a promise of reward after the act is complete, the past act would be past consideration.

> The rule is supported by the decision in *Re McCardle 1951*. Here one party carried out certain improvements to property unrequested. The persons who would ultimately benefit from this work then promised in writing to pay £488 for the work done. In deciding the validity of this promise, the court held that it was a clear case of past consideration, the work having been completed before the promise was made. Accordingly, no binding contract had been entered into.

Finally, mention should be made of the well known common law rule that the payment of a smaller amount to a creditor cannot alone be sufficient consideration to support his promise not to sue for the full debt. If however it is at the creditor's request and benefit that a smaller amount is paid at an earlier date than due, a different place than agreed, or in a different form, then this may be sufficient consideration for the creditor's promise to take it in full settlement. The courts have recognised that it would be unfair to bind a creditor to a promise extracted by the debtor's economic pressure, i.e. "take this in full settlement or get nothing!"

> A good example of this situation is the case of *D. & C. Builders Ltd. v. Rees 1965*. Here the defendant knowing that the plaintiff builders were in financial difficulties offered a £300 cheque to them as full satisfaction of a contractual debt of £482 for work done. The plaintiff builders accepted the cheque in full settlement and then sued for the balance. The Court held that there was no true agreement by the builders to accept the cheque in full satisfaction as they had merely submitted to economic pressure. The argument that the cheque was an altered mode of payment and sufficient to discharge the debt was rejected on the ground tht it was not done at the builders' request.

57

3.6 Capacity to Contract

An unconditional agreement that is intended to have legal consequences and is supported by consideration will constitute a binding contract provided that the parties to it have **legal capacity.** By the term 'legal capacity' is simply meant the legal authority to enter into the contract in question. Adults (i.e. persons of at least 18 years of age, **Family Law Reform Act 1969 s.1(1))** are said to have complete contractual capacity and can enter into contracts of any nature. There are however two categories of legal persons with restricted contractual capacity. Firstly **minors** (persons under the age of 18) and secondly **corporate bodies** (artificial persons including local authorities and companies).

The Contractual Capacity of Minors

Certainly the significance of the law relating to the contractual capacity of minors was greatly diminished following the lowering of the age of majority from 21 to 18 from January 1970. Unfortunately the legal position of minors is still overly complex, vague and certainly in need of reform. Here it is proposed to examine in outline only the various categories of contract that a minor may enter into.

a.   **Valid Contracts.** A valid contract is one that is legally binding on both parties to it and fully enforceable by them. The two types of contract entered into by infants which are binding on them are contracts for necessaries and beneficial contracts of service.

1.   **Contacts for Necessaries.** The term necessaries refers to goods and services suitable to the minor's condition in life and to his actual requirements at the time of sale and delivery. The law does not therefore provide for a categorisation of goods and services into necessaries and non-necessaries. To determine the status of a particular purchase by a minor the most relevant factors are the minor's **condition in life** and his actual requirements.

In *Nash v. Inman 1908* the defendant, a Cambridge undergraduate who was still a minor purchased a number of clothes from the plaintiff tailor including eleven fancy waistcoats. The plaintiff's action to recover the price of the goods failed, the court deciding that there was no binding contract as the goods supplied could not be regarded as

58

necessaries. Apparently the purchaser was already sufficiently supplied with clothes at the time of the sale.

2. **Beneficial Contracts of Employment** A contract of service entered into by a minor is regarded as valid and binding but only if it is substantially for the minor's benefit.

    > Therefore in *De Francesco v. Barnum 1890* a minor's apprenticeship contract for stage dancing provided that she was to be totally at her master's disposal and there was no requirement that she should be paid. After examining its provisions the court decided that the contract was generally harsh and onerous in nature and therefore not legally binding on the minor.

    Generally, to be regarded as beneficial a minor's contract of employment must provide for some element of education or training. The term education however is used in its widest sense and has been held to include professional boxing and professional billiard playing.

b. **Voidable Contracts** A voidable contract is one which is binding but can be **avoided** (set aside) at the option of one of the parties to it. If a minor enters into a contract which is voidable in his favour he remains bound by its provisions but has the option of avoiding it prior to or within a reasonable time of attaining the age of majority. Within this category are long term contracts, or contracts where the minor obtains an interest in something of a permanent nature. They include contracts for:-

    i.   the purchase of a lease;
    ii.   the creation of a partnership;
    iii. the acquisition of shares.

c. **Void Contracts** A void contract is one which has **no legal effect.** Under the **Infants Relief Act 1874 s.1** certain contracts entered into by minors are absolutely void. These include contracts for:-

    i.   the repayment of money lent or to be lent;
    ii.   goods supplied or to be supplied (other than necessaries);
    iii. accounts stated (e.g. in acknowledgement of a debt - I.O.U.s).

It does seem from the case-law authorities that a void contract under the **Infants Relief Act 1874** may have some legal effect for the courts have allowed an infant to sue on such a contract and certainly money and goods transferred are not automatically recoverable.

d.   **Unenforceable Contracts** An unenforceable contract is one which is valid in all respects but unenforceable in a court of law. Under the **Infants Relief Act 1874 s.2** an individual cannot sue on a promise by a person now of full age to repay a debt incurred while a minor.

The Contractual Capacity of Corporate Bodies

A corporate body or corporation is simply an **artificial person** created under the law (usually by statute) with a distinct legal identity separate from the members who compose it. As a separate legal person therefore, having perpetual succession, a corporate body has the capacity to own land, enter into contracts, sue and be sued. Corporations are particularly significant as business organisations operating as public limited or private companies registered under the Companies Acts. As a general principle registered companies are limited in their activities to achieving the objects as defined in the **Memorandum of Association** (the registered document containing the company constitution). This rule is designed to protect the interests of the members (the shareholders) and to some extent the company creditors who would not wish to see company funds dissipated on unauthorised activities. An activity which is **ultra vires** (beyond the powers) of the company may therefore be declared void and of no legal effect.

> The famous case of *Ashbury Rail Co. v. Riche 1875* confirms this basic principle of law. Here the company entered into a contract for the construction of a railway in Belgium despite its objects being defined as to make or sell or lend or hire railway carriages and rail rolling stock. The court held that as the contract was clearly beyond the activities of the company as expressed in the objects clause of the Memorandum, it was void on the grounds of ultra vires.

Certainly this rule has been modified to a large extent by the effect of **s.9(1) European Communities Act 1972.** As a result of this section outsiders who deal in good faith with the proper agents of a company are given a measure of protection, for in such circumstances the activity engaged upon is presumed to be **'intra vires'** (with the powers of the company) as far as the outsider is concerned.

In relation to the corporate status of local authorities the same basic principles apply. They are statutory bodies under the **Local Government Act 1972 s.2** and as such the objects which such corporations may legitimately pursue must be ascertained from the Act itself. Over the years however, the ultra vires doctrine has not been applied rigidly to local authorities and the courts have consistently held that local authorities may not only do things for which there is express or implied authority, but also whatever is reasonably incidental to the doing of those things.

> Thus in *Attorney General v. Smethwich Corporation 1932* a resolution was passed by the corporation for the establishment of a printing and stationery works for the purpose of executing works required by them. An action was brought by the Attorney General on behalf of a ratepayer on the grounds that the proposal was ultra vires. The court held that the formation of this department was reasonably incidental or consequential upon the carrying out of the corporation's statutory duties and was not therefore ultra vires.

This common law rule was reflected in the general power to contract conferred on local authorities by virtue of **s.111 Local Government Act 1972.** This section provides that authorities are empowered to do anything (whether or not involving the expenditure, borrowing or lending of money or the acquisition or disposal of any property or rights) which is calculated to facilitate, or is conducive or incidental to, the discharge of any of their functions. Provided therefore that the activity carried on is related to the particular functions of the council in question it seems that it can be justified. This general power to contract conferred on local authorities is of course supplemented by a multiplicity of specific powers from various statutes, e.g. **The Local Authority (Goods and Services) Act 1970** enables an authority to contract with other public bodies for the supply of goods and services. In addition, a local authority by its own conduct cannot extend its statutory powers.

> Thus in *Rhyl Urban District Council v. Rhyl Amusements Ltd. 1959* the authority granted a lease relying on powers contained in private legislation. Realising that these powers did not authorise the grant of the lease the council purported to rely on general leasing power conferred by the **Public Health Act 1875.** Such general power required the consent of the Local Government Board to the leasing and this was never obtained.

The court held that the lease was void on the grounds of ultra vires as the council had not obtained the required consent to it. A further important point was that the **plea of estoppel** was rejected (estoppel is a rule of evidence which prevents a person from later denying the truth of some assertion previously made). The court confirmed that a statutory body could not be estopped (prevented) from later denying the validity of the lease and so indirectly enlarge its own powers.

In relation to contractual formalities, since the **Corporate Bodies Act 1960** there is no longer a requirement that a corporation need always **contract under seal** (by specialty contract). In local government however, it is usual practice to provide in standing orders that contracts over a particular sum should be entered into by deed. (The legal effect of standing orders is dealt with elsewhere in the section on building contracts in chapter 4). A corporation is therefore in the same position as an individual in relation to contractual formalities and if a contract is required to be by deed or in writing for an individual, it is similarly so required for a local authority.

3.7 Exclusion Clauses

All contracts contain express or implied terms designed to outline the respective rights and obligations of the parties. We will examine the usual terms found in building contracts, the contract for a lease, and employment contracts elsewhere in this book. At this stage however one particular term found in different types of contract is deserving of special attention because of its importance and controversial nature. It is the 'exclusion' or 'exemption' clause designed to exclude liability for breach of contract or to limit the amount of damages payable in the event of a breach. For a number of years both the judiciary through the application of the common law and Parliament through statutory provisions have sought to regulate and control their use. Particular examples of such clauses are:-

In relation to the Supply of Goods The seller shall be exempt from all liability in respect of breach of any express or implied condition or warranty in the contract.

In relation to the Supply of Services the contractor shall not be liable for the death or any injury, damage, loss, delay or accident ... wheresoever, whensoever and howsoever caused and whether by negligence of their servants or agents in the performance of the contract.

a. **Protection of the Courts** The general attitude of the courts in interpreting such clauses and protecting the consumer of goods and services, has been to show either:-

that the exclusion did not become part of the contract e.g. a supplier cannot rely on an exclusion clause contained in an unsigned document or notice which is made known after the contract has been entered into (i.e. after acceptance has taken place).

> In *Olley v. Marlborough Court Ltd. 1949* the plaintiff booked into a hotel paying for the room in advance. A notice in the hotel room attempted to exclude the liability of the hotelier for articles left in the rooms. When the plaintiff's wife's fur coat was stolen the court held that the hotelier was not entitled to rely on the exclusion clause as it was not a term of the contract which had already been entered into at the reception desk;

or **by interpreting the clause in such a way that it does not apply.** All exclusion clauses are interpreted by the courts narrowly against the person attempting to rely on them, if there is any doubt as to their application. In addition, the courts have developed the complex principle of **fundamental breach** which essentially means that if one party to a contract has fundamentally broken it (i.e. done something fundamentally different from what he agreed to do), an exclusion clause could not protect him.

> In *Farnworth Finance Facilities Ltd. v. Attryde 1970* the defendant bought a motor cycle on hire purchase. The agreement contained a clause to the effect that the cycle was supplied "subject to no condition or warranties whatsoever express or implied". As the cycle had many faults, the defendant attempted to terminate the contract, but he was sued by the plaintiff finance company, who claimed that the exemption clause excluded liability for all defects. The court held that the exclusion clause was ineffective, as there had been a fundamental breach of contract.

Today the position as regards fundamental breach is that each individual contract has to be interpreted to decide whether in all the circumstances the exclusion clause is wide enough to cover the breach complained of. Major factors in deciding this question include the bargaining power of the parties and the consideration transferred under the contract.

b. **Statutory Protection The Unfair Contract Terms Act 1977** makes
    wide changes in the law relating to clauses which attempt to exclude
    or limit liability in relation to negligence, contractual obligations,
    implied terms in sale of goods and hire purchase contracts, guarantees
    and misrepresentation. It should be stressed however that the Act
    is concerned with business liability which includes obligations arising
    from things done by a person in the course of a business or occupation
    of premises for business purposes. The term 'business' however, is
    given a wide definition and certainly covers the activities of a local
    authority. The Act has wide application affecting many areas of law
    including:—

1. **The Tort of Negligence** Liability for death or physical injury resulting
    from negligence can no longer be excluded or restricted by contract
    terms or notices and liability for other loss or damage caused by
    negligence cannot be excluded or restricted except to the extent that
    the term satisfies the test of reasonableness. The scope of this change
    in the law is very wide, for the term negligence includes:-

    - any implied obligation to exercise reasonable care in the
      performance of a contract;
    - the common law duty to exercise reasonable care;
    - the common duty of care imposed by the **Occupier's Liability
      Act 1957.**

2. **Contractual Obligations** Here the rights of a supplier of goods or
    services to exclude or limit liability in a standard form contract or
    in a contract when dealing with a consumer are severely restricted.
    The supplier can no longer claim to be entitled to perform his
    contractual obligations in a substantially different manner from that
    which was reasonably expected of him, or to fail to perform his
    obligations at all in respect of the whole or part of his obligations
    except in so far as the contract term satisfies the **test of reasonableness.**
    This restriction therefore applies to **standard form contracts** between
    business organisations and certainly would cover a building contract
    entered into by a local authority employer and a building contractor.

    It also applies to any contract where one party **deals as a consumer**
    whether negotiated, or in a standard form. A party deals as a
    consumer, provided that he does not contract in the course of business
    and buys goods of a type ordinarily supplied for private use or

consumption. The effect of the restriction is to require the following types of exclusion clauses to satisfy the test of reasonableness:-

- If a supplier in breach of contract attempts to exclude or limit his liability (e.g. to £200).
- If a supplier attempts to reserve the right to perform his contractual obligations in a substantially different manner, e.g. in a sale of goods contract, supply goods of a different nature to those agreed.
- If a supplier attempts to reserve the right not to perform his contractual obligations, e.g. non delivery of goods because of strikes.

Although consumer protection is not the province of this book it should also be mentioned that the Act greatly restricts the rights of a seller to exclude his liability for supplying goods which are defective or inserting such exclusion clauses in so-called guarantees. In a number of cases therefore the validity of an exclusion clause will depend upon it satisfying the test of reasonableness as interpreted by applying the guidelines contained in the Act, e.g.

i.   The bargaining power of the parties;
ii. Any inducement given to the customer;
iii. The availability of contracting elsewhere without the clause;
iv. The customer's knowledge of the clause;
v.   Whether the goods were manufactured to the customer's special order.

It would seem that the most crucial factors to be taken into account would be the bargaining strength of the parties and the consideration transferred under the contract, bearing in mind the presence of the clause.

CHAPTER 4 The Contents of a Building Contract and the Discharge of Contract

4.1 The Building Contract

A specialist form of contract particularly relevant to housing management is the building contract. Such contracts are entered into by individuals requiring building work to be carried out (called the **employer)** and individuals willing to perform the service (called **contractors).** There is no requirement that building contracts be in any particular form but of course they will vary in nature depending on the extent of the works to be carried out. Thus a contract to replace windows in a dwelling house might be purely oral in nature while a contract to build a number of houses will be embodied within a **standard form agreement.** Whatever the nature of work however the basic rules on the formation of contract dealt with in Chapter 3 are relevant. An invitation to tender amounts therefore to an invitation to treat while the tenderers' or builders' estimates will constitute a contractual offer capable of acceptance or rejection. Under **s.135 Local Government Act 1972** a housing authority must comply with its own standing orders in relation to the practice of contracting. In the case of contracts for the execution of works, the standing orders must contain provisions for ensuring competition and for regulating the manner in which tenders are invited. This is subject to the right of an authority to exempt any contract from relevant standing orders if the authority is satisfied that the exemption was necessary.

The question as to whether a contractor can require a local authority to comply with its own standing orders in relation to tendering was considered in *R v. Hereford Corporation, ex-parte Harrower 1970.* Here the authority invited tenders from the N.C.B. and Gas and Electricity Boards for the installation of central heating equipment. A number of rival contractors on the council's "approved list" applied to the court for an order of "mandamus" (to compel action) directing the local authority to comply with its own standing orders in relation to public

67

tender. The court held that while an order of mandamus would lie, it was felt that as the local authority had the power to suspend standing orders it should have the opportunity to do so before the order was issued.

This decision effectively recognises that compliance with standing orders is a matter for each local authority and is not a matter subject to the control of outsiders. Once tenders have been submitted there is no obligation on the employer to accept the lowest tender. An acceptance of a tender subject to conditions will amount to a rejection of the offer and constitute a counter offer. The element of consideration transferred is **executory** in nature in the form of promises, i.e. a promise to carry out the defined work in return for a promise of payment. All building contracts will contain terms, including those expressly agreed orally or in writing and those terms implied by the law. An example of an implied term would be that the work and materials used should be of a proper standard.

4.2 Standard Form Building Contracts

Despite there being no legal requirement that building contracts be in a particular form, where extensive works are to be carried out involving the payment of large sums of money it is natural that the contracting parties will want the detailed terms of the contract specified in writing. For this reason reliance is usually placed on standard form building contracts designed to spell out all the relevant terms and minimise the danger of ambiguity for the benefit of both parties. The present standard contract relied on is the **Joint Contracts Tribunal (J.C.T.) form 1980 edition** of which there are different types depending on the contracting work to be carried out. There is a specific **Local Authorities Edition Standard form** to take account of local government requirements. Certainly the content of standard form building contracts is too detailed to be expressed in a book of this nature but what can be done is at least to describe the usual clauses which are included. The contract will usually commence with the **Article of Agreement** in which the contractor expressly agrees to carry out the specified works as described and the employer agrees to furnish the **'contract sum'** for the completion of the works. Here it is usual to describe the architect and surveyor and the procedure by which their replacements could be appointed. The Articles will also contain an **arbitration clause** for the settling of disputes and describing the circumstances and machinery for the appointment of an arbitrator. It is here that the document is signed and if it is a specialty contract, sealed and delivered. Usually a specialty contract is executed, for it gives the parties the added protection of a twelve year limitation period to take legal action following a breach. For a simple contract the limitation period is only six years, which in terms of building work is a relatively short period to discover defects.

The clauses of a standard form contract are set out as contractual conditions and relate to:-

a.   the contractor's obligations to carry out the work and use materials of the specified standard;

b.   the payment of the contract sum and V.A.T.;

c.   the duty of the contractor to comply with the architect's instructions and give him reasonable access to the site;

d.   the specified materials and payment for them;

e.   the statutory obligations in relation to such matters as the payment of fees and serving of notice that local authority inspection is required;

f.   the payment of royalties for use of patented materials;

g.   the power to vary the specified works and require defects to be remedied;

h.   the power to appoint a clerk of the works;

i.   the restriction on the parties right to assign;

j.   the rights of the employer to take possession of completed parts;

k.   the provision of insurance cover for injury to persons or property and the contractor's agreement to indemnify the employer;

l.   the date of completion, possession, liquidated damages, time extensions, rights to determine on the happening of specified events;

m. the system of certificated payments by instalments as the work is completed in stages;

n. the definition of who is to be treated as nominated subcontractor or supplier.

The above are some of the usual clauses found in a JCT standard form building contract. Unfortunately the matter is further complicated because of the need of main contractors to engage sub-contractors to carry out specialist works. Once again, to protect the parties, despite there being no legal requirement, it is usual for the terms of a contractor/subcontractor relationship to be included with a standard form sub-contract coming within the JCT 1980 edition.

4.3 Discharge of Contract

Having considered the essential elements of a valid contract in Chapter 3 it is now necessary to show how a contract may be discharged, i.e. terminated. The parties to a contract will have secured certain rights and be subject to certain obligations under it. The usual method of discharge of a contract is therefore by the parties actually performing their respective obligations under it.

1. Discharge by Performance

The general rule is that complete performance, complying precisely to the contractual terms, is necessary to discharge the contract.

An illustration of this common law rule is the case of *Sumpter v. Hedges 1898*. Here the plaintiff builder agreed to erect some houses for a lump sum of £565. Having carried out half the work to the value of £333 the builder was unable to complete the work because of financial difficulties. In an action by the builder to recover compensation for the value of the work done, the Court of Appeal confirmed that he was not entitled to payment. The legal position was expressed by Smith, L.J. who stated "The law is that where there is a contract to do work for a lump sum, until the work is completed, the price of it cannot be recovered".

On the face of it the decision of the court appears to be harsh in its effect upon the builder. In fact the difficulty for the court is an obvious one, namely that a single sum has been agreed in consideration of the completion of specified works. If these works are not completed in their entirety the court would be varying the clearly expressed intentions of the parties if it was to award the builder payment of a proportionate part of the lump sum. In other words, by agreeing a lump sum the parties have impliedly excluded the possibility of part payment for partially fulfilled building work.

The above rules, however, requiring precise performances of contractual obligations can in practice produce injustice. The law has therefore recognised certain exceptions.

a.   **A Divisible Contract** In some circumstances the courts are prepared to accept that a contract is a divisible one where part of the performance of the contract may be set off against part of the consideration to be given in return. Had the parties in *Sumpter v. Hedges* agreed a specific sum to be paid on completion of certain stages of the house building, then the builder could have recovered compensation for part of the work done. In practice it is usual in a building contract to provide for payment of parts of the total cost at various stages of completion.

b.   **Substantial Performance** If a party to a contract has substantially performed his contractual obligations subject only to minor defects, the courts have recognised that it would be unjust to prevent him recovering any of the contractual price. Therefore under this exception the contractual price would be recoverable, less of course a sum representing the value of the defects. It must be stressed that the exception will only operate where the defects are of a trifling nature. This question is determined by considering not only the nature of the defects but also the cost of rectifying them in relation to the total contract price.

A claim of substantial performance of the contract was made in *Bolton v. Mahadeva 1972*. Here the plaintiff, a heating contractor, had agreed to install a central heating system in the defendant's house for £560. On completion of the work the system proved to be so defective that it would cost £174 to repair. The defendant refused to pay the plaintiff any of the cost of the work and the plaintiff sued. The County Court accepted the plaintiff's claim of substantial performance and awarded him the cost of the work less the cost of repair. On appeal however, the Court of Appeal held that in the circumstances the plaintiff had not substantially performed the contract and he was not therefore entitled to recover any of the cost of the work. The exception would not operate where there were numerous defects requiring a relatively high cost of repair.

c. **The Acceptance of Partial Performance** If a party to a contract partially performs his obligations and the other party accepts the benefit, then he is obliged to pay a reasonable price for it. Thus if a buyer in a sale of goods contract opts to accept rather than reject a delivery of less than the agreed quantity, then he is obliged to pay a reasonable price for it. In such circumstances the courts would allow an action on a **quantum meruit basis** (as much as he deserves). This exception however will only operate where the party receiving the benefit has the option of whether or not to accept or reject. In *Sumpter v. Hedges* the owner had no choice but to accept the work done on the half completed houses and was therefore not obliged to pay for it.

d. **Where performance is prevented** Obviously if a party to a contract is prevented from fulfilling his contractual obligations by the other party then he will not be in default, e.g. if in a building contract the owner prevents the builder from completing. In these circumstances the builder can recover a reasonable price for the work done on a quantum meruit basis.

As well as the above exceptions to the general rule that the performance of contractual obligations must be precise, it is important to note that if a party to a contract makes a **valid tender (offer) of performance** this may be regarded as equivalent to performance. Thus if one party (a seller) cannot complete performance without the co-operation of the other party (a buyer), a valid tender of performance by the seller will be sufficient to discharge him from the contract, e.g. if a seller of goods attempts to deliver at the agreed time and place and the goods are of the correct quantity and quality and such delivery is wrongly refused by the buyer. Under the **Sale of Goods Act 1979 s.50** the seller in such circumstances could sue the buyer for damages for non acceptance of the goods.

2. Discharge by Agreement

This method of discharge occurs where the parties to a contract agree to **waive** their rights and obligations under it. It is called **bilateral discharge.** To be an effective waiver the second agreement must be a contract, the consideration for which being the exchange of promises not to enforce the original contract. The situation however is more complex where one party to a contract has already executed or partly executed his consideration under it. Here for a waiver to be effective it must be embodied within a **specialty contract** or be supported by **fresh consideration.** This is called **unilateral discharge** and can only be achieved by **accord and satisfaction.** The accord is simply the agreement to discharge and the satisfaction is the consideration required to support it, e.g. X contracts to sell goods to Y for £50. X delivers the goods to Y and then hearing of Y's financial difficulties agrees to waive payment. Here the agreement of X to waive payment (the accord) is not enforceable unless supported by fresh consideration furnished by Y (the satisfaction). The fresh consideration of course must be of value but need not be adequate. The position would be the same if X promised to accept £25 as full discharge of the debt of £50. There is a well known common law rule established in *Pinnel's Case 1602* that payment of a lesser sum is not satisfaction of an agreement to pay a larger sum even though the creditor agrees to take it in full discharge. The effect of this somewhat harsh common law rule would be to permit a creditor to renege on his promise. There are in fact a number of exceptions to the rule under which the courts will be prepared to accept that satisfaction, i.e. fresh consideration, has been supplied under the new agreement. Thus, if the creditor agrees:-

a. A payment of a lesser sum before the due date. This would constitute consideration to discharge the £50 debt.

b. Payment in an altered mode, e.g. a £5 book would constitute consideration to discharge the £50 debt. Payment of a cheque however for less than £50 would not be a sufficient alteration in mode unless done at the request of the creditor, see *D. & C. Builders v. Rees 1965.*

c. Payment of a lesser sum with something of value in addition, e.g. £10 and a bottle of brandy, would constitute consideration to discharge the £50 debt.

d. Payment of a lesser sum by a third party will discharge the £50 debt.

e. Payment of a lesser sum where the debtor is disputing the value of work that has been carried out by the creditor will discharge the debt, e.g. where a plumber has installed a central heating system for an agreed price, and when payment becomes due the creditor refuses to pay the full sum because of the alleged poor quality of the work performed.

A creditor's promise to accept a reduced amount may also be binding upon him through the operation of the principle of **equitable estoppel.**

> This principle was enunciated by Denning, J. in *Central London Property Trust Ltd. v. High Trees House Ltd. 1947.* The case involved the lease of a block of flats in 1939 from A to B at a rent of £2,500 p.a. In 1940 because of the lack of tenants in London caused by the war conditions the parties agreed in writing to a reduction of the rent to £1,250 p.a. As no time limit was set for the new agreement, B continued to pay the reduced rent after the war had ended, despite the fact that the flats were fully sublet. A, the landlord, now claimed rent at the rate of £2,500 p.a. for the last two quarters of 1945. The Court held that as the agreement for a reduced rent was intended to operate during the war conditions, the full rent was payable on expiration of the war and therefore for the last two quarters of 1945. Denning, J. also considered whether the common law rule that the "payment of a lesser sum will not discharge the full debt" would render A's promise to accept a lesser rent unenforceable and enable him to claim back the full rent for the whole period. Relying on the earlier case of *Hughes v. Metropolitan Railway Co. 1877,* Denning, J. thought in such circumstances it would be inequitable to allow A to go back on his promise.

The principle of law relied on was termed equitable estoppel and still today is subject to much academic debate as to its limits. It may be stated as follows- if X, a party to a legal relationship, indicates by a promise to the other party, Y, that he is not going to insist on his strict legal rights, and as a result Y alters his position to his detriment, then, although Y may not sue to enforce the promise, he may use the promise as a defence if X purports to go back on it. For the principle to operate therefore it is necessary that the fresh promise was intended by the promisor, X, to be acted upon and has in fact been acted upon to the promisee, Y's, detriment. This act must also be known to the promisor, X. It should be noted that the fresh promise cannot be enforced by court action brought by the promisee, Y, but is available as a defence to him if the promisor, X, attempts to go back on it. The principle of equitable estoppel is "a shield not a sword".

It must be stressed that the equitable doctrine is not an attempt to remove consideration as a requirement of the simple contract, but rather a principle under which equity seeks to hold a promisor to a promise which he intends to bind him, and which he knows has been acted upon by the promisee. The equitable doctrine only arises within the context of a pre-existing contractual relationship. It is worth pointing out that the *High Trees* decision is an authority which also supports the view that a deed can be varied by a simple contract. Prior to 1947 it had always been considered that because a simple contract is inferior to the more formal deed, that only a deed could vary a deed.

3. Discharge by Breach

If a party to a contract fails to perform his obligations under it or performs his obligations in a defective manner then he may be regarded as being in breach of contract. Generally, the remedy of an innocent party to a contract who has suffered as a result of a breach is to sue for damages. For some breaches of contract however, the innocent party is given the additional remedy of **repudiation** (i.e. termination of the contract) and thus discharging himself from obligations under it. Terms in a contract are classified into different categories and it is only when an important term in the contract has been broken **(a 'condition')** that the remedy of repudiation is attached (see Chapter 8).

If a breach of contract occurs before the time set for performance of the conract it is called an **anticipatory breach.** This would occur where a party to a contract expressly declares that he will not perform his part of the bargain. Once an anticipatory breach has occurred the innocent party does not have to wait for the date set for performance but has the option of immediately suing for breach of contract.

In *Hochster v. De la Tour 1853* the defendant agreed in April to engage the plaintiff for work to commence in June. The defendant told the plaintiff in May that he would not require his services. The court held that a cause of action for breach of contract arose on the anticipatory breach in May.

4.   **Discharge by Frustration**

A contract may be discharged by frustration where as a result of an event subsequent to making of the contract, performance of the contract can no longer be carried out. The event must be subsequent to the contract for if the contract is impossible to perform at the time it is made then there is no contract. Originally the common law did not take such a lenient view of changes in circumstances and required that the parties to a contract should provide for all eventualities. If because of a subsequent event performance of an obligation became impossible, the party required to perform the impossible obligation would be liable to pay damages for non performance.

In *Paradine v. Jane 1647* the King's Bench Court held a tenant liable to pay three years' arrears of rent to a landlord despite the fact that the tenant had been dispossessed of his house by soldiers during the Civil War.

Today however the courts recognise that certain supervening events may frustrate a contract and thus release the parties from their obligations under it, e.g.

a.   **Changes in the law** If because of new legislation perfomance of the contract would become illegal this would be a supervening event to frustrate the contract. In *Denny, Mott and Dickson Ltd. v. James B. Fraser Ltd. 1944* the House of Lords held that a contract for the sale of timber was frustrated because of the subsequent passage of various Control of Timber Orders rendering performance of the contract illegal.

b.   **Destruction of subject matter** If the subject matter or means of performance of the contract is destroyed this is an event which frustrates a contract. In *Taylor v. Caldwell 1863* the plaintiff agreed to hire the defendant's music hall to give some concerts.

Prior to performance the hall was destroyed by fire and this event, the court held, released the parties from their obligations under the contract.

c.   **Inability to achieve main object** If as a result of a change in circumstances performance of the contract would be radically different than the performance envisaged by the parties then the contract is frustrated. It must be shown that the parties are no longer able to achieve their main object under the contract. In *Krell v. Henry 1903* the defendant hired a flat for two days to enable him to watch Edward VII's coronation procession. Due to the King's illness the Coronation was cancelled and the defendant naturally refused to pay. The Court of Appeal held that as the main object of the contract was to view the procession, and this could no longer be achieved, the foundation of the contract had collapsed. The contract was thus frustrated and the parties released from their obligations under it.

The cancellation of Edward VII's Coronation resulted in a similar case to contrast with *Krell v. Henry*. In *Herne Bay Steam Boat Co. v. Hutton 1903* a steam boat had been chartered to watch the naval review as part of the Coronation celebrations and also for a day's cruise round the fleet. The Court of Appeal had to determine whether the cancellation of the naval review released the defendant from his obligation to pay the hire charges. The Court held that there had not been a sufficient change in circumstances to constitute a frustration of the contract. Here the defendant could have derived some benefit from the contract and was therefore liable to pay the hire charges.

d.   **Death or illness** In a contract for personal services the death or illness of the person required to perform will frustrate the contract. Temporary illness or incapacity will generally not release a party from his obligations, the illness must be such that it goes to the root of the contract. The common law doctrine of frustration will not apply in the following situations:-

1.   If performance of the contract has become **more onerous on one party or financially less rewarding**. In *Davis Contractors Ltd. v. Fareham U.D.C. 1956* the plaintiff building company

77

claimed that a building contract should be regarded as discharged by frustration due to the shortage of available labour and resultant increased costs. The House of Lords rejected the argument that frustration had discharged the contract. Performance of the contract had simply been made more onerous than originally envisaged by the plaintiffs.

2. If the parties to a contract have made **express provision for the event which has occurred** then the common law doctrine of frustration is inapplicable. The courts will simply give effect to the intention of the parties as expressed in the contract.

3. Finally a distinction must be drawn between a **frustrating event** over which the parties have no control and a **self-induced frustration.** If it can be shown that a party to the contract caused the supposed frustrating event by his own conduct then there will be no frustration but there may be a contractual breach.

To determine the rights and duties of the parties following frustration it is necessary to consider the position at common law and under statute. Frustration of course will terminate a contract. However under the common law it does not discharge the contract **ab initio** (i.e. from the outset) but only from the time of the frustrating event. Therefore, if before that date work had been done or money transferred, the common law rule is simply that losses lie where they fall. It is thus not possible to recover money due or paid prior to frustrating events, except if there is a total failure of consideration, i.e. there has been performance of consideration by one party and non performance of consideration by the other.

The common law position has been altered to some extent by the **Law Reform (Frustrated Contracts) Act 1943.** The Act however does not apply to certain contracts such as insurance, charter-parties (shipping contracts) and contracts for the sale of specific goods, so the common law position is still relevant. Under the Act the following conditions apply:-

i. Money transferred prior to the frustrating event may be recovered.

ii. Money due prior to the frustrating event is no longer due.

iii. Expenses incurred prior to the frustrating event may be deducted from money due to be returned.

iv.   Compensation may be recovered on a quantum meruit basis (as much as he deserves) where one of the parties has carried out an act of **part performance** prior to the frustrating event and thus conferred a benefit on the other party.

4.4 Remedies for Breach of Contract

No account of the principles of contract would be complete without some mention of the various remedies available to an innocent party in the event of a breach. The options available are to claim damages and/or treat the contract as discharged under the common law, or pursue an equitable discretionary remedy.

Damages

The usual remedy is to sue for **unliquidated damages** (decided by the court) under the common law. Such damages, if awarded, should amount to a sum of money which will put the innocent party in the position he would have been had the contract been performed properly, i.e. the loss resulting from the breach directly and naturally. The courts have held however that it would be unfair to make a contract-breaker responsible for damage caused as a result of circumstances of which he was unaware.

> In *Hadley v. Baxendale 1854* the plaintiff mill owner contracted with a defendant carrier who agreed to take a broken millshaft to a repairer and then return it. The carrier delayed in delivery of the shaft and as a result the plaintiff sought to recover the loss of profit he would have made during the period of delay. The court held that this loss was not recoverable as it was too remote. The possible loss of profit was a circumstance of which the carrier was unaware at the time of the contract. The result would have been different however had the plaintiff expressly made the defendant aware that this loss of profit was the probable result of a breach of contract.

In substantial contracts involving large sums, e.g. building contracts, it is usual to attempt to liquidate damages payable in the event of a breach. This is achieved by the parties expressly inserting a clause in the contract providing for a sum of compensation to be payable on a breach. Generally, provided such clauses represent a **genuine pre-estimate of the future possible loss** rather than **amount to a penalty** to ensure performance of the contract, they are enforceable by the courts.

The right to treat a contract as discharged will depend upon the nature of the breach. For breaches of important contractual terms the innocent party has an option to **repudiate** (terminate) the contract, whereas for less important terms the innocent party is limited to an action for damages.

Discretionary Remedies

These remedies are available because of the intervention of the Court of Chancery and include the **injunction and specific performance.** An injunction is an order of the court commanding someone not to do something while specific performance is an order requiring an individual to do something. As equitable remedies, they are discretionary in nature, and are never granted where a common law remedy (e.g. damages) is sufficient to compensate the injured party. The injunction is sought as a remedy mainly in tort actions such as **trespass or nuisance** but could be used to prevent a threatened breach of contract. Specific performance has wider application in contract but is never granted to enforce contracts of **personal service** or contracts which **require supervision** to ensure that the work is properly carried out. Its importance as a remedy can be seen in contracts for the disposition of interests in land and it is for that reason examined in detail later in chapter 6.

Part 3 - **Landholding**

CHAPTER 5   An Introduction to Landholding

The complexity of the law relating to landholding is due to its antiquity and also to the fact that land is permanent property, and therefore lends itself to the creation of numerous **consecutive and concurrent interests.** All this means is that many different individuals may have an interest in the same piece of land, e.g. as an owner, tenant, sub-tenant, mortgagee, neighbour or beneficiary under a trust. Before considering the nature of land ownership it is necessary first to briefly show how land, as a form of property, is classified under English law.

5.1 The Classification of Property

The expression **"property"** simply means under English law anything that is capable of ownership, e.g. land, buildings, cars, debts, etc. The most obvious way of classifying property would be to distinguish between **movable** property (e.g. goods, shares in companies, cheques, etc.) and **immovable** property (e.g. land and buildings) as they do in many European countries. Unfortunately, the English classification of property is not as simple as that, due mainly to the long historical development of English land law over 900 years. Under English law, the basic division is between **Real** and **Personal** property.

The only category of real property is **Freehold land** because originally it was the only type of property which was protected by a **Real action** in court. This meant that, if a freehold owner was wrongfully dispossessed of his land, he could bring a real action to recover the land itself rather than compensation for its loss. All other types of property is classified as **personal property.** Originally if an owner was wrongfully dispossessed of personal property he could only rely on a **personal action** which gave him no right to recover the property lost and he had to be content with compensation as a remedy. As early as the 15th century however, the courts began to recognise exceptions to this rule so that today an owner wrongfully dispossessed of personal property can normally recover the thing lost. The classification of real and personal property however remains the same. Real property then is freehold land, and any form of property which is not freehold land is classified as personal property.

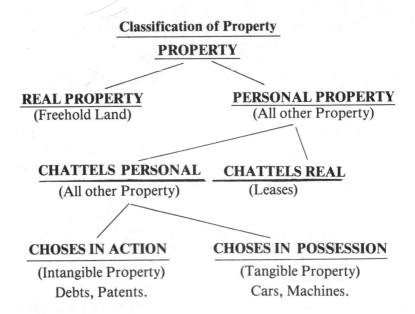

Classification of Property

PROPERTY

REAL PROPERTY
(Freehold Land)

PERSONAL PROPERTY
(All other Property)

CHATTELS PERSONAL
(All other Property)

CHATTELS REAL
(Leases)

CHOSES IN ACTION
(Intangible Property)
Debts, Patents.

CHOSES IN POSSESSION
(Tangible Property)
Cars, Machines.

Personal Property

Personal property (otherwise known as chattels) is further sub-divided into **chattels real** (leases) and **chattels personal** (all other personal property). The main characteristics of a lease are considered in the next chapter. As far as chattels personal are concerned there is one further sub-division into **Choses in Action** (intangible property, e.g. cheques, debts, patents, copyright, goodwill) and **Choses in Possession** (tangible property, e.g. cars, typewriters, radios, etc.). The word chose simply means 'thing' so that a chose in action is a thing which may be owned but has no physical existence. A chose in possession is a thing that has tangible existence and can be transferred by physical delivery.

5.2 Tenure and Estate

The ownership of all land in England and Wales is vested in the Crown so that holders of land are still technically **tenants of the Crown.** The expression 'tenure' refers to the **terms upon** which a tenant has rights over the land. In feudal times, the tenure would be to render military services, e.g. knight's service, or agricultural services. Now mainly as a result of the **property legislation of 1925** the only tenure recognised by the common law is called **freehold tenure.** In the modern day a tenant acquires rights over land (a tenure) by monetary payment.

The expression **'estate in land'** refers to the measure of a tenant's interest in land from the **point of view of time.** Basically there are two main types of estate under English law, the **freehold estate** and the **leasehold estate.**

a.   The freehold estate.
The main characteristics of this estate is that it is of uncertain duration. The two main categories of freehold estate are:—

> 1.   **the fee simple** This is the freehold estate which is normally associated with absolute ownership of land and incidentally usually referred to as the **'freehold'.** The word **'fee'** means that the estate is capable of being inherited and will not terminate on the death of the individual tenant. **'Simple'** indicates that there is no restriction on who may inherit the estate.

> 2.   **the life estate** Here an estate is granted which will last for the life of the tenant and so is of uncertain duration. As an alternative to the life estate it is possible to create an estate which will terminate in the hands of the tenant on the death of another, i.e. an estate **'pur autre vie'** (for another's life).

b.   The leasehold estate.
This is the estate enjoyed by a tenant under a lease creating the **relationship of landlord and tenant.** The major characteristic of a leasehold estate is that it is of a **certain duration,** e.g. a ten-year lease, or a duration that is capable of being made certain, e.g. a monthly tenancy, by service of notice to quit. A leasehold estate is held under the terms (covenants) of a lease, the effect of which is to give the tenant the right to occupy the land to the exclusion of all others (including the landlord) for the term of the lease. When the fixed term expires or in the case of a periodic term, e.g. a monthly tenancy, the landlord gives notice to quit, the landlord may repossess the land subject to the tenant's rights in relation to security of tenure. The creation and contents of a leasehold are considered later in the book.

Reversionary Interests

It was mentioned previously that land as permanent property lends itself to the creation of a number of concurrent and consecutive interests. Under the law it is possible for the owner of an estate in land to confer a lesser estate upon another, e.g. X, the owner of a fee simple estate in Blackacre may grant a life estate to another, Y. During the life of Y, X is said to hold a **'reversion'** because on Y's death, Blackacre will revert back to X or his personal representatives. During Y's life then, both X and Y hold interests over Blackacre which may be **assigned** (transferred) to another or even used to borrow money by way of a mortgage. It is possible for X to go one step further and create a **settlement.** This is simply a succession of estates which would occur if X, the fee simple owner of Blackacre, granted a life estate to Y and thereafter to Z in fee simple. Z's estate is referred to as the **'remainder'** because on Y's death it will remain away from X, the holder of the reversion and vest in Z or his personal representatives. Reversions and remainders are referred to collectively as **reversionary interests** as interests which will fall into possession in the future.

Legal Estates and Equitable Interests

In the introductory chapter mention was made of the major contribution of equity to the development of English law. This feature of the English legal system is no better demonstrated than in English land law. Prior to the **Judicature Acts 1873-5** rights in relation to landholding were divided into **legal estates** which were protected by the common law courts and **equitable interests** protected by the courts of equity. The court system was reformed in 1873-5 and a unified system created, but the two distinct branches of law, common law and equity, survived. Following the property legislation of 1925, particularly the **Law of Property Act, 1925,** major reforms were introduced intended to simplify land law.

One of the most radical reforms was introduced by **s.1 Law of Property Act 1925** which provides that only **two legal estates** are now recognised at common law. These are:—

    a.   **a fee simple absolute in possession** (freehold estate); and

    b.   **a term of years absolute** (leasehold estate).

The term 'fee simple' has already been considered. The word **'absolute'** refers to the fact that the estate granted must not be subject to any conditions and the word **'possession'** means that the estate is to take effect immediately. A **'term of years absolute'** is simply a lease granted for a fixed term, e.g. ten years or for a term capable of being made fixed by service of notice to quit, e.g. a monthly tenancy. To determine whether one of these two legal estates has been created, it is necessary to examine the document which granted the interest in land. In particular, reference must be made to the words which define the interest, called **'words of purchase'**. If the words of purchase are 'to A in fee simple' then a legal estate is created. This is because in the absence of words to the contrary the estate is taken to be unconditional and therefore 'absolute' and to take effect immediately and therefore be 'in possession'. Alternatively if the words of purchase are 'to A in fee simple absolute from 1985' obviously this is not a legal estate as it is not 'in possession' and does not take effect until 1985. As the grant is not of a legal estate it can survive only as an **equitable interest**.

All types of landholding other than legal estates become equitable interests and are required to be held under a **trust**, e.g. a family settlement, a life estate, a fee simple in remainder, a conditional fee simple. Under a trust the legal estate is held by **trustees** for the individual or individuals who have the **benefit of ownership**, e.g. the beneficiaries of the trust. Due to the intervention of equity, as between the immediate parties there is little distinction between an **equitable interest** in land and a **legal interest** in land. Thus a landlord and tenant have basically the same rights and obligations towards each other whether they hold under a legal lease or under an equitable lease (see Chapter 6). In relation to third parties however, the general rule is that an equitable right such as an equitable easement will be unenforceable against a bona fide purchaser of the legal estate without notice of the equitable interest. This means that on a transfer of the legal estate to such a person without notice of the equitable easement, it will not be binding on him. In practice the holder of an equitable interest is taken to have given constructive notice of its existence to a prospective purchaser by registering the interest as a **land charge** under the **Land Charges Act 1972**. By registering the equitable interest in this manner the holder becomes protected against third party purchasers who have no actual notice of its existence but are taken to have constructive notice of it.

5.3 Co-ownership

This occurs when two or more persons have concurrent interests in the same property, e.g. land is granted to A and B in fee simple. The two main forms of co-ownership are **joint tenancy** and **tenancy in common.** The main difference between them is that the **right of survivorship** (jus accrescendi) applies to joint tenancies but not to tenancies in common. This means that on the death of a joint tenant the remaining tenant will inherit his interest. Alternatively a tenant in common has a distinct share in the land, which is capable of being assigned, and will devolve on his personal representatives on his death as part of his estate. For all practical purposes whenever a disposition of land creates co-ownership, the land is held upon **statutory trust for sale.** The trustees are normally the co-owners themselves except when the co-ownership is created by a will and then the trustees are usually the deceased's personal representatives. The trustees, of whom there can be no more than four, hold the legal estate as joint tenants.

While a legal estate cannot be held in individual shares (the trustees holding as joint tenants), the equitable interests of the beneficial co-owners may be held jointly, as joint tenants or in common, as tenants in common. The words of the grant will usually make it clear which form of co-ownership is desired. If **'words of severance'** are used in the grant, e.g. to hold 'equally' or in 'equal shares' the beneficial interest will be held as tenants in common. Where the terms of the grant are silent, then as a general rule a joint tenancy is created subject to two exceptions:—

1.   Equity supported the tenancy in common as a form of co-ownership and will presume it, unless there is express indication to the contrary, where the co-owner's purchase money is in unequal proportions or where the co-owners are mortgagees or partners.

2.   A joint tenancy cannot exist without the presence of the **'four unities'.** These are unities of **possession, interest, title** and **time.** Unity of possession means that each co-owner has possession of the whole and does not have separate ownership of part of the land. Also the interest held by the co-owners must be identical and they must have derived their title (ownership) from the same interest. Finally, unity of time means that the interest of each co-owner has vested at the same time.

The most popular form of co-ownership is of course holding as beneficial joint tenants, e.g. a married couple. Of course it can lead to difficult problems particularly when co-owners (whether joint tenants or tenants in common) cannot agree to live together or dispose of the property. In such circumstances it is necessary to have recourse to the court who may have little choice but to order a sale.

5.4 Easements

These are rights which may exist over land normally as part of a land transaction or by express agreement but, in some cases by implication if in existance for more than twenty years and used as of right. An easement could confer the right to use the land of another in a particular way (a **positive easement,** e.g. a right of way) or the right to prevent another from using his land in a particular way (a **negative easement,** e.g. a right of light to prevent building on an adjacent property). Easements, like restrictive covenants, may bind successive owners of the land (see Chapter 6). However, in all cases, to be valid, there must be one piece of land which enjoys the benefit of the easement and one piece of land which bears the burden e.g. the dominant tenement and the servient tenement. Also the easement must be capable of being granted by deed and in some way add to the amenities of the land it is to benefit. Finally the pieces of land (referred to as tenements) must not be both owned and occupied by the same person.

The Prescription Act 1832 provides that a claim to an easement other than light may be based on user as of right without interruption for either 20 years or 40 years. In relation to the easement of light, the 20 year user need not be as of right, nor need it be by or on behalf of one fee simple owner against another. It is the actual user that is important and in consequence a **tenant** could acquire an easement of light under the Act against land which is occupied by another tenant of the same landlord, or the landlord himself. To enable an owner to prevent his neighbour from acquiring an easement of light the **Right of Light Act 1959** provides for the registration as a local land charge, a right of light notice specifying the size and position of a notional obstruction.

5.5 Fixtures

Fixtures which would otherwise be classified as personalty, e.g. furniture, cupboards, may by virtue of their attachment to the land, become treated as part of the land and be classified as **realty.** It is only by applying the law of fixtures that it is possible for an incoming tenant to know what forms part of the demise to him and for an outgoing tenant to know what he can remove or alternatively sell. According to the common law rule **'quicquid plantatur solo, solo cedit'** (whatever is affixed to the soil belongs to the soil) a fixture becomes the property of the owner of the fee simple and so it cannot be lawfully removed by any temporary occupier of the land even though it was he who put it there. This rule however is now subject to a number of exceptions in particular the recognition by the common law of the right of a tenant to remove domestic or trade fixtures in certain circumstances.

A fixture is something which is capable of having a separate identity of its own in a detached state. In relation to a house it is something which has been **affixed to the freehold** as an accessory to it rather than something which was part of the house itself in the course of construction, e.g. plate glass windows. The fact that a chattel is not fixed to the land or buildings but merely rests upon it raises a presumption that it is not a fixture, e.g. garden sheds, removable greenhouses. However if the intention is that the chattel resting on the land is to become a permanent feature of it there may be a sufficient **degree of annexation** for it to become a fixture, e.g. a dry stone wall. Alternatively if a chattel is fixed to the land or buildings then the presumption is raised that it is a fixture, e.g. fireplaces, immersion heaters, fans. Once again however, if the chattel is fastened to the land as a matter of convenience and there is no intention for it to become a permanent feature of the land then it will remain a chattel and be removable, e.g. nailed down carpets, plumbed in washing machines, pictures, gas fires. In deciding whether a chattel provided by a tenant constitutes a fixture the courts take into account that it is unlikely that a tenant would consciously attempt to benefit the landlord by adding to the value of the land.

Once it has been established that an item is a fixture then:—

a. ownership of the fixture will pass with the freehold on a conveyance under **s.62 Law of Property Act 1925;**

b. as it is classified as realty, ownership will pass to a devisee of the land by will or to a remainderman on the death of the tenant for life;

c. as it is part of the land it is not distrainable for arrears of rent;

d. the tenant may not remove it (landlord's fixture) except by agreement with the landlord unless it is classified as a tenant's fixture.

Tenant's fixtures

These are chattels which although regarded as fixtures are removable and fall into three groups:—

1. **Domestic fixtures.** These include domestic items which despite being annexed to the land are removable depending on the extent of damage which would be caused by the removal, e.g. fitted kitchen appliances, panelling and cupboards. There is still doubt as to the right to remove bedroom suites and fitted kitchen furniture.

2. **Trade fixtures.** Here an intention to remove expensive machinery is readily inferred, e.g. engines, transmission gear and plant. The fixture may of course constitute an improvement for which the tenant is entitled to compensation under the **Landlord and Tenant Act 1927** (see Chapter 11).

3. **Agricultural fixtures.** By virtue of **s.13 Agricultural Holdings Act 1948** an agricultural tenant is entitled to remove all trade fixtures up to two months after the expiration of the tenancy subject to the observance of certain conditions in relation to notice and an option on the landlord to purchase them. (see Chapter 11).

In relation to the removal of fixtures the tenant's right will subsist as long as he is a tenant (including a statutory tenant) entitled to possession. Once the landlord resumes possession however it seems that the tenant's rights will be lost, unless there is an express stipulation in the lease that the tenant may remove fixtures at the 'end of the term'. This is interpreted as extending the term for a reasonable period after its expiration. The landlord will have a right to an action for damages under the tort of waste in respect of any fixtures wrongfully removed by the tenant, and may also apply for an injunction to restrain such an act. The court will only award a mandatory injunction to require the tenant to replace the fixtures wrongfully removed where damages would not be an adequate remedy.

5.6 Restrictions on the holder of a fee simple (freehold estate)

As previously mentioned the holder of a fee simple estate is for all practical purposes regarded as the absolute owner of a piece of land having the right to possession of the surface of the land, the air space above and the earth below. Nevertheless, the fee simple owner is subject to many restrictions, particularly in relation to the use to which he may put the land. Examples of such restrictions on a freehold owner will now be considered. The position of the holder of a leasehold will be examined in Chapter 8.

a. **the right to minerals underneath the surface.** This right is restricted by the Crown's claim to gold, silver or petroleum and the rights of the National Coal Board to coal.

b. **the right to possession of the air space above the surface.** This right is limited by the **Civil Aviation Act 1949** which provides that aircraft have statutory authority to fly over the land at a reasonable height.

c. **the right to water.** The owner of land which adjoins a river enjoys certain rights with other owners called **riparian rights.** Generally a riparian owner may take water from a river in unrestricted quantities if it is used for ordinary purposes connected with the land. There is no right however for a riparian owner to take water for purposes not connected with the land.

d. **the right to treasure trove.** The Crown has a claim to all treasure trove found in the land, i.e. gold or silver, in any manufactured form, deliberately hidden, and where the owner is unknown. If coins or objects have been lost however they are not regarded as treasure trove.

e. **the right to develop the land.** The holder of a fee simple estate is subject to the control of the local planning authority under the **Town and Country Planning Act 1971** in relation to any proposed development of the land. Planning permission is required for any material alteration of buildings on land or the use to which they are put. If an individual is considering acquiring a piece of land, there is a means by which he can obtain **outline planning permission** for any proposed development to ascertain whether **full planning permission** is likely to be granted. The local authority will ensure minimum building standards by requiring that building regulations are complied with.

f.   **the right to ownership.** We shall see later in the book that wide
       powers are conferred on local authorities with regard to the
       compulsory purchase of land. The holder of a fee simple estate
       can be required to sell his interests in the land to a local authority
       exercising compulsory purchase powers, usually in order to
       facilitate some development scheme. An owner can, of course,
       object to a **compulsory purchase order** and then a Public Inquiry
       will have to be held to consider the views of those affected. Such
       inquiries are conducted by an inspector who will recommend
       a course of action to the appropriate Minister (the Secretary
       of State for the Environment), his decision being final.

Further restrictions imposed on a freehold owner by virtue of restrictive
covenants and easements are considered in this Chapter and in Chapter 6.
Similarly, liability which may arise from land holding both under the
common law and statute is dealt with elsewhere in Chapter 10.

5.7 Mortgages

No introductory account of the law relating to landholding would be
complete without mention of the law of mortgages. A mortgage of land
may be simply described as a transaction under which a **borrower (the
mortgagor)** in return for a loan from the **lender (the mortgagee)** gives
security in the form of land. The effect of a mortgage is to confer certain
rights on the mortgagee against the borrower and the land, should the
mortgagor default. Most mortgages are entered into by the holders of legal
estates in land (a fee simple or term of years absolute) but equitable interests
in land may also be mortgaged.

Legal Mortgages

Under the 1925 property legislation, in a mortgage of a fee simple the
mortgagor does not divest himself of the legal estate but rather grants
to the mortgagee a demise for a term of years absolute (usually 3,000 years).
The mortgagee agrees that the term of years will end when the loan plus
interest is repaid. As an alternative **s.87 Law of Property Act 1925** provides
that it is possible to create a legal mortgage of a fee simple by means of
a **short deed** stating that a **legal charge** on the land is created "charge by
deed expressed to be made by way of a legal mortgage". Such a charge
does not convey a term of years but the mortgagee has all the rights and
powers as if he had received a term of years.

For a legal mortgage of a term of years the mortgagor may grant the mortgagee a **sub lease of a lesser term,** i.e. the term of the lease less 10 days. The mortgagee expressly agrees that on repayment of the loan plus interest the term shall cease. Alternatively, a legal mortgage can be created by a charge by way of a mortgage under **s.87 Law of Property Act 1925.**

If the value of the mortgaged property exceeds the loan there is nothing to prevent the mortgagor borrowing further sums by way of a second or even a third mortgage.

Equitable Mortgages

A mortgage of an equitable interest, e.g. a life interest, is said to be an **equitable mortgage.** Additionally an informal mortgage (without a deed) of a legal estate or interest will create an equitable mortgage. In the same way that equity looks on a specifically enforceable contract for a lease as an equitable lease (see Chapter 6) it will also regard a specifically enforceable contract for a mortgage as an equitable mortgage, i.e. 'equity looks on as done that which ought to be done'.

Rights of the Mortgagor and the Mortgagee

The mortgagor covenants in the mortgage deed to repay the principal money with interest on a date specified (the legal or contractual date for redemption). However, the common law rule that the mortgage cannot be redeemed after that date was superceded many years ago by the rule in equity which compels the mortgagee to allow redemption at any time after the legal date on payment of the **'price of redemption'.** This equitable right is one of the totality of mortgagor's rights called the **'equity of redemption'** which arises automatically as soon as the mortgage is entered into. One of the mortgagor's most fundamental rights is his equitable right to redeem and this can only be extinguished by the mortgagee exercising his rights such as the power to sell, to take possession or foreclose. On the basis that "he who seeks equity must do equity" the equitable right to redeem can only be exercised following reasonable notice which for a legal mortgage will amount to six months. The rights of a council tenant to a mortgage from the local authority, when exercising the right to buy under the **Housing Act 1980,** are considered in Chapter 13.

94

The mortgagee's rights are contained both in common law and statute and include:—

1. **the right to take possession.** This right may be exercised when the sum due is not being paid and the mortgagee wishes to pay himself from the proceeds of the property, e.g. rents and profits. The usual course is to appoint a receiver under the **Law of Property Act 1925 s.109.** An action for possession is usually taken as a preliminary to exercising the right of sale. If the mortgage is of a **dwelling house** the court has power under the **Administration of Justice Act 1970 ss.36-39** to adjourn the proceedings or suspend or postpone the order if it appears that the mortgagor is likely to be able to repay the sum due within a reasonable time.

2. **the right of sale.** Subject to certain conditions, the mortgagee may on the mortgagor's default, sell and convey to a purchaser the whole of the mortgaged property, and recoup himself from the proceeds. He should try and obtain the best price possible and not act recklessly.

3. **the right to foreclose.** If the mortgagor is in default for an unreasonable time the mortgagee may obtain an order from the court requiring the debt to be paid. If it is not paid the order becomes **absolute** and the property vests in the mortgagee. The courts have wide powers to postpone or even reopen a foreclosure.

4. **to sue for the money owning.** Usually the remedies previously mentioned are more satisfactory but a mortgagee also has the right to sue on the mortgagor's personal covenant to repay.

CHAPTER 6 The Creation of a Leasehold

6.1 The Agreement (Contract) for a lease

The relationship of landlord and tenant may arise expressly by the creation of a lease, by statute, or by an agreement for a lease. To constitute a landlord and tenant relationship there must be one party possessing an estate in real property granting a **lesser estate** to another party which is **less than the estate of freehold.** During the period of the relationship therefore, two concurrent estates will subsist, that of the landlord's which will be a **freehold or leasehold reversion,** and that of the tenant's which is the **tenancy.** The duration of the tenancy must be **certain,** over a fixed term (e.g. 99 years) or a periodic term which could be made certain by the service of notice to quit (e.g. an annual tenancy). As a general principle assignees of the respective estates of the parties will be bound by the terms of the original tenancy. Any person who is not under a legal disability may take or grant a lease of land. Under **s.205 Law of Property Act 1925** land is defined as "including land of any tenure, and mines and minerals, whether or not held apart from the surface, buildings or parts of buildings (whether the division is horizontal or vertical)...."

Under the **Law of Property Act 1925 s.1(1)** a 'term of years absolute' is the only leasehold interest which is capable of existing as a legal estate. This would include a lease for a fixed term or even a periodic tenancy. As a general rule the law requires the same formalities for the creation or transfer of a term of years as apply to the fee simple. Thus to effect the transfer of title to a leasehold estate **a deed** is necessary, i.e. an instrument signed, sealed and delivered. However exceptionally, under the **Law of Property Act 1925 ss.52 and 54,** a lease for three years or less taking effect in possession at the best rent reasonably obtainable without taking a fine (a payment) will be a valid legal lease however granted (even if oral). This exception therefore covers periodic tenancies where the basic term does not exceed three years. Otherwise to create a legal lease it is usual to go through three stages involving precontractual negotiations, the contract (or agreement) for a lease, and the lease. It is at the second stage, when an enforceable contract is concluded, that the parties are legally bound to fulfil their promises.

To be enforceable at law such a contract must comply with the requirement of **s.40(1) Law of Property Act 1925** which provides that:- no action may be brought upon any contract for the sale or other disposition of land or any interest in land, unless the agreement upon which such action is brought, or some memorandum or note thereof, is in writing, and signed by the party to be charged or by some other person authorised by him. The essential requirement of **s.40** is therefore, written evidence of a complete and binding contract rather than an agreement to contract. Certainly use of the expression **'subject to contract'** would negate any intention to be bound. The written evidence required could of course amount to the contract itself. If a formal contract has been drawn up it is usual to make two copies of it which are signed and simultaneously exchanged by the parties. Otherwise the written evidence may be simply a note or memorandum which shows the existence of an oral contract. No particular form is necessary for the note or memorandum provided it acknowledges the existence of the contract. Letters, entries in a diary, notes in a rent book have been held to be sufficient. Even two or more documents may be treated as one provided there is sufficient evidence to connect them either contained within the documents or through the production of oral evidence. In this way a letter and envelope were connected in *Pearce v. Gardner 1897*. The material terms of the contract must be referred to in the note or memorandum including the names of the parties, the property, the rent and any premium, the term and its commencement and any special covenants. In addition the document must be signed "by the party to be charged or by some other person lawfully authorised". There is no requirement that it be signed by both parties but it can only be enforced against the party who has signed it. For the purpose of signature it is sufficient to show that the name or even initials of the party to be bound by the contract have been inserted. Remedies for breach of a contract for a lease include an action for **damages** or, at the court's discretion, an action to compel **specific performance** of the contract where damages would not give an adequate remedy to the plaintiff.

Part performance

Despite the absence of a note or memorandum for the purposes of **s.40(1)** it is still possible to obtain specific performance of an unenforceable contract for the sale of land through the operation of the **equitable doctrine of part performance**. This doctrine is a further example of the role of equity to ensure that failure to comply with legal formalities should not override the principles of fairness and justice. **Section 40(2)** makes specific reference to the fact that **s.40(1)** does not affect the law relating to part performance. The basic requirement of the doctrine is that the plaintiff must show that he has done an act in performance of the contract. This act must specifically refer to an oral agreement which itself constitutes a complete and binding contract.

> In *Rawlinson v. Ames 1925* the prospective tenant of a 21 year lease required the landlord to carry out conversion work which the tenant supervised. On completion of the work, the prospective tenant backed out. The court held that the act of the landlord, in paying for the conversion for the tenant's benefit, was a sufficient act of part-performance to require the tenant to enter into the lease and awarded specific performance.

Certainly the act of part performance must specifically refer to the nature of the contract alleged. Payment of rent on its own will not be sufficient for it is not referable to any particular contract. In *Steadman v. Steadman 1976* however, the payment of rent alone without other acts was held to be sufficient. To successfully claim part performance it is necessary for there to be an overt act rather than a continuation in possession.

> Thus in *Maddison v. Alderson 1883* there was no act of performance when a housekeeper carried on with her duties without pay following a promise by her employer that in return he would leave her a life estate in his farm. The court held that her continuing service was not a sufficient change in circumstances to suggest a contract to transfer a life estate.

> In *Wakeham v. McKenzie 1968* however, the court awarded specific performance in the following circumstances. A widower of 72 asked his neighbour, a widow of 67, to come and look after him with the promise that he would leave his property to her when he died. The widow left her council flat and moved in agreeing to pay "her own board and her share of the coal". The widower died but there was no provision in his will to leave the property to the unfortunate old lady. The court ordered that the property should be transferred to her because of her act of part performance in leaving her council flat and looking after the old man in return for his promise.

99

A recent illustration of the operation of the doctrine is the case of *Cohen v. Nessdale Ltd. 1981* which is considered in some depth. Here the plaintiff, a statutory tenant of a flat received an offer to purchase the leasehold from the defendants for £20,000. The offer was made 'subject to contract', and after negotiations over a number of months, an oral agreement for the sale of a 99 year lease was finally entered into. The same day as this oral agreement was reached the defendant confirmed it in writing, but again 'subject to contract'. A further written confirmation a few days later made no reference to 'subject to contract' and then, in accordance with the agreement, the plaintiff paid £50 ground rent. The defendants subsequently attempted to back out of the agreement and the plaintiff now sought specific performance of it. The two basic questions faced by the High Court in this case were whether there was:-

a. an enforceable contract capable of being part performed; and whether

b. the payment of £50 amounted to an act of part performance.

The High Court decided both questions in the affirmative and awarded specific performance of the contract. The Court of Appeal however took a different view. As far as the payment was concerned the Court of Appeal accepted that following *Steadman v. Steadman* the mere payment of money could constitute a sufficient act of performance, but only in exceptional cases, of which this was not one. In addition, the question as to whether there was an enforceable contract depended upon whether the earlier dealings made 'subject to contract' continued to apply to the later agreement. The Court relied on the view of Ld. Denning M.R. that in such circumstances for the parties to release themselves from the condition of 'subject to contract' they had to do so by express agreement. As there was no such express agreement in this case the later dealings were taken to be a continuation of the earlier ones 'subject to contract'. Accordingly there was no contract in existence for the purposes of specific performance and no order was made.

Specific Performance The **equitable remedy of specific performance** is an order compelling the defendant to perform his obligations, and in relation to a contract for a lease, execute a legal lease. As an equitable

100

remedy it is discretionary in nature and will only be awarded in accordance with established equitable principles such as "he who comes to equity must come with clean hands" and "delay defeats equity". In particular there must be a complete and binding contract and the prospective landlord must have a good title to the property in question. The conduct of the plaintiff is examined to ensure an absence of misrepresentation or deceit, and the court must be satisfied that as a result of the order no undue hardship will ensue. If it is a lease capable of existing as a legal estate then the order for specific performance of a contract for a lease is complied with by the execution of a legal lease.

Equitable Lease

The Courts of Equity would always enforce the terms of an intended lease which is specifically enforceable, as an equitable lease. This was achieved by applying the maxim "Equity looks on as done that which ought to be done". Today a tenant in occupation by virtue of a contract for a lease only, is regarded as holding under an equitable lease.

> Following the important decision in *Walsh v. Lonsdale 1882* both parties to such a contract can enforce their equitable rights against each other. Here a landlord agreed to grant a seven year lease of a mill to the tenant at a rent paid quarterly in arrear but one year in advance if demanded. No lease was executed but the tenant went into possession. The landlord subsequently claimed a year's rent in advance which the tenant refused to pay. The court held that the tenant was bound by the terms of the equitable lease in the same way as if a legal lease had been properly executed. The tenant was therefore bound by the term that the rent could be demanded one year in advance.

While the decision in *Walsh v. Lonsdale* seems to imply that a contract for a lease, (an equitable lease), is as good as a lease, there remain a number of important differences. Firstly an equitable lease will only exist on the terms of a contract for a lease which is **'specifically enforceable'**. Secondly an equitable lease, while binding on the parties to it, is not protected against an assignee of the landlord's reversion who is a bona fide purchaser for value without notice of it. It is necessary therefore to ensure that a contract for a lease of unregistered land is registered as an **estate contract** (a Class C (iv) land charge) under the **Land Charges Act 1972.** This will give constructive notice of its existence to a prospective third party purchaser

101

for value of the landlord's reversion. Alternatively, for registered land, a tenant can protect his interest by entering a notice on the register under **s.48 Land Registration Act 1925.** By entering into possession however a tenant of registered land is protected by his occupation and has an **'overriding interest'** which will bind third parties.

The Formal Lease

All legal leases other than those within **s.54(2) Law of Property Act 1925** must be created by deed. The deed is the instrument by which the legal estate i.e. 'the term of years absolute' is transferred. In practice the deed is referred to as the 'lease' and must be executed by the landlord and delivered to the tenant. The tenant then executes and returns the counterpart document (a copy) to the landlord. Execution of the lease is achieved under **s.73 Law of Property Act 1925** by signing, sealing and delivering the document. In relation to its content there is no requirement as to precise form but usually standard leases are adopted (see Appendix). A valid lease is said to require the following:- a capable lessor and lessee; a thing which is demisable; a defined term; an intention to demise and acceptance of the thing demised; a sufficient description of the parties, the thing demised, and the covenants. The usual parts of a lease are:-

1. **The premises** comprising of the commencement, the date of the lease, the names and descriptions of the parties, the premium or fine (if any, the description of the parcels (i.e. a description of the demised property), any exceptions (i.e. part of the land not demised), and reservations (i.e. rights reserved by the landlord over the land such as an easement), and the operative words (i.e. words of demise such as **let**);

2. **The Habendum** which specifies the quantity and quality of the estate held, the date from which the term is to run and its duration;

3. **The Reddendum** which is the formal reservation of the rent to be paid;

4. **The Covenants** which are the formal obligations of the parties;

5. **Conditions for re-entry** for non payment of rent or breach of covenant.

6.2 Leases and Licences

Having considered the process by which a leasehold is created it is now necessary to examine the fundamental features of a lease which distinguish it from other relationships such as a licence. The fact that a lease is required to have a fixed or determinable term (i.e. a periodic tenancy) has already been stated. In addition to create a lease it is fundamental that the prospective tenant is given **'exclusive possession'** of the demised premises. Thus a guest in a hotel or a lodger without exclusive possession of any part of the premises would not be regarded as a tenant. While the fact that exclusive possession has been given is not conclusive that a lease has been created, it is strong evidence of the fact. Nevertheless it is possible to grant exclusive possession of premises or a part of premises without entering into a tenancy, such as:- occupation for the purposes of carrying out work; letting under an oral gentleman's agreement not intended to be enforceable at law; family arrangements; where the rent payable is unquantified personal services; or operating a business under an exclusive right (i.e. renting a kiosk in a cinema foyer). Here the intention of the parties is to create a mere licence rather than a tenancy, and no estate in land is transferred. A licence is merely a contractual relationship between the parties to it and does not bind third parties. Also, most of the protective legislation (for residential occupiers, the **Rent Act 1977**, the **Housing Act 1980** and for business occupiers, the **Landlord and Tenant Act 1954 Part II**) does not apply to a mere licence. Clearly then, the distinction between leases and licences is of crucial importance and on first impression the possibilities of owners of property avoiding the difficulties of Rent Act protection simply by creating licences seem obvious. This possibility however is not always practicable. For whether a licence or tenancy has been entered into does not depend upon the label that is hung upon the relationship (e.g. 'licence agreement') and the terminology used, but rather it is the **substance of the relationship** that is the important factor. Thus a relationship which bears the characteristics of a tenancy will amount to a tenancy and one that bears the characteristics of a licence will be regarded as a licence.

This is of course easy to state but difficult to apply in practice. Certainly the intention of the parties to the relationship at the time of the grant is of paramount importance as are the terms of the agreement. Neither is the parties intention to be deduced simply by scrutinising the terms of a document drafted by the landlord and signed by the parties at the time of the grant. Obviously if the intention of the landlord is to avoid Rent

Act protection and create a licence the document will support this intention. Denning L.J. made the point in *Facchini v. Bryson 1952* when he said that to place sole reliance on the landlord's intention as expressed in a document, the courts would "find all landlords granting licences and not tenancies, and we should make a hole in the Rent Acts through which could be driven - I will not in these days say a coach and four, but an articulated vehicle". It should be stressed however that if it is the intention of both parties to the relationship that a licence is to be created and it is clearly intended to avoid the operation of the Rent Acts, then the courts will support this intention. It is in such cases where a formal document is used to hide the true intention of the parties that the courts will intervene and attempt to determine the true relationship. The words of Lord Denning M.R. in *Marchant v. Charters 1977* provide some guidance when he said "What is the test to see whether the occupier of one room in a house is a tenant or a licensee? It does not depend on whether the occupation is permanent or temporary. It does not depend upon the label which the parties put upon it. All these factors may influence the decision but none of them are conclusive. All the circumstances have to be worked out. Eventually the answer depends on the nature and quality of the occupancy. Was it intended that the occupier should have a stake in the room or did he have only permission for himself personally to occupy the room whether under a contract or not in which case he is a licensee".

It may be then that the particular circumstances of a grant will be sufficient to negative the normal intention of a tenancy. In *Errington v. Errington 1952* the court held that a licence existed when a father allowed his son to occupy a house in return for making the mortgage repayments. Similarly in *E. Moss Ltd. v. Brown 1946* where tenants left friends to occupy their house in return for regular payments the court held that only a licence had been created. Today however, the problem of distinguishing between the relationships still exists, for the prospect of creating licences rather than letting has many advantages for the owner. It is not uncommon therefore for new agreements, which are drafted to evade Rent Act protection, to come under judicial scrutiny. Unfortunately the judicial attitude towards them is not always consistent. Two cases in 1978 involving flat sharing illustrate the point.

In the first case of *Lloyd v. Sadler 1978* two young people took a joint protected tenancy of a flat but before it expired one of them had left. The remaining occupant claimed security of tenure as a statutory tenant under the **Rent Act 1977** on the expiration

104

of the contractual tenancy. On the ground that both occupants were the contractual tenant under the protected tenancy, and both of them had to remain in occupation to establish a statutory tenancy, the landlord claimed possession. The Court of Appeal held that, despite a weight of authority to the contrary, the remaining tenant was entitled to hold over as a statutory tenant. The argument was accepted that otherwise the result would be unreasonable, or unlikely to accord with legislative intention.

Certainly this attitude of according with legislative intention was not apparent later in 1978 when the Court of Appeal decided the case of *Somma v. Hazelhurst 1978*. The case concerned the status of so-called **non exclusive occupation agreements,** a device designed to evade Rent Act protection. Under such agreements a number of occupiers sharing a house or flat enter into a series of identical agreements with the landlord providing that each occupant has the right to use the premises, but no particular part of them, in common with others and in some cases the landlord. Without joint possession or exclusive occupation there can be no tenancy and thus no Rent Act protection. In the case before the court a young couple shared a bedsitting room after signing an exclusive occupation agreement, the terms and effect of which they understood. In determining the status of the agreement the Court of Appeal recognised that this was another attempt to avoid creating a tenancy of a dwelling house by arranging for a licence to share occupation. However both occupiers "knew what they were letting themselves in for" and "preferred to have the accommodation on the terms it was offered ... than not to have the accommodation at all". The Court took the view that here there was no dressing up of a tenancy as a licence but rather a clear intention by both parties to enter into a contractual licence having no Rent Act protection. It was held therefore that a mere licence had been created by the parties. This was despite the obvious unequal bargaining situation in such cases and the possible implication for contracting out of Rent Act protection (see Chapter 12).

6.3 Types of Leases

As previously stated a term of years absolute whether for a month or one hundred years, is the only leasehold interest that is capable of existing as a **legal lease**. All other leasehold interests including a specifically enforceable contract for a lease operate as an **equitable lease.** Unlike a fee simple freehold estate there is no requirement that a lease is to take effect **in possession** (i.e. to commence immediately) and it is possible to grant a lease to commence in the future. This will take effect as a **future or reversionary lease.**

Reversionary Lease Reversionary leases are void under the **Law of Property Act 1925 s.149(3)**if rent is reserved or a fine is payable and it is expressed to take effect more than 21 years from the date of the instrument creating it. Similarly a contract to grant such a term to take effect more than 21 years from the date of the grant of the lease is also void. This must be distinguished from a contract to grant a lease more than 21 years from the date of the contract, which is valid, and would include an **option for renewal** contained in a lease for more than 21 years. A reversionary lease must be distinguished from another type of arrangement, the **concurrent lease.**

Concurrent lease Such leases exist as a demonstration of the fundamental feature of the doctrine of estates, the fact that it is possible to create any number of concurrent legal estates in the same piece of land. Thus, it is possible for a reversion on a legal lease itself to be leased concurrently with the legal lease. Its effect is to substitute the new tenant of the reversion as the landlord of the legal lease for as long as the two interests last concurrently. Such a scheme is used mainly to provide security for a loan. The capital sum lent is related not to the value of the reversion but rather to the rent payable by the tenant to the lender as lessee of the reversion.

Leases for a Fixed Term The most straightforward term of years is the lease for a fixed term (e.g. 6 months, 1 year, 99 years, etc.) of whatever length the parties decide provided that it is certain or capable of being rendered so before it takes effect. Such a lease comes to an end automatically on the expiration of the fixed term and as a general rule **no notice to quit** is required. An exception is the lease of an agricultural holding (see Chapter 11). Also there is nothing to prevent the parties providing in the lease that it may be determined at particular intervals during its currency by notice served by either party. Such a provision is termed a 'break clause' and would, for example, in a 21 year lease, be operational on the seventh and fourteenth years of the lease.

Leases for Life, Lives or Marriage Such leases are automatically converted by virtue of **s.149(6) Law of Property Act 1925** into leases for a **ninety year term.** They may be terminated however by either party serving at least one month's notice on the death (or marriage, if relevant) of the original lessee. The written notice in such a case must be given to determine the lease on one of the **quarter days** applicable to it.

Yearly Tenancies Otherwise known as **annual tenancies** or **tenancies from year to year,** such tenancies will continue until either side brings it to an end by serving the required notice to quit. Under the common law this is **six months** (183 days expiring on an anniversary of its commencement) in the absence of agreement to the contrary. Yearly tenancies may arise expressly or by implication of the law. Thus if there is no express agreement as to the nature of the tenancy granted, and the tenant tenders, and the landlord accepts some payment of annual rent, then a yearly tenancy will arise by implication, e.g. if a yearly rent of £400 is agreed to be payable by four quarterly instalments, the payment of a quarter's rent will give rise to an annual tenancy. A particular case in which a yearly tenancy may arise by implication occurs where a tenant under a lease for a fixed term holds over (remains in possession) on the expiration of the term, and then makes some payment of annual rent which the landlord accepts. In such circumstances the terms of the fixed term lease will apply to the yearly tenancy in so far as they are not inconsistent with it. It should be noted however that such an intention to create a new tenancy is not readily inferred. This is particularly so where the tenant holds over under his rights as a **statutory tenant** under the Rent Acts. In *Morrison v. Jacobs 1945* this was the case, and the court held that the mere fact that the landlord accepted rent in such circumstances did not create an annual tenancy. If the rent payable is calculated by reference to weekly sums then the tenant holds over as a weekly tenant rather than an annual tenant, *Alder v. Blackman 1953.*

Other Periodic Tenancies Such tenancies for less than a year may arise expressly or by implication of the law. They include weekly, monthly, quarterly and six-monthly tenancies and will arise by implication on payment of rent in relation to the term, e.g. payment of one month's rent will give rise to a monthly tenancy. Unlike yearly tenancies, the period of notice to terminate periodic tenancies for less than a year is under the common law, the period upon which the tenancy is based, e.g. a quarterly tenancy requires one quarter's notice to determine it.

Although the parties can vary the common law rules by contrary intention, if the letting is of a dwelling house by virtue of **s.5 Protection from Eviction Act 1977** at least four weeks' notice must be given despite any contrary agreement.

Perpetually Renewable Leases These are leases which give the lessee a perpetual right to renewal. Thus a fourteen year lease may give the lessee not less than one month before the expiration of the term, the right to require the landlord to grant a new lease for the same period on the same terms as the original lease **including the provision for renewal.** By **s.145 Law of Property Act 1922** all perpetually renewable leases are converted into **terms of 2,000 years.** They remain however determinable by the lessee giving at least 10 days' notice expiring on any day which, but for the Act, the lease would have terminated had it not been renewed. If the lease provides for the payment of a fine on renewal, then if granted before 1926 it is commuted into additional rent, otherwise it is void.

Tenancy at Will Such tenancies arise when an individual occupies property with the consent of the owner (i.e. at his will). No estate is transferred as there is no term of years absolute. A tenancy at will survives as an **equitable interest** and may be determined expressly by either party without notice (**s.5 Protection from Eviction Act 1977** does not apply) or by implication of the law by the death of either party. They arise chiefly when a prospective purchaser takes possession of property before completion, or a prospective tenant goes into possession prior to the granting of an express lease.

> In *Young v. Hargreaves 1963* a young married couple were impliedly granted a tenancy at will of part of a house when told they could live in part of the house "for as long as you wish" with no provision for the payment of rent. The court held that the subsequent payment of rent on a periodic basis yearly, monthly or quarterly had the effect of creating a periodic tenancy of that term.

Tenancy at Sufference Such a tenancy arises where a tenant, once in lawful possession of land, holds over on the termination of his previous tenancy without his landlord's consent. It differs from a tenancy at will in that the landlord does not consent to it and as soon as rent is payable under it, a new lawful tenancy (either periodic or at will) will arise. A landlord can bring an action in respect of **mesne profits** for use and occupation of the property from his tenancy at sufference (see Chapter 8). Of course tenancies at sufference are now extremely rare, because most tenants who hold over on the expiration of their contractual tenancy have statutory rights to do so.

CHAPTER 7   Family Law Relating to Landholding

7.1 The Marriage

To fully appreciate the rights and duties of the parties to a marriage to the matrimonial property in the event of marital breakdown it is necessary to briefly consider how a lawful marriage is effected under English law. Marriage is usually preceded by an **engagement,** i.e. an agreement to marry, which, following the **Law Reform (Miscellaneous Provisions) Act 1970 s.1(1),** has no longer any legal significance as a contract. The well known action of **'breach of promise to marry'** by the rejected suitor is no longer known to the law.

The union of marriage was defined by Lord Penzance in *Hyde's case 1886* as the "voluntary union for life of one man and one woman to the exclusion of all others". The two main characteristics of a valid marriage then are that it must be **voluntary,** and both parties to it must have the **capacity** to enter into it. The term 'voluntary' means that there must be no duress to marry through force, fear, or pressure and both parties must be aware of what they are doing. To have legal capacity to marry, both parties must be either single, widowed or divorced, over the age of sixteen, of opposite sex and not closely related. The formalities relating to marriage are contained in the **Marriage Act 1949** which provides that a marriage may be effected by a **civil ceremony** or a **Church of England ceremony.** For a valid civil ceremony, a **superintendent registrar's certificate** must have been issued either with a **licence**(allowing the marriage to take place one day after notice is given to the registrar) or without a licence (allowing the marriage to take place 21 days after notice is given to the registrar). There are more onerous formalities attaching to the Church of England ceremony which requires the reading of **marriage banns** and the acquisition of either a **common licence** from a diocesan bishop, a special licence from the Archbishop of Canterbury or more usually a superintendent registrar's certificate.

Void and Voidable Marriages

Under the **Matrimonial Causes Act 1973** a marriage whose validity depends on English law is **void** and has no validity if either party did not have the legal capacity to marry (i.e. not single, closely related, under age, or the same sex) or it was knowingly celebrated without some of the essential formalities. While there is no legal requirement to obtain it, it is still usual in such cases to seek a formal **declaration of nullity.**

A **voidable** marriage on the other hand remains a valid marriage until a court annuls it by issuing a decree of nullity on the application of either party to the marriage. The grounds for such an application are:-

1. That either party to the marriage is incapable of consumating the marriage due to impotence and the marriage has not been consumated;

2. That the marriage has not been consumated due to a wilful refusal of the respondent to consumate it;

3. That either party to the marriage did not validly consent to it because of duress, mistake, unsoundness of mind 'or otherwise'.

4. That at the time of the marriage either party though capable of giving valid consent, was suffering from a mental disorder within the **Mental Health Act 1959** which makes them unfitted for marriage.

5. That the respondent was at the time of the marriage suffering from venereal disease in a communicable form.

6. That the respondent was at the time of the marriage pregnant by some person other than the petitioner.

These grounds are all subject to the overriding principle contained in the **Matrimonial Causes Act 1973 s.13** which forbids the court to grant a decree where the marriage is voidable if the petitioner's conduct had led the respondent to reasonably believe that he would not seek to annul the marriage and it would be unjust to do so.

7.2 Married couples as owners or tenants

When married couples acquire ownership of the matrimonial home it has become standard practice to treat them as **co-owners.** The type of co-ownership usually adopted is that of the **joint tenancy** which is dealt with in some detail in Chapter 5. Under the principle of **"right of survivorship"**, **'jus accrescendi'**, following the death of one joint tenant their interest passes to the survivor or survivors. In cases where the matrimonial home is in the sole ownership of one spouse, the **Matrimonial Homes Act 1967 s.1** provides that the other spouse has certain **'rights of occupation'** and cannot be evicted without a court order. This right of occupation operates as a charge on the interest of the other spouse and is registerable as a **land charge (Class F)** under the **Land Charges Act 1972.** Registration of course gives a prospective purchaser or mortgagee constructive notice of the spouse's right of occupation.

The usual practice where married couples occupy property as tenants under a lease is for the husband to hold the tenancy. This feature is rapidly changing however, particularly in the public sector, where it is becoming more and more common for housing authorities to offer prospective tenants the choice between sole tenancy and a joint tenancy. This is also becoming a common practice among housing associations. The benefits for a married woman (or indeed a 'common law' wife) of having a joint tenancy of council property with her husband are obvious. As she holds as a joint tenant there is no need to apply for a transfer of the tenancy on the death of, or desertion by her husband. In addition in divorce or judicial separation proceedings the court has power to make an order with regard to transferring the property under **s.24 Matrimonial Causes Act 1973.** As a joint tenant the married wife has the right to remain in occupation of the property on the break up of the marriage and the important right under the **Domestic Violence and Matrimonial Proceedings Act 1976** to apply to the court for an order excluding her spouse from the property. The most obvious detriment of a joint tenant is that a wife may become liable for arrears of rent.

The **Housing Act 1980** clearly encourages the grant of joint tenancies of council property to married couples and while there are administrative problems involved in consulting and communicating to joint tenants rather than a single tenant the weight of opinion seems to favour their use as an example of good housing management.

Property transfer on the break up of marriage

The courts have wide powers by virtue of **s.24 Matrimonial Causes Act 1973** to order, on the granting of a divorce, decree of nullity or judicial separation, the transfer by one party to a marriage to another, or child of the family, such property as specified in the order. This provision applies to both protected private sector tenancies and secure public sector tenancies. On the transfer of a tenancy the transferee spouse is subject to all the rights and liabilities of the former spouse's estate. The former spouse is in turn relieved of liability for matters arising after the decree of divorce or nullity becomes absolute.

By virtue of **s.37 Housing Act 1980** however, if a secure tenancy is assigned under a **s.24 order,** it ceases to be secure. **Schedule 25 Housing Act 1980** provides that if a spouse is a secure tenant of a dwelling house in his own right or jointly, and the marriage is terminated by a decree of divorce or nullity, then the court, when the decree becomes absolute, may order the transfer of the secure tenancy to the other former spouse. Such an order may be applied for before the decree is made absolute.

In relation to unsecure council tenancies such an interest does not pass as of right to a surviving spouse or member of the family on the death or desertion by the council tenant. Subject to the authority's agreement, a widow or deserted spouse will be permitted to continue the tenancy and in practice most councils will agree to a transfer of the tenancy. In such cases however, the authority may take this as an opportunity to offer smaller accommodation to the remaining tenant if it is reasonable in the circumstances.

It is also possible that the council will make a transfer conditional on the payment of any rent arrears. In the case of a deserted wife who has suffered physical violence the authority may insist that she obtains a court order, e.g. a personal protection order or an exclusion order under the **Domestic Violence and Matrimonial Proceedings Act 1976.** In this way the deserted wife may establish her claim to a tenancy in the Magistrates Court.

Where there is a death of a secure tenant the rights of the surviving spouse and/or members of the family in relation to the tenancy, depend upon whether it is fixed term or periodic. On the death of a fixed term tenant the tenancy passes to the beneficiary under the will or on intestacy. In a case where the beneficiary would have been qualified as a statutory successor if the tenancy had been periodic, then the tenancy remains a secure tenancy in the hands of the beneficiary. On the death of a periodic tenant the tenancy will vest in the statutory successor as defined in **s.31 Housing Act 1980,** unless the deceased tenant was himself a statutory successor. The statutory successor is of course the tenant's spouse or member of the tenant's family who had resided with the tenant throughout the twelve months prior to his death (see Chapter 13).

7.3 Divorce

Commencement of divorce proceedings

Under **s.3 Matrimonial Causes Act, 1973** no petition for divorce can be presented before the expiration of **three years** from the date of the marriage except on the ground of **exceptional hardship** suffered by the petitioner or of **exceptional depravity** on the part of the respondent. The idea of course is to deter people from entering into marriage lightly and then obtaining a speedy divorce. The scope of the provision has been considered in numerous cases.

> In *C v. C 1979,* the parties had carried on sexual relations for a long time prior to the marriage but soon after the marriage it became apparent that the husband was incapable of sustaining a sexual relationship with his wife. He then left his wife forming an attachment for a young male. The question facing the Court of Appeal was whether this is evidence of exceptional hardship or depravity to justify the presentation of a divorce petition within the first three years of marriage. In considering the separate limbs of **s.3,** the court decided that it would be seldom necessary to allege exceptional depravity since it would be difficult to imagine a case of exceptional depravity that did not cause exceptional hardship. Despite there being no evidence of exceptionally depraved conduct in this case the court held that a case of exceptional hardship had been made out for the exception to apply.

The Court of Appeal in the above case also doubted whether the view of Ld. Denning as expressed in 1949 in *Bowman v. Bowman* was still a relevant one to determine exceptional depravity. Here his Lordship had classified adultery as depravity, and adultery with aggravating circumstances as exceptional depravity (i.e. within a few weeks of marriage, with more than one woman, with a wife's sister). **Section 3** then, is designed to prevent undue haste in getting a divorce, and particularly where there is a child, encourage a reconciliation. The Act further provides under **s.6** that if at any stage of the divorce proceedings it appears to the court that there is a reasonable opportunity of a reconciliation between the parties to a marriage, the court may adjourn the proceedings for a specified period to enable attempts to be made to effect such a reconciliation.

The grounds for divorce

The sole ground for divorce, introduced by the **Divorce Reform Act 1969** and now included in the **Matrimonial Causes Act 1973,** is that the marriage has **broken down irretrievably.** The irretrievable breakdown of a marriage can be established however only by proof of any one of the five facts prescribed in **s.1** of the 1973 Act. Proof of a fact will only establish the irretrievable breakdown of the marriage if the court is satisfied on the evidence as a whole that it has occurred. The five facts are as follows:

a.   **That the respondent has committed adultery and the petitioner finds it intolerable to live with the respondent.**

To constitute adultery there must be proof of voluntary sexual intercourse by the respondent and a member of the opposite sex. If it is denied by the respondent then it may be proved by circumstantial evidence which raises a probability that adultery occurred. In addition to the act of adultery, the petitioner must also prove that as a result of it, **life with the respondent is intolerable.** If the petitioner, aware of the adultery, lives in the same household as the respondent for a total period exceeding six months then the petitioner cannot rely on the adultery as a fact to prove the irretrievable breakdown of the marriage.

b.   **That the respondent has behaved in such a way that the petitioner cannot reasonably be expected to live with the respondent.**

This fact provides the residual category of misbehaviour and is not limited or restricted but must be **'grave and weighty'** in degree. Certainly there must be some breach of the obligations of married life which causes the petitioner to find life with the respondent unbearable, e.g. serious illness or violent behaviour.

116

c. **That the respondent has deserted the petitioner for a continuous period of at least two years immediately preceeding the presentation of the petition.**

To constitute a desertion there must be an involuntary separation of the husband and wife with the intention on the part of the deserter to remain apart permanently. It is possible to be separate under the same roof provided that the parties live totally apart. There must be a lack of consent to the desertion however, and the deserter must have no reasonable cause for leaving (called **simple desertion**). In cases where the party who leaves has reasonable cause for doing so because of the other party's behaviour, it is the party who remains who is the deserter (called **constructive desertion**). A period of desertion is not interrupted by resumption of married life in the same household for either one period not exceeding six months or several periods not exceeding six months in all. Such periods however will not count towards the calculation of the minimum period of desertion of two years.

d. **That the parties to the marriage have lived apart continuously for at least two years immediately preceding the presentation of the petition and that the respondent consents to a decree being granted.**

For the purposes of this ground the parties are treated as living apart unless they are living with each other in the same household. It is necessary however that during the period of separation the parties do not regard their married life as still subsisting, e.g. separations due to work, hospital treatment or confinement in prison.

In relation to any periods where cohabitation is resumed the same rules apply as for desertion. This is the most usual fact to show that a marriage has irretrievably broken down, when both parties consent to the marriage being brought to an end.

e. **That the parties to the marriage have lived apart for a continuous period of at least five years immediately preceding the presentation of the petition.**

The distinction between this fact and the preceding one is that here there is no requirement to show that the respondent consents to the divorce.

The process of divorce requires a court hearing and if the proceedings are defended (only 2% of petitions) then a trial before a High Court judge is necessary. The parties must appear in person with or without legal representation. An undefended petition is heard in the County Court for which legal aid is no longer available. Now, by virtue of a **'special procedure'**, there is no longer a need for the parties or their representatives to attend the court. The pronouncement of a **'decree nisi'** by the court does not dissolve the marriage but provides that the marriage will be dissolved within six weeks, and the decree made **'absolute'**, unless sufficient cause is shown to the court. A decree nisi can of course be rescinded prior to it being made absolute if the parties effect a reconciliation.

7.4 Matrimonial Orders

Matrimonial orders made by a Magistrates Court do not affect the validity or continuation of a marriage but are intended rather to provide primarily for the maintenance of one of the spouses (the wife) and also determine matters in dispute in relation to the children. Of course matrimonial orders are often an early stage in the process of securing a dissolution of the marriage by divorce. Legal aid is available for such proceedings but it will only be granted by the legal aid committee where it is envisaged that a real benefit will be brought to the applicant, who is usually the wife. The powers of Magistrates to grant matrimonial orders are for the most part contained in the **Domestic Proceedings and Magistrates Courts Act 1978.** This Act replaces the **Matrimonial Proceedings (Magistrates Courts) Act 1960** and in particular substitutes three grounds on which an application for a matrimonial order may be made, replacing the long list of grounds contained in the 1960 Act. Either party to a marriage may now apply to a Magistrates Court under **s.1** to make an order for **financial provision** for a spouse or children of the family on the ground that the other party to the marriage has:-

    a.   **failed to provide reasonable maintenance for the applicant or any child of the family;** or

    b.   **behaved in such a way that the applicant cannot reasonably be expected to live with the respondent;** or

    c.   **deserted the applicant.**

Notice that either spouse may now be required to provide maintenance on the basis of equality, which is a departure from the earlier 1960 Act. Also for ground a., there is no longer any need to show that a spouse '**wilfully**' failed to provide reasonable maintenance, but rather that he failed to do so. Ground b. is based upon one of the 'facts' contained in the **Matrimonial Causes Act 1973** which provides evidence that the marriage has irretrievably broken down. The same principles will apply therefore to determine its proof, the Magistrates making an objective assessment on the circumstances of each case as to whether the applicant can reasonably be expected to live with the respondent. They must base their judgement on the actual spouse's involved, and not on whether a reasonable spouse would endure the respondent's behaviour. The type of conduct relied on would include persistent physical or mental cruelty. As far as ground c. is concerned, the meaning of desertion is the same as for 'desertion' under the **Matrimonial Causes Act 1973** dealt with earlier in relation to divorce.

On proof of any of the **s.1** grounds the court has power to make any one of a number of orders under **s.2**:-

a.   that the respondent will make periodic payments to the applicant for a specified term;

b.   that the respondent shall pay a specified lump sum to the applicant;

c.   that the respondent will make periodic payments to the applicant for the benefit of a child of the family for a specified term;

d.   that the respondent shall pay a specified lump sum to the applicant, for the benefit of a child of the family, or directly to the child.

The lump sum payable must not exceed £500 and periodic payments may be ordered by Magistrates on such a basis as they consider suitable. There is no power to effect property transfers or to make orders for secured periodic payments. To determine the nature and extent of a **s.2** order for financial provision, Magistrates should have regard to the guidelines laid down in **s.3**. Numerous matters are referred to in **s.3** including the income and financial resources of the marriage parties, the likely commitments of the parties, their present standard of life, the age of the parties and the duration of the marriage.

On an application for an order for financial provision under **s.2** the Magistrates have power to make an order regarding the legal custody of any child of the family up to the age of eighteen, and access to such a child. Power is also granted to Magistrates to make a **split order** which

119

involves conferring **legal custody** of the child on one party while ordering **actual custody** (i.e. where he resides) in the hands of another. The Act also contains provision that where a custody order is made and the court believes it desirable, then it can order that the child is put under the **supervision of a local authority or probation officer.** The powers of the Magistrates to make orders for the protection of a party to a marriage or a child of the family under **s.16** are dealt with later in the chapter.

7.5 Domestic Violence Legislation

The inadequacy of the law protecting the spouse subjected to domestic violence promoted the enactment of the **Domestic Violence and Matrimonial Proceedings Act 1976.** Prior to that Act a 'battered wife' could only secure the court's protection by commencing divorce or separation proceedings. A much quicker and more simple procedure was introduced by the 1976 Act **s.1(1)** which confers power on the County Court to grant an injunction containing one or more of the following provisions:-

1. a provision restraining the other party to the marriage from molesting the applicant;

2. a provision restraining the other party from molesting a child living with the applicant;

3. a provision excluding the other party from the matrimonial home or a part of the matrimonial home, or from a specified area in which the matrimonial home is included;

4. a provision requiring the other party to permit the applicant to enter and remain in the matrimonial home or a part of the matrimonial home; whether or not any other relief is sought in the proceedings.

    This Act specifically states that the above provisions apply equally to a man or woman cohabiting as man and wife and this was confirmed in *Davis v. Johnson 1979.* Here a young unmarried mother held a joint tenancy of a council house with the father of her child. Because of his violent behaviour the mother applied to the County Court for an injunction restraining the father from molesting her or the child, and also excluding him from the matrimonial home. The House of Lords confirmed the county court's jurisdiction to grant an injunction in such a case despite the property rights of the person excluded.

In *Adeoso v. Adeoso 1981,* it was argued that the Act had no application to the situation where, because of bad relations, the parties who were unmarried although occupying the same accommodation did not live together. This argument was rejected by the court which held that the occupation by a couple of two small rooms could not be regarded as living separately and therefore the Act was applicable.

It should be stressed that the powers of the county court are very wide under the 1976 Act, and an order can be made even without evidence of violence if it is in the best interests of any children.

In *Spindlow v. Spindlow 1979,* an unmarried couple occupied a council house with their two children. The woman applied to the county court under the 1976 Act for an injunction to order the man to vacate the property. There was no real evidence of any violence but the woman was adamant that unless the man left she would leave with the children who would then have to be taken into care. The court ordered the male cohabitee out of the house emphasising that the interests of the children were the paramount consideration. The court recognised the importance of the family unit.

It is intended that injunctions granted under the Act are temporary in nature and will last for only three months subject to discharge or extension. Under **s.2** of the Act, if on the grant of an injunction a judge is satisfied that the guilty party has caused actual bodily harm to the applicant, or a child of the applicant, and is likely to do so again, he may attach a **power of arrest** to the injunction. This effectively empowers a police officer to arrest without a warrant any person he reasonably suspects of being in breach of an injunction.

In relation to marriage only, equivalent power to protect a spouse, or child from the threat or use of violence by the other spouse was conferred on Magistrates courts by the **Domestic Proceedings and Magistrates Courts Act 1978.** The Act provides under **s.16** that where, on an application for an order under this section, the court is satisfied:-

a.   that the respondent has used violence against the person of the applicant or a child of the family, or

b.   that the respondent has threatened to use violence against the person of the applicant or a child of the family and has used violence against some other person, or

c.   that the respondent has in contravention of an order threatened to use violence against the person of the applicant or a child of the family **AND** that the applicant or a child of the family is in danger of being physically injured by the respondent.

Then the court may make one of the following orders:-

1.   an order prohibiting the respondent from entering the matrimonial home, or

2.   an order requiring the respondent to leave the matrimonial home.

Alternatively, there is power to require the respondent to permit the applicant to enter and remain in the matrimonial home. A power of arrest may also be attached to an **exclusion order** where the court is satisfied as to past violence by the respondent on the applicant, or child of the family, and can foresee its reoccurrence. Provision is made, in cases of urgency, to waive certain rules governing domestic proceedings, and as to the composition of the Magistrates court. Where there is imminent danger of physical injury to the applicant or child an **'expedited order'** against personal violence may be made by a single magistrate, despite the fact that no summons had been served on the respondent. Such orders are normally effective for 28 days. The main distinction between the powers conferred under the 1978 Act on Magistrates and under the 1976 Act on County Courts are that:-

1.   Magistrates jurisdiction is confined to married couples while the county court has power where there are persons cohabiting as man and wife.

2.   Magistrates protect children of the family while the county court has jurisdiction over children living with the applicant.

3. Magistrates make orders against 'violence' while for county courts the term is 'molestation'.

An interesting case which draws a comparison between the jurisdiction of the courts under domestic violence legislation is that of *Horner v. Horner 1982*. Here a wife successfully applied to the magistrates under **s.16 Domestic Proceedings and Magistrates Courts Act 1978** for an order to restrain her husband from using violence or threatening violence against her. A power of arrest was attached to the order. Subsequently the husband began to harass the wife without using or threatening violence and the wife then applied to the county court under **s.1 Domestic Violence and Matrimonial Proceedings Act 1976** for an injunction restraining the husband from molesting her. The county court judge refused the order on the grounds that the applicant was sufficiently protected by the order made under the 1978 Act. The wife then appealed to the Court of Appeal against this decision. The court held, allowing the appeal, that the term 'molesting' in the 1976 Act, included conduct short of violent behaviour and accordingly the extent of an injunction made under the 1976 Act could be wider than an order made under **s.16** of the 1978 Act. Since the wife in this case needed protection from conduct short of violence, the county court judge should have made an order restraining the husband from assaulting, molesting or otherwise interfering with the applicant.

CHAPTER 8 The Covenants of a Lease and its Determination

A lease, like any other contract, will contain the rights and obligations of the parties to it. Such contractual stipulations in a lease are generally referred to as **'covenants'** and may be **positive** (to repair) or **negative** (to restrict user) in nature. Covenants may be expressly referred to in the lease i.e. **express covenants,** or referred to by implication i.e. **usual covenants.** In addition, a large number of covenants may be **implied** into a lease by the operation of the **common law** or **statute.** While covenants govern the rights and obligations of the parties during the term of the lease, it is also possible for a lease to contain **'conditions'.** The expression 'condition' in this context has a very technical meaning and refers to those obligations which if broken will make the lease automatically terminable. On breach of a covenant the tenancy is not automatically terminable unless there is a **right of re-entry** inserted within it. However, as it is usual practice to insert such a provision for re-entry into the lease the distinction between 'covenant' and 'condition' is of little practical importance. Unless there is contrary intention expressed in the lease the following covenants are implied into the lease by the operation of the law.

8.1 Implied Covenants by the Landlord

1. **For quiet enjoyment** This covenant provides that the tenant may enjoy the property **free from disturbance** (interruption) in title. A breach would occur when as a result of the behaviour of the landlord (or connected person), the tenant's use or enjoyment of the property is diminished. It is a question of fact whether in a particular case quiet enjoyment has·.been interrupted. Examples of cases where the covenant has been broken include flooding due to the landlord's negligence, vibrations due to the landlord's machinery and noise and dust caused by the landlord's building work. If the landlord is wilfully attempting to drive out the tenant by threats, removing doors, cutting off electricity, etc., then the covenant is also broken. Such conduct would constitute the crime of harassment under the **Protection from Eviction Act 1977** but does not provide the tenant with an alternative action in tort for breach of statutory duty.

This was confirmed in *McCall v. Abelesz 1976* where the county court judge had awarded the plaintiff tenant £75 damages for harassment contrary to **s.30 Rent Act 1965.** The defendant landlord had failed to pay gas, electricity and water bills for which he was responsible and the plaintiff had had these services cut off for a period. On appeal however Ld. Denning, M.R. did not believe that the offence of harassment gave rise to a civil action for damages as there was a perfectly good civil action for breach of the covenant of quiet enjoyment available. The decision to award damages was consequently reversed.

2.   **Not to derogate from the grant** An action for breach of this implied covenant is often linked to the previous one for quiet enjoyment. A landlord would be guilty of derogating from the grant of the lease if he used or permitted the use of adjoining premises as a nuisance to the tenant, or made the demised premises unfit for the particular purpose for which they were let.

In *Grosvenor Hotel Co. v. Hamilton 1894* the landlord leased an old house to the tenant and then used machinery on adjoining land which caused the house to be unstable. The court held that there had been a breach of the covenant not to derogate.

Alternatively in *Ocedar v. Slough Trading Co. 1927* there was held to be no breach of the covenant where the landlord stored wood on his adjoining land which consequently raised the fire insurance premiums on the tenant's commercial premises.

3.   **In relation to fitness and repair** The nature and extent of the landlord's covenant to provide fit premises and carry out repairs implied by the common law and statute, are examined in depth in Chapter 10.

8.2 Implied Covenants by the Tenant

In the absence of contrary intention the following covenants are implied in a lease which impose obligations on the tenant.

1.   **To pay rent, rates and taxes** In the absence of any express covenant by the tenant to pay rent, a covenant to pay rent is implied from any words in the contract or the lease which show a clear intention that rent is to be payable. The amount payable by the tenant is a

reasonable sum by way of compensation for use and occupation of the premises. Similarly the tenant is under an implied obligation to pay all rates, taxes and charges for which the landlord is not liable.

2. **Not to commit waste.** The implied obligations of a tenant in relation to repair (i.e. use the premises in a tenant-like manner) is examined in Chapter 10. A tenant is in breach of the tort of **'waste'** if he causes any alteration to the premises or to the land by way of damage, destruction, addition, improvement or neglect. **Voluntary waste** is committed by an act causing damage, e.g. demolishing buildings, felling trees. **Equitable waste** is a more serious form of voluntary waste and would involve the tenant for life demolishing the mansion house. An alteration which improved the value of the property was called **ameliorating waste** but is no longer actionable. Finally **permissive waste** is simply damage caused by neglect or failure to maintain. The extent of a tenant's liability for waste depends upon the term of years held and is considered in Chapter 10.

3. **Not to repudiate the landlord's title** There would be a breach of this implied covenant if the tenant deliberately asserted a title to the land which was adverse to that of the landlord's. The effect of the breach would be to automatically terminate the lease by forfeiture. If the tenant alleged that himself or a third party owned the freehold reversion there would be a breach of this covenant.

8.3 The Usual Covenants.

The expression 'usual covenants' relates to covenants which are implied into a lease where either:-

a. the contract specifies that the lease shall contain the usual covenants; or
b. the contract is silent as to the covenants which are to be contained in the lease (i.e. an **open contract**).

In practice the usual covenants are more or less the covenants implied by the common law, e.g.

i. a covenant by the landlord for quiet enjoyment;

ii. a covenant by the tenant to pay rates and taxes;

iii. a covenant by the tenant to keep the premises in repair and deliver them up in repair;

iv. a covenant by the tenant to permit the landlord to enter and view the state of repair (not an implied covenant);

v. a condition of re-entry for non payment of rent (not an implied covenant).

8.4 Express Covenants

Here it is proposed to cover those covenants which are commonly found in leases being expressly inserted by the parties.

a. **To pay Rent** Rent is the sum of money payable by the tenant in return for the interest and is fundamental to the landlord and tenant relationship. It will become due on the date appointed in the lease but is not in arrear until after midnight of that day. Rent is payable to the landlord or his agent or, on an assignment of the freehold reversion, the rent will become payable to the assignee after notice of the assignment has been given to the tenant.

b. **To repair or improve the premises** The nature and extent of an express covenant imposing repair obligations on the landlord or the tenant is dealt with in Chapter 10.

c. **For quiet enjoyment** An express covenant for quiet enjoyment will displace entirely any reliance on the implied covenant considered earlier in the chapter. In its express form the covenant is not dependent on the tenant observing his covenants and so even a tenant in default can still sue under it. The covenant will last for the duration of the lease and bind the landlord's successors in title. Usually however, the express covenant will limit the landlord's responsibility under it to himself and persons claiming from him. The effect of this limitation is that a tenant could not sue for breach of the covenant if he is subsequently dispossessed by the true owner, as the landlord had no right to create the tenancy in the first place.

d. **To insure** It is usual for the tenant to covenant to insure the premises against fire and other damage, either for a specified sum or to the full value. The landlord may reserve the right to insure, on the tenant's failure, and recover the premium from the tenant. Alternatively the landlord may covenant to take out a policy of insurance but require the tenant to pay the premiums by way of additional rent. Any monies resulting from a claim of course must be used to reinstate the premises.

e.   **Covenant not to Assign or Sublet** If the tenant wishes to retain the right to transfer his interest by assignment, or create a sublease of part of the property, he must ensure that there is no covenant prohibiting this in the lease. In practice the longer the lease the more likely it is that there will be no restriction on the tenant's right to assign. In many cases however the landlord will want some control over who takes an assignment of the lease to ensure that they are financially sound and able to pay the rent due. In such a case it is usual to insert in the lease an express covenant prohibiting assignment or sub-letting but **subject to the landlord's consent, e.g. "Not without the written consent of the landlord to assign, sub-let or part with possession of the property or any part thereof"**. It is implied in such a covenant that the landlord's consent is not to be unreasonably withheld. In some cases this is expressed in the lease by the addition of the words **"such consent not to be unreasonably withheld"**. The covenant against assignment is also likely to be reinforced by an express condition that in the event of its breach the term will come to an end, or by reliance on a general provision for re-entry and forfeiture on the tenant's breach of his obligations.

If the covenant against assignment is expressed to be without the landlord's consent then two statutory provisions come into operation:-

i.   Under the **Landlord and Tenant Act 1927 s.19,** despite anything to the contrary the landlord's consent is not to be unreasonably withheld.

ii.   Under the **Law of Property Act 1925 s.144** subject to contrary agreement the landlord may not demand a fine (payment) as the price of giving consent.

Before the above provisions are examined in depth it is necessary to make the following points which show how such a covenant has been interpreted under the common law.

1. The covenant is interpreted strictly and is not broken by the creation of a legal charge, or the passing of the tenant's estate on his death to personal representatives or to his trustee in bankruptcy.

2. The covenant prohibiting assignment is not broken by the creation of a sub-lease and vice versa.

3. Such a covenant **'runs with the land'** and is binding on the tenant's successors in title.

4. The covenant is not broken if the tenant assigns after requesting the landlord's consent and such consent is unreasonably refused.

5. The covenant is broken if the tenant assigns without requesting the landlord's consent even though the assignment is one to which consent could not reasonably have been refused.

Consent to Assignment The alternative grounds upon which the landlord could rely to justify withholding consent are that either the prospective tenant is undesirable, or the proposal is to use the premises in an undesirable way. It is up to the tenant to prove unreasonableness on the part of the landlord but there are no strict rules as to when this is constituted. It is only possible to make reference to a number of case decisions which provide guidance.

> In *Re Gibbs and Houlder Bros. & Co. 1925* the fact that the proposed assignee was another tenant of the landlord who might terminate that tenancy was not a reasonable ground to refuse consent.

> Alternatively in *Whiteminister Estate v. Hodges Menswear 1974* the fact that the proposed assignee's use of the premises would damage the landlord's own trading interests by running a rival business next door, was a sufficient ground to withhold consent.

> Also in *Lee v. K. Carter Ltd. 1949* the proposed assignment was by a limited company tenant to one of its directors and as the effect would be to create a statutorily protected tenancy the landlord had acted reasonably in withholding his consent.

Under the **Race Relations Act 1976 s.24** it is unlawful for a landlord to withhold consent on racial grounds unless the landlord or a near relative resides or intends to reside on the premises which are not large enough to accommodate more than seven people or two households, and accommodation would have to be shared with the tenant.

8.5 Remedies for breach of Covenant

The remedies for breach of covenant are an action for **damages** and if necessary **specific performance** or an **injunction.** The measure of damages payable is the amount the plaintiff suffers from the breach. As far as the landlord is concerned this is the amount by which the **value of his reversion is diminished** as a result of the breach. Only nominal damages would be payable therefore if the landlord obtains possession for breach of covenant and then demolishes the premises. There is nothing to prevent the parties expressly stipulating in the lease the measure of damages payable provided that the specified sum is a **genuine pre-estimate of the future possible loss rather than a penalty.** A plaintiff will seek the remedy of specific performance to compel compliance with the covenants, (e.g. a repairing covenant) and an injunction to prevent their breach, (e.g. a covenant limiting user). Both remedies, being equitable in nature, will never be granted where damages would suffice. The further remedy of re-entry and forfeiture is dealt with later in the chapter.

8.6 Remedies for non payment of Rent

The remedies available to a landlord for the tenant's breach of the covenant to pay rent are deserving of special attention. The ultimate remedy of re-entry and forfeiture for Non Payment of rent is dealt with later in the chapter. It should be stressed however that exacting a forfeiture for non payment of rent by way of court proceedings will only terminate the contractual tenancy in the case of protected tenancies under the **Rent Act 1977** (see Chapter 12). The landlord is not automatically entitled to possession as the tenant is entitled to stay on as a statutory tenant. The court can then order possession of the statutory tenancy if it is reasonable in the circumstances. Similarly, for secure tenancies under the **Housing Act 1980** the forfeiture of the tenancy will terminate the contract and a periodic tenancy automatically arises. In order to recover possession the landlord will then have to terminate the periodic tenancy and claim possession on one of the grounds set out in **schedule 4** of the 1980 Act. It is usual therefore to couple forfeiture proceedings with possession proceedings under schedule 4 for non payment of rent. (See Chapter 12)

Distress

Distress is a common law remedy which enables a landlord, in certain circumstances, to recover rent arrears without taking legal proceedings but by entering and taking property found on the demised premises. Under the **Rent Act 1977 s.147** distress may not be levied for rent due on a residential tenancy which is either protected or statutory without leave of the county court. This has greatly reduced the use of distress as a remedy in the private sector and therefore its importance is limited to public sector tenancies.

The right to distrain (exercise the remedy of distress) is vested in the person who holds the reversionary interest to which the right to take rent is attached, i.e. the landlord. He may exercise the distraint himself or employ a certificated bailiff. The relationship of landlord and tenant must exist at the time of the distraint and the rent must be both a certain amount and in arrear. The right to distrain will be lost therefore if payment of arrears is made or tendered before entry is made on the premises. Many classes of goods are **privileged absolutely or conditionally** against distress. Absolutely privileged means that the goods must not be taken and includes cattle, perishables, things in use, Crown property, tenant's fixtures, hired agricultural machinery, money (unless in bags or chests) and things left in the course of a trade. Conditionally privileged means that the goods may only be taken if there are no other goods available and include tools and implements of trade, and certain animals. As far as the goods of third parties are concerned the **Law of Distress Amendment Act 1908** provides that a third party may protect his goods by making a written declaration in the prescribed form to the landlord or bailiff. Having taken possession of the tenant's goods by the landlord or baliff the tenant then has five days to pay the rent arrears otherwise they are sold usually by auction. If the distress is illegal either because the rent is not in arrear or the procedure required by law has not been complied with, then the tenant has a number of remedies. He may **'rescue'** which is to retake goods not impounded or **'replevy'** which is to obtain a court order for possession. The landlord may also incur liability under the **Torts (Interference with Goods) Act 1977.** Surprisingly the use of distress as a remedy is still quite widespread by local authority landlords particularly when they have decided that eviction is an unsatisfactory way of dealing with rent arrears.

Action for non payment of rent

A court action for arrears of rent may be brought in the same way as any action for the recovery of a debt. A rent action in the county court may be brought against a tenant still in occupation by the service of a summons for arrears. A court hearing is then held with judgement given and entered. If the tenant fails to comply with the judgement, then the landlord may take enforcement proceedings such as applying to the court for an **attachment of earnings order.**

8.7 Termination of the Leasehold

A fixed term lease will terminate automatically on the expiration of the term without the need to serve a **notice to quit.** Of course statutory protection is conferred on most tenants entitling them to remain in occupation after the term has expired (see Chapter 12 and 13). Similarly a periodic tenancy will continue indefinitely until it is brought to an end by the service of a 'notice to quit'. Once again however the majority of periodic tenants are entitled to remain in occupation even after the contractual tenancy has been terminated because of statutory protection.

Surrender

A lease will come to an end if the tenant surrenders it to the landlord and the landlord accepts the surrender. An express surrender must either be by deed or by writing under **ss.52-54 Law of Property Act 1925.** In the case where a tenant has granted a sub-lease, the rights of the sub-tenant remain unaffected by a surrender of the tenant's interest. An implied surrender of the lease occurs where the tenant accepts a new lease from the landlord to commence during the continuance of the current lease.

Merger

A merger occurs when the tenant acquires the freehold reversion and the lease is said to **merge in the reversion,** it ceasing to exist. The tenant could be exercising an option to purchase the reversion, or relying on a statutory right to acquire the freehold by **enlargement or enfranchisement.**

Enlargement

Under the **Law of Property Act 1925 s.153** a lessee may execute a deed of enlargement to convert his lease into a fee simple. The principal conditions are that the lease should have been granted for at least 300 years of which 200 years or more remain unexpired, no rent is payable, and no right of redemption should exist in favour of the reversioner. In the section on mortgages in Chapter 5, the rights of a mortgagee are considered when the mortgagor loses his right of redemption. In such a case, if the mortgageee holds a 3,000 year lease he may convert it into a fee simple by executing a deed of enlargment.

Enfranchisement

This is the term applied to the statutory right of a tenant to acquire the landlord's reversionary freehold and is considered in Chapter 12.

Disclaimer

In some circumstances a person in whom a lease is vested may disclaim it if it proves to be **onerous,** e.g. a trustee in bankruptcy or a company liquidator.

8.8 Forfeiture

A landlord may terminate a lease when he **exacts a forfeiture of it** by reason of the tenant's breach of some obligation. For a breach of condition a right of re-entry arises automatically but this is not the case for a breach of covenant. It is necessary therefore to include an express provision in the lease reserving an **express right of re-entry** for breach of any covenant. Alternatively the same result can be achieved by stipulating that the tenant's performance of his covenants is a **condition of the lease.** In any event if the landlord wishes to exact a forfeiture and exercise his right of re-entry for breach of some obligation he must act on the breach and take positive steps to terminate the lease.

Obtaining possession

If possible the landlord, with the tenant's consent, may repossess peacefully. However **s.2 Protection from Eviction Act 1977** makes it unlawful to enforce a right of re-entry on forfeiture of premises let as a dwelling otherwise than by court proceedings while any person is lawfully residing on them. Such action would also amount to a breach of the covenant for quiet enjoyment. Under the **Criminal Law Act 1977 s.6** it is an offence for any person without lawful authority to use or threaten violence for the purpose of securing entry into any premises when he knows that there is someone present on the premises who is opposed to the entry.

If the tenant is opposed to the forfeiture it is necessary therefore to bring proceedings to recover possession of the dwelling in the county court (where the rateable value of the premises does not exceed £2,000). The normal procedure is that the plaintiff completes a praecipe in the prescribed form and delivers it to the county court along with his particulars of claim, a copy for service on each defendant, and the correct fees. The court then issues a summons to the defendant who has then 14 days to deliver a defence which he can do by completing the pro forma attached to the summons. Other parties who are interested in the proceedings, e.g. deserted wives, mortgagees, sub-tenants, etc. can apply and defend. If the proceedings are contested then there will be a **pre-trial review** before the registrar. The burden of proof is on the plaintiff at the actual trial and if he is successful a judgement for possession may be given, stipulating a time within which the defendant has to give up possession of the premises. When that time expires and the defendant is still in possession the plaintiff must then apply for a **warrant for possession** which is executed by the court bailiffs.

Waiver The landlord who has the right of re-entry for forfeiture may lose it in respect of a particular breach by waiving the right. A waiver may occur expressly or impliedly but to be effective the landlord must be aware of the breach. An **implied waiver** occurs if the landlord with knowledge of the breach performs any act showing that he has elected to treat the lease as still in existence. Acceptance of rent due after the breach or distraining for rent due before or after the breach would constitute an implied waiver. The remedy of distress was considered earlier in the chapter but as its exercise is dependent upon the relationship of landlord and tenant existing, then the act of distraining for rent shows an intention to treat the lease as still in existence. A waiver will only operate in relation to past breaches and therefore if the tenant continues in breach after the waiver, or commits fresh breaches, then a right of re-entry may arise once again in favour of the landlord.

Effecting a Forfeiture

For non payment of rent As previously stated there is no implied right to exact a forfeiture for breach of covenant and so it is usual to insert an express provision in the lease providing for it, e.g. "if the rent is in arrear (whether formally demanded or not) or there is a breach by the tenant of any other covenant, or if the tenant becomes bankrupt, then the landlord can re-enter the premises and determine the lease". The reference to the fact that the rent need not be formally demanded obviates the need to make such a demand. Under the common law this involves making a demand for the rent on the premises, before sunset on the last day on which the rent has to be paid and the demand continuing until sunset. It is usual therefore to expressly exclude this requirement and in any event the **Common Law Procedure Act 1852 s.210** provides that no formal demand need be made if more than one half year's rent is in arrear and there are no sufficient goods available for distress. The court has a discretionary power (equitable in origin) to grant **relief against forfeiture** for non payment of rent. Such applications are now regulated by the **Common Law Procedure Act 1852** and must be made within six months of ejectment. To obtain relief the tenant must have paid all the rent due, together with the landlord's costs, and the court must be satisfied that it is just and equitable to grant relief in the circumstances.

For other breaches of covenant To effect a forfeiture for breaches of covenant other than to pay rent **s.146 Law of Property Act 1925** must be complied with. This section requires the landlord to serve a **statutory notice** on the tenant giving him a reasonable time to comply with it. The **s.146** notice must:

a.   specify the breach complained of; and

b.   require the tenant to remedy it if it is capable or remedy; and

c.   require the tenant to pay damages for the breach.

If the tenant fails to comply with the notice within a reasonable time then the landlord can take steps to enforce the forfeiture. Some breaches of covenant by their very nature cannot be remedied in which case it is not necessary to specify that they be remedied on the **s.146** notice, e.g. a serious breach in relation to user.

In *Scala House v. Forbes 1974* it was held that the breach of a covenant against assignment or sub-letting could not be remedied. Under **s.145** both the tenants and any sub-tenants may apply to the court for relief against forfeiture. Generally the landlord brings proceedings for possession and the tenant makes his application for relief in the same action. There are special provisions contained in the **Leasehold Property (Repairs) Act 1938** relating to where the breach complained of is a repairing covenant (see Chapter 10).

136

The rights of sub-tenants on forfeiture The effect of a forfeiture of the head lease is that any sub-lease is automatically terminated. The **Law of Property Act 1925 s.146** however confers a right of any sub-tenant to apply to the court for relief against the forfeiture of the head lease. This right is applicable whatever the ground relied on to forfeit the head lease. The court has power to grant relief by ordering the grant of a new lease to the sub-tenant for a term not exceeding the unexpired residue of the sub-tenancy. The sub-tenant effectively steps into the shoes of the head tenant under the new lease.

8.9 The Running of Covenants

Covenants in leases

Between the original landlord and the original tenant there is said to be **'privity of contract'**, i.e. the parties have bound themselves personally by the covenants in the lease. As a general rule the respective parties will retain this contractual liability throughout the term of the lease, even on the death of the landlord or tenant (the personal representatives of the deceased remain liable). In addition, this liability on the landlord subsists despite the fact that he has assigned the freehold reversion to another person and on the tenant despite the fact he has assigned the lease. Where the freehold reversion is assigned it is possible to transfer the benefit of the tenant's covenants to the assignee who can then sue the original tenant on his covenants. Similarly on an assignment of the lease the benefit of the landlord's covenants can be expressly assigned to an assignee of the lease enabling him to sue the original landlord.

The relationship of landlord and tenant exists between the owner of the freehold reversion for the time being and the owner of the lease for the time being and there is said to be **'privity of estate'** between them. When privity of estate exists the landlord is liable to the tenant on such covenants that **'touch and concern'** the land and vice-versa. The authority for this rule in the case of **assignment of the lease** is the rule in *Spencer's Case 1583* and in the case of the **freehold reversion** it is **ss.141-2 Law of Property Act 1925.** In fact all covenants that are commonly found in leases do touch and concern the land, e.g. a landlord's covenant for quiet enjoyment and repair the exterior of the premises or a tenant's covenant to pay rent, rates and taxes, repair or restrict user. The rule is that a covenant touches and concerns the land if it **regulates the position of landlord and tenant** and so a covenant by the landlord to sell the reversion to the tenant would

137

not be included in that category. This is because such a covenant does not regulate the position of landlord and tenant but rather contemplates its determination.

Privity of 'Estate' and 'Contract'

The distinction between liability imposed by contract or estate is that the original landlord and tenant remain liable throughout the term on their covenants through privity of contract. The relationship of privity of estate however imposes liability on a landlord or tenant for breaches of covenant which occur while he holds his interest.

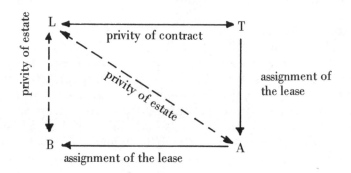

In this example L is the original landlord and T is the original tenant. T has assigned the lease to A and A has assigned the lease to B. Let us suppose that the lease contains a repair covenant and B is in breach. In relation to the breach the landlord (L) has the option of suing the Tenant (T) who remains liable by privity of contract, and he may also sue B who is in breach, because of privity of estate. The landlord cannot however sue A who is liable by privity of estate but who ceases to be liable for future breaches when he parts with his interest.

Indemnity

In the above example if the landlord chooses to sue the original tenant (T) then under the common law, T may claim indemnity from the assignee of the lease who committed the breach (B). The problem for T is that B may prove to be financially unsound. It has therefore become the practice of conveyancers to insert into an assignment of a lease an express covenant

138

by the assignee to indemnify the assignor against liability for any breach of the tenant's covenants after the assignment, whether by the assignee or a later assignee. This indemnity is implied in assignments for value by virtue of **s.77 Law of Property Act 1925.** Of course if the immediate assignee (A) is himself financially unsound and not worth suing, then the original tenant (T) has only himself to blame. In relation to an assignment of the freehold reversion there is no such implied indemnity, therefore an express covenant of indemnity should be included in the conveyance.

Covenants in the Sale of a Freehold

These are commonly referred to as **vendor and purchaser covenants** usually entered into by a vendor on the sale of part of his land, i.e. to use the land for the purposes of a dwelling house only. The rules of common law and equity differ in relation to the enforcement of such covenants.

Common Law At common law there is privity of contract between the original parties (the covenantor and covenantee) and as a general principle they remain bound by the covenants even though they have parted with their interest. Also the benefit of a covenant can be expressly assigned with the land to which it relates and so an assignee will have a right of action against the original covenantor. If the covenant is taken for the benefit of land owned by the covenantee, the **benefit of the covenant** will pass without express assignment on a transfer of the land. However the **burden of the covenant** will not pass with the land of the covenantor even though the covenant is intended to regulate the use of the land.

Under the common law therefore, a transferee of the covenantee's land may be able to enforce the covenant against the original covenantor but neither the original covenantee nor a transferee of his land can enforce the covenant against a subsequent owner of the covenantor's land. Such a person can only be made liable by the original covenantor expressly taking an indemnity on the transfer of his land against continued personal liability on the covenants.

Equity The rule in equity is that both the benefit and burden of restrictive covenants run with the land of the covenantee and the covenantor respectively. If a restrictive covenant affecting the covenantor's land is taken for the benefit of land owned by the covenantee, then equity is prepared on certain conditions to treat the covenant as creating an interest in the covenantor's land similar to a **negative easement.** As a result not only will the benefit of the covenant pass, but also the burden will pass on a transfer of the covenantor's land, and a subsequent owner will be bound by it. As the interest arising is merely equitable it is necessary however to give a subsequent purchaser for value of the covenantor's legal estate notice of the covenant. This can be achieved by registering the covenant as a land charge under the **Land Charges Act 1972.**

Scheme of Development Usually, when land is developed (e.g. a housing estate is built) the developer may require each purchaser to enter into restrictive covenants designed to maintain the general character of the estate and the value of the property on it (e.g. do not keep a chicken coop in the back garden). Every holder of a freehold property on the housing estate can enforce such covenants against every other holder. This is because the benefit of the covenants is regarded as running in equity with each plot sold under the scheme to give effect to the common intention of the parties. The running of the burden of the covenants however will once again depend upon registration. There are, however, statutory provision which ensure that in some cases, restrictive covenants can be modified or discharged with or without the payment of compensation, namely **s.84 Law of Property Act 1925.** The matter is dealt with by the **Lands Tribunal** which takes into account the changes in the character of the neighbourhood or the fact that the covenant impedes some reasonable user of the land.

Part 4 - **Liability**

CHAPTER 9   Tortious Liability

The concept of a civil wrong was introduced in Chapter 1. In that chapter it was stated that certain acts or omissions have been identified under the law as constituting civil wrongs, referred to as **torts.** An individual who suffers harm as the result of the tort of another will have recourse to the courts who will order the wrongdoer to provide the innocent party with a remedy by way of redress. Generally individual torts are common law in origin e.g. nuisance, negligence and trespass, but some have now been incorporated into statute e.g occupiers liability. As the seperate torts of nuisance and occupiers liability are mainly related to land holding, particularly property in disrepair, it is proposed to examine them seperately in the next chapter. This chapter therefore will be confined to a consideration of the torts of negligence and trespass, the tortious liability of local authorities generally and the concept of vicarious liability.

9.1 The Tort of Negligence

The tort of negligence has developed as the most important civil wrong and this is confirmed by the fact that more actions are brought based upon this tort than all the other torts taken together. From the outset it is necessary to distinguish between the concept of negligence simply as a state of mind, i.e. carelessness, and negligence as a tort. The tort has been defined as the **breach of a legal duty to take care which results in damage.** It is applicable therefore to numerous areas of activity including: injuries at work; road accidents; poor workmanship; dangerous premises; and defective goods. In all of these activities, to succeed in an action based upon the tort of negligence the plaintiff will have to prove the existence of three essential elements:-

a.   that the defendant owed him a legal duty of care; and

b.   that the defendant broke that duty; and

c.   that the plaintiff suffered loss as a result.

When all three elements have been proved to the court's satisfaction then the tort of negligence has been committed subject to the possibility of defences. It is proposed to examine each essential element in turn.

a) The Existence of a Duty of Care

One of the first points to recognise is that the law does not make an individual responsible for all the consequences of his actions and it is necessary to draw a line somewhere. Thus it would be unreasonable to make a driver who crashes and blocks the highway through negligent driving responsible for all the consequences of the traffic jam that might ensue. The law does not therefore impose a duty of care on the plaintiff in relation to all those who are affected by his actions.

> In *Bourhill v. Young 1942* a motor-cyclist through his negligent driving collided with a car and was killed. Unfortunately the plaintiff, a pregnant fishwife, who heard the crash suffered shock and subsequently later miscarried as a result. She then sued the personal representatives of the cyclist in negligence claiming that were it not for his conduct, she would not have suffered harm. The House of Lords dismissed the action on the grounds that no duty of care could be established. At the time of the negligence the fishwife was outside the area of foreseeable danger and a reasonable man could not have contemplated her being injured.

> This test of foreseeability to establish the existence of a duty of care was first propounded in the famous case of *Donoghue v. Stevenson 1932*. Here the House of Lords had to decide whether a manufacturer could be made liable to a consumer under the tort of negligence in the following circumstances. The consumer's friend had purchased a bottle of the manufacturer's ginger beer for her from a retailer. When she consumed some of the ginger beer, the remainder from the opaque bottle was poured into her glass with what was later discovered to be the remains of a decomposed snail. As the prescence of the snail caused shock, distress and later illness, the consumer sued the manufacturer under the tort of negligence claiming that he was in breach of the legal duty of care he owed towards her. By a majority decision the House of Lords held that a duty of care was owed by a manufacturer to the ultimate consumer of his products, here the duty had been broken and as damage resulted there was liability in negligence. This case owes its importance to the statements of Ld. Atkin who attempted to propound a

test of general applicability to determine when a duty of care ought to be established. It is referred to as the **neighbour test,** Ld. Atkin stating "we owe a duty of care to our neighbour", and he is **"anyone who we can reasonably foresee would be likely to be injured by our acts or omissions".** Numerous duty situations had been established by precedent including employer/employee, doctor/patient and car driver/passenger. Ld. Atkin's test however has been applied to recognise new situations where a legal duty of care is taken to exist thus "the categories of negligence are never closed".

In *Home Office v. Dorset Yacht Co. Ltd. 1970* the House of Lords held that the Home Office owed a duty of care to the public to protect them from escaped prisoners, in this case ten borstal boys.

In *Hedley Byrne v. Heller & Partners 1964* the House of Lords recognised that a duty of care would arise where a person, aware that others are relying upon him, gives negligent advice which produces financial loss.

Also in *Dutton v. Bognor Regis UDC 1972* the Court of Appeal held that a duty of care was owed by a local authority when exercising supervisory powers under the Public Health Act to ensure that building work conformed with regulations. This duty was owed to a subsequent purchaser of a property who suffered harm as a result of a negligent inspection by the local authority.

The present position in relation to establishing a duty of care was stated by Lord Wilberforce in *Anns v. Merton London Borough Council 1977.* Here the House of Lords confirmed the important principle of law that local authorities may owe a duty of care under the common law for the negligent exercise of their statutory powers. Similar negligence was alleged to that in *Dutton v. Bognor Regis UDC* in that building foundations had been negligently approved by a local authority inspector and as a result maisonettes had been built which proved to have many defects. The House of Lords confirmed the decision in *Dutton v. Bognor Regis UDC* (on a different legal basis) and held that the council were liable for the damage caused to the subsequent purchasers of the property. In relation to negligence generally,

Lord Wilberforce confirmed that the correct approach to determine the existence of a duty of care was firstly to apply the neighbour test from *Donoghue v. Stevenson* which is sufficient to give rise to a **prima facie duty**. Secondly, it is then necessary for the court to determine whether there are any considerations which ought to negative or limit the scope of the duty.

It is suggested that such a limiting factor would be **public policy**, the courts having an overriding duty to confirm or deny a duty situation depending on whether it was felt to be in the public interest. On this basis it is possible to reconcile a decision such as *Rondel v. Worsley 1969* where the court held that a barrister when presenting a case does not owe a duty of care under the tort of negligence to his client. This is despite the fact that he can reasonably foresee harm and can only be justified on the ground that the court felt that to establish such a duty situation was not in the public interest.

b. **Breach of a Legal Duty to Take Care**

The second element of the tort of negligence that the plaintiff must prove is that the defendant was in breach of the duty of care. To determine this element the courts must consider, on the evidence presented, whether the defendant acted **reasonably** in the circumstances. The duty is broken if the defendant failed to do what the reasonable man would do, or did what the reasonable man would not do. Each case must be viewed on its own facts, but the courts recognise that the standard of care required of the defendant will vary depending on the plaintiff. An employer would therefore owe a higher standard of care to an apprentice than he would to an experienced employee as the risk of injury is greater.

In *Paris v. Stepney BC 1951* the court held that an employer owed a higher standard of care to a motor mechanic who had only one eye and was therefore obliged to provide him with protective goggles. This was not because the likelihood of injury was greater but because the consequences of eye injury were that much more serious in this case.

Another approach adopted by the courts is to weigh the risk of injury against the cost of avoiding it.

146

In *Latimer v. AEC 1952* a factory floor was flooded and the employer took steps to clear the water. He warned his workforce of the danger but nevertheless allowed them to carry on working. The plaintiff suffered injury when he slipped on a patch of water and he sued in negligence. The court held that the employer had acted reasonably in the circumstances. Certainly there was a risk of injury but the cost of preventing the possibility of harm altogether would be to close the factory and send the workers home, and this was too high a price to pay.

It is for the plaintiff to prove that the defendant is in breach of the duty of care but in one circumstance he may rely on a rule of evidence to assist him, which has the effect of shifting the burden of proof to the defendant. This rule of evidence is called **'res ipsa loquitur'** and means 'the facts speak for themselves'. It is relevant when the defendant has a means of knowledge denied to the plaintiff, control over the events which caused the harm, and the damage is such that would not occur in the normal course of things.

This rule was applied for the benefit of the plaintiff in *Scott v. London & St. Katherine Dock Co. 1865*. Here a customs officer was injured by the fall of bags of sugar in a warehouse and the court, relying on the res ipsa loquitur rule inferred negligence on the part of the defendant.

c. **Damage**

The final element of the tort is that as a result of the breach of duty the plaintiff has suffered damage in the form of physical injury or financial loss.

In *Barnett v. Chelsea & Kensington Hospital Management Committee 1969* a night watchman went to a hospital casualty department in the early hours of the morning complaining of stomach pains. The casualty officer refused to examine him and advised him to report to his GP later in the day. The man subsequently died of arsenic poisoning a few hours later. In an action by his widow based on negligence the court decided that the casualty officer was clearly in breach of the duty of care he owed to the patient. However it was shown by medical evidence that an examination by the doctor would not have revealed the poisoning in time, nor could the death have been

147

prevented. Therefore the court held that as the breach of duty did not cause the damage there was no liability on the doctor or his employer. The death had not occurred as a result of the doctor's negligence.

The extent of loss recoverable will depend on whether it is regarded as too remote. To determine the question of remoteness the best test seems to be that of **reasonable foreseeability.** In relation to physical injury however once it is shown that the type of injury is foreseeable the rule is still applied that you must "take your plaintiff as you find him". A plaintiff who is therefore sensitive to the type of harm caused is entitled to recover for all the physical harm suffered.

> In *Smith v. Leech Brain & Co. Ltd. 1961* a workman suffered harm when he was splashed on the lip by molten metal. Unfortunately the man had dormant cancer in his lip and as a result of the burn it became malignant and he subsequently died. The employer's negligence was accepted but what was in question was the extent of damage for which he was liable. The court held that as the employer could reasonably foresee the type of injury, i.e. the burn, they were liable for all the damage which was suffered as a result, i.e. the death.

Defences

1. **Contributory Negligence** Prior to the **Law Reform (Contributory Negligence) Act 1945** if it could be shown that the plaintiff was partly the cause of his own injury then he could not recover in negligence and the contributory fault acted as a complete defence. Now as a result of that Act a plaintiff who has contributed towards his own injury will have his damages reduced in accordance with the degree of fault. Total damages are assessed and then reduced by the percentage of the plaintiff's fault, which for the Act to apply must be at least 10%.

    > In *Baker v. Willoughby 1969* a pedestrian suffered injury when he was struck by a motor car. Both the pedestrian and the car had a clear view of the road and the court took the view that the pedestrian was 50% to blame.

Certainly the failure of a car passenger to wear a seatbelt is now regarded as a sufficient ground to reduce damages in cases of physical injury.

2. **Volenti Non Fit Injuria** (no cause of action arises to someone who voluntarily accepts the risk). If the plaintiff expressly or impliedly consents to the risk of injury then he can hardly complain of it and maintain an action in tort. Volenti is relevant therefore when a person consents to an act which would otherwise be a tort, e.g. a surgical operation, or agrees to run the risk of injury, e.g. participate in a sport. For the defence to be applicable the plaintiff must however be aware of the risk of injury, appreciate it and be taken to have accepted it. There is no volenti however when a person is, by the negligence of another, put in a position where he is under a duty to act, and then does so, e.g. a rescuer who can foresee injury to others and acts reasonably to prevent it.

> In the case of *Haynes v. Harwood 1935,* the defendant tied his horse and cart negligently and as a result, the horse bolted in a crowded street. Foreseeing injury to others the plaintiff intervened and in attempting to stop the horse suffered injury himself. The court held that he had acted reasonably in the circumstances and could not be regarded as volenti.

9.2 The Tort of Trespass

Trespass is one of the earliest forms of civil wrong recognised under the law. It may take one of three forms, trespass to person, trespass to land or trespass to goods.

a. **Trespass to person**

> Trespass to person must be further broken down into its three aspects - battery, assault and false imprisonment.

A battery may be defined as the intentional application of force to another person without lawful justification. The essence of the tort is the act of touching a person in a hostile manner or against his will, e.g. wounding with a weapon or striking with an object. The act must be a direct one either carried out **intentionally** or **negligently.**

In *Nash v. Sheen 1953* a hairdresser negligently applied a tone rinse to the plaintiff's hair when she had asked for a permanent wave. As a result the plaintiff suffered a skin complaint for which she sued in tort. The court held that the negligent act constituted a battery.

Battery is actionable 'per se' (without proof of damage) but substantial compensation may be awarded when the battery is an affront to personal dignity, even though there is no physical injury.

An assault (rather than the criminal offence of common assault) is constituted by an act that creates in a person's mind a reasonable fear that he is about to suffer a battery. An assault is therefore often the threat of force before the battery is committed, e.g. to raise a fist or point a gun. There is authority to suggest that mere words alone without movement cannot amount to an assualt. In *Innes v. Wylie 1844,* there was no assault when a policeman stood still and acted as a closed door so that the plaintiff could not pass. An assault may occur without a battery or vice-versa but often assault and battery occur in the same incident. Also the defences to assault and battery are similar and include:- volenti non fit injuria, self defence, necessity, lawful arrest and the ejection of a trespasser using reasonable force.

False imprisonment is committed where, without lawful justification, a person is restrained from going wherever he wants to. Any form of unlawful restraint is sufficient provided it is total. Even if the plaintff is unaware that he is being imprisoned, the tort may still be committed.

In *Meering v. Graham White Aviation (1919)* 122 L.T. 44 the plaintiff employee was interviewed in respect of a theft at his place of employment. Without realising it he was restrained in an office during the interview and this act the court held was sufficient to constitute the tort of false imprisonment.

False imprisonment is a tort actionable 'per se', most actions arising in relation to arrest and subsequent detention which proves to be unlawful.

b. **Trespass to Land**

This may be defined as an unlawful interference with the possession of land of another without lawful justification. It is a tort actionable

150

per se, and to bring an action the plaintiff must prove actual possession of the land in question, e.g. an owner in possession or a tenant. The direct interference which constitutes the tort may take many forms and include:-

1. **entering onto land without lawful justification.** This may occur by walking on land of another without express or implied permission even if in ignorance.

2. **abusing a right of entry.** This occurs where the defendant enters lawfully for a specific purpose but subsequently abuses his right of entry by pursuing a different purpose, or going to a part of the land without authorisation. The effect of abusing a right of entry is that the trespass may be regarded as a **trespass 'ab initio'** (from the beginning). Thus the defendant would be guilty of a trespass from the time of entry rather than from the time of the wrongful act.

3. **termination of authority.** If permission to be on land is expressly withdrawn then the defendant has a reasonable time to leave after which he becomes a trespasser.

4. **placing things on land.** To leave a scrap car on land without permission could constitute trespass to land.

5. **infringing the air space above land.** In *Kelsen v. Imperial Tobacco Co. Ltd. 1957* it was held that to erect an advertising sign projecting into the air space above the plaintiff's land was a trespass. As far as aircraft are concerned, statutory authority to infringe air space at a reasonable height is conferred by the **Civil Aviation Act 1949.**

The remedies for trespass to land include:- an action for damages, an action for profits (damages for a person wrongfully ejected from land), an action for recovery of the land; an injunction, ejection of the trespasser using reasonable force.

Finally the various defences to an action in trespass include:- volenti non fit injuria, necessity, statutory authority, entry under the authority of the law, (e.g. entry by a court bailiff).

c.   **Trespass to Goods**

This tort may be defined as a physical interference with the possession of goods without lawful justification. Once again this form of trespass is actionable per se and could involve removing goods from possession of the owner without authority, damaging goods or intermeddling with goods. The interference must be direct and forcible and the plaintiff must show that, when it occurred, he was in possession (or entitled to possession) of the goods. Defences to the tort include:- volenti non fit injuria, self defence, inevitable accident.

9.3 The Tortious Liability of Local Authorities

As corporate bodies local authorities have the capacity to sue and be sued under the law of tort. Examples of tort actions brought by local authorities are rare but in the case of *Bognor Regis Urban District Council v. Campion 1972* the plaintiff council successfully brought an action in the tort of defamation against a ratepayer who had published a leaflet defamatory of the council.

> The possibility of a local authority being made liable in tort was confirmed in *Campbell v. Paddington Corporation 1911*. Here the defendant council had authorised the erection of a stand on the highway from which councillors could view the funeral procession of Edward VII. This act, causing special damage to the plaintiff, constituted the tort of private nuisance for which the council could be held liable. Part of the council's defence was that, as it had no authority to erect the stand it had acted **ultra vires,** and could not therefore be sued in tort. The court rejected the argument and decided that the council was liable. Avory, J. made the point when he said "To say that because the borough council had no legal right to erect it, therefore, the corporation cannot be sued, is to say that no corporation can ever be sued for any tort... That would be absurd".

The liability of a local authority is normally **vicarious** (substituted) as it acts through its employees, contractors or agents. It is convenient therefore at this point to examine the concept of vicarious liability.

9.4 Vicarious Liability

As a general principle the person who is responsible for the commission of a tort can always be made liable for it. Under the doctrine of vicarious liability however another person can be made liable depending on the circumstances. The most common example of where this can occur is the common law rule which imposes vicarious liability on employers in respect of torts committed by their employees (servants) during the course of their employment.

Following the **Employer's Liability (Compulsory Insurance) Act 1969** an employer must insure himself in respect of vicarious liability for injuries caused by his employees to their colleagues and will normally insure against injury to third parties. To determine the employer's liability it is first necessary to establish whether the relationship is one of employer and employee (servant) with a contract of service rather than an employer and independent contractor with a contract for services. This whole question is examined in depth in Chapter 18.

Servants

If the employee is a servant under his employer's control it is then necessary to determine whether the tort was committed during the course of his employment. The usual question that is posed is whether the employee was doing his job at the time of the tortious act. Obviously if the employee was doing something which was personal to himself it would be unjust to make his employer liable for it.

> In *Warren v. Henlys Ltd. 1948* following an argument over payment for petrol a pump attendant physically assaulted a customer. The court held that the employee had gone beyond the scope of his employment and his employer could not be made vicariously liable for the tortious act.

This is not to say of course that an employer can never be made liable for excessive force used by an employee. The use of force may be envisaged as part of the employee's employment, e.g. a night club bouncer.

> In *Century Insurance Ltd. v. Northern Ireland Transport Board 1942* a tanker driver while delivering petrol at a garage lit a cigarette and carelessly threw away the lighted match causing

an explosion and considerable damage. His employer was held to be vicariously liable for the negligent act as here the employee was within the course of his employment. By supervising the unloading the employee was doing his job, and by smoking he was doing his job in a negligent manner.

Even an employee who wilfully disobeys his employer's express orders could still be regarded as being within the scope of his employment.

In *Rose v. Plenty 1976* a milkman contrary to orders engaged a young thirteen year old boy to help him deliver milk. The boy was subsequently injured by the milkman's negligent driving and sued both the milkman and his employer. The Court of Appeal held that despite the instructions of the employer he remained vicariously liable as the action of the milkman remained within the scope of his employment.

As far as local authorities are concerned they may be made vicariously liable for the tortious acts of their employees in the same way as any other employer.

In *Smith v. Martin and Hull Corporation 1911* a teacher negligently instructed a young pupil to stoke the fire in the teachers' common room. In so doing the child sustained injury. The injured child successfully succeeded in an action in the tort of negligence against the employee and the council employer. Vicarious liability was established because the negligent act was within the scope of the teacher's authority.

It is important to distinguish between vicarious liability and the possible **primary liability** of a local authority.

In *Carmarthenshire County Council v. Lewis 1955* a child at nursery school wandered from the school yard on to the highway and caused the death of a lorry driver who swerved to avoid the child. An action was brought against the council in negligence on the grounds that the child's teacher had left her unattended for a short time. In fact the teacher was at the relevant time giving assistance to another child. The court held that the teacher had in fact fulfilled the duty of care required of her by acting as a prudent parent would in the circumstances, so there could be no vicarious liability of her employer. However, the fact that the child could reach the street so easily, indicated that the council were failing in their duty to take sufficient precautions and they were held to be liable for primary negligence.

Independent Contractors

Corporations often find the need to employ persons as contractors to carry out specialist tasks. The question as to whether a genuine employer - independent contractor relationship has in fact been entered into is examined in Chapter 18. If the relationship is one of employer contractor, then as a general principle, the employer is not liable for the torts of the contractor. This principle is subject to exceptions however, particularly where the employer is a local authority. Vicarious liability may be imposed therefore where:-

1.   **the work undertaken is particularly hazardous.** In *Honeywell v. Larkin Brothers 1934* a firm hired an independent contractor to photograph the inside of a cinema where they had done some work. The photographer used old fashioned equipment which caused a fire. The court held that because of the hazards involved in flash photography at that time the firm was vicariously liable for the damage caused by their contractor;

2.   **where the contractor is carrying out a duty imposed by law on the local authority.** This exception is particularly relevant for local authorites and may be illustated by the case of *Hardaker v. Idle District Council 1896.* Here the council having statutory power to do so employed a contractor to construct a sewer. In carrying out the work negligently the contractor pierced a gas main and the plaintiff's property was consequently damaged by the resultant explosion. In an action by the plaintiffs against the contractor and the council employer the court held that in exercising their statutory power the council owed an overriding duty to the public. This duty was to construct the sewer so as not to damage the gas main and put the public at risk. The council could not discharge this duty by simply employing a contractor to carry out the work, and accordingly they remained responsible to the plaintiff for its breach;

3.   **where the authority specifically authorises the tortious act.** This would be the case where the council authorises the erection of a building,

155

e.g. a school or hospital, which because of its situation constituted the tort of private nuisance to adjoining residents;

4. **where the authority interferes to prescribe how the work is to be done.** The more interference there is by the council employer in the performance of the task, the more likely it is that the courts will impose vicarious liability;

5. **where the authority is negligent in the selection of the contractor.** The employer must ensure that he selects a competent contractor who is reputable to carry out the task otherwise he will be made liable for his actions.

CHAPTER 10 The Law Relating to Property in Disrepair

In this chapter it is proposed to examine the law covering the rights, duties and powers of **'persons'** in relation to individual houses in disrepair. In this context 'persons' who may be affected by disrepair include owner occupiers, landlords, tenants, local authorities, visitors and even trespassers. The subject matter contained here is necessarily very broad in nature and includes a consideration of the law relating to:— the express and implied repair obligations of the landlord and tenant; the concept of nuisance in its common law and statutory form; individual unfit property; compulsory repair and occupier's liability.

10.1 Repair Obligations of the Landlord and Tenant

Obligations in relation to repair of property may be expressly imposed on the landlord and/or tenant by virtue of the covenants of the lease. Alternatively repair obligations may be implied by the common law or statute. Firstly it is proposed to examine the position of the tenant.

Repair Obligations on the Tenant

It is usual practice under a lease to impose an express repairing obligation on the tenant. The extent of the obligation depends on the type of premises demised and the length of the lease. The tenant is often required to repair, and, keep the property in repair during the period of the tenancy, and additionally to repair defects within a specified time of notice of them. It is also usual to confer an express right on the landlord to enter and view the state of repair of the property during the term, after the service of reasonable notice. This could be supplemented by an express covenant to allow the landlord to enter the premises to carry out repairs which the tenant has failed to execute after notice has been served upon him, and then recover the cost.

The express covenant to keep the premises in repair will impose an onerous obligation on the tenant. It could involve putting the premises into a state of repair on the commencement of the term and certainly delivering up the premises in a state of repair on the expiration of the term. It should be stressed however that repair does not mean improvement and renewal.

In *Pembery v. Lamdin 1940* the landlord attempted to enforce a repair covenant requiring the tenant to keep the premises dry by waterproofing the walls. The premises suffered from dry rot as they had not been constructed with a damp course or waterproofing. The court held that what was required here was structural alteration which constituted improvement rather than repair which the tenant was not bound to carry out.

The fine distinction between **'repairing'** by renewing parts and **'renewing'** by renewing the whole was drawn by Buckley L. J. in *Lurcott v. Wakely 1911*. He said that "repair is restoration by renewal or replacement of subsidiary parts of a whole. Renewal as distinguished from repair is reconstruction of the entirety".

This approach was recently adopted by the court in *Ravenseft Properties Ltd. v. Davestone (Holdings) Ltd. 1979*. Here the question faced by the court was whether the insertion of expansion joints in a building constituted renewal or repair. The court held that the work amounted to repair, for the joints formed a small part of the whole building.

It is common practice in short term or periodic tenancies to limit the repair covenant imposed on the tenant by the words **"fair wear and tear excepted"**. This clause is inserted to relieve the tenant from liability for disrepair arising from the action of time and the weather and also reasonable use of the premises. The exception will not extend to misuse and is restricted to the ordinary effects of the wind and weather. The tenant will be expected however, to take steps to prevent additional deterioration flowing from normal fair wear and tear which could easily be prevented by prompt action.

In the absence of any express covenant there is an obligation **implied by the common law** in all leases that the tenant will use the property in a **'tenant like manner'**. The extent of this obligation will vary with the nature and term of the lease. For a weekly tenant it involves taking proper care of the premises. He may be made responsible for damage to the property which he causes by his own action or by action of those under his control. Liability may be imposed under the tort of **voluntary waste.** A weekly tenant is not liable however for disrepair caused by his failure to take action which could constitute the tort of **permissive waste.** In fulfilling his obligation to treat the premises in a tenant like manner a periodic tenant must, said Ld Denning M.R. in *Warren v. Keen 1954* "clean the chimney when necessary, mend the electric light when it fuses, unstop the sink when it is blocked and turn off the water and empty the boiler if he is going away for the winter''. Both annual and fixed term tenants may be made liable for voluntary and permissive waste. In addition to treating the property in a tenant like manner, annual and fixed term tenants must keep the premises **wind and water tight** and do **timely repairs.**

Repair Obligations on the Landlord

The landlord may by covenant expressly agree to do all or part of the repairs to the property during the term of the lease. If so, it is implied that before an obligation to repair arises on the landlord, the tenant must give reasonable notice of the want of repair. Certainly a landlord who covenants to repair will have an implied right to enter the property to view the state of repair and/or carry out the repair work. Failure by the landlord to fulfil his repair obligation will give the tenant the right to carry out the work in default and deduct the resulting expenses from future rent. This right was confirmed in *Lee-Parker v. Izzet 1971,* where it was stressed that the tenant should ensure that the landlord is kept fully informed of his intentions. Certainly there is no right for the tenant to withold payment of rent to compel the landlord to repair, for he will then be in breach of covenant. Additional remedies where the landlord is in breach of a repair obligation include termination of the tenancy and/or an action for damages.

The common law implies no obligation on a landlord who lets unfurnished premises or land either that it is reasonably fit for habitation or that it is physically fit for the purpose for which it was let. For a letting of furnished property however, there is an implied common law duty to ensure that on the commencement of the tenancy the premises are fit for human habitation. The question as to fitness will be dealt with later in the chapter but generally property is fit if it is reasonably habitable. Fitness need only be established on the commencement of the tenancy and there is no duty on the landlord to keep the premises fit during the period of the term. The **Housing Act 1957 s.6** provides an exception in relation to the fitness of property let at a low rental (i.e. £40 p.a. London, £26 p.a. elsewhere, for a letting before 6th July, 1957, and £80 p.a. in London, and £52 p.a. elsewhere for lettings after that date). Here there is an implied statutory condition that the property is fit on the commencement of the tenancy and will remain so throughout the term. The landlord having been notified of the defects which it is alleged constitute unfitness must repair within a reasonable period. Failure to do so will give the tenant the right to terminate the tenancy and sue for damages.

In exceptional cases the courts have been willing to imply terms imposing a repair obligation on the landlord into a tenancy.

> A recent example was the decision of the House of Lords in *Liverpool City Council v. Irwin 1977* which concerned the letting of a flat in a high rise block. The local authority landlord let flats in a tower block which as a result of vandalism suffered from defects in relation to blocked rubbish chutes, staircase lighting, lifts, etc. Because of the state of the premises the tenants withheld rent claiming that the landlords were in breach of covenant. This was claimed despite there being no express contractual obligation to repair the common parts imposed on the landlord. Folowing an action for possession the case was finally heard on appeal by the House of Lords. The Lords held that in certain circumstances the courts were prepared to imply terms into tenancies which they regarded as necessary for the functioning of the tenancy contract. Here the implied right of the tenants to use the stairs, lifts and rubbish chutes should place an implied contractual obligation on the landlords to take reasonable care to maintain these common areas and facilities. In the circumstances reasonable care had been taken by the landlords to attempt to keep the common parts in repair and they had therefore fulfilled their implied repair obligation.

The most important statutory provision imposing a repairing obligation on the landlord is contained in **s.32 (1) Housing Act 1961.** This provides that in the lease of a dwelling house granted after 24th October, 1961 for a term of years of less than 7 years the landlord covenants:—

1.   to keep in repair the structure and exterior of the dwelling house including drains, gutters and external pipes; and

2.   to keep in repair and proper working order installations for the supply of water, gas, electricity and sanitation including basins, sinks, baths and sanitary conveniences and installations for space and water heating.

This section does not impose an obligation on the landlord to rebuild or reinstate the premises in cases of destruction or damage caused by fire, tempest or flood. Nor is the landlord required under it to carry out repairs for which the tenant is liable. Express provision is made in **s.33** however to prevent the landlord avoiding his statutory obligation under **s.32.** **Sections 33(6) and 33(7)** provide that any attempt to contract out of this repairing obligation either directly or indirectly is void and of no legal effect. Usually the statutory obligation imposed on the landlord by **s.32** is inserted into a lease as an express covenant.

To take action under **s.32,** the tenant must first show that notice of the disrepair has been served on the landlord who has been given a reasonable opportunity to inspect the premises and carry out the repairs. The nature and extent of the obligation imposed by **s.32(1)** has been the subject of interpretation in the courts.

> In *Brown v. Liverpool C 1963* it was held that the whole steps and a path leading to the front of a house were within the meaning of the structure and exterior for the purposes of the section. On the other hand, slabs in the backyard which were not an essential means of access were held not to be within the section in *Hopwood v. Cannock Chase District C 1975*. In relation to flats, the Court of Appeal in *Campden Hill Towers v. Gardner 1977* held that the scope of **s.32(1)** extended to matters affecting stability which includes outside walls, the outer sides of horizontal divisions between flats, the outside of the inner party walls of the flat and the structural framework.

10.2 Individual Unfit Property

In the preceeding section, the rights and duties of the parties to a lease in relation to property in disrepair were considered. Now it is proposed to examine the statutory powers and duties of local authorities (contained in housing and public health legislation), to enable them to take action in relation to unfit housing and housing in sustantial disrepair. It should be stressed that at this stage the discussion will be confined to local authority powers over **individual unfit housing** rather than development clearance powers of local authorities over **areas of unfit housing.**

The major aims of the legislation in relation to unfit housing and housing in substantial disrepair is to ensure that no one resides in property that is unfit and that fit property in substantial disrepair is put into a state of repair. As far as individual unfit housing is concerned the **Housing Act 1957 Part II** imposed a duty on local authorities having formed the view that a house is unfit to take action in relation to it. A statutory duty is also placed on local authorities under **s.70 Housing Act 1969** to inspect their areas for the purpose of determining 'inter alia' (amongst other things) whether there are any unfit houses. Complaints of unfitness may also be made by individuals through a local justice of the peace under **s.157(2) Housing Act 1957.** Thus, having obtained information in relation to unfitness, whether following complaints, or through their own investigations, local authorities must then consider it. If a decision of unfitness is reached the local authority is required by statute to take action.

Unfitness

The unfitness provisions apply to **houses** which under **s.7 Housing Act 1969** would include purpose built dwelling houses, flats and converted premises. The test of determining unfitness is contained in the **Housing Act 1957 s.4** which provides that a dwelling is statutorily unfit for human habitation when it is so far defective in one or more listed items that it is unsuitable for reasonable occupation. Listed items are:— repair; structure stability; freedom from damp; internal arrangements; natural lighting; ventilation; water supply; drainage and sanitary conveniences; and facilities for the preparation and cooking of food and for the disposal of waste water. Guidance in relation to the above matters is provided by **Ministry Circular 69/67** which had the aim of producing a consistent approach to unfitness throughout the country. Here further explanation is given of the listed items. For example, dampness is only to be regarded as significant if is amounts to a health hazard. Also structural instability is only significant if it indicates the possibility of further movement constituting a threat to the occupants. It should be stressed however that the final decision as to unfitness rests with the local authority in question implementing its own particular policy.

Certainly the courts have provided little guidance as illustrated by the decision in *Summers v. Salford Corporation 1943.* Here the question before the House of Lords was whether a defective sash cord on a bedroom window in a council flat could render the property unfit. The court held that as the window was as a result permanently jammed open, the bedroom was not reasonably suitable for occupation and the house therefore unfit. Ld Atkin stated "a burst or a leaking pipe, a displaced slate or tile, a stopped drain, a rotten stair tread might each of them, until repair, make a house unfit to live in though each of them might be quickly and cheaply repaired, but disrepair to a single room would not be sufficient unless the effect was to render the whole house not reasonably fit for human habitaiton as in the case before the court''.

Previously it was the case that certain property was deemed to be unfit for human habitation by statute i.e. back to back houses intended to be used as dwellings for the working classes (see Chapter 1).

Having determined that an individual house is unfit for human habitation the next question that the local authority is under a duty to determine is whether the property can or cannot be made fit at **reasonable expense.** The question as to reasonable expense is a crucial one, for its determination will designate the local authority's responsibility in relation to the property. Guidance is provided by **s.39(1) Housing Act 1957** which provides that in determining 'reasonable expense' regard is to be had to the estimated cost of the works necessary to render the house fit and the estimated cost value of the house once the works are complete. Following recent case law it seems that this is not the only matter to be considered.

In *Dudlow Estates Ltd. v. Sefton MBC 1979,* the County Court rejected a local authority's finding that a property could not be made fit at reasonable expense following a straight financial calculation. Estimated costs of repair of the property were £1400-£1500 and the only evidence as to its value when repaired was that of the local authority who valued it at £1000. The judge, having seen the property decided that it could provide an attractive home when repaired and bearing in mind the possible demolition costs of £500 held that it was repairable at reasonable expense. This wide discretion of the County Court judge was confirmed on appeal by the Court of Appeal. The question asked by Ld Denning M.R. in *Bacon v. Grimsby Corp. 1950* was quite simply "Is the house worth the cost of repairs?".

Compulsory Repair of Unfit Property

If a local authority determines that an unfit property which is **not in a designated clearance area** is capable of being **made fit at reasonable expense it is under a duty under s.9(1) Housing Act 1957** to serve a **compulsory repair notice** on the person who has control of the house, e.g. the owner occupier or person in receipt of rent. This notice must detail the repair works necessary and give a reasonable time, not less than 21 days, to enable them to be carried out. Copies of this notice must be served on persons with an interest in the property which would include tenants and mortgagees. Rights of appeal against the repair notice are contained in

s.11 Housing Act 1957 which allows an appeal to the County Court by an aggrieved person within 21 days. Grounds of appeal include a claim that the house is not unfit, that excessive works have been detailed, or that they cannot be carried out at reasonable expense. The County Court has power to confirm, vary or quash the notice. If the repair notice is confirmed on appeal or no appeal is lodged then the person in control of the house must carry out the stipulated works. Failure to do so within the prescribed period will enable the local authority to act under power conferred by **s.10** by **carrying out the works in default** and recovering the costs from the person in control of the property as a civil debt.

Under **s.10(1) Housing Act 1957** a local authority having served a **s.9** notice requiring remedial work in a house unfit for human habitation has a discretion whether or not to carry out the work in default which it is bound to exercise under the circumstances of each case.

> In *Elliot v. Brighton B.C. 1981,* the local authority gave out standing instructions to its staff that where a **s.9** notice was not complied with they should carry out the work themselves immediately. The plaintiff failed to comply with a **s.9** notice and the Environmental Health Office carried out the work. The local authority then demanded payment of the cost. The plaintiff then appealed against the demand and the county court dismissed the appeal. On appeal to the Court of Appeal it was held that as the council had a discretion to carry out the work in default under **s.10** this carried with it a duty to exercise the discretion considering the individual circumstances of each case. Since they had failed to do this they had accordingly acted **ultra vires** and no demand for expenses could be made (see Chapter 1).

Compulsory purchase, demolition or closing of unfit property

If the local authority determines that an unfit property **cannot be rendered fit at reasonable expense** it is under a duty under **s.16 Housing Act 1957** to call a meeting of persons who have a legal interest in the property at a particular time and place (not less than 21 days from the service of the notice). It is at this **time and place meeting** that all interested parties are given an opportunity to air their views and proposals in relation to the future of the property. It may be that the owner will **undertake** to either carry out the works necessary to render the property fit or instead to cease to use the property as a dwelling house. The local authority has an absolute discretion as to whether it accepts either of these undertakings. If no undertakings are given or if they are given and not accepted, then the local authority has three basic alternatives in relation to the property, **demolition, closing** or **purchase.** It is at this point that the local authority may exercise power conferred on it by the **Local Government (Miscellaneous Provisions) Act 1976** to do such works as it considers necessary to keep out unauthorised persons and/or to prevent the premises becoming a danger to public health.

Demolition If the local authority opts for demolition then a **demolition order** will be made and served on every person on whom the time and place meeting notice was served. The demolition order will require the property to be vacated within at least 28 days and also it will have the effect of removing any protection that the tenants have under Rent Act legislation. **Section 22 Housing Act 1957** creates the offence of knowingly occupying or allowing occupation of property subject to such an order punishable on summary conviction by a fine of up to £20 plus £5 for each day the offence continues. Demolition must take place within 6 weeks of the date set for vacation of the property but the period may be extended. This would be the case where even at this late stage the owner put forward plans for reconstruction or improvement but the period of extension must not be an unreasonable one. In such circumstances the demolition order would be held in abeyance to enable the owner or other person such as a potential purchaser to carry out the work. Eventually the order would be revoked if necessary. If the owner fails to comply with a demolition order then under **s.23** the local authority has power to demolish on default and recover the cost as a civil debt in the County Court. Right to appeal against a demolition order is conferred by **s.20** which will be considered later.

Closing The alternative to demolition is to serve a **closing order** forbidding the use of the house or part of it for human habitation. Such an order would be made in any of the following three cases. **s.17 Housing Act 1957:—**

1. If it is considered inexpedient to make a demolition order having regard to the effect of the demolition of that house upon any other house or building; this would be relevant where the property in question is regarded as necessary to support adjoining buildings.

2. If the house has been **listed** or has been stated to be of historic or architectural interest by the Minister; here the requirement of closing rather than demolition is mandatory.

3. If the unfitness relates to only part of the dwelling such as an **underground room** and the rest of the dwelling is fit for human habitation.

In determining whether an underground room is fit for habitation the general standards of fitness laid down in **s.4** are not necessarily relevant. **Section 18** provides that a closing order may be made in respect of an underground room (one whose floor is more than 3 feet below street level) if either the average height of the room is not at least 7 feet or the room does not comply with local regulations made by the local authority.

In relation to the rights of any tenants a closing order has the same effect as a demolition order in that any protection under the Rent Acts is removed by it. It is an offence to knowingly use property in contravention of a closing order, however a discretion is conferred on local authorities by **s.27** to enable them to permit houses subject to a closing order to be used for purposes other than as a dwelling house. This permission is not to be unreasonably withheld. In the event of either demolition or closing the occupants must be rehoused and compensated by the local authority under the **Land Compensation Act 1973.**

Purchase A further alternative to demolition or closing is provided by **s.17(2).** Where a local authority would be required to make a demolition or closing order in respect of a house they may, if it appears to them that the house is or can be rendered capable of providing **temporary accommodation,** purchase the house instead. Notice of such an intention to purchase must be served on all persons who received the time and place notice. Purchase itself may be effected either **voluntarily** by agreement, or **compulsorily.** Under **s.29(2)** compensation payable for compulsory purchase is the value at the time when the valuation is made of the site as a **cleared site available for development** in accordance with the requirements of the building by-laws.

Appeals

Any person aggrieved by a demolition or closing order or a purchase notice may within 21 days after the service of the notice or order appeal to the County Court under **s.20.** Once an appeal is lodged the local authority may not proceed until it has been finally determined. The County Court has power to vary, accept, quash undertakings and confirm the order or notice as it sees fit. Such an appeal may be made on either law or fact, or both, and grounds could include:— that the premises are not unfit;

that they are capable of being rendered fit at reasonable expense; that an undertaking has been made which should have been accepted; that a reasonable time to complete the works has not been given; that demolition is not expedient.

10.3 Property in Substantial Disrepair

The powers conferred on local authorities under the **Housing Act 1957** are limited to taking action in relation to housing which is statutorily unfit. This limitation was abrogated by the **Housing Act 1969 s.72** which conferred power on local authorities to enable them to prevent individual properties becoming unfit through deterioration. This new power was inserted as **s.9(1A) Housing Act 1957** and may be invoked where a local authority is satisfied that a house is in such a state of disrepair that although not unfit for human habitation substantial repairs are required to bring it up to a reasonable standard having regard to its age, character and locality. In such a case the local authority may serve on the person in control of the house a notice requiring specified works of repair (not being works of internal decorative repair) to be completed within a reasonable period of time (not less than 21 days). No guidance is given as to what would constitute **substantial disrepair** but it is suggested that it amounts to either one major item of disrepair or a small number of small items of disrepair. A right of appeal against such a finding is conferred by **s.11 Housing Act 1969.** Certainly it seems that the effectiveness of **s.9(1A)** power depends largely on the willingness of the local authority in question to carry out works of repair in default and recover the costs from the owner under **s.10.**

> The question as to what works are necessary to bring property up to a reasonable standard and what constitutes reasonable expense was discussed by the Court of Appeal in *Hillbank Properties Ltd. v. Hackney LBC 1978*. Here **s.9(1A)** notices were served by a local authority in respect of two separate houses owned by a property company. On an appeal against the notices it was held at first instance that as the cost of the works specified was greater than the increase in the value of the properties with sitting tenants, the notices should be quashed. This decision was reversed by the Court of Appeal who held that the value of the repaired properties with vacant possession should be taken into account, or at least a figure between that and the value with a sitting tenant. This meant that the cost of repairs was now a reasonable figure in comparison with the valuation of the property when the work was completed, e.g.

167

Unrepaired value:	£1700
Cost of repairs:	£2750
Value with a sitting tenant after repairs:	£2300
Value with vacant possession after repairs:	£7500

The main critisism of the use of **s.9(1A)** power is based on the failure of local authorities, who having served a notice, fail to enforce it. In such a situation there is no effective means by which an aggrieved tenant can require a local authority to take action. Now development has taken place in the form of **s.149 Housing Act 1980** which adds further **ss.9(1B) and 9(1C)** to the **Housing Act 1957. Section 9(1B)** provides that where a local authority on a representation made by an occupying tenant is satisfied that a house is in such a state of disrepair that although it is not unfit for human habitation the condition of the house is such as to interfere materially with the personal comfort of the occupying tenant, they may serve on the person having control of the house a **s.9(1A)** notice. **Section 9(1B)** is then an additional power to **s.9(1)** and **s.9(1A)** to deal with substandard housing. The occupying tenant referred to in **s.9(1B)** is defined in **s.9(1C)** as the person referred to in **s.104 Housing Act 1974,** that is, someone who is not an owner occupier but who occupies or is entitled to occupy the dwelling as lessee, statutory tenant, agricultural tenant or holder of a restricted contract. The local authority is excluded from taking the initiative under **s.9(1B)** and can only act following a complaint by the occupying tenant that his personal comfort is being materially interfered with. It is suggested that **'disrepair causing personal discomfort'** would be something less than **'substantial disrepair'** as required for **s.9(1A). Finally is should be stressed that a local authority receiving a complaint under s.9(1B)** is not required to take action but rather a power to act is conferred. Certainly the reasonable expense factor would be a consideration in deciding whether to require the landlord to repair.

10.4 Statutory Nuisance

Additional important statutory powers and duties conferred on local authorities in relation to property in substantial disrepair are contained in Public Health legislation which creates a **nuisance** in a **statutory form.** The concept of a common law nuisance is considered later in this chapter.

> Under **s.92 Public Health Act 1936** a statutory nuisance is any matter which could be dealt with summarily including:—

1. any premises in such a state as to be prejudicial to health or a nuisance;

2. an animal kept in such a state as to be prejudicial to health or a nuisance;

3. accumulations or deposits on land prejudicial to health or a nuisance;

4. dust or effluvia (ejected steam) caused by any trade, business, manufacture or process and being prejudicial to the health of, or a nuisance to, the inhabitants of the neighbourhood;

5. a workplace which is not provided with sufficient means of ventilation, or which is so overcrowded while work is carried on as to be prejudicial to the health of those employed.

Other examples of more recent legislation creating nuisances in a statutory form include the **Noise Abatement Act 1960** (covering noise and vibrations) and the **Clean Air Act 1960** (covering emissions of dark smoke).

The duty of enforcing statutory nuisances by criminal prosecution is placed upon local authorities who are required to inspect their areas for statutory nuisances. Environmental Health Departments are usually given the function of inspection, but they normally rely heavily on direct complaints by members of the public.

The matter of particular importance to the local authority in relation to housing is **s.92(1)(a) Public Health Act 1936, any premises in such a state as to be prejudicial to health or a nuisance.** This definition of statutory nuisance has been the subject of judicial scrutiny which it is now necessary to consider to determine the rights and duties that arise under it.

The initial approach of the courts may be illustrated by the case of *Betts v. Penge UDC 1942* in which it was held that a statutory nuisance in this form could be constituted by anything which could cause **discomfort** to the occupants of the dwelling. Exclusive emphasis on 'discomfort' as the criteria is now regarded as insufficient following *Salford City Council v. McNally 1976.* Here Lord Wilberforce in considering s.92(1)(a) thought that the approach to be adopted is to regard 'predudicial to health and nuisance' as separate limbs of the definition. He stated that "the use of the words **'personal comfort'** are appropriate enough in the context of what is a 'nuisance' for the purposes of the Public Health Act but they are quite inappropriate in relation to the other limb 'prejudicial to health'.

169

Health is not the same as comfort and interference with the latter does not bring a case within the health limb of the 1936 Act. In my opinion *Betts v. Penge UDC* was wrongly decided". A further important statement from the decision was the indication that a nuisance coming within the meaning of the **Public Health Act 1936** must be either a **private or public nuisance as understood by the common law.** A case of statutory nuisance which alleges the nuisance part of the definition therefore must necessarily show evidence of interference with persons other than the occupants of the premises to constitute a common law nuisance, e.g. loose slate or tiles, noise, smoke, smells, leaking pipes and gutters (see later in this chapter).

> In *NCB v. Thorne 1976* an abatement notice was served on the NCB as a person responisble for a house with faulty and rotten rain gutters, skirting boards and windows. The notice alleged that these conditions amounted to a nuisance under the definition. The High Court held that the disrepair could not amount to a common law nuisance as no interference with persons other than the occupants had been alleged. Also in the absence of any allegation that the extent of disrepair was prejudicial to the health of the occupants the abatement order must be quashed.

If the 'prejudicial to health' limb of the definition is alleged then only the occupants need be affected by the defaults. These could be evidenced by matters such as structural defects, defective sanitation and drains, rotten woodwork, dampness. In *Springett v. Harold 1951,* the court confirmed a mere lack of internal decorative repair is not regarded as sufficient.

> The question as to whether premises may be prejudicial to health and therefore a statutory nuisance once the occupants have left was considered by the Divisional Court in *Lambeth BC v. Stubbs 1980.* Here the local authority had admitted a statutory nuisance in particular property and the Magistrates ordered its abatement within a fixed period. By rehousing the occupants the local authority alleged that this act had effectively abated the statutory nuisance as the premises were now vacant. Appeal on this ground was rejected by the Crown Court and on a further appeal to the Divisional Court it was held that the nuisance was not abated by the house being vacated. The whole purpose of the nuisance order was to require work to be done to prevent injury to health. The premises were still injurious or likely to cause injury to health as there remained a possibility of reletting and the fact that demolition was imminent had no bearing on the local authority's responsibility to abate the statutory nuisance.

Once a local authority is satisfied that land or buildings constitute a statutory nuisance then the **Public Health Act 1936 s.93** imposes a duty on it to serve a notice on the person responsible (usually the owner) requiring its abatement. This **abatement notice** must be in a particular form specifying the nuisance, the works necessary to abate it and stipulate a reasonable time to carry them out. If the person responsible fails to carry out the work then the local authority must bring the matter before the local Magistrates Court. This is done by causing a complaint to be made to a justice of the peace who will issue a summons requiring the person on whom the notice was served to appear before a court of summary jurisdiction. It is at the court proceedings that the Magistrates will hear the Environmental Health Department's allegation of nuisance and the owner's reply. If the court believes that the complaint constitutes a statutory nuisance then under **s.94** the magistrates will make a **final nuisance order** requiring its abatement within a specified period of days or weeks. The Magistrates have a wide discretion as to the content of this order and may detail priority work depending on the gravity of the danger to health. In addition the order may provide that: the person responsible must pay the costs of the hearing, pay a fine up to £200 and not use the premises for human habitation until they are rendered fit. A further fine of up to £400 may be imposed for knowingly failing to comply with the nuisance order plus a sum of £50 for each day that the offence continues.

A speedier procedure to deal with statutory nuisances was introduced by the **Public Health Act 1961.** Under this Act power is conferred on local authorities to serve a notice on any person on whom an abatement notice could have been served requiring him to remedy defects. The person in control has then 9 days (**nine days notice**) to signify his intention to do the work specified, in the absence of which, the local authority can do the work in default and recover the cost. A default power also exists under the **Public Health Act 1936 s.95** whereby the local authority may do the work specified in a nuisance order and recover the cost from the person responsible.

In a situation where the local authority is reluctant to use its enforcement powers or it is alleged that the local authority itself is responsible for the nuisance then there is a process under which an individual can take action. Under **s.99** a person aggrieved may **lay an information** before the Magistrates Court complaining of statutory nuisance, and the court has the same powers of action as if the information had been laid by a local authority following default in complying with an abatement notice. The principle that criminal proceedings could be taken against a local authority was confirmed in *R v. Epping (Waltham Abbey) J.J. Ex-parte Burlinson 1948*. Here Lord Goddard stated that **s.99** applies where either the local authority is alleged to have failed to carry out its enforcement duties or it is the local authority itself who is alleged to have created the nuisance. Certainly there has been a sharp increase in the number of cases brought by individuals against local authorities alleging that council property constitutes a statutory nuisance. The popularity of the procedure stems from the fact that once the court accepts that a statutory nusiance exists they are under a duty to make a nuisance order stipulating a definite time period for the nuisance to be abated. Unfortunately this can cause problems particularly where a large number of properties are suffering from the same defect (e.g. dampness) and the local authority is attempting to proceed and deal with the problem in a planned and orderly fashion. Action by individual occupants to obtain nuisance orders may effectively disrupt the local authority's programme and be detrimental to those occupants who have not resorted to legal action.

10.5 Nuisance

It is convenient at this point to examine the legal position of third parties who as neighbours, visitors or even trespassers may suffer harm as a result of the state of property.

The concept of a **'nuisance'** covers a wide range of legal situations having both common law and statutory origins, and involving both the criminal and civil law. Under the common law a nuisance was originally confined to an interference with another's use of land. If the interference constituted the **tort of private nuisance** it was redressable by an action for damages and/or an injunction. The common law **crime of public nuisance** was a later development encompassing a wide range of petty offences redressable by prosecutions leading to fines and abatement orders. A further complication arose when the courts recognised that an individual who suffered **special damage** as a result of a public nuisance could maintain an action for damages based on private nuisance. Finally as already noted nuisance has been created in a statutory form, in particular by means of the **Public Health Act 1936.**

Public Nuisance

The common law crime of public nuisance has been defined as comprising of an act or omission which materially affects the reasonable comfort and convenience of a class of Her Majesty's subjects. Such a wide definition would encompass many types of conduct harmful to others and although not restricted to the use of land it has been held to include various ways in which land may be unlawfully used, e.g.

    a.   selling or serving food from premises in unhygienic conditions;

    b.   causing an obstruction of the highway.

In *Fabbri v. Morris 1947* a trader committed a public nuisance by selling ice cream through his shop window causing queues to form which blocked the highway.

    c.   keeping a disorderly house;

    d.   carrying on a dangerous activity near the public highway.

In *Castle v. St. Augustine's Links Ltd. 1922* the court held that the proximity of a hole on a golf course to the public highway amounted to a public nuisance.

It is a requirement of public nuisance that a number of persons must be affected by the act or ommission. In the above case these were the persons using the highway. If however an individual can show that as a result of a public nuisance he has suffered some special damage beyond the discomfort of the public at large then he can succeed in a tort action for damages against the creator of it.

In *Castle v. St. Augustine's Links 1922* the plaintiff taxi driver who lost an eye as a result of a golf ball striking the windscreen of his cab succeeded in a tort action against the defendants and recovered damages.

The person responsible for a public nuisance is prima facie the creator of it so that if the nuisance eminates from premises the occupier in possession will usually be made responsible for it. If the premises are let however, and the nuisance arises out of the landlord's failure to fulfil an express or implied repair obligation, then the landlord may be prosecuted for it. Finally it should be mentioned that acts which constitute a public nuisance may also amount to offences under statute, e.g. the **Highways Act 1959** (obstructing the highway), the **Sexual Offences Act 1956** (keeping a disorderly house), and the **Public Health Act 1936** (emitting noxious substances into the atmosphere).

Private Nuisance

An individual in possession of land who suffers harm as a result of interference by an adjoining occupier can have recourse to the law of tort to provide a remedy. To succeed in such an action the plaintiff would have to establish the tort of private nuisance. Private nuisance has been defined as **an unlawful interference with a person's use or enjoyment of land or of some right over or in connection with it.** As a general rule the creator of a nuisance remains responsible for it. Thus if a landlord lets property in such a state that it constitutes a private nuisance, he may be made liable in tort to an adjoining occupier who suffers an unreasonable interference with the enjoyment of his land as a result. Also if the nuisance arises from the landlord's failure to fulfil an express or implied repair obligation he may be made responsible for it under **s.4 Defective Premises Act 1972.** Alternatively if the tenant creates the nuisance then he will be solely responsible unless the creation of the nuisance was the inevitable consequence of the purpose of the letting, e.g. carrying on a noxious trade. In these circumstances if the activity involved was contemplated by the landlord and authorised by the lease then he may be made jointly liable with the tenant.

For an action to succeed in the tort of private nuisance the plaintiff must establish the existance of three essential elements.

1. **That there has been an indirect interference with the enjoyment of land.** This could be evidenced by matters such as excessive noise, smoke, smells, heat, vibrations and encroaching roots or branches of trees. This is in contrast to a direct interference such as trespass to land dealt with in Chapter 9.

2. **That the interference has caused some sort of damage** in the form of physical harm to the land or discomfort or inconvenience to the occupier.

    The case of *Halsey v. Esso Petroleum 1961* provides an example of actual physical harm. Here smuts from the defendant's chimneys caused damage to the plaintiff's clothes which had been hung out to dry.

The case of *Kennaway v. Thompson and Another 1980* provides an example of damage in the form of discomfort and inconvenience. Here the plaintiff occupied a house adjacent to a lake where the defendents carried on motor boat racing during the summer months. Claiming grave discomfort caused by the excessive noice the plaintiff sued under the tort of nuisance for damages and an injunction to restrain the activity. The Court of Appeal awarded an injunction to restrain the defendants racing to such an extent that it could not be said to constitute an unreasonable interference with the plaintiff's use of her land.

3. **That the interference is an unlawful one.** The determination of this question is a crucial one involving an examination of all the circumstances of the particular case. Relevant consideration would include the following:—

a. **The sensitivity of the plaintiff**
Generally under the law the standard an individual has to adhere to is that of the reasonable man. An occupier of land is only entitled to reasonable comfort in the enjoyment of his land and can hardly complain if he is peculiarly sensitive to his neighbours' conduct. An occupier therefore who merely suffers harm because he is overly sensitive to the interference cannot complain of it.

In *Robinson v. Kilvert 1889* the plaintiff tenant occupied the ground floor of his landlord's premises which he used for the purposes of storing brown paper. The paper became badly damaged as a result of heat rising from a boiler in the defendant landlord's cellar. In an action based in private nuisance the court held that as the level of heat rising would be harmful to most goods there could be no nuisance for damage caused to sensitive brown paper.

b. **The reason for the interference**
The fact that the defendant shows that his activities which constitute the alleged nuisance are in the public interest is of no bearing in determining whether or not they are unlawful.

In *Adams v. Ursell 1913* the defendant's claim that his fried fish shop in the East End of London performed a public service in providing cheap food for the working classes was held to be irrelevant in determining whether it constituted a private nuisance.

On the other hand the fact that the defendant is acting from a malicious motive has been held to be a relevant consideration.

In *Hollywood Silver Fox Farm v. Emmett 1936* there was a dispute between the defendant who had a farm adjacent to the plaintiff's silver fox farm. In an attempt to interfere with the foxes breeding the defendant asked his son to fire guns as near as possible to the plaintiff's land. The court held that the malicious intention was sufficient to make the interference an unlawful one and damages and an injunction were awarded for private nuisance.

c. **The locality of the nuisance**
The location of the interference is an important factor in determining whether it is unlawful. The words of Thesiger L.J. in *Sturges v. Bridgman 1879* "What would be a nuisance in Belgrave Square would not necessarily be so in Bermondsey" still have relevance. It would be unreasonable therefore for an occupier of property in a heavy industrial area to complain of smoke from his neighbour's fire if the atmosphere is already to a large extent polluted.

d. **Duration of the nuisance**
Although the act complained of must usually be of a continuous nature such as constant emissions of smoke from a factory, nevertheless a single serious act could constitute a nuisance if it is evidence of a dangerous situation. Thus an explosion may be evidence of a dangerous state of affairs.

In *Miller v. Jackson 1977* the regular hitting of cricket balls from a cricket ground on to adjacent property was held to be a sufficient course of conduct for the purpose of nuisance.

The defences to an action in nuisance include:—

1. **'Volenti non fit injuria'** i.e. consent of the plaintiff to the interference.

2. That the nuisance was caused by the **act of a stranger** of whom the defendant was unaware.

3.　That the nuisance has been **in existence for 20 years** or more **(Prescription Act 1832).**

Of course it is the nuisance rather than the interference which must have been in existence for the 20-year period.

> In *Sturges v. Bridgman 1879* a confectioner caused noise and vibrations in the course of his trade which affected the adjoining garden of a physician. The interference had been in existance for more than 20 years but no damage was caused until the physician built a consulting room in his garden. The court held that as the nuisance was not created until the damage was caused, the **Prescription Act 1832** provided no defence.

4.　Statutory Authority
If the act which constitutes the nuisance is authorised by statute this may provide a defence to an action.

> In *Allen v. Gulf Oil Refining Ltd. 1979,* the **Gulf Oil Refining Act 1965** authorised the defendants to acquire land for the construction of a refinery. The oil refinery was built and began operations, but following complaints by adjoining occupiers of noxious odours, vibrations and unreasonable noise an action in nuisance was finally brought. The defence of statutory authority was accepted in the High Court. The Court of Appeal however interpreted the Gulf Oil Act differently, stating that although the Act authorised the building of a refinery there was no specific statutory authority to operate it. The operation of the refinery was carried on by the company under its common law right to use its land as it pleases. Consequently, if the operation of the refinery constituted a nuisance, those affected by it could exercise their common law rights to bring an action to enforce them. Lord Denning M.R. made the point that where private enterprises seek statutory authority to conduct and operate an installation which might cause damage to people in the neighbourhood, it should not be assumed that Parliament intended that damage should be done to innocent people without redress. The diverse opinions of the judiciary in relation to the use of this defence of statutory authority is shown by the decision of the House of Lords on further appeal in January 1981. The Lords reversed the decision of the Court of Appeal and held that the defendants **could** rely on the Gulf Oil Act as a defence to an action in nuisance resulting from

the operation of the refinery, but only to the extent that the nuisance was the **inevitable result** of such operation.

The various remedies for the victim of a private nuisance include an action for damages, abatement of the nuisance (e.g. cutting off offending roots or branches of a tree that cross the boundary), or an injunction to prevent the defendant continuing the nuisance. It should be noted that an injunction is a discretionary remedy and need not be granted if the court feels that the circumstances of the case do not merit its grant.

In *Miller v. Jackson 1977* (previously mentioned) it was held that the cricket club was liable in nuisance but the Court refused to grant an injunction to prevent the playing of cricket after weighing the loss of the club to the community against the risk of injury to adjoining occupiers. This decision may be contrasted with the approach of the Court of Appeal in the later case of *Kennaway v. Thompson and Another 1980* (previously mentioned) where an injunction **was** granted but only to the extent that the interference was unreasonable.

10.6 Occupier's liability

All occupiers of land and buildings have responsibility under the law for the safety of those who come into their buildings and onto their land. As far as lawful entrants are concerned (classifed as **visitors**) they are given protection by virtue of the **Occupiers Liability Act 1957.** This Act imposes a duty on all occupiers in relation to the safety of visitors who come on to their premises. If the occupier fails to fulfil this duty and a visitor suffers personal injury as a result then prima facie he will have a right of action in tort to recover damages for the harm caused. All other entrants are classified as **trespassers** and any duty that is imposed on the occupier in relation to their safety is contained in the common law tort of negligence.

Under the **Occupiers Liability Act 1957** the **common duty of care** is owed by an occupier of premises to all his lawful visitors. Notice that the duty is owed by the **occupier** and he is regarded as the person **in control of the premises.** He would certainly include the owner in possession or a tenant or licensee. The landlord is regarded as the occupier in relation to parts of the premises which remain under his control, e.g. entrance hall, lifts, forecourt or other common parts. Also if the landlord is under a contractual, common law or statutory obligation to repair, he may under the **Defective Premises Act 1972 s.4** be made liable for injuries that occur as a result of his failure to fulfil a repair obligation. Where the premsies are let therefore, both the landlord and the tenant may be regarded as occupier of the premises for different purposes under the Act. Thus if a repair obligation in relation to the exterior of the premises is imposed on the landlord under the **Housing Act 1961 s.32** then the landlord will be regarded as the occupier if personal injury is suffered by a visitor as a result of the landlord's failure to repair the exterior.

The common duty of care is expressed in **s.2(2) Occupiers Liability Act, 1957** as a duty to take such care as in all the circumstances of the case is reasonable to see that the visitor will be reasonably safe in using the premises for the purposes for which he is invited or permitted to be there. The term **'premises'** is referred to in the Act as including not only land and buildings but also fixed or movable structures such as caravans, vehicles, houseboats or even aircraft. In addition to this general standard of exercising reasonable care towards visitors, the Act specifies that in relation to child visitors an occupier must be prepared for them to be less careful than adults. This suggests that a higher standard of care is owed in relation to children and a warning sign that may be sufficient to protect an adult may not be so for a child. Independent contractors are also singled out for mention, the Act stating that such persons engaged to carry out specialist work should be aware of the risks inherent in their own trades.

> This is reflected in *Roles v. Nathan 1963* where despite being warned of the danger two chimney sweeps carried on working on a boiler and were killed by carbon monoxide poisoning entering from the ventilation system. The employer/occupier was held in the circumstances not to be liable. Ld. Denning M.R. stated that "when a householder calls in a specialist to deal with a defective installation on his premises he can reasonably expect the specialist to appreciate and guard against the dangers arising from the defect".

An occupier may satisfy the duty of care imposed upon him in one of two ways. He may either ensure that his premises are reasonably safe and free from dangers or give effective warning of the danger which is sufficient to enable the visitor to be reasonably safe. The latter course could be achieved by the prominent display of a warning notice. Prior to 1977 all occupiers of premises had a further option open to them. They could simply exclude or restrict the duty owed to their visitors.

> In *Ashdown v. Williams 1957* the defendants had posted notices on their land to the effect that persons entered at their own risks and

should have no claim against the defendants for any injury whatsoever. The plaintiff visitor suffered injury by the negligent shunting of railway trucks and sued. The court held that her action must fail as the occupier had successfully excluded his liability by notice.

This right to exclude liability has been modified to a large extent by the **Unfair Contract Terms Act 1977**. This Act applies to duties which arise for occupiers of business premises and states that liability for negligence including breach of the common duty of care under the **Occupiers Liability Act 1957** causing death or physical injury cannot be excluded or restricted. This means that as far as business property is concerned neither owner occupiers, landlords or tenants can exclude or restrict liability for physical injury resulting from a failure to fulfil their respective obligations. The Act also provides that liability for other loss or damage can be excluded or restricted but only to the extent that such provision satisfies the **test of reasonableness** laid down in the Act.

Where injury is caused to a visitor because of the negligent workmanship of a contractor then the liability of the occupier will depend on whether he acted reasonably in entrusting the work to the contractor in the first place. Certainly the occupier will have acted reasonably if he selected a reputable organisation to do the work rather than the local handyman.

> In *O'Connor v. Swan & Edgar 1963* the plaintiff was injured by a fall of plaster when she worked as a demonstrator on the first defendant's premises. The fall of plaster was due to the faulty workmanship of the second defendants who had been engaged as contractors to work on the premises. The court held that as the first defendants had acted reasonably in entrusting the work to a reputable contractor as occupier he had satisfied the duty of care which was owed. The second defendants however were held liable in the tort of negligence for the faulty workmanship.

Trespassers

A trespasser is not a lawful visitor so therefore the **Occupiers Liability Act 1957** has no relevance in determining any liability that may be imposed if he suffers injury. The duty owed towards trespassers is found by referring to the common law, and the traditional attitude of the courts was that, so long as an occupier did not set out to injure trespassers intentionally, then he would not be made liable for their injuries.

This approach is illustrated in *Addie v. Dumbreck 1929* where the defendant occupier of a colliery was held by the House of Lords to owe no duty of care under the common law towards a child trespasser who was crushed in the wheel of the defendant's haulage system.

The harshness of this attitude was mitigated to the extent that if **children** habitually trespassed and an occupier took no steps to warn them off his land, the child trespasser could be regarded as a lawful visitor and was thus owed a duty of care.

The contemporary approach is reflected in the following decision of the House of Lords which effectively overrules the precedent of *Addie v. Dumbreck*.

In *British Railways Board v. Herrington 1972,* British Rail had negligently failed to maintain fencing which ran between their railway track and a park frequently used by children. A six-year old climbed through the fence, wandered onto the track, and suffered severe injury on the electrified rail. The House of Lords held the Board liable in negligence to the child trespasser. The Court stated that, "... if the presence of the trespasser is known or ought reasonably to be anticipated by the occupier then the occupier has ... a duty to treat the trespasser with **ordinary humanity**". Among the factors to be taken into account in such cases are the degree of potential harm faced by the trespassers, the financial resources of the occupier, and in the case of children, whether the premises act as an allurement. In this case the Board where aware of a known and potenitally lethal danger particularly to children. The standard of care required of an occupier in these circumstances was **to act as a conscientious humane man, with his knowledge, skill and resources, could reasonably be expected to act.** British Rail had not fulfilled this duty and were liable for damages.

It should be noted that the duty owed to a trespasser is a restricted duty and much less than the standard of care owed to a lawful visitor. In addition, the court pointed to the economic resources of the occupier as a factor to determine whether he had acted reasonably, The rule in *British Railways Board v. Herrington* has been applied in later cases.

In *Pannett v. McGuinness Ltd. 1972* a demolition contractor was made liable for injuries caused to a five-year old trespasser by an unguarded fire. This was despite the fact that the contractor, aware of the danger, had posted workmen the guard the fire. The fact that the workmen were absent when the injury occurred meant, as far as the injured child was concerned, nothing was done to safeguard him.

An important factor to determine whether child trespassers are foreseeable is whether or not the occupier has things on his land which might attract a child, e.g. building site, water, fire.

In *Harris v. Wirral BC 1976* the defendant local authority, who failed to board up an empty house under their control, were held liable to a child trespasser who wandered inside and was injured. The presence of the child, the court decided, was foreseeable, as he was attracted to the derelict property, and the failure to prevent his entry was not the conduct to be expected of a conscientious humane local authority.

Part 5 - **Statutory Protection**

CHAPTER 11　Business Tenancies and Tenancies of Agricultural Holdings

11.1 Business Tenancies

The first major piece of legislation designed to confer rights on the tenant of business premises was the **Landlord and Tenant Act 1927.** The most fundamental provision of this Act, **s.1,** was to confer on the business tenant the right to claim compensation on the expiration of the tenancy for improvements he made to the premises during its term. This right was subject to the tenant having previously served a notice on the landlord informing him of his intention to carry out improvements. In addition, by virtue of **s.4** compensation could also be claimed if the tenant could show as a result of a period of five years trading, goodwill had attached to the premises increasing their value for letting purposes. The indirect consequence for the business tenant, of these provisions, was to greatly increase his security in relation to the property comprised in the tenancy. Rather than face a claim for compensation the landlord of business property was now more willing to re-let to the tenant on the expiration of his current term.

Statutory protection in relation to security of tenure and compensation for improvements has now been conferred on the business tenant by the **Landlord and Tenant Act 1954 (Part II and Part III).** This Act, for the most part, contains the current law in relation to the legal position of the business tenant and is referred to throughout this section. **Part II** of the 1954 Act represents the view of the legislature that on the expiration of a business tenancy the landlord should have the right to recover possession of the premises if he wishes to operate a business himself, or redevelop, but otherwise the sitting tenant should have the right to remain in possession on reasonable terms. **Part III** of the Act represents the current view that compensation should be payable to a tenant who has carried out improvements to the property.

Tenancies to which the Landlord and Tenant Act 1954 Parts II and III applies.

Under **s.23(1)** the Act applies to **tenancies where the property comprised in the tenancy is or includes premises occupied by the tenant for the purposes of his business.** It must be emphasised that the Act applies to tenancies only and would not cover a mere licence. For the purposes of the Act therefore there must be an **occupation of premises** (which includes land and buildings).

> In *Morrisons Holdings Ltd. v. Manden Property (Wolverhampton) Ltd. 1976* it was held that the condition of occupation may be fulfilled even if the tenant is not physically in possession of the premises. Here the property concerned was destroyed by fire so that occupation for business was impossible. Nevertheless the tenant's retention of the key and repeated enquiries in relation to the rebuilding work were sufficient facts to demonstrate his desire to occupy and therefore satisfy the Act.

In addition the occupation of premises must be for **business purposes. Business** is defined under **s.23(2)** as to include **a trade, profession or employment or any activity carried on by a body of persons whether corporate or unincorporate.** For a body of persons therefore, corporate or unincorporate, **'any activity'** may be regarded as a business for the purposes of the Act.

> In *Re Hanger Hill Country Club; Westminister Roman Catholic Diocese Trustee v. Parkes 1978* occupation of premises as a community centre in connection with a church was held to be a business and come within the Act's protection. This was in accordance with the earlier decision in *Addiscombe Garden Estates Ltd. v. Crabbe 1958* where the activity of a member's tennis club was held to be within the Act.

Certainly, this wide construction of the term 'business' does not apply to **individuals** as landlords. In addition case law suggests an uncertainty particularly as to whether the practises of sub-letting or taking in lodgers could constitute businesses for the purposes of the Act.

> In *William Boyer and Sons Ltd. v. Adams 1976* the tenant who sublet outbuildings and provided sub-tenants with management

186

services was held to be in occupation of the outbuildings, carrying on a business there, and therefore entitled to protection.

Alternatively in *Lewis v. Weldcrest Ltd. 1978* a tenant who took in lodgers and provided them with services did not carry on a business for the purposes of the Act. A crucial factor in this case was that the tenant, in taking in lodgers, did not have as his prime motive the making of profit.

As far as operating a business from home is concerned, the question as to business purposes is decided by examining the extent of business activity.

In *Royal Life Saving Society v. Page 1978* a partner in a firm of seafood importers who interviewed business clients at home, kept business documents and a business phone there, was held to operate a business for the purposes of the Act.

There is some doubt as to whether carrying on an activity ancillary to a business is sufficient to come within the Act where there is no actual business activity.

In *Chapman v. Freeman 1978* a hotel owner took a tenancy of a nearby cottage to accommodate his staff. On the question as to whether the tenant occupied the premises as a business tenant the Court of Appeal held that the tenant could be regarded as being in occupation of the premises through his staff. However, to amount to an occupation for business purposes the tenant had to show that the staff occupied the premises **necessarily** for the performance of their duties. This the tenant had failed to do. The occupation was merely a matter of convenience and accordingly there was no business occupation for the purposes of the Act.

Excluded Tenancies

Certain tenancies are expressly excluded from the provisions of the **Landlord and Tenant Act 1954 Part II** by virtue of **section 43.**

a.   **Tenancies of Agricultural Holdings.** These are defined as "the aggregate of the agricultural land comprised in a contract of tenancy, not being a contract under which the land is let to the tenant during his continuance in any office, appointment or employment held under the landlord. Such tenancies are given protection under the **Agricultural Holdings Act 1948** and are dealt with later in the chapter.

b. **Tenancies created by Mining Leases.** These are leases granted for mining or a connected purpose and would cover "sinking and searching for, winning, working, getting, making merchantable, smelting or otherwise converting or working for the purposes of any manufacture, carrying away and disposing of mines and material in or under land and the erection of buildings and the execution of engineering and other works suitable for these "purposes" **(Landlord and Tenant Act 1927 s.25).**

c. **Part residential protected under the Rent Act.** Although premises let for joint business and residential use may come under the protection of the 1954 Act (e.g. shops with flats above), part residential premises which are subject to the **Rent Act 1977** as controlled tenancies or tenancies which would be controlled were it not for the fact that they are let at a low rent, are excluded.

d. **Licenced Premises.** Tenancies of on-licence premises for the sale of intoxicants are exempt, e.g. public houses. Premises with off licences are however protected along with hotels, restaurants, theatres and places of public and private entertainment where the holding of the licence is ancillary to the main purpose for which the premises are used.

c. **Service Tenancies.** Tenancies which are granted to the tenant as the holder of an office, appointment or employment which ends on the termination of the tenant's employment or service have no protection under the Act.

f. **Short Term Tenancies.** Tenancies which are granted for a term not exceeding six months do not come within the Act's protection. Such a tenancy must not contain any term which allows for renewal or extension beyond the initial six month period and the tenant must not have been in occupation for more than twelve months.

Express Exclusion

Any attempt to expressly exclude the provisions of the **Landlord and Tenant Act 1954** is void under **s.38(1)** except in one case under **s.38(4)** (inserted by the **Law of Property Act 1969 s.5**). On a joint application by both the landlord and the tenant the court may authorise a **contracting out** from the Act's provisions. This provision illustrates the current view that business people who have taken legal advice should have the freedom to contract in some cases without statutory intervention.

> In *Hagee (London) Ltd. v. A.B. Enkson & Larsen 1976* the tenancy which was created was expressed to be **'at will only'** and the court held that it did not fall within the scope of **Part II of the Landlord and Tenant Act 1954.** The tenants had entered into the tenancy with full knowledge that they would have no security of tenure and therefore on its termination had no right to a new lease. Ld. Denning M.R. expressed the position as follows: "It is obvious, however, that if parties, by agreeing on a tenancy at will, can escape the provision of the Act, it means there is readily to hand a way of contracting out of the Act. This would be contrary to the intention of the Act of 1954, ... because **s.38** forbad contracting out ... But in 1969 the legislature changed its mind on contracting out. By **s.5 Law of Property Act 1969** it amended **s.38** to permit a landlord and tenant to agree that the 1954 Act shall not apply ... Such an agreement is good and binding provided it is approved by the court. We are told that the court invariably approves such an agreement when it is made by business people properly advised by their lawyers."

11.2 Covenants in Business Tenancies

It is usual in a business tenancy for the landlord and tenant to expressly agree their mutual obligations which are then included as express covenants in the lease.

Express Covenants

In addition to the usual express covenants covering the payment of rent and repair, etc., business tenancies will normally include express covenants in relation to business user, improvements, assignment and subletting. A business tenancy could therefore contain covenants imposing obligations on the tenant:-

i.   to pay rent and to provide for rent review;

ii. to pay rates and taxes except such expressly payable by the landlord;

189

iii. to keep and deliver up the premises in a state of repair;

iv. to permit the landlord to enter and inspect the state of repair and to repair;

v. not to alter the physical state of the property;

vi. not to assign, underlet, or part with possession;

vii. to use for the purpose specified in the tenancy;

viii. to comply with statutory notices.

Covenants imposing obligations on the landlord:-

i. to repair;

ii. to provide for quiet enjoyment of the property;

iii. to insure the property;

iv. to provide for a right of re-entry for breach of any covenant.

The covenant imposing a restriction on the tenant in relation to business use may come in a positive or negative form. It could restrict the tenant to carrying on a particular business or using the property for a particular purpose, e.g. carrying on the business of a retail travel agent. Alternatively the covenant could prevent the tenant from carrying on a particular form of trade or any activity causing a nuisance or annoyance.

The covenant imposing a restriction on assigning or subletting of the property is normally inserted so that the landlord can prevent the tenancy coming into the hands of an undesirable tenant. An absolute prohibition on other subletting or assigning will, in the absence of a waiver by the landlord, prevent the tenant from either subletting or assigning. If the covenant provides however, that these activities are only prohibited when carried out without the landlord's consent, then such consent is not to be unreasonably withheld **(Landlord and Tenant Act 1927 s.19).**

Usual Covenants

It is permissible of course for the parties to a business tenancy to simply make reference to the 'usual covenants' rather than setting out in full the express covenants. In such a case it is a question of fact to determine what covenants would be regarded as part of the tenancy. The recent case of *Chester v. Buckingham Travel Ltd. 1980* provides some guidance as to what the courts would regard as amounting to the 'usual covenants' in a commercial lease entered into in 1971. The lease in question related to certain garage workshops and was for 14 years at a rent of £6,000 p.a. exclusive of rates. On the question of what covenants should be included in the lease as 'usual covenants' the court held that the type of premises let and the purpose and duration of the lease were all relevant factors to be considered. In this case in addition to the well known usual covenants, namely, those by the tenant to pay rent, taxes, repair and permit entry to view the state of repair, and that by the landlord for quiet enjoyment, **extra covenants in relation to the following should be included.** That the tenant:-

a. would not alter the plan, height, elevation or appearance of the building without the landlord's consent;

b. would not obstruct windows or lights or knowingly permit any encroachment easements to be acquired against the demised premises;

c. would not alter the user of the premises without the landlord's consent, such consent not to be unreasonably withheld;

d. would not suffer any part of the premises to be a nuisance or cause annoyance and that the landlord should have a right of re-entry for breach of any covenant.

11.3 Procedure for Determination

A tenancy to which the **Landlord and Tenant Act 1954 Part II** applies will not automatically terminate on the expiration of the current term or on the service of the required notice to quit. The Act stipulates the alternative procedures by which such a tenancy may be determined and involves a course of action to be taken either by the landlord or the tenant.

Action by the Landlord

If the landlord wishes to bring the contractual tenancy to an end he must do so in accordance with the Act's provisions (in the absence of any right to exact a forfeiture under a provision for re-entry). Under **s.25** the competent landlord may serve a statutory notice on the tenant, in writing, and in the form prescribed in the **Landlord and Tenant (Notice) Regulations 1969,** or substantially similar. Certainly, a minor difference from the statutory form will not invalidate the notice.

> In *Tegerdine v. Brook 1978,* a notice was held to be valid despite the omission of certain statutory notes from the margin. Also in *Safeway Foodstores v. Morris 1980,* it was held that provided a reasonable tenant would not be misled by an error in the notice such an error could be overlooked.

The following matters must be included in the **section 25 notice:-**

a.   The date of termination of the current tenancy; (this date must not be earlier than the date the term expires in the case of a fixed term tenancy **or** the earliest date of termination by notice in the case of a periodic tenancy).

b.   A statement that the landlord is not willing to grant the tenant a new tenancy and, on an application by the tenant for a new tenancy, a statement of the statutory ground on which the landlord intends to rely.

c.   A statement which requires the tenant to notify the landlord by counter-notice within two months as to whether he intends to give up possession of the premises on the date of termination.

The **s.25 notice** must be served not earlier than six nor more than 12 months before the date of termination specified within it. Following the receipt of a s.25 notice if the tenant wishes to oppose the landlord's termination of the contractual tenancy he must serve a **counter-notice** on the landlord **within the two month period** informing him of his opposition to delivering up possession and his intention to apply for a new tenancy.

> In *Chiswell v. Griffon Land and Estates Ltd. 1975* such a counter notice was sent within the two month time period by the tenant's

192

solicitors but was apparently lost in the post. The court held that, despite proof of posting as the tenant had failed to reply to the landlord's notice within two months from its service the court had no power to entertain his application for a new tenancy.

Having served a counter-notice, and in the event of the parties failing to reach agreement, the next stage is for the tenant to apply to the court for a new tenancy under **s.24(1)**. This is achieved under **s.29(3)** by the tenant filing an application to the County Court or the High Court not less than two nor more than four months after the s.25 notice has been served.

> Once again it is a strict requirement that action is taken within the time period prescribed as was demonstrated by the House of Lords' decision in *Dodds v. Walker 1981*. Here a s.25 notice was served by the landlord on Sept. 30 1978 and the tenant applied to the County Court for a new tenancy on January 31 1979. The House of Lords held that the relevant period for such an application was between two and four months ending on the corresponding date of the appropriate subsequent month, and accordingly the tenant's application should be dismissed as out of time.

Action by the Tenant

In the absence of agreement between the landlord and tenant as to the grant of a new tenancy the Act provides a means by which the tenant can take action. Under **S.26** the tenant can terminate the current tenancy by making a request for a new tenancy to the landlord. The request must be served on the competent landlord, be in writing and in the form prescribed by the **Landlord and Tenant (Notice) Regulations 1957,** or substantially similar.
NOTE. The **s.26 request** cannot be served if the landlord has already served a s.25 notice and vice-versa.

The following matters must be included in the s.26 request:-

a. The date of commencement of the new tenancy; (this date must be at least six but not more than 12 months after the request has been made).

b. A statement of the terms of the proposed new tenancy including such matters as the property to be comprised, the rent payable and its duration.

It should be pointed out that a s.26 request may not be made by a tenant when either:-

i.   the term of the current tenancy granted is for a period of less than one year (**s.29(1)**); or

ii. a **s.25** notice has already been served by the landlord; or

iii. the tenant has already served a notice to quit or a notice under **s.27** that he does not wish the tenancy to be continued.

A landlord wishing to oppose the tenant's request for a new tenancy is obliged, within two months, to serve a counter-notice which must include a statement of the statutory ground upon which the landlord intends to rely. Failure to serve such a notice effectively means that the landlord loses all rights to oppose the tenant's application for a new tenancy.

11.4 Landlord's grounds of opposition

The alternative grounds upon which a landlord can rely to oppose a tenant's application to the court for a new tenancy are set out in **section 30** of the Act.

S.30(1)(a) Breach of a repairing obligation. Relying on this ground the landlord must prove that in view of the state of repair of the premises resulting from the tenant's failure to observe a repairing obligation under the current tenancy, a new tenancy ought not to be granted. To grant possession on this ground the court must be satisfied that the breach of the repairing covenant is a serious one.

S.30(1)(b) Persistant delay in paying rent. Here the landlord must prove that in view of the tenant's persistant delay in paying rent due under the current tenancy, a new tenancy ought not to be granted. Here again the court must be satisfied that the delay is a serious one either over an extended time period or consist of a number of separate delays.

S.30(1)(c) Other substantial breaches. In this case the landlord must prove that the tenant ought not to be granted a new tenancy in view of other substantial breaches of obligations under the current tenancy or for any other reason connected with the tenant's use or management of the holding.

Again the important question for the court to determine is the seriousness of the breach and whether the tenant has any proposals for its remedy. In relation to "any other reason connected with the tenant's use or management of the holding" an illegal use of the premises would certainly amount to such a reason.

> In *Turner & Bell v. Searles (Stanford-le-Hope) Ltd. 1977* the tenants were found to be using the premises unlawfully by parking coaches in breach of planning law, having had an enforcement notice served upon them. As it was clear that the tenants intended to continue the illegal use under a new tenancy, the landlord was held to be entitled to possession under **s.30(1)(c).**

S.30(1)(d) Provision of suitable alternative accommodation. Relying on this ground the landlord must prove that the tenant ought not to be granted a new tenancy as the landlord is willing to provide him with suitable alternative accommodation. The question of deciding whether the alternative accommodation offered is suitable is to be determined by reference to all the circumstances, and in particular whether any goodwill attaching to the premises will be preserved.

S.30(1)(e) Letting or disposing of the property as a whole. Here the landlord may object to the granting of a new tenancy in a case where the current tenancy was created by a sub-letting of only part of the premises let under a superior tenancy, and the interest of the tenant's immediate landlord is to terminate in the near future. The ground relied on is that the superior landlord requires possession of the premises as he might reasonably be expected to re-let the property as a whole or dispose of the property as a whole. To succeed on this ground the superior landlord would have to show that the re-letting value of the property as one unit is much higher than if re-let in separate parts.

S.30(1)(f) Demolishing or reconstructing the premises. The objection of the landlord in this case is that the tenant ought not to be granted possession because the landlord **intends,** on the termination of the tenancy to demolish or reconstruct the premises, or a substantial part of them, or to carry out substantial work of construction on them and he could not reasonably do this work without obtaining possession of the premises.

> In *Betty's Cafes v. Phillips Furnishing Stores 1959* it was held that the relevant **intention** of the landlord had to be established at the date of the court application. This intention must be proved to be a fixed one evidenced by **positive steps to secure its implementation,** e.g. planning applications (where necessary), building contracts, building plans, etc.

For the purposes of reconstruction the intention to carry out substantial work must be shown.

> In *Atkinson v. Bettison 1955* installing a new front to a shop was held to be insufficient to constitute reconstruction whereas in *Joel v. Swaddle 1957* changing the identity of a small shop into a large hall intended to be an amusement arcade was held to constitute reconstruction.

Under the provisions of the 1954 Act, the fact that the landlord required possession of only part of the premises for only a short period would not prevent him from obtaining possession.

This position was altered by the **Law of Property Act 1969** which added **s.31A(1)** to the 1954 Act. this section provides that the landlord cannot establish his need for possession under the 1954 Act if:—

a)   the tenant is willing to have a term included in the new tenancy conferring a right of access on the landlord sufficient to enable him to carry out the work; or

b)   the tenant is willing to accept a new tenancy of an economically separable part of the holding and the landlord is able to carry out the works by having possession of the remainder.

In cases where the landlord has already reserved a right under the terms of the lease to enter and carry out works of improvement or alteration, then it is unlikely that a court would grant possession under **30(1)(f).**

In *Price v. Esso Petroleum 1980* the landlord of a filling station served a **s.25** notice to terminate a tenancy relying on **s.30(1)(f)** as the ground of opposition in that they wished to demolish and reconstruct. The County Court held that the proposed work could be carried out without interfering to a substantial degree with the tenant's business and granted a new tenancy subject to access under **s.31 A(1)**. The Court of Appeal agreed that the tenant was entitled to a new tenancy but rejected the County Court finding of access under **s.31 A(1)**. The fact that the lease contained a provision allowing the landlord to enter and improve, and the works fell within that description, meant that the landlord could not rely on **s.30(1)(f)** as a ground of opposition.

S.30(1)(g) The Landlord intends to occupy for his own purposes. Here the ground is that the tenant ought not to be granted a new tenancy because the landlord **intends** to occupy the premises for the purposes of a business to be carried on by him therein or as his residence. For the purposes of showing intention the same factors to establish proof applicable to **s.30(1)(e)** are relevant.

In *Lightcliffe & District Cricket and Lawn Tennis Club v. Walton 1978* the landlord, a farmer, relied on **s.30(1)(g)** to resist the tenant's application for a new tenancy of a piece of land. However, the fact that the farmer failed to show through clear evidence his plans for making use of the land, convinced the court that his application should be rejected and a new tenancy was granted to the tenant.

A statutory limitation on the landlord relying on this ground is contained in **s.30(2)** of the 1954 Act. This provides that **s.30(1)(f)** cannot be relied on if the landlord's interest was purchased or created within the five years previous to the termination of the tenancy and throughout that five year period there has been a tenancy or succession of tenancies of the holding.

An application by a landlord under **s.30(1)(g)** may be upheld even though the business is not actually carried on by him but by persons on his behalf.

Thus in *Re Hanger Hill Country Club; Westminister Roman Catholic Diocese Trustee v. Parkes 1978* the trustee landlords were held to be entitled to the possession of premises under **s.30**

197

(1)(g) for use as a community centre. This was the case even though the business of running the centre was to be carried on by workers under their control rather than by the trustee landlords themselves.

Proof of any of the seven alternative statutory grounds may be sufficient to enable the landlord to recover possession of the business premises and successfully oppose the tenant's application for a new tenancy. It should be stressed however that grounds (d), (f) and (g) are **absolute** in that if they are proved by the landlord then the court must grant him possession. The remaining grounds (a), (b), (c) and (e) are **discretionary** and even if proved by the landlord the court nevertheless has a final discretion to determine whether a new tenancy is granted.

11.5 The Court Application and the New Tenancy

It should be stressed that in the majority of cases and usually as the result of compromise, agreement is reached as to the grant and/or terms of the new tenancy without the need for court intervention. In the event of failure to reach agreement however, a court application will proceed. If the rateable value of the property does not exceed £5,000 the relevant court is the County Court, otherwise it is the High Court. In either case the court must determine two distinct issues. Firstly, whether the tenant is to be granted a new tenancy and if so, secondly, determine its content.

The first issue, of course is determined by the court deciding whether the landlord has satisfield the **s.30** ground relied on. This may also involve the exercise of the court's discretion, where one has been conferred, i.e. for grounds included in **s.30(1)(a)**, **s.30(1)(b)**, **s.30(1)(c)**, **s.30(1)(e)**. A further complication is introduced by **s.31(2)** which provides for a compromise situation where the ground relied on is either **s.30(1)(d)**, **s.30(1)(e)** or **s.30(1)(f)**. Here if the court is satisfied that the ground relied on would have been fulfilled had the date specified in the **s.25 notice** or **s.26 request** been later, (but not more than one year later), then the court must make a **declaration** to that effect, and no order for a new tenancy is made. The effect of this declaration is that the tenant has 14 days from it being made to require the court to make an order that the later date be substituted in the **s.25 notice** or the **s.26 request.** The notice or request will then take effect accordingly. This provision could be relied on by a court if it felt that **suitable alternative accommodation** would be available for the tenant in the near future or a necessary planning permission to carry out works will be obtained by the landlord.

Having decided that a new tenancy is to be ordered, the court is then faced with the second issue, as to its content. In the absence of agreement the Act confers a wide discretion on the courts in this matter. So far as the length of the new tenancy is concerned, its duration is to be such, up to a maximum of 14 years, as the court considers reasonable in all the circumstances. It is unlikely however that the new tenancy will be granted for a term which exceeds the original tenancy and factors such as the landlord's intention to demolish or redevelop in the future are relevant to decide its length. The subject matter of the new tenancy, the demised premises, is generally that part of the premises occupied by the tenant for the purposes of the business under the original tenancy. This is the case unless the tenant has expressly agreed to accept a tenancy of only part of the property to enable works to be carried out on the remainder **s.32(1)(A).** The rent payable under the new tenancy is that amount, having regard to the terms of the tenancy, that a willing lessor might reasonably expect to let the property at on the **open market.** Certain matters however are to be disregarded under **s.34(1)** including:-

1. The fact that there is a sitting tenant;

2. The fact that goodwill is attached to the property by reason of the tenant's or his predecessors business;

3. The fact that the tenant or his predecessor has carried out voluntary improvements to the property;

4. The fact that the tenant holds a licence to sell intoxicating liquor from the property, the benefit of which belongs to the tenant.

Of course the question as to the rent payable can only be determined once the court is satisfied as to the remaining terms of the tenancy. Again, in the absence of agreement the court will have regard to the content of the original tenancy to determine such matters as restrictive covenants in relation to user, prohibition on assignment, service charges, repair, etc. Certainly if the landlord seeks to grant a new tenancy with terms that differ from the original tenancy he will have to justify the changes. If a new tenancy proves to be onerous on the tenant, even in an **indirect** way, the court may not accept it.

> In *Charles Clements (London) Ltd. v. Rank City Wall Ltd. 1978*
> the landlord suggested that the new tenancy should contain a

less restrictive covenant in relation to business user. This apparent concession however had the indirect effect of raising the market rent and was held to be therefore oppressive and not justifiable.

11.6 Compensation for Improvements

During the term of a business tenancy it is likely that the tenant, or his predecessors in title will carry out improvements to the property. These improvements will ultimately benefit the landlord, since they will increase the potential letting value of property when the letting under which they were carried out comes to an end. The **Landlord and Tenant Act 1927** provides for compensation to be paid to the tenant by the landlord in such circumstances, subject to **certain requirements being satisfied, and certain conditions fulfilled.**

Before considering these, some general observations need to be made. At common law a tenant is entitled to carry out alterations and improvements to the property as he wishes, although such work must not constitute the tort of waste. Since a landlord may wish to exercise some control over such activities it is common to find inserted into business tenancies a covenant that absolutely prohibits such work, or which is qualified by requiring the landlord's consent to the work. Although such consent cannot be unreasonably withheld by virtue of **s.19(1) Landlord and Tenant Act 1927,** the landlord may lawfully impose conditions upon the granting of the consent. He can require payment of any costs connected with granting the consent, such as surveyors fees, or the payment of a sum to cover the reduction in the value of the property caused by the work. Alternatively he may require reinstatement of the property if the work carried out has not increased the letting value of the property. The parties cannot exclude by agreement the requirement that consent shall not be unreasonably withheld, **s.19(2) Landlord and Tenant Act 1927.**

The right to compensation is contained in **s.1 Landlord and Tenant Act 1927,** (as amended by the **Landlord and Tenant Act 1954,**) which provides that "...a tenant of a holding to which ... this Act applies shall, if a claim is made in the prescribed manner, (and within the time limited by **s.47 Landlord and Tenant Act 1954**), be entitled, at the termination of the tenancy, on quitting his holding, to be paid by his landlord compensation in respect of any improvements (including the erection of any buildings) on his holding made by him or his predecessor in title ... which at the termination of the tenancy adds to the letting value of the holding".

The improvements can only be compensated if they increase the letting value, and not all improvements need have this effect. They may for instance be beneficial only to that particular tenant. Trade fixtures, such as shop fittings, which can be lawfully removed by a tenant before the end of the tenancy, do not qualify for compensation as improvements. An improvement provides a benefit to a landlord when the tenancy comes to an end. If sub-tenancies have been granted, then an improvement carried out by a sub-tenant must be compensated by his immediate landlord, who in turn must seek compensation from his own landlord.

The Conditions for Compensation

In order to obtain compensation it is not enough that the tenant has simply carried out the improvements. He must in addition have followed the statutory procedure laid down under **s.3** of the 1927 Act. Under this procedure the tenant must first have served notice on the landlord of his intention to carry out improvements, accompanied by a specification and plan of the works to be carried out. The landlord then has 3 months to serve a notice of objection. If he fails to do so the improvement is regarded as being authorised. In any event no objection can be served if the improvement is being carried out in pursuance of a statutory obligation. If the landlord does serve a notice of objection during the statutory time period the tenant can apply to the court for a **certificate** that the improvement is a proper one. The court will grant the certificate if it is satisfied:-

a.   that the improvement is such as to be calculated to add to the letting value of the property when the tenancy ends, and

b.   that the improvement is reasonable and suitable bearing in mind the character of the property, and

c.   that the improvement will not diminish the value of any other property owned by the landlord or superior landlord.

Once the certificate is granted (and the court may in granting it impose conditions and modify the specification or plan), the improvement becomes an authorised one. The certificate will not be issued if the landlord has offered to carry out the improvement himself, in consideration of increasing the tenant's rent, although if the landlord subsequently fails to carry out the work the certificate authorising the tenant to do so will be granted. An authorised improvement must be completed within the time agreed between the landlord and the tenant, or as fixed by the court, and on completion of the work the tenant may ask the landlord for a **certificate of due completion.**

If the improvement is authorised, or no objection to it has been received from the landlord, the improvement can be lawfully carried out despite any provision to the contrary contained in the lease. If the landlord has agreed to carry out the improvements, the 1927 Act confers the power on him, or those authorised by him, to enter the property to carry them out.

The Claim for Compensation

This must be made by the tenant in the prescribed form, and include the date the work was carried out, the cost of it, what the work consisted of, and the amount now being claimed by the tenant.

The claim must be served on the landlord within the strict time limits set out under **s.47 Landlord and Tenant Act 1954,** namely:-

a)   within three months of the service of a notice to quit or to terminate the tenancy. In the case of a tenancy terminated under **s.26** of the 1954 Act, within three months of the counter-notice served by the landlord; or

b)   not more than six months but not less than three months before termination if the tenancy will end by simple passing of time; or

c)   where the tenancy is determined by forfeiture, within three months commencing with the effective date for the recovery of possession by order of the court, or if there is no such order within three months commencing with the date of re-entry by the landlord.

It should be noted that compensation is only payable when the tenancy comes to an end, and of course, generally a tenant will be entitled to a new tenancy under the 1954 Act. It is nevertheless prudent for the tenant to ensure that he qualifies for the right to compensation, for **should the tenancy end** he will not be entitled to compensation if he did not originally qualify.

If the parties have not agreed the amount of compensation to be paid the 1927 Act provides that compensation is not to exceed the **net addition**

to the value of the property as a direct result of the improvement, or the **reasonable cost** of carrying out the improvement, valued at the end of the tenancy.

It is of course possible that when the tenancy ends the improvement is not in an acceptable state of repair. If this is the case the cost of putting it into a reasonable state of repair has to be deducted from the reasonable cost of carrying out the improvement.

For the purpose of determining the **net addition** regard must be had to any intention on the part of the landlord to demolish or structurally alter any part of the premises, or any change of use, and the effect this will have on the additional value of the property produced by the improvements. Compensation will be reduced where the tenant has received a benefit from the landlord in consideration of carrying out the improvement. Finally, the landlord is entitled under the 1927 Act to deduct any sum the tenant owes him in relation to the tenancy (e.g. rent arrears), from the compensation he is obliged to pay. Likewise the tenant can deduct from any sum he owes the landlord regarding the tenancy, any sum due to him from the landlord regarding improvements.

Compensation for Disturbance

The Act provides, under **s.37,** for the payment of compensation to a business tenant in the following circumstances: either

a)   the tenant has applied to the court for a new tenancy and his application has been rejected because of the landlords opposition relying on either grounds **s.30(1)(e), s.30(1)(f)** or **s.30(1)(g);** or

b)   Following the service of a **s.25** notice or a **s.26** request in which the landlord relies on one of the above grounds of opposition, the tenant either does not apply for a new tenancy or applies for a new tenancy and then withdraws his application.

In either of the above cases if the tenant has quit the premises he is entitled to make a claim for compensation for disturbance. If the occupier has carried on a particular business in the premises, or has succeeded to that business during the fourteen years prior to the termination of the tenancy, the amount of compensation payable is **twice the rateable value of the property.** Otherwise the compensation payable is simply the **rateable value**

of the premises. Finally, it should be mentioned that if there has been a business occupation of the premises for less than five years, the parties to the tenancy may expressly exclude or modify the tenants rights to any claim for compensation for disturbance.

11.7 Agricultural Holdings

The rights of the tenant of an agricultural holding are for the most part contained in the **Agricultural Holdings Act 1948** as amended by the **Agriculture Act 1958,** and the **Agricultural Holdings (Notices to Quit) Act 1977.** The 1948 Act applies to agricultural holdings which are defined as the aggregate of the agricultural land comprised in a contract of tenancy, not being a contract under which the said land is let to the tenant during his continuance in any office, appointment or employment under the landlord. **Agricultural land** is further defined as including "horticulture, fruit growing, seed growing, dairy farming and livestock keeping and breeding and the use of land for grazing, meadow, market gardens or woodland".

Security of Tenure

Tenancies of agricultural holdings may only be determined in accordance with the **Agricultural Holdings (Notices to Quit) Act 1977. Section 1** provides that a notice to quit an agricultural holding is invalid if it purports to terminate the tenancy before the expiration of twelve months from the end of the term. Periodic tenancies of agricultural land let for a term of less than one year are automatically converted into **yearly tenancies.** Similarly a fixed term tenancy of two years or more will not determine on the expiration of the term, but require the service of a notice to quit of not less than one year, otherwise it will continue as an annual tenancy. Within one month of the service of a notice to quit, the tenant who wishes to oppose it may serve a counter notice on the landlord. The effect of the service of a counter notice is that the landlord's notice to quit will only become effective if supported by the **Agricultural Land Tribunal.** To obtain this support it is necessary for the landlord to prove the existence of a specified statutory ground. These grounds are listed as cases in **s.2** of the 1977 Act as follows:-

CASE A   That the Tribunal previously consented to the notice being given;

CASE B	That the land is required for a non agricultural purpose for which planning permission (if required) has been given;

CASE C   That the landlord has obtained a certificate that the tenant has failed to farm according to the rules of good husbandry;

CASE D   That the tenant has failed to comply with a notice to pay arrears of rent within two months;

CASE E   That the tenant has committed irremediable breaches to the prejudice of the landlord;

CASE F   That the tenant is bankrupt or has compounded with his creditors;

CASE G   That the sole surviving tenant died within three months of the notice.

Certainly it is the intention of the legislation that disputes in relation to possession should be settled where possible by arbitration, or by a tribunal, rather than the ordinary courts. The landlord must specify the particular statutory case he is relying on for possession, and for cases B, D and E the tenant can serve a counter notice requiring the dispute to be **settled by arbitration.** It should also be stressed that proof of a **s.2** case by the landlord does not automatically confer a right to possession. The tribunal must also be satisfied that it is reasonable to deliver up possession to the landlord in the circumstances. Also for the purposes of **case G,** a notice to quit served following the tenant's death will only become effective in the absence of any application to succeed to the tenancy within the three months following the death.

Succession

Succession to an agricultural tenancy will only be granted to eligible applicants who are:-

a.   **eligible persons;** there are eligible relations including husbands, wives, brothers, sisters or children of the deceased whose only or principal source of income for five years has been derived from the holding; and

b.   **those not disqualified;** disqualification occurs following the **second statutory succession** or if the original tenancy is too long (i.e. a fixed

205

term with more than 27 months left to run) or too short (i.e. a periodic tenancy less than year to year); and

c. **suitable persons;** to determine whether an eligible person is a **suitable person** the tribunal will consider his training, experience, age, health, financial resources and the views of the landlord. If the person designated in the landlord's will is suitable then there is no problem, but otherwise the tribunal must determine competing claims. Up to four persons may be selected by the tribunal as **joint tenants.**

The 1948 Act provides for four different types of compensation on the expiration of an agricultural tenancy. There are complex provisions relating to the assessment of compensation; for **specified improvements** to the holding (to which the landlord consented); introducing a **special system of farming** (which has increased the value of the holding); **suffering damage to crops** from game; and for **disturbance** when the tenancy was brought to an end by the landlord's notice to quit.

Chapter 12   Private Sector Protection (The Rent Act 1977)

Since the early 1920's successive governments have attempted by legislative means to prevent exploitation of individuals by landlords as a result of the limited availability of residential accommodation in the private sector. To achieve this aim rights have been conferred on residential tenants who are **'protected'** in relation to:-

a.   **security of tenure** so that a **protected (regulated) tenant** has the right to hold over in possession of the dwelling house as a **'statutory tenant'** on the expiration of his **contractual** (regulated) tenancy; and

b.   **registration of a fair rent** so that a protected tenant has the opportunity of applying to have a fair rent **registered** for the dwelling which will become the maximum rent recoverable.

The present statutory provisions are contained in the **Rent Act 1977** (as amended by the **Housing Act 1980**) in relation to residential tenants generally, and the **Rent (Agriculture) Act 1976** in relation to agricultural workers in tied houses. Except where otherwise mentioned reference to legislative provisions will be to the **Rent Act 1977.**

12.1 Protected Tenancies

One of the main tasks in interpreting Rent Act legislation is ~~to~~ firstly to determine to which tenancies it is applicable and are therefore given protection under it. **Section 1 provides that a tenancy under which a dwelling house (which may be a house or part of a house) is let as a separate dwelling is a protected tenancy for the purposes of this Act.**

The first criterion is that there must be a **tenancy** of any type rather than a mere licence (see Chapter 6). Also the letting must be of a **'dwelling house'** (or part of a house). This has been widely interpreted as a dwelling, e.g. a hotel, a beach hut, a flat, a room, a cottage. Further, the dwelling must be let **'as a separate dwelling'**, and to decide this question it is necessary to discover the parties' intention as expressed in the lease or shown by the surrounding circumstances. Certainly if the lease contains an express provision to the effect that the premises are to be used as a 'private dwelling house only' then this would be conclusive. It is also possible for property to be let for one purpose, for example business premises, and then during the term there is a change of user, for instance to a dwelling house. If such a change is made with the full knowledge of the landlord he could be taken to have impliedly agreed to it but in any event, the burden of proof would be on the tenant. The word **'separate'** means that there must be no sharing of the accommodation either with the landlord or another tenant in order to obtain full protection as a protected tenant. Sharing is taken to occur when 'living rooms' or 'dwelling rooms' are shared, e.g. dining room, kitchen, bedroom, rather than particular rooms only visited for specific purposes, e.g. bathroom, toilet. If the tenant shares accommodation with the landlord then the tenancy cannot be protected but may qualify for less protection as a **restricted contract** (see later in the chapter).

Excluded Tenancies

a. **Rateable Value** Under **s.4(1)** a tenancy is not a protected tenancy if on the 'appropriate' day the dwelling house had too high a rateable value. The appropriate day means 23rd March 1965 or such later date on which a rateable value for the dwelling house was first shown on the valuation list. By **s.4** a tenancy is now protected unless the rateable value of the dwelling hosue exceeded:-

   i.   £200 (£400 Greater London) on 23.3.65; and

   ii. £300 (£600 Greater London) on 22.3.73; and

   iii. £750 (£1,500 Greater London) on 1.4.73 or such later date as the value was first shown.

   For a dwelling on which a value is not shown until after 1.4.73 then only the £750 (£1,500) limit is relevant.

b. **Low Rent** Under **s.5(1)** a tenancy is not protected if under the tenancy either:-

   i.   no rent is payable; or

   ii. the rent payable is less than two-thirds of the rateable value of the dwelling house on the appropriate day.

Here the term 'rent' means rent payable only in money rather than the value of services provided in lieu of rent. In relation to the low rent exception this does not include tenancies which although at a low rent are **'controlled tenancies'** under pre-1965 legislation. These tenancies have been gradually converted into protected regulated tenancies under the post-1965 legislation, and by virtue of **s.64(1) Housing Act 1980** every existing controlled tenancy is to cease to be controlled and becomes regulated.

c. **Dwellings let with other land** This exclusion contained in **s.6** relates to where a dwelling house is let together with land other than the site of the dwelling house. Whether land and a dwelling house are let together is a question of fact in each case.

d. **Payments for Board or Attendance** Under **s.7(1)** a tenancy is not protected if under it the dwelling house is let at a rent which includes payments for **board or attendance.** Attendance means services personal to the tenant provided by the landlord in accordance with his contract, e.g. carrying down refuse, providing a maid, delivering correspondence. The exception in relation to attendance will not apply when the amount of rent attributable to it forms a substantial part of the whole rent. This is not the case for board where it seems that bed and breakfast would suffice but not the early morning cup of tea!

e. **Student Lettings** This exception under **s.8(1)** relates to a tenancy granted to a person who is pursuing or intends to pursue a course of study provided by a specified educational institution and is so granted by a specified educational institution.

f. **Holiday Lettings** Here the exclusion **s.9** is quite simply where the purpose of the tenancy is to confer on the tenant the right to occupy the dwelling house for a holiday.

g. **Agricultural Holdings** Agricultural tenancies are governed by the **Agricultural Holdings Act 1948** and are not protected tenancies under the **Rent Act 1977 s.10.**

h. **Public Houses with on-licences s.11** provides that 'a tenancy of a dwelling house which consists of, or comprises premises licensed for the sale of intoxicating liquor for consumption on the premises shall not be a protected tenancy'.

i.   **Crown Property ss.13 to 16** exclude property where the landlord's interest is owned by the Crown or a number of specified bodies including local authorities (county, district, the GLC or London boroughs), the Commission for New Towns, the Housing Corporation, a development corporation, or a registered housing association, trust or co-operative.

The position of housing associations under the law is considered in the next chapter. At this point however it should be stressed that registered housing associations are in a privileged position under the **Rent Act 1977** in that they do not create protected tenancies. Previously this privilege was subject to qualifying conditions but these have effectively been removed by **s.74(1) Housing Act 1980.** Those housing associations whose tenants are protected under the **Rent Act 1977** e.g. unregistered associations, must give notice to their tenants that they are not excluded from rent act protection.

j.   **Church Parsonages** This exception relates to Church of England parsonages governed by the **Pluralities Act 1836.**

k.   **Business Tenancies** Under **s.24(3)** a tenancy shall not be regulated if it is a tenancy to which the **Landlord and Tenant Act 1954 Part II** applies (see Chapter 11)

12.2 Security of Tenure

Security of tenure is acquired automatically by a protected tenant in the following way. When the protected contractual tenancy comes to an end the protected tenant shall have the right to hold over as a **statutory tenant** under the Rent Act so long as he occupies the dwelling house as his residence. There is no estate or interest in property conferred on the statutory tenant but rather a **personal right** to remain in possession of the dwelling house on the same terms as the former contractual tenancy in so far as they are consistent with the Rent Act. Having only a personal right to possession, a statutory tenant has no right to **assign or sub-let the whole** and he has no estate or interest to dispose of by will or pass to a trustee in bankruptcy. Clearly only a protected tenant in residence is capable of being a statutory tenant so that a corporate body, e.g. a limited company, is excluded from the security of tenure provisions. If the statutory tenant ceases to reside in the premises then the landlord will be able to obtain an order for possession. The courts have recognised however that a person may reside in more than one home at the same time.

Statutory Succession

The Act provides machinery whereby the statutory tenant can, by a written agreement with a person proposing to occupy the dwelling (the incoming tenant), agree that the incoming tenant is deemed to be the statutory tenant as from an agreed date. To be effective the landlord must be a party to such an agreement. In such circumstances the incoming tenant will take over all the rights of the outgoing statutory tenant.

The more usual method of transfer is called a **transmission by succession.** This occurs on the death of the person who was the protected or statutory tenant. If that person is a man and leaves a widow who was residing with him at his death, the widow shall be the statutory tenant for as long as she occupies the dwelling house as her residence. Where there is no such widow (including every case where the tenant is a woman), the statutory successor will be a person who was a member of the tenant's family and residing with him at the time of, and for the six month period prior to his death. Of course if there is more than one such person the statutory tenancy is to be decided by agreement, or in default, agreement by the County Court. As for the term 'family', this is used in its popular sense and would cover the persons that an ordinary man would regard as members of his family, e.g. children (including illegitimate children), step children, brothers, sisters, (including in-laws). The fact that a couple are living together as man and wife may also be sufficient to establish the relationship of family. In *Dyson Holdings Ltd. v. Fox 1976* the Court of Appeal held that the meaning of the term family has been extended to include the survivor of the union of a couple living together as man and wife provided the union had the appropriate degree of permanence and stability and whether they had children or not.

If there is more than one person eligible to claim statutory succession and they cannot reach agreement, then the courts will settle the dispute by taking into account all the circumstances of the case including the wishes of the deceased tenant.

> In *Williams v. Williams 1970* the court had to determine on the death of a female tenant whether her spouse or son should succeed to the statutory tenancy. The son was in good employment and had supported his mother well while the husband who had only a modest income had treated her badly. On the ground that the son could easily find alternative

211

accommodation the court held that the husband, who was also near to retirement, should inherit the tenancy.

The person who becomes the statutory tenant by succession is known as the **'first successor'** and on his or her death, while still a statutory tenant, there is provision for a second transmission. Following the death of the second successor however there can be no further transmission.

12.3 Grounds for Possession.

One of the fundamental aims of the Rent Act legislation is to ensure security of tenure for the occupier who is a protected contractual tenant or is a statutory tenant. In either case a landlord wishing to obtain possession must proceed by way of an action in the County Court. If a contractual tenancy is still in existence the landlord must first serve a **valid notice to quit** giving at least four weeks notice. Under **s.98(1)** a court shall not make an order for possession of a dwelling house let as a protected tenancy or subject to a statutory tenancy unless:-

a.   **the court is satisfied that it is reasonable to make such an order; and**

b.   **either the court is satisfied as to the availability of suitable alternative accommodation for the tenant; or the circumstances are as specified in any of the Cases in Part I of Schedule 15.**

Part I of Schedule 15 contains the discretionary grounds for possession. The Act also provides in **s.98(2) mandatory grounds** for possession for if the circumstances of the case are as specified in any of the cases in Part II of Schedule 15 then an order for possession must be made.

If reliance is placed upon **s.98(1),** either suitable alternative accommodation, or a case in Part I of Schedule 15, it is for the landlord to satisfy the court as to the reasonableness of his action. The determination of this matter is a question of fact for the County Court judge to decide by examining all the relevant circumstances as they exist at the date of the hearing. Certainly matters such as the financial hardship of the tenant or the possible pecuniary gain of the landlord are relevant considerations.

In *Macdonnell v. Daly 1969* it was held that the professional needs of an artist tenant should be taken into account as should the financial loss he would suffer if forced to move.

Account is also taken of past or present breaches of covenant by either the landlord or tenant.

Suitable Alternative Accommodation

Possession may be awarded under **s.98(1)** if the court is satisfied that **suitable alternative accommodation** is available for the tenant when the order is to take effect. An offer of part of the existing demised premises would constitute alternative accommodation but whether it is suitable will depend on the nature of the proposed letting and the needs of the tenant.

In *Mykolyshyn v. Noah 1971* the offer of alternative accommodation was the present premises but excluding a number of rooms. However in the circumstances of the case this was held to be suitable.

A landlord can prove the existence of suitable alternative accommodation by pointing to a **housing authority certificate** stating that the authority will provide such accommodation for the tenant. Alternatively the landlord must show that he is able to offer premises let as a separate dwelling as a protected tenancy (or equivalent) which fulfils the relevant conditions. These conditions are related to the needs of the tenant and his family and include such matters as proximity to work place, rental, and the nature and situation of the accommodation offered.

In addition to the offer of suitable alternative accommodation **Schedule 15 Part I** contains a number of discretionary cases on which the landlord can rely for possession.

Discretionary Grounds

Case I, Arrears of rent or breach of the terms of the tenancy To prove this ground the landlord must show either that rent is due and unpaid or any obligation of the protected or statutory tenancy has been broken or not performed. It is probably the most common ground relied on because arrears of rent is the most popular reason for eviction proceedings. Usually if the arrears are paid before the hearing it would not be reasonable to make an order on this ground. However, in a case involving a long history of default, with large arrears, an order could still be made despite payment after the summons has been issued. *Dellenty v. Pellow 1951.* Certainly no order should be made if the reason for the arrears is that there has been a genuine dispute as to the amount owing or the rent has been withheld because of a genuine complaint of disrepair against the landlord. Case I also includes the breach of any express or implied obligation of the tenancy. Express covenants relied on could include breaches of those covenants providing for residential user, repair, or non assignment or sub-letting. Implied covenants relied on could include using the premises in a tenant-like manner or providing the landlord with access to carry out repairs.

Case II. Nuisance, annoyance or immoral or illegal user To constitute a nuisance or annoyance for the purposes of this case it is necessary to point to some conduct which is causing material interference to adjoining occupiers, e.g. noise, smoke, smells, vibration, etc. For the purposes of showing that the premises have been used for immoral or illegal purposes, it is sufficient to demonstrate that the tenant has taken advantage of the tenancy of the premises for the purposes of the offence, e.g. storing stolen goods or committing a sexual offence. In *Abrahams v. Wilson 1971,* the Court of Appeal held that being unlawfully in possession of cannabis resin on premises was not sufficient to **associate the offence with the premises** for the purposes of unlawful user. Had the premises been used to store the cannabis it would have been a different matter.

Case III. Deterioration due to waste, neglect or default This case is satisfied where the condition of the dwelling house has, in the opinion of the court, deteriorated owing to acts of waste by, or the neglect or default of, the tenant or any person residing or lodging with him or any sub-tenant.

Case IV. Deterioration in the condition of furniture provided This case is satisfied when the condition of any furniture provided for use under the tenancy has, in the opinion of the court, deteriorated owing to ill-treatment by the tenant or any person residing or lodging with him or any sub-tenant.

Case V. Tenants notice to quit Here the ground is that the tenant has given notice to quit and as a result the landlord has contracted to sell or let the dwelling house. In addition the landlord must have taken other steps which, as a result, will seriously prejudice him if he cannot obtain possession. It seems that the notice to quit served must be a valid one in the proper form (in writing) and giving the contractual notice for a minimum of four weeks.

Case VI. Assigning or sub-letting This ground applies where, without the landlord's consent, the tenant has assigned or sub-let the whole of the dwelling house, or sub-let part of the dwelling house the remainder being already sub-let. For the purposes of Case VI there is no requirement that there be a covenant against assignment or sub-letting, and the landlord's consent may be given expressly or impliedly.

Case VII. Off-licence offences Possession may be granted under Case VII where the dwelling house consists of or includes premises for the sale of intoxicating liquor for consumption off the premises only, and the tenant has committed an offence as holder of the licence, or renewal of the licence has been refused.

Case VIII. Former service tenant Here the landlord must establish that the dwelling house is required for occupation or a residence for a person engaged in whole-time employment for him. Also the tenant in residence at present was in the employment of the landlord and the dwelling was let as a consequence, and now such employment has ceased.
It should be noted that this ground is not available for use against a person employed in agriculture or forestry who is protected under the **Rent (Agriculture) Act 1976** (see later in the chapter).

Case IX. Required as a residence Under this ground the landlord must show that the dwelling house is reasonably required as a residence for himself, any son or daughter of his over 18, his father or mother, or if the dwelling house is let on a regulated tenancy, the father or mother of his/her wife or husband.

For the dwelling house to be reasonably required it must be the subject of a **genuine present need** on the part of the landlord. Also for an application to succeed on this ground it is a condition that the landlord did not become landlord by purchasing the dwelling house after:-

a.   7.11.56 in the case of a controlled tenancy;

b.   8.3.73 in the case of a tenancy which became regulated by virtue of **s.14 Counter Inflation Act 1973;**

c.   24.5.74 in the case of a regulated furnished tenancy;

d.   23.3.65 in the case of any other tenancy.

For this purpose the acquisition of the freehold or leasehold reversion for value would constitute a 'purchase'. The aim of the condition is plainly to prevent people buying houses over the heads of the tenants and then obtaining possession for themselves without providing the tenants with suitable alternative accommodation. A further condition in relation to a Case IX application is that a court should not make an order for possession under it if greater hardship would be caused by granting the order than refusing it. The court must have regard to all the circumstances of the case including the question as to whether other accommodation is available for the landlord or the tenant.

Case X. Overcharging a sub-tenant The case is proven if the court is satisfied that the rent charged by the tenant for any sub-let part of the dwelling house is in excess of the maximum rent recoverable for that part under the Act.

Mandatory Grounds

Under **s.98(2)** the court must order possession if certain grounds are satisfied. These grounds listed in **Schedule 15 Part II** apply only to regulated tenancies and in every case a **written notice** must have been given to the tenant warning him that possession may be claimed under the appropriate case. The cases for mandatory possession are listed as a continuance of the discretionary cases.

Case XI. Required as a residence for previous occupier Here the landlord must be a previous occupier of the dwelling house who has let it on a regulated tenancy and:-

a. not later than the 'relevant date' (usually the commencement date of the tenancy) the landlord gave notice that possession may be recovered under this case; and

b. the dwelling has not since 8.12.65 (14.8.74 for regulated furnished) (22.3.73 for regulated under the Counter Inflation Act), been let by the landlord on a protected tenancy under which the above condition has not been satisfied; and

c. the court is satisfied that the dwelling house is required as a residence for the owner-occupier or any member of his family who resided with the owner-occupier when he last occupied the dwelling house as a residence. Even in cases where the requirements under a. or b. have not been satisfied the court has **power to dispense with them** where it is **just and equitable** to make an order for possession in the circumstances.

Case XIII. Retirement home Under this ground the landlord must show that he acquired the dwelling house for the purposes of using it as a **retirement home** and prior to retirement he has let it under a regulated tenancy and:-

a. not later than the 'relevant date' gave the tenant written notice that possession might be recovered under this case; and

b. the dwelling house has not since 14.8.74 been let by the owner on a protected tenancy under which the above condition was not satisfied; and

c. the court is satisfied that the owner has retired, and requires the dwelling house as a residence or has died and the dwelling house is required as a residence for a member of his family residing with him at the time of his death.

Once again the court has power to make an order under this case even though the requirements of a. and b. have not been complied with where it is **just** and **equitable** to do so.

Case XIII. Short term out of season holiday lettings This ground applies where the dwelling house is let under a tenancy for a term of years not exceeding 8 months and:-

a. not later than the relevant date the landlord gives notice that possession might be recovered under this case; and

b. the dwelling house was at some time within the period of 12 months ending on the relevant date **occupied for a holiday** under a right to occupy.

The aim of this case is to enable landlords of holiday houses to let them during the off-season for short periods, and enable them to recover possession for the holiday period.

Case XIV. Student lettings by specified educational institutions Here the ground applies where the dwelling house is let under a tenancy for a term of years not exceeding 12 months and:-

a.   not later than the relevant date the landlord gave notice that possession might be recovered under this case; and

b.   at some time within the 12 month period ending on the relevant date the dwelling house was subject to such a tenancy or is referred to in **s.8(1)** of this Act.

Section 8 refers to lettings to a student studying at a specified educational institution by a landlord which is a specified educational institution although not necessarily that at which the student tenant is studying.

Case XV. Letting to a minister of religion This case relates to the situation where the dwelling house is held for the purpose of being available for occupation by a minister of religion as a residence from which he performs the duties of his office and:-

a.   not later than the relevant date the tenant was given notice that possession might be recovered under this case; and

b.   the court is satisfied that the dwelling house is required for occupation by a minister of religion as such a residence.

Case XVI. Agricultural employee This case covers the situation where the dwelling house was at any time occupied by a person under the terms of his employment in agriculture and:-

a.   the tenant is not and never has been employed by the landlord and is not the widow of a person who was so employed; and

b.   not later than the relevant date the tenant was given notice in writing that possession might be recovered under this case; and

c.   the court is satisfied that the dwelling house is required for occupation by a person employed or to be employed by the landlord in agriculture.

Case XVII. Agricultural amalgamation Under this case proposals for amalgamation approved for the purposes of a scheme under **s.26 Agriculture Act 1967** must have been carried out. The ground for possession is that the dwelling house was, when the amalgamation was proposed, occupied by a person responsible for the control of the farming of the land and:-

a.   after the amalgamation the dwelling house was let on a regulated tenancy to someone other than such a person, or his widow, or any agricultural employee of the landlord; and

b.   the court is satisfied that the dwelling house is now required for an agricultural employee of the landlord; and

c.   not later than the relevant date the tenant was given notice that possession might be recovered under this case; and

d.   the proceedings for possession are commenced within 5 years of **the date of the approval of the amalgamation proposals** or not more than 3 years after the person responsible for the farming or his widow vacated the property.

Case XVIII. Agricultural tenant The Case XVIII ground is also related to agriculture and is applicable where the last occupier of the dwelling house, before the relevant date, was responsible for the control of farming of land which together with the dwelling house formed an agricultural unit and:-

a.   not later than the relevant date the tenant was given notice that possession might be recovered under this case; and

b.   the court is satisfied that the dwelling house is required for occupation by such a person or by an agricultural employee and the tenant is neither of those nor the widow of either.

Case XIX Protected shorthold tenancy This mandatory ground for possession is a new addition introduced by the **Housing Act 1980** and covers the situation where a dwelling house has been let under a **protected shorthold tenancy** which has expired. As an important creation of the **Housing Act 1980** the protected shorthold tenancy **(PST)** is deserving of special attention. Essentially PST's are **short fixed term leases of between**

one and five years under which the landlord has, on expiration of the term, an absolute right to possession on compliance with formal notice requirements. The major requirement of PST's is that they must have a registered rent and indeed the **Housing Act 1980** makes it clear that for their duration PST's are to be fully embodied within the Rent Acts. It is for these two reasons that they are not as an attractive proposition for landlords as one would believe on first examination. For a landlord wishing to avoid the full impact of the Rent Acts, the possibilities of creating a restricted contract or a licence are perhaps more inviting. It should be pointed out that registered housing associations cannot grant protected shorthold tenancies.

Formalities for Creation To enter into a PST the following formalities must be adhered to, failing which, a full protected tenancy under the Rent Acts will normally be created:-

a.   A PST must be a protected (regulated) tenancy and therefore of a residential property let as a separate dwelling.

b.   It must have been granted after the commencement of the Act for a fixed term of not less than one year nor more than five years (i.e. no periodic tenancy).

c.   To constitute a PST the tenancy created cannot be terminated by the landlord before the term certain expires except in pursuance of a provision for re-entry or forfeiture for non payment of rent or breach of any other obligation of the tenancy.

d.   It is a prerequisite of the creation of a PST that before the grant the landlord serves a **notice in the prescribed form** on the tenant stating that the tenancy is to be a PST. The court may however waive this requirement where it is just and equitable to make an order for possession in the circumstances (see Appendices).

e.   There can be no PST unless the landlord complies with the **registration of rent requirements** in that a rent is already registered for the dwelling house, or a certificate of fair rent has been issued, or an application for the registration of a rent is made not later than 28 days after the beginning of the term. These requirements are subject to an overriding power of the Secretary of State or the court to dispense with them if it is just and equitable in the circumstances.

f.   There can be no PST if it is granted to a person who immediately before it was granted was a protected or statutory tenant of the dwelling house.

These then are the basic formalities for the creation of a PST but mention should also be made of the fact that provision can be made in the grant of a PST for the tenant to remain in possession after its expiration without prejudicing the landlord's ultimate right to possession. Also the tenant has an express right of termination by one month's notice for tenancies of less than two years, and three months' notice for tenancies of between two and five years.

12.4 Rent Control of Protected Tenancies

Central to the scheme of rent registration for protected tenancies are **rent officers** who are appointed with responsibility for registration areas, and **rent assessment committees** which have appeal powers. Rent officers are appointed by the local authority under a scheme agreed in consultation with the Secretary of State. Their principal duty is to prepare and keep up to date a rent register for the area. In administering the rent registration system however, rent officers have a large degree of discretion and independence. In addition each registration area has rent assessment committees drawn up by the Secretary of State and comprising of lawyers, one of whom is usually chairman, and also non lawyers. A typical rent assessment committee would consist of a lawyer as chairman with two other members, one of whom would usually be a surveyor. Remuneration and allowances are payable to committee members directly by central government.

It should be noted that while registered housing associations do not grant protected tenancies, they have nevertheless been brought into rent regulation. Housing associations as landlords and their tenants now have a common rent registration procedure and incidently, a common rent phasing procedure with private landlords, the rules relating to which are contained in **s.61 Housing Act 1980.**

Fair Rent Application

The application procedure for registration of a rent for a dwelling house let under a protected regulated tenancy is as follows:-

a. Application may be made to a rent officer by the landlord, tenant, jointly by both, or by a local authority. A local authority will usually apply where it has been asked to pay a **rent allowance** and believes that the rent payable exceeds a **fair rent.**

b. The application must be in the prescribed form containing prescribed particulars and stipulating a specified rent which the applicant seeks to have registered.

c. Following receipt of the application the rent officer may serve notice on the landlord or tenant requesting information within a period of not less than seven days. Otherwise the rent officer must notify the other party of the application, and give him an opportunity to make representations.

d. If there is a joint application and the rent specified in the application is a fair rent, then the rent officer may register the rent specified without further proceedings (i.e. no reference to a rent assessment committee).

e. If the rent officer is not satisfied that the specified rent is a fair rent he must notify the parties of his intention to consider in consultation with them, what rent ought to be registered.

f. In determining what constitutes a fair rent in such circumstances, the rent officer should bear in mind the registered rents of comparable dwelling houses.

g. Having decided that a rent different from that specified ought to be registered, the rent officer must either determine a fair rent and register it, or confirm the rent which has been registered for the time being and in both cases notify the parties.

h. The notice of the rent officer's decision must confer a right to object to it within 28 days and, if so received, the rent officer must refer the matter to a rent assessment committee. If objection is received after the 28 day period, or a period which the rent assessment committee directs, the rent officer has a discretion whether to refer it.

i. The rent assessment committee in dealing with a matter referred to it may serve notice on the parties requiring further information within a period of not less than 14 days. It must serve notice on the parties giving at least 14 days to enable them to make representations which may be heard in person at a hearing.

j.   If a hearing is held, it is normal practice to give both parties an opportunity to be heard, the committee deciding its own procedure which is informal, but in public.

k.   Having considered all the information and in most cases inspecting the property the rent assessment committee may confirm the registered rent, or determine a different fair rent giving reasons for its decision, and informing the parties.

Where there is already a registered rent the general rule is that neither party nor their successors may apply for a different rent to be registered for three years from the relevant date (the date of application), except on the ground that there have been changes in relation to:-

i.   the condition of the dwelling house;

ii.   the terms of the tenancy;

iii.   the quantity or quality of furniture provided;

iv.   any other relevant circumstances.

This rule does not prevent a joint application by the parties, or an application made during the last three months of a three-year-period.

There is also machinery whereby a prospective landlord can apply to the rent officer for a **certificate of fair rent** specifying what would be a fair rent if the property was let on a regulated tenancy. The procedure for such an application is similar to that for registration of a fair rent. Applications for such a certificate are useful where the landlord has made improvements or intends to make improvements. Having obtained a certificate this can be used to support an application to have a fair rent registered.

Fair Rent

To determine what will constitute a fair rent under a regulated tenancy of a dwelling house under **s.70** it is necessary to have regard to all the circumstances (other than personal ones of both the landlord and tenant) and in particular to:-

1.   the age, character, locality and state of repair of the dwelling house;

2.   if any furniture is provided for use under the tenancy, the quantity quality and condition of the furniture.

Generally then, it is left to the discretion of the rent officer and rent assessment committee to decide their method of ascertaining a fair rent, provided it is not unlawful. It has already been mentioned that the registered rents for comparable properties may provide some guide. The idea is to assess a rent which is not only fair to the tenant but also to the landlord as well. If services are provided by the landlord then a fair rent may include them. However it should be noted that high market demand for the type of accommodation provided is to be ignored and it is to be presumed that whatever the reality of the situation demand for the accommodation does not exceed supply.

Other matters to be disregarded include:-

—   the tenant's voluntary improvements;

—   defects due to tenant's failure to repair or comply with a covenant to put the premises into repair;

—   the provision or improvement of any amenity or deterioration of any amenity in the locality;

—   any improvement to, or deterioration in, furniture provided due to the action of the tenant.

The registered rent is to be an inclusive one of rates and taxes, and the date from which it takes effect is entered in the rent register. Sums which are paid by the tenant in excess of the registered rent are of course recoverable.

Premiums

In order to complete an examination of rent protection under the Rent Acts, mention should be made of the provisions designed to prevent the most obvious way of avoiding rent control. That is by letting property at or below the registered rent, but demanding in addition a **lump sum as a premium for making the grant.** The **Rent Act 1977 s.119** is quite explicit in relation to such payments and states that it is a **criminal offence** to require a premium or the making of a loan as a condition of the granting, continuance or renewal of a protected tenancy. It is also an offence to receive such a payment, which may be ordered to be repaid on conviction. The payment need not be made to the landlord but could be made to his agent or even the outgoing tenant as in *Farrell v. Alexander 1977.* Also if the parties attempted to disguise the payment by charging an excessive price for furniture this would also constitute a premium and therefore an unlawful payment.

12.5 Partial Protection

Restricted Contracts

Originally the Rent Protection legislation conferred only a limited protection on furnished accommodation, that is until 1974 when most furnished tenancies were converted into fully protected regulated tenancies. This left a group of tenancies/licences receiving limited **Rent Tribunal protection** known as 'restricted contracts'. By far the major category of restricted contracts covers tenancies where there is a **resident landlord.** To determine the rights of a holder of a restricted contract it is crucial to determine the date it was entered into. This is because the **1980 Housing Act** substantially amends the rights of the parties to a restricted contract entered into after the Act's commencement.

Definition A restricted contract is "a contract whereby one person grants to another person, in consideration of a rent which includes payment of or the use of furniture or services, the right to occupy a dwelling as a residence". The expression 'right to occupy' clearly envisages a restricted contract amounting to a tenancy or a licence provided there is monetary payment. Also the major criterion for a valid claim to a restricted contract is the need to show **exclusive occupation** of at least part of the accommodation, i.e. a person is entitled to occupy a room himself and no one else is entitled to occupy it. Tenancies which are automatically excluded from restricted contract status include those which exceed the rateable value limits (similar to protected tenancies), holiday lettings, contracts where a substantial part of the payment is for board and attendance, and contracts where the lessor is the Crown, a housing association, housing trust or the Housing Corporation. The two principal types of restricted contracts are:-

a. tenancies of a house or flat where there is a resident landlord. This is despite the fact there is no payment for furniture or services; and

b. tenancies with attendance, furniture or services.

Services are defined to include attendance, heating, lighting, or the supply of hot water. Tenancies with attendances and licences with furniture or services are a significant group of restricted contracts. Only those licences which grant exclusive occupation however, may be restricted.

Statutory Rights

Rent Control Either party to a restricted contract or the local authority can refer the contract to a rent tribunal. Under **s.72 Housing Act 1980** rent tribunals were abolished and their functions transferred to rent assessment committees. However, when carrying out a rent tribunal function, e.g. examining a restricted contract, the rent assessment committee is referred to as the rent tribunal. The duties of a tribunal in relation to such a reference are to give the parties the opportunity of making representations, make inquiries involving an inspection of the property, and then approve the rent, reduce or increase it, or dismiss the application. The tribunal, after inspecting the premises/furniture/services supplied, must determine what amounts to a **'reasonable'** rent as opposed to registered rent for protected tenancies which has to be **'fair'**. Certainly the fact that restricted contracts are usually short life is a major criterion to justify a rent which would constitute the market rent for the property. If a rent is registered for the restricted contract, it becomes the rent payable between the parties and their successors and cannot be reconsidered by the rent tribunal for two years, **s.70 Housing Act 1980.**

Security of Tenure Tenants of restricted contracts have no security of tenure but rather there are certain restraints on the lessor's right to recover possession. These restraints are significantly reduced for restricted contracts entered into after the commencement of **s.69 Housing Act 1980.** For **pre s.69** contracts, a limited security of tenure is provided by **ss.103-106 Rent Act 1977.** Generally under these provisions a notice to quit a restricted contract which is a periodic tenancy may be suspended by a Rent Tribunal. The period of suspension can be six months and if justified in the circumstances, the tribunal can renew the suspension period for further periods. Now following **s.69 Housing Act 1980,** for restricted contracts entered into after 28.11.80 this limited security of tenure under the **Rent Act 1977** no longer applies. A landlord in such circumstances can respond to a reference by a tenant to a rent tribunal for registration of a reasonable rent, by service of a notice to quit which will be fully effective. If the landlord brings proceedings for possession (after the minimum four weeks' notice under the **s.4 Protection from Eviction Act 1977** has been se. ed), the court will normally grant it and has only a limited power to stay or suspend or postpone its execution in cases of **exceptional hardship.** The period of postponement cannot exceed three months from the date of the order for possession.

12.6 Agricultural Tied Tenancies

The provision of accommodation tied to employment is a common feature of many types of employment of which the agricultural industry is one. The reasons for this are twofold. Firstly, the fact that residential accommodation is available on a large number of agricultural estates and secondly, the nature of agricultural employment, which is often in isolated regions. In this section it is proposed to examine the provisions relating to agricultural tied tenancies contained in the **Rent (Agriculture) Act 1976.** This Act goes some way to provide the agricultural tenant with the same protection in relation to security of tenure as enjoyed by the protected regulated tenant under the **Rent Act 1977.**

Protected Occupiers

To qualify as a protected occupier under the 1976 Act the agricultural tenant must be a **'qualifying worker'.** This is an **individual who has worked not fewer than 91 out of the last 104 weeks whole time (35 hours per week) in agriculture or forestry.** In addition such a person must have been granted a contractual tenancy or licence covered by the Act. The 1976 Act operates in the same way as the Rent Act so that on expiration of the contractual tenancy the protected occupier becomes a **statutory tenant** for as long as he occupies the dwelling house as his residence. Tenants who share accommodation with the landlord are not covered by the Act and are limited to the claim of a **restricted contract** under the Rent Act.

Statutory Tenancy

The contractual tenancy or licence of a protected occupier may come to an end in a number of alternative ways including:-

- the occupier's death;

- voluntary termination by the occupier;

- service of notice to quit by the landlord;

- service of a notice of increase of rent by the landlord;

- service of notice of the termination of employment by the landlord.

On its termination a statutory tenancy comes into being, the terms of which are contained in **Schedule 5** of the Act, and implied by the common law. No account is to be taken of terms in the original contract which depended upon employment in agriculture. As far as rent is concerned the difficulty is that in most cases rent would not have been payable under the original contractual tenancy. There must be an express agreement as to the rent payable, in default of which the landlord must serve a notice requiring payment of rent which must not exceed one and a half times the rateable value. A **registered rent** may then be applied for as soon as the statutory tenancy comes into being. As one of the main aims of the 1976 Act is to also provide security for the tenant's family residing with him when his employment ceased, or when he died, provision is made for statutory succession similar to the Rent Act. A resident spouse is given priority, but members of the tenant's family living with him for six months before his death may also succeed to the tenancy. Under the **Rent (Agriculture) Act 1976** however only one statutory succession is provided for.

Possession A landlord may obtain an order for possession of property let to a protected occupier by proving one of the grounds contained in the 1976 Act. These grounds are essentially the same as those contained in the **Rent Act 1977** and some are mandatory and some are discretionary. The mandatory grounds are Cases XI and XII relating to owner occupation and retirement homes and the discretionary grounds, Cases I to X, are essentially the same as in the **Rent Act 1977**. Possession will often be sought because the landlord requires the dwelling house for a replacement employee and in such circumstances it will be granted if the landlord can, under Case I, provide the tenant with suitable alternative accommodation. If this is not available the landlord can turn to the local authority for assistance. Under the Act the local authority in such circumstances, and **in the interests of efficient agriculture,** can be compelled to use their **best**

endeavours to provide suitable alternative accommodation for the displaced tenant. The landlord must apply in writing to the local authority who can obtain advice from the **Agriculture Dwelling House Advisory Committee** on whether the application is justified in the interests of efficient agriculture. A decision by the local authority must be made within three months. It should be stressed that there is no statutory duty on a local authority to provide suitable alternative accommodation in these circumstances, but rather to use their best endeavours to do so, taking into account competing claims on accommodation.

Finally it should be mentioned that those employees having exclusive occupation of dwellings under the terms of their employment who do not qualify under the 1976 Act have a limited amount of protection under the **Protection from Eviction Act 1977 s.4.** Where there is occupation by a former tenant or his surviving spouse or family, the court has power to suspend the execution of an order for possession on such terms as it thinks are reasonable depending on all the circumstances.

12.7 Long Leases

The major statutory rights of a long leasholder are contained in the **Landlord and Tenant Act 1954 Part I** and the **Leasehold Reform Act 1967.**

The Landlord and Tenant Act 1954 Part I
This Act confers protection on the holders of tenancies for a **term exceeding 21 years (long tenancies).** As the present Rent Act legislation may confer protected status on tenancies of any term the importance of the 1954 Act is now limited to long tenancies which do not qualify for Rent Act protection because they are **let at a low rent** (i.e. less than two-thirds of the rateable value of the property). In determining the amount of rent payable such part of the rent that is expressed to be payable in respect of rates, services, repairs, maintenance or insurance is to be disregarded.

Protection A tenant who qualifies for protection under the 1954 Act may remain in possession on the expiration of the fixed term and his tenancy is automatically continued. Otherwise the tenant can determine the tenancy by serving one month's notice in the prescribed form. If the landlord wishes to determine the tenancy however he must also serve notice not earlier than 6 and not later than 12 months from the contactual date for termination. This notice will give the tenant 2 months to inform the landlord whether he intends to give up possession voluntarily. If no such

229

notice is given and the tenant is not in residence on the termination date, the tenancy will automatically determine. Otherwise the contractual tenancy will determine but be replaced by a statutory tenancy under the **Rent Act 1977.** The terms of the statutory tenancy may be agreed between the parties and, in default of agreement, by the County Court. A landlord who has resolved to obtain possession must inform the tenant of this fact by notice and stipulate the ground for possession he intends to rely on. The grounds could be any of Cases I to IX under the **Rent Act 1977** or the ground that the landlord intends to demolish or reconstruct the premises for the purposes of redevelopment. Then an application to the court for an order for possession by the landlord must be made within four months of the service of the notice or two months of the tenant's election to remain in possession. If the court refuses to grant possession then the contractual tenancy will continue.

The Leasehold Reform Act 1967

The rights of the long leaseholder were greatly extended by the passing of the **Leasehold Reform Act 1967** which was designed to confer on the residential tenant of a leasehold house a right to **acquire on fair terms the freehold or an extended lease of the house.** Notice that the provisions of the Act relate to houses rather than to flats. Also the value of the landlord's freehold reversion is **restricted** and generally taken to be the capitalised value of the right to receive the ground rent of the site of the property. The Act applies to long leases at a low rent which are referred to as 'tenancies granted for a term of years certain with at least 21 years left to run and at a rent not exceeding two-thirds of the rateable value'. Also the qualifying tenant has to occupy the house as his only or main residence, and show that he has occupied it as his residence for the **last three years** or for periods amounting to **three years in the last ten years.**

The Act confers two distinct statutory rights on a qualifying tenant:-

1.   to request **enfranchisement,** i.e. acquire the freehold reversion; or

2.   to request an **extended 50 year term** of the existing lease.

The most popular option is to acquire the freehold and extended terms are requested only infrequently. A tenant who does obtain an extended term automatically loses his right to acquire the freehold and also obtain any further extension. Disputes relating to the exercise of these complex rights under the Act may be referred to the County Court for settlement.

CHAPTER 13   Public Sector Protection (The Housing Act 1980)

In this chapter it is proposed to examine some of the main statutory rights and duties relating to the provision of housing in the public sector and also the provision of housing by public bodies. Certainly the number of council tenancies far exceeds tenancies in the private sector and, in recent years mainly as a result of the **Housing Act 1980,** the legal position of the council tenant has changed dramatically. The general belief that public bodies have an important role to play in the provision of residential accommodation only became accepted at the turn of the century.

After the First World War legislation was introduced conferring wide powers and imposing onerous duties on local authorities in relation to the provision of public housing. This legislation clearly demonstrated the important position that local authorities were assigned in the provision of public housing and additional powers in relation to slum clearance and overcrowding were conferred on them in the 1930's. The **Housing Act 1957** (as amended) contains the present powers and duties of housing authorities.

13.1 Housing Authorities

Outside the Greater London Council, under **s.1 Housing Act 1957** the principal housing authorities are the **district councils.** The role of county councils in the provision of housing is only a minor one and they may only undertake the provision of housing on behalf of districts within their area following a request from a district council, and also approval of the Secretary of State. The position in London is that the **Common Council** is the housing authority for the City of London while elsewhere in the metropolis the responsibility for housing is divided between the London boroughs and the Greater London Council. By virtue of **s.21 London Government Act 1963** the individual London boroughs are the principal housing authorities within their areas. Generally the GLC, while a housing authority in its own right, may not provide housing accommodation in a London borough except with the consent of that borough.

The Provision of Housing Accommodation

The duty to provide housing and the ancillary powers necessary to fulfil this duty are contained in **Part V Housing Act 1957. Section 91** provides that it shall be the duty of every local housing authority to consider the housing conditions in, and the needs of, their district with respect to the provision of further housing accommodation. This may be achieved in several ways under **ss. 92 and 96,** e.g. by acquiring houses, by erecting houses on land which the authority owns, by conversions and by altering, enlarging, repairing or improving housing or buildings acquired by the authority. Wide powers to acquire land and property by agreement or compulsorily are conferred on housing authorities by virtue of **s.97.** In addition, with the consent of the Secretary of State, an authority may under **s.93** provide shops, recreation grounds and other amenities to service its housing estates, and also under **ss.94 and 95** sell furniture for cash or on hire purchase to council tenants and provide facilities for laundering clothes and obtaining meals and refreshments. The **Housing Act 1980 s.93** empowers an authority to purchase land for the purposes of building for sale, or for selling land to persons who will build on it.

It must be stressed that housing authorities do not work in isolation in attempting to meet local housing needs. A brief mention should also be made of the **development of new towns.** The present legislation is contained in the **New Towns Act 1965.** This Act confers power on the Minister under **s.1** to, by order, designate an area as the site of a proposed new town. This may be done after full consultation with any local authorities concerned. Once the site has been designated, its development is undertaken by a **development corporation** established by order made under **s.2** of the 1965 Act. Development corporations have of course wide powers to acquire land and undertake building work.

The achievements of **Housing Associations** and **Housing Societies** in relation to the provision of housing accommodation are clearly demonstrated by their statutory recognition since the early 1960's. Such bodies are **voluntary organisations** primarily concerned with providing well managed and maintained accommodation, let at a non profit rent for people encountering housing difficulties. Because of their importance in fulfilling specialist housing needs it is proposed to consider the position of Housing Associations in a separate section in the chapter.

The Allocation of Housing

A general discretion is conferred on housing authoritites in relation to the allocation of housing stock. Preference should be given however under **s.113 Housing Act 1957** to those individuals who occupy insanitary or overcrowded accommodation, have large families, or who generally occupy property which is in an unsatisfactory condition. A further group to whom priority should be given are those persons to whom the authority owes a duty under the **Housing (Homeless Persons) Act 1977.** Where the selection rules and procedures of an authority prove to be rigid to house families in need, then such cases are often referred to local housing associations which will have more flexible rules in relation to priority. Local housing associations will usually adopt a tolerant approach to meeting the needs of individuals having housing difficulties even where they have bad housing records. The **Housing Act 1980 s.44** imposes a duty on housing authorities to maintain a set of rules regarding allocation priorities, transfer and exchange procedures and to publish a summary of these rules making them available for inspection. An applicant on the waiting list is thereby entitled to check on the accuracy of the information that the landlord has recorded about him. Also registered housing associations and housing trusts which grant secure tenancies must publish a written statement of their policies on tenant selection,allocation and transfer. Copies of this information must be made available for public inspection.

13.2 Housing Associations/Societies

To understand the various ways that voluntary housing bodies may be organised and acquire rights and legal status, it is necessary to initially examine their complex definition under the **Housing Acts 1957** and **1964.** Housing associations are defined under the **Housing Act 1957 s.189(1)** as 'a society, body of trustees or company established for the purpose of or amongst whose objects or powers are included, those of constructing, improving, managing or facilitating or encouraging the construction or improvement of houses or hostels, being a society, body of trustees or company who do not trade for profit or whose constitution or rules prohibit the issue of any capital with interest or dividend exceeding the rate for the time being prescribed by the Treasury, whether with or without differentiation as between shares and loan capital.' The definition provides therefore that housing associations may be organised in three ways, **'societies', 'body of trustees',** and **'companies'.**

a. The term **'housing society'** now refers to bodies operating under the **Housing Act 1964** and receiving advice and support from the **Housing Corporation.** They are the traditional voluntary housing bodies providing rented accommodation in the 'general family' field working in support of local authorities. Housing Societies normally adopt the standard rules provided by the **National Federation of Housing Associations** and acquire legal status by registering with the Registrar of Friendly Societies under the **Industrial and Provident Societies Act 1965.**

b. The term **'body of trustees'** refers to those bodies which operate as **charitable trusts** and include some of the earliest voluntary housing organisations. They are normally registered directly with the Charity Commissioners who are responsible for supervising their activities. To constitute a charity under the **Charities Act 1960** such bodies must pursue one of the 'four activities' recognised under the law as charitable. The provision of housing comes within the general activity of the 'relief of poverty'. Charitable housing associations will normally therefore have as their main object the provision of housing for persons in **'necessitous circumstances upon terms appropriate to their needs'.** Today the financial advantages of charitable status, which include tax exemption and the right to receive donations, are no longer as significant, particularly as non charitable housing associations may now obtain relief from taxation.

c. The term **'company'** refers to the small number of housing associations registered as companies under the **Companies Acts 1948, 1967 and 1980.** They may be recognised as voluntary housing bodies provided their objects conform with the definition in **s.189 Housing Act 1957.**

As well as being organised in different ways housing associations may also have different purposes and may be further categorised as 'general family', 'industrial', 'self build' and 'special need'.

'General family' are those bodies already referred to acting as a support to local housing authorities by providing rented accommodation in the general family field. The two main types are **cost rent** and **co-ownership societies.** A cost rent society is simply one that builds or provides houses to persons at cost without profits to the society or subsidy to the tenant. Unfortunately therefore, as maintenance costs increase, so must the rents to keep pace. A co-ownership society is one which provides houses or flats to be occupied exclusively by their members, who also jointly own the dwellings they occupy individually. The members are like **tenants** in that they make payments to the association under a tenancy agreement, and do not own the dwellings they occupy individually. On the other hand, they are similar to **owners** in that by making payments, they are acquiring an interest in the freehold of the property held by the society. The members right of occupation is tied to their rights as **corporate owners of the property**.

Industrial associations are those bodies set up in connection with industrial firms, commercial organisations or public corporations. They are concerned primarily with providing accommodation for their own employees, e.g. Coal Industry Housing Association, British Airways Staff Housing Society Ltd.

Self build associations are transitory bodies, the members of which have combined to build houses for themselves. The idea is that by providing the labour, the overall capital costs are necessarily reduced, and once the houses have been completed the association is usually dissolved.

Special needs associations are those bodies set up to give priority to housing particular groups, e.g. retired, disabled, ex-prisoners, ex-mental patients.

The above bodies have a number of alternative sources of finance including rents, charitable funds, tax subsidies and loans from central and local government. In addition special needs associations may be financially assisted by bodies other than local housing authorities. Associations also have access to grants for improvements or conversions either as **private owners** or if they work under **approved arrangements** with local authorities they may have direct access to government funds.

The Role of the Housing Corporation

Part I of the Housing Act 1964 provided for the setting up of the **Housing Corporation** with the general aim of promoting and assisting the development of housing societies providing unsubsidised cost rent and co-ownership housing, with power to make loans to them and acquire land on their behalf. The corporation is in turn financed by central government and to a large extent by the building societies. The **Housing Act 1974** greatly extended the corporation's powers to enable it to assist housing assocations providing subsidised rented accommodation for those in greatest need. Under **s.13,** the housing corporation may establish a **register of housing associations** with the aim of allowing a degree of control over them with reference to accountancy, auditing and management matters. In return registered associations enjoy certain privileges with regard to access to government funds and exclusion from certain provisions of the **Rent Act 1977.** Under **s.13** of the 1974 Act, the housing corporation may register any housing association which:

a.   is a registered charity and not exempt from registration as such under the **Charities Act 1960;** or

b.   is a society registered under the **Industrial and Provident Societies Act 1965.**

The association must also fulfil the following conditions:

i.   it does not trade for a profit;

ii   it is established for the purpose, or has among its objects or powers those of providing, constructing, improving or managing houses, to be kept available for letting; or houses for occupation by members of the association, provided the rules of the association restrict membership to persons entitled or prospectively entitled to occupy association houses or hostels.

Both housing associations and housing societies may register therefore, and **nearly all cost rent and co-ownership societies are registered.**

Subject to the consent of the Housing Corporation under **s.2 Housing Act 1974** all housing associations are given the power under **ss.122 and 123 Housing Act 1980** to dispose of land owned by them in whatever manner they think fit. This includes registered associations which are charitable trusts, who previously were required to obtain the consent of the Charity Commissioner or a court order before making a disposal. There is no longer an obligation under **s.39 Settled Land Act 1939** to obtain the best consideration reasonably obtainable. The power of associations to grant leases up to seven years without the consent of the housing corporation, has however been modified, and now associations may only grant 'periodic tenancies' without obtaining the corporation's consent.

13.3 The Creation of a Council Tenancy

In this section except where otherwise stated any reference to legislative provisions will be to the **Housing Act 1980.** Council tenancies are created usually by the parties signing a standard form tenancy agreement (see appendices), the terms of which are sometimes inserted in the rent book. There is now a statutory obligation to supply each **'secure tenant'** with a written statement of the terms of his tenancy. If the tenancy is a 'secure tenancy', **s.41** requires the local authority to supply the tenant with, and also publish, certain information relating to security of tenure, the right to buy, repair provisions and improvement provisions contained in the 1980 Act. The tenant's obligations in the agreement will usually include the following undertakings:

i.   to pay a reasonable rent weekly in advance;
ii.   not to sub-let or part with possession of the property without written consent;
iii. not to use for business, illegal or immoral purposes;
iv.   not to make alterations or improvements to the property without consent;
v.   to provide an opportunity for council employees to carry out repair and maintenance work.

Few tenancy agreements make express reference to the obligations of the local authority landlord. Such obligations that are imposed on the council landlord are implied by the common law and statute and include the following implied undertakings: quiet enjoyment; non derogation from the grant; fitness on the commencement of a furnished tenancy; repair of the structure and exterior; keeping common parts reasonably safe; not to commit a statutory nuisance (for repair obligations see Chapter 10)

13.4 Security of Tenure

After a long period of debate the government decided to confer rights on council tenants in relation to security of tenure which are contained in **Part I Chapter II** of the 1980 Act. A secure tenancy is one where the following conditions are satisfied:

a.   there must be a letting of a separate dwelling with no sharing of accommodation;

b.   the landlord must be a local housing authority, e.g. a district council, a London Borough Council, the GLC or the Commission for New Towns, a development corporation, a county council acting under its reserve power under **s.149 Local Government Act 1972,** the Development Board for Rural Wales, the Housing Corporation and registered Housing Associations;

c.   the tenant must be an individual or several individuals as joint tenants, at least one of whom occupies the dwelling as a principal or only house;

d.   the tenancy must not be listed in **Schedule 3** as exempt, e.g.

    1.   long tenancies for a term exceeding 21 years;

    2.   if the tenant is an employee of the landlord (or another local authority, development corporation, Commission for New Towns, county council or Development Board for Rural Wales) and he is required to occupy the property as part of his employment;

    3.   where the house is on land being used for development and is being used as temporary housing accommodation;

    4.   where the tenancy or licence was granted temporarily pursuant to the **Housing (Homeless Persons) Act 1977** it cannot be the subject of a secure tenancy until twelve months expire;

    5.   where accommodation is granted by a district council or London Borough Council to a person who prior to the grant was not resident in the area, and having employment within

the area, requires temporary accommodation. Here the tenant has no right to security for the first twelve months following the grant;

6. where the tenancy consists of or includes premises with a licence;

7. where the tenancy is one to which the **Landlord and Tenant Act 1954 Part II** applies, i.e. a business tenancy;

8. where the tenancy has been granted to a student specifically to enable him to attend a designated course at a university or further education establishment;

9. where the tenancy is granted as temporary accommodation for occupation by a tenant while works are carried out to his former home in which he is not a secure tenant;

10. where the tenancy is an agricultural holding under the **Agricultural Holdings Act 1948** and the tenant is a manager;

11. where the local authority has acquired a short term lease from a body incapable of granting secure tenancies (e.g. an individual), for the purpose of providing temporary accommodation and under the terms of the letting the landlord may recover possession from the council either on the expiration of a specified period or whenever he requires it back. If these conditions are fulfilled any sub-letting by the council will not be a secure tenancy.

Having satisfied the above conditions a., b., c., and d., a tenancy is then a secure one whether granted before or after the commencement of the 1980 Act. This means that under **s.29** when a secure tenancy comes to an end, a periodic tenancy arises automatically unless the tenant is granted another secure tenancy of the dwelling.

Provision is also made for statutory succession under **ss.30 and 31** in relation to secure periodic tenancies where the tenant has died. In such circumstances the tenancy will vest in his spouse or member of the tenant's family residing with him for **twelve months** prior to his death. The term **'family'** is given the same meaning as it received under the **Rent Act 1977.** In the event of more than one person being qualified to

239

succeed, then the spouse is to be preferred, or if there is no spouse it should be settled by agreement between those qualified. Where there is failure to reach agreement **the final decision rests with the local authority.**

The totality of rights under **ss.32-34** conferred on secure tenants of local authorities, new towns and housing associations are referred to as the **tenants' charter.** Tenants of registered housing associations are secure tenants to whom the tenants' charter is applicable, whereas tenants of unregistered housing associations, with the exception of co-ownership or mutual co-operatives, are not secure tenants. Those co-ownership and co-operative societies which are registered with the Housing Corporation are excluded from the tenants' charter provisions. However tenants of a co-ownership or mutual co-operative society which is not registered with the Housing Corporation have security of tenure with the right of succession. It should be stressed that such tenants have none of the other rights of secure tenants and thus would not have the right to buy. This is the only example of a tenant of an unregistered housing association becoming a secure tenant although having limited rights.

To determine a secure tenancy the landlord must first serve **notice** on the tenant in the prescribed form stating that possession is demanded, and also specifying the ground to be relied on in court. These grounds contained in **Schedule 4 Part I** are very similar to those applicable under the **Rent Act 1977** and so they will be considered in outline only. In addition there are two overriding conditions. Firstly, that it is reasonable to make the order for possession and secondly, that there is suitable alternative accommodation available. These two overriding conditions are the same as those applicable under the Rent Act and considered earlier in Chapter 12.

Grounds for Possession

Relying on the following grounds the landlord must prove to the court that it is **reasonable** to order possession in the circumstances. The individual grounds are that the tenant (or those for whom he is responsible) has been guilty of:

1. non payment of rent or breach of other obligation;

2. nuisance or immoral or illegal user;

3. neglect, default or acts of waste;

4. ill treatment of any furniture;

5. making of a false statement knowingly or recklessly which induced the council to grant the tenancy;

6. refusing to move out of the dwelling for which possession is sought and back into another dwelling of which he is a secure tenant. This other dwelling is the tenant's home and works were being carried out on it and are now completed.

Relying on the following grounds the landlord must prove to the court that he has made an offer of suitable alternative accommodation. The individual grounds are that:

7. the dwelling house is illegally overcrowded;

8. the landlord intends to carry out demolition and/or reconstruction works on the dwelling for which he requires possession.

Relying on the following grounds the landlord must prove to the court that it is reasonable to order possession in the circumstances and also that an offer of suitable alternative accommodation has been made. The individual grounds are that:

10. the accommodation has special features making it suitable for occupation by a physically disabled person;

12. the accommodation is part of a group which it is the practice of the landlord to let to persons with special needs and also:

   a. a social service or special facility is provided in close proximity to assist with those needs; and

   b. there is no longer a person with those needs residing in the house; and

   c. the landlord requires the house for someone with those needs.

13. the accommodation is more extensive than is reasonably required by the present tenant to whom the tenancy was statutorily transmitted on the death of the former tenant, provided the successor tenant is not the spouse of the deceased tenant. For this ground, notice of intention to begin proceedings must be served more than six months but less than twelve months after the death of the original tenant.

The other grounds not referred to relate to housing charities, ground 9, and housing associations and trusts, ground 11.

Finally it should be stressed that the provisions in relation to security of tenure apply only to public sector tenants who occupy dwellings **'let as a secure tenancy'**.

In the recent case of *Harrison v. Hammersmith and Fulham London Borough Council 1981,* the Court of Appeal was called on to determine whether the provisions of the 1980 Act applied to a contractual tenancy which had expired before the commencement date of the Act with the tenant remaining in possession. The Court held that because the premises were not let under a secure tenancy the 1980 Act did not apply, and the words **'previously let as'** could not be added simply to confer protection on the tenant.

Mention should also be made that under **s.87** the court has wide powers to adjourn proceedings for possession of a dwelling house let on a secure tenancy, and also postpone the date of possession or stay or suspend the execution of the possession order. Of course once the court orders that possession must be given up on one of the statutory grounds, then the secure tenancy will come to an end. It will also automatically terminate:

a. if the tenant exercises his right to buy the freehold of the house or a long lease of his flat is vested in him; or

b. if the secure tenancy is a fixed term which has expired, and no new secure tenancy is granted, then a periodic tenancy arises automatically but it will not be secure; or

c. if the tenant sub-lets the whole of the property (even with consent) or part of it where the remainder is sub-let, it ceases to be secure; or

d.   if the tenant assigns the tenancy it ceases to be secure.

It is possible therefore for a secure tenant to forfeit his security without necessarily losing the tenancy. Thus, if a secure tenant sub-lets the whole of the premises, whether or not this is prohibited by the tenancy agreement, the sub-tenancy may be terminated by notice to quit with the sub-tenant acquiring no security. Similarly, if a secure tenant assigns the tenancy then it ceases to be secure unless the person to whom it is assigned might have succeeded to the tenancy under **s.30** or, unless the assignment is under an order in the couse of matrimonial dealings by virtue of **s.24 Matrimonial Causes Act 1973.**

The terms of a secure tenancy may be **varied** but only in accordance with **s.40** of the Act. This provides for variation by **mutual agreement,** by the landlord unilaterally relying on an **express variation clause** in respect of changes in rent, rates or services, and also by the landlord alone by way of service of **a notice of variation** on the tenant. If variation is proposed by the service of notice it is necessary for the landlord to have informed the tenants individually in advance, and given them the opportunity of consultation, unless the variation relates solely to rent.

13.5 Further Rights of Secure Tenants

a.   **Consultation in relation to Housing Management**

Prior to the passage of the **Housing Act 1980** some local authorities had gone as far as to put into practice the idea that council tenants should have a much greater say in housing management by setting up **Joint Estate Management Committees** to transfer some power to tenants. The 1980 Act clearly envisages consultation between the housing authority and its tenants in matters relating to housing management. Under **s.41,** it is a requirement that within two years of the Act's commencement the landlord must publish up to date information about its secure tenancies explaining in full the rights of secure tenants and supplying each tenant with a copy(see appendices). In addition under **ss.42 and 43,** public sector landlords, including housing associations and trusts granting secure tenancies, have a duty to consult their tenants on certain matters of housing management. These matters would include a new housing programme, a change

243

in policy of housing management, maintenance, improvement, development or the provision of services or amenities. Arrangements must be made to make the tenants aware of changes which substantially affect them, and also enable the tenants to inform the landlord of their views before any action is taken. The statutory duty of consultation is enforceable by an order of mandamus.

b. **Sub-letting and lodgers**

In every secure tenancy there is an implied term by virtue of **s.35(1)** that the tenant has the right to allow persons to reside or lodge in his dwelling. In relation to sub-letting however, **s.35(2)** states that the landlord's written consent is necessary but it is not to be unreasonably withheld. Disputes relating to sub-letting may be referred to the County Court. As a general rule a secure tenancy cannot be assigned and neither can a secure tenant part with possession or sub-let the whole of the dwelling without the tenancy ceasing to be secure.

c. **Improvements**

In every secure tenancy there is an implied term under **s.81** that a tenant may make improvements but only with the landlord's written consent. Such consent however is not to be unreasonably withheld. Improvement means any alteration or additions to the dwelling, the landlord's fixtures and fittings, or the services or the carrying out of external decoration. Disputes may be referred to the County Court which will consider the effect of the improvement on the safety and value of the dwelling and also whether it would be likely to involve the landlord in expenditure. For improvements made after the Act's commencement which have added to the market value of the dwelling, the landlord has a discretion to make a payment at the end of the tenancy. Certainly there could be no increase in rent as a result of the tenants improvement.

d. **The Right to Buy**

The most publicised right of a council tenant under the 1980 Act is the right to acquire the freehold of his dwelling where it is a house, or a long lease where it is a flat. The right arises **s.1** when the tenant has been a secure tenant for three years provided that the council is the freehold owner when the right is exercised. A dwelling is a house under the Act if it...... 'is a structure reasonably so called.' Thus, if a building is divided vertically, each unit may be a house, whereas if it is divided horizontally the units will be flats. The right of a qualifying tenant of a flat is to the grant of a long lease of not less than 125 years at a rent not exceeding £10 per annum.

Qualifying Tenants As previously mentioned qualifying tenants require three years residence however it need not be continuous residence, and separate periods of residence may be accumulated. Also a tenant who succeeds to a secure tenancy on the death of his or her spouse at a time when they occupied the dwelling as their principal home, can include the deceased spouse's residence period. If a tenant succeeds to a secure tenancy from his parent, at the discretion of the council a period during which he occupied the dwelling with his parent as a secure tenant may also be counted. Periods of residence as a secure tenant do not have to be with the same landlord and can be as a secure tenant of different housing authorities. Where there are joint tenants the right to buy can vest in all of them, and can be exercised by all of them, or by agreement where the joint tenant is nominated. Similarly, a tenant who has the right to buy can request that up to three members of his family share in the purchase and be treated as joint tenants. The council has a discretion as to whether it accepts this or not.

Excluded Tenants and Excluded Dwellings Certain secure tenants are excluded from the right to buy and include:

a.   a tenant against whom a possession order has been made in respect of the dwelling;

b.   a tenant who is an undischarged bankrupt or who has made a composition with his creditors;

c.   a tenant who has fallen into rent arrears (right to buy temporarily suspended).

Also certain dwelling houses are excluded from the right to buy and include dwellings:

a. held by local authorities other than for the provision of housing accommodation under **Part V Housing Act 1957;**

b. held by a Development Corporation, the Commission for New Towns, the Development Board for Rural Wales for purposes other than housing accommodation and which the landlord believes should be excluded from the right to buy;

c. designed for occupation by physically disabled persons;

d. normally let to pensioners and social services or other special facilities are provided in close proximity;

e. in respect of which the Secretary of State has determined that the right to buy does not apply. This determination is made after application is made to him by the council within six weeks of the service of the tenant's notice purporting to exercise the right to buy.

In relation to Housing Associations, it was argued strongly by the National Federation of Housing Associations that such voluntary bodies should not be compelled to sell off their housing stock. While the principle that the right to buy provisions should apply to housing associations remains a feature of the **Housing Act 1980,** nevertheless a large number of categories of association were given exemption. These exemptions include:

a. charitable associations;
b. housing co-operatives and co-ownerships;
c. housing associations which had received no public grants or subsidy;
d. tenants of special housing designed or adapted for the elderly or disabled.

Thus the right to buy is vested in only a minority of association tenants, notably those associations providing general family housing on non-charitable rules.

The Price to be Paid The price to be paid is under **s.6,** the 'value at the relevant time' which is the open market value disregarding tenant's improvements and neglect of internal decoration. The relevant time is the date on which the tenant's notice claiming the right to buy was served on a willing vendor. Certain valuation assumptions are made. On the sale of a freehold:

a. that the council sells a fee simple estate with vacant possession;

b. neither the tenant nor a member of his family residing with him wants to buy.

On the grant of a long lease:

a. that the vendor grants a lease for 125 years with vacant possession;

b. neither the tenant nor a member of his family residing with him wants to take a lease;

c. the ground rent will not exceed £100.

The sale price is determined by the council and included in the notice of the terms of sale provided in response to the tenant's 'right to buy' notice. A discount is available under **s.7** and amounts to 33%, plus 1% for each complete year by which his period as a secure tenant exceeds three years up to a maximum of 50%. A tenant who re-sells within five years of the conveyance or lease to him, may be required to repay some or all of the discount. The amount repayable is the discount reduced by 20% for each complete year elapsing after the date of transfer to the purchaser.

A secure tenant who has the right to buy will also have the right to a mortgage (see appendices) which may be exercised by serving written notice on the landlord not later than three months after the tenant has been served with notice under **s.10**. The council must reply by **counter notice** informing the tenant as to the amount he is entitled to leave outstanding on mortgage and how it is arrived at. The counter notice must also contain the main provisions of the mortgage deed and the effect of **s.16** which empowers the council to require the purchasing tenant to complete the purchase within a specified period. The term of the mortgage can be up to 25 years with the principal and interest repayable by equal instalments over that period.

Excercising the Right to Buy The procedure under which the right to buy (see appendices) is exercised is contained in **s.5** and involves the prospective purchaser serving written notice on the landlord that he wishes to buy. The council landlord has then four weeks to reply in the form of written notice either admitting the tenant's right to buy or denying it with reasons. If necessary a dispute could be referred to the County Court. Once the right to buy is admitted the council must serve as soon as is practicable a **s.10 notice** stating: the price (and how arrived at); the main provisions of the conveyance or lease; the right of appeal on the value; the right to a mortgage and how the right is exercised; the right of the tenant to postpone completion. On service of a **s.10 notice** the tenant can then serve a further notice exercising his right to a mortgage (see appendices). If the tenant does not agree with the valuation, he has the right under **s.11** to appeal to the district valuer who has exclusive jurisdiction in this matter. The next stage is to proceed to completion of the purchase under **s.16**, the effect of which being to bring the secure tenancy to an end. Obviously the controversial nature of the policy of selling off council housing has meant that councils have different attitudes towards secure tenants attempting to exercise their right to buy. For this reason wide powers are conferred in the Secretary of State under the **s.23** and **s.24** to intervene where local authorities attempt to resist the sales policy. If there is reasonable evidence that tenants are finding it difficult to exercise the right to buy effectively and expeditiously the Secretary of State may, by giving written notice of his intention, intervene in the situation. The effect of this notice is to vest the rights and obligations of the local authority in the Secretary of State who may exercise and discharge them at the authority's expense.

This power of the Secretary of State for the Environment to intervene under **s.23(1)** was challenged in *R v. Secretary of State for the Environment ex parte Norwich City Council 1982*. In this case there had been a number of complaints by tenants who were attempting to exercise the right to buy their council homes in Norwich. The substance of these complaints was that Norwich City Council were unreasonably delaying in the implementation of the procedure for purchase under the 1980 Act. Subsequently, the Department of the Environment had intervened and informed the council that they were not progressing with their sales procedure at a comparable rate with other authorities and unless they improved their performance, action would be taken. This warning was not heeded and so the Secretary of State served written notices that he intended to exercise his powers under **s.23**. Finally the Secretary of State served a formal order under **s.23** in December 1981. Later the same month the Divisional Court dismissed Norwich City Council's application for an order of **certiorari** to quash the Secretary of State's decision on the grounds of ultra vires. The council then appealed against this decision. The Court of Appeal held, dismissing the appeal that the Secretary of State had acted fairly and reasonably in the circumstances and had lawfully exercised his powers under **s.23(1)**. Ld. Denning, M.R. put forward the view of the court in relation to the **s.23** power as follows: "If the city council failed to carry out sales effectively and expeditiously and thereby put the tenant in difficulty, then the Secretary of State could exercise the default powers conferred on him by **s.23**. But he should only do so after telling the city council of the complaints against them and hearing what they had to say: and even then he should not make the default order unless their default was unreasonable or .... inexcusable .... A default order .... is a very great power to be used only after careful consideration. The Secretary of State here did give it careful consideration. He gave the council every opportunity to mend their ways. He gave them ample notice .... and clear warning .... his order was within his statutory powers. It cannot be upset in this court".

The court has therefore confirmed the Secretary of State's wide default powers under the right to buy provisions and this decision will serve as a warning to those councils who are reluctant to implement the right to buy provisions.

CHAPTER 14 Homelessness The Housing (Homeless Persons) Act 1977

The **Housing (Homeless Persons) Act 1977** imposes burdonsome duties on housing authorities in relation to the homeless. Basically the Act (which is referred to throughout this section) places a duty on housing authorities to house the homeless subject to qualifications and limitations. Unfortunately, because of the complexity of the legislation, and also the sensitivity of the area, the Act has produced a spate of litigation and also numerous problems for local authorities in its implementation. The statutory duty imposed on housing authorities is to house the **unintentionally homeless person with a priority need provided he does not have a local connection with another area.** This duty is further broken down in the Act.

14.1 Homeless

A homeless person is defined in **s.1** as someone who has no accommodation. There is no accommodation if there is none which he, together with any other person who normally resides with him as a member of his family, or in circumstances in which the housing authority considers it reasonable for that person to reside with him:

1. is entitled to occupy by virtue of an interest in it; or

2. has an express or implied licence to occupy.

Also a person is homeless even if he has accommodation but he cannot secure entry to it, or occupation of it will lead to violence, or it consists of a moveable structure and there is no place he is entitled to put it. A person is only homeless therefore if he has no accommodation which he has a right to occupy (as owner, statutory tenant or having an express or implied licence). A lodger, despite having no home, could not therefore be classified as homeless, while a person with accommodation would be so classified if he is unable to use it. Notice also that the Act imposes obligations on the housing authority not only in relation to the homeless but also those **threatened with homelessness** (i.e. persons likely to

251

become homeless within 28 days). Also persons covered by the Act include not only the applicant who is homeless but those who normally reside with him either as **members of his family** or in circumstances in which the local authority considers it reasonable for that person to reside with him.

Duty to make appropriate inquiries

The Act under **s.3** places a duty on housing authorities to make appropriate inquiries in the following circumstances. If the authority has reason to believe that the person who applied to them may be homeless and have a priority need, they shall secure that accommodation is made available for his occupation pending any decision which they may make as a result of their inquiries (irrespective of any local connection he may have with the area of another housing authority). The **appropriate inquiries** should be such to satisfy the authority whether the applicant is homeless or threatened with homelessness, whether he has a priority need, and whether his homelessness has been brought about intentionally. The **Code of Guidance** on the Act, issued by the Department of the Environment advises authorities how to conduct their inquiries. They are to be conducted in a serious manner but not to the level of C.I.D. type investigations. During the inquiries the authority is under a duty to provide **temporary accommodation** for applicants they have reason to believe have a **'priority need'** and a discretion to provide such accommodation in other cases.

Priority Need

The term 'priority' is dealt with in **s.2(1)** which provides that a homeless person has a priority need for accommodation when the housing authority is satisfied that he is in one of the following categories:

a. he has dependant children residing with him or might reasonably be expected to reside with him;

b. he is homeless or threatened with homelessness as a result of flood, fire or any other disaster;

c. he or any person who might be expected to reside with him is incapacitated as a result of old age, mental illness or handicap or physical handicap or other special reason.

Under **s.2(2)** a homeless person or a person threatened with homelessness who is a pregnant woman or resides or might reasonably be expected to reside with a pregnant woman has a 'priority need' for accommodation. Further guidance in relation to 'priority need' is contained in the Code of Guidance but it should be stressed that there is no obligation on a housing authority to follow the advice given in the Code. In *De Falco v. Crawley B.C. 1980* Ld Denning, M.R. indicated that authorities should refer to the Code but having done so were free to depart from it.

Intentionally Homeless

The term 'intentionally homeless' also requires further explanation, for the statutory duty does not arise in relation to those who voluntarily and without good reason give up accommodation. Under **s.17** persons become homeless or threatened with homelessness intentionally, if they deliberately do or fail to do anything in consequence of which they cease to occupy accommodation which is available and which it would be reasonable for them to carry on occupying. This would be the case where a person is evicted for rent arrears and the default should have been avoided as there were sufficient funds available to pay the rent. Of course homelessness could not be said to be intentional in the case of a deserted wife who was not provided for by her husband, or indeed the D.H.S.S., and got into rent arrears. Obviously the problems arise in relation to the extensive grey area where people get into rent arrears because of neglect or incompetence, and here it is extremely difficult to determine the intentional element. In the case of recurring homelessness it is suggested that regard should still be had to the original reason for homelessness to decide whether it is intentional or not.

> In *Dyson v. Kerrier District Council 1980* a young mother was granted a tenancy of a council flat which she surrendered to take a 'winter only' tenancy of a flat next door to her sister. Subsequently a possession order was made against her and she applied to the housing authority for accommodation. The authority concluded that she was homeless, in priority need but intentionally homeless. The Court of Appeal confirmed that the girl was indeed 'intentionally homeless' on the surrender of the initial council tenancy which had in due course led to the applicant's homelessness.

The issue as to whether or not the past acts of the applicant's family are a consideration in determining intentional homelessness was examined in *Lewis v. North Devon D.C. 1981*. Here a married farm worker resigned his job and was forced to vacate his tied accommodation. After a determination by the local authority that he was therefore intentionally homeless, a further application was made by his wife on behalf of herself and the members of her family under the 1977 Act. The authority rejected her application on the grounds that, by agreeing with her husband in resigning, she was also intentionally homeless. On an application to the court it was held that a wife was not necessarily barred from relief in such circumstances. However in interpreting the 1977 Act, the housing authority were charged with the duty of taking into account the conduct of the family unit as a whole. In the absence of contrary evidence the authority were entitled to assume that the applicant was a party to her husband's decision and accordingly intentionally homeless.

In *Din v. Wandsworth B.C. 1981* the Court of Appeal confirmed that the material date for determining whether a person becomes homeless intentionally is the date on which he left his accommodation. Here the applicant had left his accommodation after receiving a distress warrant for rates and moved in with a relative. Subsequently the applicant left that accommodation and applied to the local authority for housing as a homeless person. The Court of Appeal reversing the decision of the county court held that as the applicant's homelessness was a direct consequence of his leaving accommodation when not forced to do so, he could not be regarded as unintentionally homeless.

Under E.E.C. regulations, an E.E.C. national, employed in the territory of another member state, has all the housing rights of that member state's nationals. This means that the 1977 Act applies to E.E.C. nationals coming to work in the U.K. Such persons however, if they voluntarily give up accommodation in their own country are regarded as intentionally homeless, and this will limit the housing authority's duty to provide temporary accommodation and advice and assistance.

This was the decision of the Court of Appeal in *De Falco v. Crawley B.C. 1980*. Here two Italian families had come to England with the prospect of work and accommodation. Unfortunately their accommodation plans fell through and they applied to the local authority as homeless persons under the 1977 Act. The authority decided that the families had a priority need but that their homelessness was intentional since they had arrived in the U.K. without ensuring they had permanent accommodation to go to. Accordingly only temporary accommodation was provided in a guest house. The Court of Appeal agreed with the authority's decision and held that by leaving secure homes in Italy the families were intentionally homeless and the duty of the authority was to house them only for a short time to enable them to find other accommodation.

14.2 Duties of Housing Authorities to the Homeless

The main duties of housing authorities under the Act are contained in s.4 and arise in relation to persons who are homeless or are threatened with homelessness and apply for accommodation. They may be summarised as follows:

1. Where the authority decides there is no priority need or if there is, the homelessness arose intentionally, the duty is to furnish the applicant with advice and assistance. The extent of such assistance is that which the authority considers appropriate in the circumstances.

2. Where the authority decides that the applicant is homeless and is subject to a duty towards him, because he has a priority need although he is homeless intentionally, it shall secure that accommodation is made available for his occupation for such a period as it considers will give him a reasonable opportunity of securing accommodation. In *Lally v. Kensington & Chelsea Royal Borough 1980* it was held that the period of temporary accommodation should be long enough to enable the applicant to find accommodation. Here 14 days was insufficient, particularly in London where three or four months would be a reasonable time.

3. Where the authority decides that the applicant is threatened with homelessness, and there is a priority need, and it is not satisfied that he became threatened with homelessness

255

intentionally, it is under a duty to take reasonable steps to secure that accommodation does not cease to be available for his occupation.

4. Where the authority decides that the applicant is homeless, has a priority need and is not satisfied that he became homeless intentionally, its duty is to secure that accommodation becomes available for his occupation. An authority can fulfil this obligation by either providing the accommodation itself or securing that accommodation is made available by some other person. In the controversial case of *R v. Bristol City Council ex-parte Browne 1977* it was decided that a housing authority could fulfil this duty by making and financing travel arrangements for the applicant to be housed by another authority, even where it is outside the country (Eire) and not a housing authority as defined in the Act. This was despite there being no offer of specific accommodation by the foreign authority, but merely a promise of the availability of accommodation.

Whatever decision the housing authority reaches in relation to the applicant, it is under a duty to notify him of that decision and include the reasons for it.

Absence of a local connection

Under **s.5(1)** there is not duty to house if the authority is of the opinion that:

a. neither the applicant nor any person reasonably expected to reside with him has a local connection **with its area;** and

b. the applicant or a person expected to reside with him has a local connection with **another housing area;** and

c. neither the applicant nor any person reasonably expected to reside with him will **run the risk of domestic violence** in that housing authority's area.

The authority must also inform the housing authority in whose area they consider the applicant to have a local connection, otherwise the duty to house will still arise. If the notified authority are satisfied that there is a local connection and there is no risk of domestic violence then they are under a duty to house the applicant. Otherwise if no local connection is established the duty to house falls on the authority to whom application has been made. Under **s.18** a local connection is taken to exist when an applicant either is or was normally resident in an area, employed there, has a family association with the area, or there are other special circumstances indicating a connection.

14.3 Alternative Remedies

The alternative courses of action open to an individual who is aggrieved at a housing authority's action or lack of it in relation to the 1977 Act include:

a. **An Application for an Order of Mandamus.** This is a prerogative remedy available from the High Court which has the effect of compelling an authority to fulfil its statutory duties.

b. **An action for breach of Statutory Duty** In *De Falco v. Crawley B.C. 1980* Ld Denning, M.R. confirmed that if an individual suffers harm as a result of a housing authority's failure to fulfil its duties under the 1977 Act then an action would lie for damages for breach of statutory duty. Damages awarded would be related to actual financial loss, i.e. hotel bills as well as compensation for discomfort and distress.

c. **A Mandatory or Interim Injunction.** A mandatory injunction may be awarded to compel an authority to comply with its duties or an interim injunction where a family is homeless and the authority are required under the Act to provide them with temporary accommodation.

d. **A complaint to the Commission for Local Administration.** If an authority fails to perform its duties under the 1977 Act, this would constitute an act of maladministration for which complaint could be made to the local government ombudsman.

Part 6 - **Housing Control and Management**

CHAPTER 15   Houses in Multiple Occupation and Overcrowding Generally

Multiple occupation of houses occurs primarily in inner city areas because of the greater demand for living accommodation. It would be wrong to assume that multi-occupation is harmful per se, for often large Victorian properties converted in a proper manner can provide reasonable accommodation particularly for single or small households. Unfortunately the prospect of high financial returns from such properties has prompted many unscrupulous owners to encourage overcrowding by unsatisfactory division of households. As a result occupants are forced to share unsatisfactory cooking and sanitary facilities. Parliament has therefore conferred **wide supervisory powers** on local authorities to deal with the problem of multi-occupancy. The difficulty is of course that in the final analysis, if powers are used to close **houses in multiple occupation (HMO's)** further demands are then imposed on the authority's existing housing stock by those necessarily displaced. Future problems can be prevented by local authorities taking a positive role in ensuring that proposed conversions of properties into HMO's are carried out to the highest standards. For the thousands of completed conversions which at present provide unsatisfactory accommodation the authorities are restricted to use of their powers of **management and control.**

15.1 The definition of HMO's

The present definition of a multi-occupied house is contained in the **Housing Act 1969 s.58.** It occurs when a house 'is occupied by persons who do not form a **single household'.** Therefore a single house or flat occupied exclusively by one family is not an HMO.

> In *Wolkind v. Ali 1975* the defendant occupied premises with his large family. Relying on powers in relation to multi-occupancy the local authority had served a notice charging him with exceeding the prescribed numbers permitted to sleep in each room. The Divisional Court held that as the house was being used by a single household, the authority's multi-occupancy powers had no application.

261

The term **'household'** is not restricted to a family however, and would cover a group of people who **live and eat together communally** whether they are related or not. A single lodger might therefore form part of a household, but lodgers as a business enterprise on a substantial scale would constitute multiple occupation. A group of students living together communally could therefore constitute a single household. It is only where there is a division of control over the house between different households that multi-occupancy arises. Certainly if individuals or families apportion rooms for exclusive accommodation and share facilities, a presumption of multi-occupancy arises.

> In *Simmons v. Pizzey 1977,* a refuge for 'battered women' was held by the House of Lords to constitute multi-occupancy rather than one household. The court referred to the large numbers involved (30 or more), the fluctuating occupants, and the owner's intentions as determining factors in concluding whether a single household was constituted.

In deciding whether an HMO exists it is also necessary to consider whether separate households occupy separate dwellings in the house as a whole. If this is the case then there is a block of flats rather than an HMO. If only some of the separate households within the house constitute separate dwellings then under the **Housing Act 1974** the house as a whole may still constitute an HMO, but the separate dwellings are excluded from HMO powers. The definition of an HMO under the **Housing Act 1974 s.129** is therefore **'a house which is occupied by persons who do not form a single household excluding any part thereof which is occupied as a separate dwelling by persons who do form a single household'**. As far as **tenements and common lodging houses** are concerned separate provisions exist but they are both subject to some of the general powers relating to HMO's. In particular a tenement (defined as a building comprising of two or more separate dwellings which either do not have exclusive use of lavatories/personal washing facilities or do not comprise of single households) is regarded as an HMO for the purposes of **management orders.** Common lodging houses are defined under the **Public Health Act 1936 s.235** as houses 'provided for the purposes of accommodating by night poor persons not being members of the same family ... in one common room for the purpose of sleeping or eating'. Such houses clearly constitute HMO's and are subject to some of the general provisions of the Housing Acts in relation to HMO's as well as specific provisions under the Public Health Act concerned with management.

15.2 Local Authority Control — Provision of Facilities

The first major piece of legislation to confer power on local authorities over HMO's was the **Housing Act 1961.** Under **Part II** of the 1961 Act authorities are permitted to require those in control of HMO's to provide facilities for cooking, washing and sanitation and in addition take necessary precautions against fire. **Section 15** permits intervention by an authority if it considers an HMO unsuitable for occupation by the number of individuals or households in the HMO because it is so far defective in relation to any of the following: lighting; heating; ventilation; washing facilities; water supply; sanitation. In fact each local authority is left to prescribe its own guidelines for maximum numbers and households within an HMO in relation to the facilities provided. Where they are infringed the authority has power under **s.15** (as amended by the **Housing Act 1964 s.67**) to serve a **'numbers direction'** on the person responsible requiring him to comply with the number of persons prescribed for the property and provide the facilities directed as suitable. The notice will give the person responsible a reasonable time for completion of the works which must not be less than 21 days. Of course the need to complete the works could be avoided if the local authority are satisfied that the number of occupants has been reduced to a reasonable level in relation to the facilities provided. It should be noted that powers in relation to the provision of facilities have no application in relation to ensuring that repairs are carried out. For this purpose additional notices under **s.9(1)(A) Housing Act 1957** would have to be served (see Chapter 10).

More extensive powers in relation to the provision of adequate fire escapes in HMO's have been conferred on authorities by the **Housing Act 1980 schedule 24.** Under the schedule, authorities have a discretion to act if they feel an HMO is not adequately supplied with a fire escape whereas they have a duty to act if the property falls within a description of houses specified by order of the Secretary of State i.e. those most at risk because of the number of storeys or households. While schedule 24 places no obligation on authorities to seek out HMO's without adequate fire escapes, if schedule 24 powers are used and a notice is served, the payment of a **special grant** to assist in carrying out the work is **mandatory.** It is usual for the authority to accept undertakings from the person responsible not to use certain parts of the property for human habitation to enable him to carry out the work. Failure to comply with such an undertaking could lead to the authority obtaining a **closing order** in relation to that part of the property.

The usual rights of appeal under **s.17** will be available to persons served with a **s.15 or schedule 24 notice.** He has 21 days to appeal to the County Court on a number of alternative grounds including the fact that the work is unnecessary or excessive, insufficient time has been allowed, or the notice is defective. The court may confirm, quash or amend the notice. It the person responsible informs the local authority that he is unable to do work, **s.18** allows the authority to do the work **in default** and recover the cost from him, if necessary by County Court action. In any event wilful failure to comply with a s.15 or schedule 24 notice is a criminal offence and could lead to a prosecution and conviction with a fine of up to £500 imposed under **s.65 Housing Act 1964** (as amended by **schedule 23 Housing Act 1980**). Of course in such a case the obligation to complete the work remains and a continuing offence may be committed by taking no action.

15.3 Local Authority Control — Management

In addition to ensuring the provision of adequate facilities within HMO's the other major supervisory control of local authorities is in relation to ensuring that HMO's are properly managed. Guidance in this matter is provided by the **Housing (Management of HMO) Regulations 1962** produced by the Secretary of State. Power to act is conferred by **s.12** which provides that a local authority may by order apply a **management code** to any HMO if it is in an unsatisfactory state in consequence of a failure to maintain proper standards of management. The procedure involved in taking action under **s.12** requires the authority to serve a **notice of intention** on the owner, display a copy of it prominently within the HMO, and give persons affected an opportunity to make representations to the authority. After 21 days a **formal order** may be made, served on the owner with copies to persons affected and displayed on the premises. Appeal on the grounds that the order is unnecessary may be made to the Magistrates Court within a further 21 days. The effect of a **management order** is to impose duties on the person who is **'the manager'.** He is the person who, being an owner of lessee of a house, receives rents or other payments from tenants of parts of the house or who are lodgers therein, and also any person who receives such payments on behalf of an owner or lessee as a trustee or agent. His duties involve: keeping all common parts and facilities clean, safe and unobstructed; maintaining and keeping in good order and repair supplies of gas, water, electricity and lighting; ensuring general safety and adequate methods of storage and disposal of refuse;

ensuring that on the commencement of letting, facilities and service installation in the rooms are clean and in a good state of repair; maintaining proper ventilation, means of escape from fire, out-buildings and yards, etc.; displaying a copy of the regulations and the manager's name and address prominently within the premises. Local authorities will maintain a register of the names and addresses of managers of HMO's subject to a management order and to ensure compliance with the regulations may bring prosecutions against those who fail to co-operate. Contravention of the regulations is a criminal offence punishable with a fine of up to £200 under **s.13** (as amended by **schedule 23 Housing Act 1980**). Once a management order is in force, **s.14** gives local authorities power to require the manager to carry out works necessary to ensure that the regulations have been complied with. This could involve carrying out structural repair or replacing defective facilities. The procedure for service of a **s.14** notice, rights of appeal against it, enforcement and powers to do work in default are equivalent to those for **s.15.**

A further extension of local authority powers in relation to the management of HMO's was introduced by the **Housing Act 1964.** This Act introduced the concept of the **control order** under which an authority has power to take control of an HMO for a period of up to 5 years during which the authority has itself the opportunity to carry out necessary physical improvements. Power to intervene in this way is conferred by **s.73** of the **Housing Act 1964** on the ground that living conditions in the HMO in which a numbers direction, management order or notice under **ss.14 or 15** has been or might have been issued, are such that a control order is necessary to protect the **safety, health or welfare of persons living in it.** Such an order may be made effective immediately subject to rights of appeal that it is unnecessary or suffers from a defect in formality. Copies of the order must be served on all interested parties and displayed prominently on the premises. Its effect is to transfer management and control of the property to the local authority which then has power to grant tenancies but also duties to maintain proper standards of management and also to insure against fire. Under **s.79 Housing Act 1964** the local authority must within 8 weeks prepare a **detailed improvement scheme** to make the premises suitable for multiple occupation and include all the financial implications of it. Then the authority must give notice of the scheme to all affected parties. Rights of appeal to the County Court by interested parties against the control order or the improvement scheme will expire 6 weeks after service of the improvement scheme. The scheme should cover all matters which affect the HMO including numbers, households, rent revenue, capital expenditure and compensation. Under **s.78** of the 1964 Act the local authority must pay the dispossessed proprietor compensation at an annual rate of one half of the gross rateable value during the continuance of the order. After five years or when the scheme is complete, the order will expire and the control of the HMO must be handed back to the owner with any balance of revenue. The alternative of course, is for the local authority to take permanent control of the HMO by means of **compulsory purchase.** Power to make such an order is conferred by **s.63 Housing Act 1969** and if it is made within 28 days of making the control order there is no need to prepare an improvement scheme until after the compulsory purchase order (CPO) has been confirmed or rejected by the Secretary of State. Wide use of CPO powers in such cases effectively means that the control order may now be regarded as an interim step towards compulsory purchase of badly managed HMO's. Usually of course the threat of such proceedings is sufficient to encourage a voluntary sale of the property by the proprietor.

15.4 Overcrowding

It is convenient at this point to examine the powers of local authorities generally to deal with the problem of **overcrowding.** Separate procedures exist for dealing with overcrowding in different types of accommodation ranging from separate dwellings, to houses in multiple occupation.

Overcrowding in Separate Dwellings

In relation to separate dwellings, local authority powers are contained in **Part IV Housing Act 1957** (reference to which is made throughout this section) which under **s.87** relates to premises 'used as a separate dwelling by members of the working class or a type suitable for such use'. Every local authority is under a statutory duty to investigate overcrowding within their areas with a view to preventing it and enforcing the statutory provisions. Overcrowding occurs in a separate dwelling when under **s.77** and **schedule 6** more than two persons over ten years old of opposite sexes and not living together as man and wife, must sleep in the same room or there are more than two persons per room (or for two rooms three persons, three rooms five persons) or more than a given number of persons per square foot of relevant accommodation, whichever is less. For the purposes of calculating numbers all persons who use the house as their home should be counted to determine overcrowding, not just those who sleep there at any given time. Once overcrowding is established the authority can require its abatement, and in the absence of such, within a reasonable time proceed to prosecute the occupier or landlord responsible for it. Under **s.78 Housing Act 1957** to cause or permit overcrowding is an offence punishable by a fine of £5 plus a fine of £2 for every day the offence continues. An exception in relation to **long occupation** is constituted where the occupants have continuously lived in the house since the **'appointed day'** or are children of such persons. The 'appointed day' is simply a reference to various appointed day orders made between 1936 and 1938. This exception only applies when suitable alternative occupation has been offered to the occupier or a member of his family, and he has failed to accept it. Similarly there is no offence if overcrowding is constituted because a child has reached a sufficient age to be counted as an adult (i.e. ten years) and suitable alternative accommodation has been applied for from the local authority.

As far as rented accommodation is concerned, **s.85** empowers a local authority to serve notice on the landlord to abate any overcrowding within 14 days. If the house is still overcrowded within three months the authority may apply to the court for an order to vacate the premises under **s.101 Rent Act 1977** thus taking away any security of tenure enjoyed by a tenant in such circumstances (see Chapter 12). Vacation of the premises in such circumstances would of course place the authority under a duty to rehouse the tenants under the **Housing (Homeless Persons) Act 1977** (see Chapter 14). As an alternative to eventual prosecution, local authorities have power under **s.80** to license an occupier to exceed the permitted number of occupants up to a specified number for a period of up to twelve months. Also **s.81** places authorities under a duty to ensure that landlords, tenants and occupiers are informed of the permitted number relating to the house in question. As far as tenants are concerned such information would normally be included in the rent book. There is a statutory obligation to provide weekly tenants with rent books or similar documents under the **Landlord and Tenant Act 1962 s.1(1)** but not so monthly tenants. In addition to a statement of the permitted number such documents are also required to contain such information as set out in the 1962 Act and the **Rent Book (Forms of Notice) Regulations 1976.** The landlord's name and address must be disclosed along with an outline of the tenant's position in relation to rent variation, allowances or registration, subletting and security of tenure. In this way the tenant is given some notice of his rights and under **s.4** of the 1962 Act it is a criminal act for the landlord not to provide a rent book where necessary.

Overcrowding in Houses in Multiple Occupation

We have already considered the powers of a local authority in relation to control and management of HMO's under the **Housing Act 1961.** **Section 19** of that Act gives an authority power to serve a **numbers direction** on the proprietor and tenants, a copy of which is posted on the premises. This direction will stipulate the permitted number of occupants of the property and require the occupier to comply with it. Noncompliance constitutes an offence the penalty for which is a fine of up to £500 under the **Housing Act 1980 schedule 23.** While there is no appeal against an **s.19** direction it may be revoked or amended on application.

An 'occupier' for the purposes of the **Housing Act 1961** under **s.19(2)** includes anyone who is entitled or authorised to permit individuals to take up residence in a house.

> In *Hackney LBC v. Ezedinma 1981* a house comprising of a basement, first and second floor containing single rooms was let to students. Each floor had its own kitchen. The local authority served a numbers direction under **s.19(1)** limiting the number of households to three. Five rooms in the house had already been let to individual students and the estate agent (the defendant) let a further three. A prosecution was then brought against the estate agent for failing to comply with the numbers direction in that there were now eight households. The Divisional Court of the Queens Bench Division held that
>
> 1. the defendant was "the occupier for the time being" of the house within **s.19(2)** of the Act;
>
> 2. what constitutes a 'household' within **s.19** was a question of fact and degree and in this case there was sufficient evidence to conclude that the prosecutor had not proved beyond reasonable doubt that there was more than three households.

A further power to control overcrowding in HMO's was included in **s.146 Housing Act 1980** which replaced **s.90 Housing Act 1957.** By virtue of this section authorities are empowered to serve, giving at least 7 days notice, an **'overcrowding notice'** on the person having control of the premises. It may be served when it appears to the authority that an HMO is excessively occupied in relation to the rooms available. The notice will also stipulate the maximum number of persons the authority considers reasonable to sleep in each room available. The effect of a **s.146** notice is that the recipient of the notice may be required to prevent any room within the HMO from being used for sleeping accommodation otherwise than as directed in the notice or permitting persons of opposite sexes (other than those living as man and wife) to share sleeping accommodation without contravening the notice. He may also be required to prevent new residents from occupying a room in contravention of the notice or occupying a room which may result in sexual overcrowding. During the term of the overcrowding notice the local authority can require the person responsible to give them information as to the occupants of the HMO including numbers at any particular time, names, households, and division of accommodation. Appeal against an overcrowding notice is to the County Court within 21 days and contravention of the notice could lead to a fine on summary conviction in the Magistrates Court of up to £500. Finally, mention should be made that to enable enforcement of the authority's powers in relation to HMO's wide powers of entry are conferred on local authority officers, usually after service of 24 hours notice under the **Housing Act 1957 s.159** and the **Housing Act 1961 s.23.**

CHAPTER 16 Grant Aid and Area Improvement

16.1 Grant Aid

Successive governments have recognised that the provision of grant aid is crucial to encourage the rehabilitation of both public and private sector housing. Percentage grants may be taken up voluntarily as a contribution towards the cost of repair, improvement or conversion of dwelling houses, which may include houses, flats and other buildings. The relevant legislation detailing the various grants available is the **Housing Act 1974 Part VII** and any reference to individual sections made will be from this Act. Amendments to the grant aid scheme have also been made by the **Housing Act 1980.** Four types of grant are provided for and each shall now be considered in turn:

a. **Improvement grants.** As the name suggests this grant is available for the improvement of a dwelling house or for works of conversion.

b. **Intermediate grants.** These are available for the provision of standard amenities and ancillary repairs.

c. **Repair grants.** Originally such grants were limited to the costs of repair of houses in Housing Action Areas (HAA's) and General Improvement Areas (GIA's) but following the **Housing Act 1980 schedule 26** they are available generally.

d. **Special grants.** Such grants are limited to the provision of facilities in houses in multiple occupation.

16.2 General Considerations for the Provision of Grants

Before considering each grant in detail it is necessary to examine some of the general principles that govern their provision. Except where the Secretary of State directs otherwise local authorities may not entertain application for grant aid in the case of a dwelling erected or provided after 2 October 1961. In addition the applicant must either hold the freehold or an unexpired leasehold of at least five years of the land in question. Following **s.106 Housing Act 1980** in relation to grants other than improvement grants applications may be considered by local authorities from protected, statutory or secure tenants, tenants holding under **Part I Landlord and Tenant Act 1954,** protected occupants and secure tenants under the **Rent (Agriculture) Act 1976.** Local authorities have however an overriding discretion to refuse such applications unless they are accompanied by a certificate from the landlord that the dwelling will be let or available for letting as a residence to a person other than a member of his family. Even if the applicant is the owner then such a **certificate of availability for letting** must be included with the application or alternatively a **certificate of owner-occupation.** This certificate states that the applicant intends that on or before the first anniversary of the 'certified date' and for four years following, the dwelling will be the only or main residence of the applicant and his household, or a member of his family within his household. A further basic principle is that it is not usual to entertain applications for grant aid in respect of work which has already begun. Obviously application must be in the prescribed form detailing the proposed works and estimating the cost.

The amount of grant payable is related to a **percentage of the eligible expenses** of improvement or repair. The percentage of eligible expense varies with the situation of the property in question and by virtue of **s.59 Housing Act 1974** range from 50% for houses outside area action to 60% within GIA's and 75% for HAA's. Within HAA's if the costs of the work cannot be met by the applicant without undue hardship then 90% grants are available. The **Housing Act 1980 schedule 12** confers power on the Secretary of State to vary the percentages subject to the approval of Parliament. The balance of the cost must be provided by the applicant himself usually by loans which many local authorities now offer themselves. A further restriction on the amount of grant payable is that each grant is subject to a **maximum expenditure limit.** These limits effectively control local authority spending in this field and are subject to review. They are calculated by distinguishing between the **repair and improvement element** in the prescribed work and limiting the expenditure allocated to each element. The relevant figures will be shown when each grant is examined in turn.

It is intended that subject to exceptions (intermediate grants) the approval of a grant application should be a decision of the local authority in question based upon its own particular policy. The standard of work prescribed for each individual grant is provided for by the legislation but a wide discretion is given to authorities to stipulate in each case whether **'full'** or **'reduced'** works are necessary. Certainly the works must be completed within a stipulated time (not less than 12 months) and to the satisfaction of the local authority.

Finally some mention should be made that as a general principle the payment of a grant resulted in residence conditions being imposed on the applicant under the **Housing Act 1974.** The effect of these conditions is that the grant or part of it becomes repayable to the local authority if the applicant ceases to use the dwelling in accordance with his intentions as certified in the grant application. These residence conditions have now largely been relaxed by the **Housing Act 1980.**

It is now proposed to examine in turn the general principles relating to the provision of each individual grant.

16.3 Improvement Grants

Improvements grants are intended for the rehabilitation of individual houses or for the creation of additional dwellings by conversion. While their approval is at the discretion of the individual local authority under **s.61 Housing Act 1974** they are certainly not intended for the improvement of modern homes, e.g. building an additional bedroom or installing central heating. Some guidance is provided by the 1974 Act which stipulates under **s.58** and **schedule 6** that an application may not be approved unless the authority is satisfied that on completion of the relevant works the dwelling will reach the following **'full standard':**

a.   **be in a reasonable state of repair having regard to its age, character and locality;**

b.   **have all the standard amenities for the exclusive use of the occupants:**

      i.   a fixed bath or shower;
      ii.   a hot and cold water supply at a fixed bath or shower;
      iii. a wash hand basin;
      iv. hot and cold water supply at a wash hand basin;
      v.   a sink;
      vi. hot and cold water supply at a sink;
      vii. a water closet;

c. **be likely to have useful life of at least 30 years;**

d. **conform with the following requirements (specified by the Secretary of State):**

  i. be substantially free from damp;
  ii. have adequate natural lighting and ventilation in each habitable room;
  iii. have adequate and safe provision of artificial lighting and sufficient electric sockets;
  iv. have adequate drainage facilities;
  v. be in a stable structural condition;
  vi. have satisfactory internal arrangement;
  vii. have satisfactory facilities for cooking and preparing food;
  viii. have satisfactory heating facilities;
  ix. have proper provision for storage of fuel and refuse;
  x. have adequate thermal insulation in the roof.

It should be stressed that the above is the **'full standard'** of works which may be prescribed for an improvement grant by the authority and in cases where its implementation would be impracticable because of the unreasonable expense involved authorities have a discretion to reduce the standard of works prescribed. This **'reduced standard'** under **s.61** would simply amount to a reduction of any of the requirements of the four criteria of the full standard works. Applicants who are owner occupiers will not qualify for an improvement grant if the property in question exceeds the rateable value limits as fixed by the Secretary of State. At the present these limits are £400 in Greater London or £225 elsewhere but under **schedule 12 Housing Act 1980** they do not apply to houses within HAA's or to a grant to improve a home for a disabled person.

The amount of the grant payable will depend upon a number of factors. In the first place a distinction must be drawn between repair/renewal and improvement. Grants for works of repair or renewal are only payable if the work is carried out as part of a programme of improvement, i.e. alteration and enlargement. If works of repair are treated as **eligible expense,** then normally no more than 50% of its estimated cost may be met by the authority. Having determined the **estimated expense** for improvement (and repair if any) under **s.63,** it is possible to calculate the amount of grant payable under **s.64.** This will

274

be the **appropriate percentage (i.e. 50%, 60%, 75%, 90%) of the proper estimated cost below the eligible expense limits.** These are contained in the **Grants by Local Authorities (Eligible Expense Limits) Order 1980.** The eligible expense limits will depend upon whether the house is a priority case (unfit, lacking standard amenities, in need of substantial structural repair, situated in an HAA), or a non-priority case. At present the figures are for priority cases, £11,500 (GLC) and £8,500 (elsewhere) and for non-priority cases, £7,500 (GLC) and £5,500 (elsewhere).

16.4 Intermediate Grants

Intermediate grants are intended to assist in the improvement of property by securing the provision of **standard amenities** (previously listed). They may also be used to carry out works of **repair and replacement** at the same time. It should be stressed from the outset that an application for such a grant **must be approved** by a local authority if it is satisfied that all the basic requirements are met. These are that the application is made in the prescribed form, specifying the amenities lacking the amenities in question for a period of not less than 12 months. On completion of the works the authority must be satisfied that the property will conform with the standard laid down in **schedule 12 Housing Act 1980.** That is that the property will be statutorily fit for human habitation or, despite not being statutorily fit, it is reasonable to approve the application in the circumstances. Provision is now made in **schedule 12** to enable the local authority to vary an application for an intermediate grant which includes works of repair or improvement, so that such works are limited to those necessary for the reasonable repair of the property. Thus the application which includes works of repair that exceeds that which is regarded as reasonable need no longer be rejected out of hand.

The amount of the grant payable is determined by **s.68** as amended by the 1980 Act which involves the authority distinguishing between the estimated **costs of the provision of the amenities and the costs of repair.** In relation to the amenities the eligible expense limits are contained in **Local Authorities (Eligible Expense Limits) Order 1980** and are in 1982:

	GLC	Elsewhere
	£	£
Fixed bath or shower...............	375	285
Wash hand basin.....................	145	110
Sink	375	285
Hot and Cold water at a fixed bath or shower	475	360
Hot and Cold water at a wash hand basin	250	190
Hot and Cold water at a sink...	315	240
Water Closet	565	430
	£2,500	£1,900

Thus in relation to the **amenities** the amount of grant payable will be the **appropriate percentage of the proper estimated cost below the individual eligible expense limits.** For the repairs element the eligible expense limits are either:

i.   the full repairs element of the intermediate grant (£3,500 GLC; £2,500 elsewhere) which would involve putting the whole house into reasonable repair; or

ii. a smaller amount for minor repairs limited to £350 for each standard amenity (in the GLC up to a maximum of £1,400) or £250 for each standard amenity (elsewhere up to a maximum of £1,000).

Thus for **repairs** the amount of grant payable will be the **appropriate percentage of the proper estimated cost below the eligible expense limits.** The total grant then amounts to the sum payable for **both the amenities and repair.**

16.5 Repair Grants

Repair grants are intended for the purpose of carrying out essential repairs where the applicant does not wish to improve. Originally they were limited to properties situated within HAA's or GIA's but now following the **Housing Act 1980** authorities have a discretion to make repair grants for any property. Indeed their award is **mandatory** where a **compulsory repairs** notice has been served under **s.9 Housing Act 1957.**

The following criteria must however be satisfied before a repair grant is made. Firstly the property in question must have been erected before 1 January 1919. Secondly, apart from HAA's, the property must fall within the rateable value limits of £400 GLC and £225 elsewhere. Thirdly the works must be of a substantial and structural character and finally, on their completion, the dwelling must attain a reasonable standard of repair having regard to its age, character and locality. The amount of grant payable is determined by **s.72** as amended and will amount to the **appropriate percentage of the proper estimated cost and below the eligible expense limits.** These are fixed by the **1980 order** and are at present £5,500 in GLC and £4,000 elsewhere.

16.6 Special Grants

Special grants are intended solely for the provision of standard amenities in houses in multiple occupation. They are an extension of the intermediate grants but less generous, for while a repairs element is also payable, it is limited to the repair works necessary for the installation of the approved standard amenities. The payment of special grants is discretionary under **s.69** but following **s.69A** as included by the **Housing Act 1980** they are **mandatory** if a notice requiring the provision of standard amenities has been served under **s.15 Housing Act 1961** or requiring means of escape from fire under **schedule 24 Housing Act 1980** (see Chapter 15). Application for special grants must be made in the prescribed form stating the number of households and individuals, occupying the amenities already provided and the means of fire escape. Any repairs necessary must be sufficient to bring the house up to a reasonable standard of repair having regard to its age, character and locality.

With the applicant's consent, and application may be varied to exclude repair work which would exceed a reasonable standard. The amount of the grant is calculated by distinguishing between the eligible expense of the provision of amenities, escape from fire, and repairs. If the grant is discretionary the eligible expense limit will be fixed by the local authority and the grant payable will be the appropriate percentage of the estimated cost below that amount. For mandatory special grants the eligible expense limit is for amenities, the amounts stipulated for intermediate grants, plus the costs of repair and replacement (up to £3,500 GLC and £2,500 elsewhere), plus the cost of providing means of escape from fire (£9,000 GLC and £6,750 elsewhere). The grant payable will be the appropriate percentage of the proper estimated cost below those eligible expense limits.

16.7 Area Improvement

The need for concerted planned improvement of specified areas was recognised in the early 1960's when it became apparent that the ad hoc improvement of individual properties was ineffective. Power was conferred on local authorities under the **Housing Act 1964** to declare **'improvement areas'** and later the **Housing Act 1974** identified particular categories of area improvement including, **'Housing Action Areas'** and **'General improvement areas'**. The main objective behind the declaration of such areas rather that the rehabilitation of individual properties is to start self regeneration in a specified area by giving occupiers long term confidence in their properties. This may be achieved by the very declaration of such areas, thereby giving the local authority an opportunity to give some formal indication in planning terms of their commitment to **rehabilitation** rather than clearance or redevelopment.

16.8 General Improvement Area (GIA's)

The procedure for the designation of an area as a GIA is governed by the **Housing Act 1969** as amended by the **Housing Acts 1974** and **1980**. The effect of the 1980 Act **schedule 13** was to restore the law to the position it was under **s.28** of the 1969 Act. This meant that the requirement of the 1974 Act in relation to approval by central government (the Department of the Environment) of the scheme was abolished. All that is necessary is that having resolved to declare a GIA, the local authority must publish notice of this fact in local newspapers, inform owners and residents, and pass a copy of the resolution to the Minister. Generally the declaration of a GIA should be restricted to primarily residential areas composed of older, but sound housing within a stable community. It is also expected that the local authority will have acquired evidence to the fact that the residents are ready and willing to improve their properties and contribute their financial share to the grant aided work. Once the GIA is declared the legislation imposes a number of duties and confers a number of powers on the local authority in relation to it. **Section 31 Housing Act 1969** places a duty on local authorities to inform owners and occupiers in the GIA of the availability of **grant assistance** towards the improvement of property and also of the local authority's proposals to improve the amenities in the area. The main effect of declaring a GIA for occupiers and owners is, of course, that **higher percentage grants** are available to encourage improvement. As far as the local authorities' costs are concerned under **s.37 Housing Act 1969** as substituted by **schedule 13 Housing Act 1980** the Secretary of State subsidises the costs of works carried out by them. Declaration automatically gives the authority power to issue **compulsory improvement notices** on owners without prior request from tenants, and also power to acquire land compulsorily or by agreement where necessary (see later in this chapter).

16.9 Housing Action Areas

The designation of a **Housing Action Area** under the **Housing Act 1974** is confined to areas unsuitable for clearance and redevelopment but where there is **acute housing stress** necessitating speedy action. Following consideration of a detailed report by a suitable qualified person as to the conditions of the area in question under **s.36 Housing Act 1974,** the local authority may resolve to declare the area an HAA and define it so on a map. The local authority must be satisfied that declaration of the HAA is the best means, within a period of 5 years of improving the housing accommodation in the area as a whole; the proper and effective management and use of housing in the area, and the well being of the residents. Once the resolution to declare a Housing Action Area has been passed, then the local authority must publish notice of it in two or more local newspapers and also inform residents where the resolution, report and map can be inspected. Unlike GIA's the declaration of an HAA requires confirmation by the Secretary of State and so it is necessary to send him a copy of the resolution, report and map and a statement of the local authority's proposals in relation to the area. The wide powers of the Secretary of State giving him control over the declaration of HAA's are contained in **s.37 Housing Act 1974** which provides that within 28 days, or longer if necessary, the resolution may be cancelled or confirmed. There is then a duty on the local authority to inform residents by publication in two local newspapers of the Secretary of State's decision. If the declaration of an HAA is confirmed then it will last for five years with the possibility of a two-year extension.

The main practical effect of the declaration for residents is that higher grants of up to 75% and 90% in cases of hardship are available. As with GIA's the local authority is entitled to recoup 90% of its expenditure on house improvement in HAA's from central government. A separate power under **s.46 Housing Act 1974** enables local authorities to assist private owners with the cost of carrying out environmental works on their premises with proportional contributions from the Secretary of State. Expenditure for this purpose of up to £50 per house is available from central government. As the whole point of the declaration is to secure improved accommodation within the area, **s.43 Housing Act 1974** confers power on the local authority to acquire land voluntarily or compulsorily if necessary to achieve this aim. Having acquired land under **s.43** then the local authority by carrying out conversion, construction, repair or improvment work is enabled to provide improved housing accommodation within the area. Provision is made under **s.47 Housing Act 1974** to ensure that as far as possible existing residents benefit from the declaration rather than outsiders. This is achieved by monitoring sales and the grant of tenancies by strict requirements as to notice. The prospective seller of property must give the local authority not less that four weeks nor more than six months notice of the disposal. Similarly in the case of a tenancy, the landlord must give seven days notice of the service of a notice to quit, and four weeks notice of a tenancy's expiration. These provisions enable the local authority to keep a constant check on vacant accommodation which could be voluntarily or compulsorily acquired and used for the benefit of the HAA.

16.10 Compulsory Improvement

Power to compel the compulsory improvement of certain property has been conferred on local authorities under the **Housing Act 1974 Part VIII** as modified by the **Housing Act 1980.** Here we are not concerned with unfitness or disrepair but rather the situation where property lacks a bathroom or any other standard amenity and this is the basis for the compulsory procedure to be adopted. For properties inside HAA's and GIA's the local authority itself can compel action, but for dwellings outside these areas it is the tenant who can initiate the process.

Under **s.85** of the 1974 Act local authorities may serve a **'provisional notice'** on the person having control of a dwelling within an HAA or GIA if the dwelling:

a. lacks a standard amenity;
b. was built before 3 October 1961; and
c. is capable of attaining the standard laid down by **s.103A Housing Act** 1974 as inserted by **schedule 25 Housing Act 1980**

Standard amenities include any of the items listed in **schedule 6 Housing Act 1974:**

1. a fixed bath or shower;
2. a hot and cold water supply at a fixed bath or shower;
3. a wash hand basin;
4. a hot and cold supply at a wash hand basin;
5. a sink;
6. a hot and cold water supply at a sink;
7. a water closet.

There is a requirement that the standard amenities must be provided for the exclusive use of the occupants of a single identifiable dwelling whereas the provisions are more flexible as to where they must be situated. Thus there is no requirement that the water closet be situated within the dwelling, provided that it is reasonably accessible. It should be stressed however that a compulsory improvement notice can only be served in respect of an identifiable dwelling, i.e. an individual house or self contained flat. In the case of houses in multiple occupation, for the procedure to be applicable it must be possible to identify a separate dwelling within the HMO. This is done by pointing to exclusive occupation by a single household of a sufficient number of persons to meet all reasonable living requirements. If this is not the case then a different procedure for compulsory improvement applicable to HMO's must be adopted. This is of significance to the owners and tenants in HMO's, not only because the separate procedures require different standards of work, but also because different levels of grants are available to carry it out.

The standard of work referred to for compulsory improvement is the full standard laid down in **schedule 25 Housing Act 1980.** This involves ensuring that when the work is completed the dwelling will: be provided with all standard amenities; be in reasonable repair taking into account age, character and locality; conform with requirements in respect of thermal insulation; be statutorily fit; and have an expected life of at least fifteen years. This maximum standard is identical to that required for intermediate grants. Local authorities have an overriding discretion,

281

if it is reasonable in the circumstances, to require a reduced standard of work for a particular dwelling by dispensing wholly or in part with any of the above conditions. The exercise of this discretion will depend very much on the cost of the work prescribed, for it must not exceed a reasonable expense limit. The level of expense that is reasonable is similar to what is regarded as reasonable expense for the purposes of compulsory repair notices for unfit property. In *F.F.F. Estates Ltd. v. Hackney LBC 1981*, the Court of Appeal held that in determining reasonable expense regard should be had to the market value of the dwelling house with any protected tenancy that has been granted. The costs of compulsory improvement to the owner are further reduced by virtue of the duty imposed on local authorities to pay a full intermediate grant for any work prescribed.

Procedure

The procedure adopted will depend upon whether the compulsory improvement notice relates to property inside or outside GIA's or HAA's. Within such areas the local authority can initiate the process without a formal request from a tenant but they can only do so in respect of owner occupied dwellings if improvement is necessary for the improvement of adjacent rented property. This is not to say that within such areas tenants may not make requests of the local authority to act, for they often will. Outside improvement areas a formal request must be made by a tenant for the provision of any standard amenity under **s.89 Housing Act 1974.** Having received a request there is no duty on the local authority to proceed in response to it. If the local authority decides to proceed it will serve a **provisional notice** on the person responsible requiring him to carry out specified works and calling a time and place meeting not less than 21 days after service of the notice. Copies of the notice must be served on all interested parties so that all views and proposals in relation to the property may be aired at the meeting. At this stage if full agreement is reached as to the work to be carried out including adequate housing arrangements for the tenants, then the local authority may accept an **undertaking** from the person responsible that he will bring the property up to the required standard within nine months. In such a case the compulsory improvment procedure need not then be proceeded with. Alternatively, if no undertaking is offered, accepted, or fulfilled, the local authority may serve a full improvement notice under **s.88.** Such notice under **s.90** must give the person responsible twelve months to complete the work specified and estimate the projected cost. Appeal against such a notice may be made within six weeks on various grounds such as unreasonable expense, alternative work unreasonably rejected, no lack of standard amenities or that the dwelling is in a clearance area. Failure to comply with a s.88 notice will enable the local authority to carry out the work under s.93 and recover the cost from the person in control of the dwelling. A person served with an improvement notice may alternatively within six months require the local authority to purchase his interest. Finally, mention should be made that local authorities have power under s.100 to grant loans to persons responsible, to pay for work specified in a compulsory improvement notice.

CHAPTER 17   Clearance and Redevelopment

The alternative to schemes of rehabilitation and renewal of properties is to proceed with a programme of **clearance and redevelopment.** Under the **Housing Act 1969** a statutory duty is imposed on authorities to inspect their areas to determine any action that is required to be taken in relation to clearance and the possible **declaration of a clearance area.** The decision by an authority to adopt a programme of clearance rather than rehabilitation is of course a highly complex one which in a book of this nature it is not proposed to examine. Rather, a general consideration of the legal powers which exist to enable an authority to implement a clearance programme will be considered. This will involve a consideration of the various compulsory purchase powers which have been conferred on authorities. It should be noted that 'CPO' powers are not limited to clearance but may also be necessary in a rehabilitation scheme where individual properties need to be acquired either because the owners will not co-operate or rehabilitation is impractical because of their state of repair.

17.1 The Process of Clearance Declaration

The original local authority powers in relation to clearance are contained in the **Housing Act 1957,** which provides in **s.42** that an area may be declared a clearance area if the authority is satisfied in good faith as to the following:—

1.   that the houses in the area are unfit for human habitation or are by reason of their bad arrangement or the narrowness or bad arrangement of the streets dangerous or injurious to the health of the inhabitants of the area and that the other buildings, if any, in the area are for the like reason dangerous or injurious to the health of the inhabitants; and

2.   that the most satisfactory method of dealing with the conditions in the area is the demolition of all the buildings in the area; and

3.   that alternative accommodation can be made available; and

4.   that the resources of the authority are sufficient.

The process of clearance declaration requires the authority to define the clearance area on a map, excluding any building which is not unfit for human habitation or dangerous or injurious to health. The map must be drawn up in the prescribed manner — unfit houses coloured pink (or diagonally hatched), houses included because of their bad arrangement coloured pink, hatched - yellow (or diagonally cross hatched). It is then possible to pass the resolution actually declaring the area to be a clearance area and inform the Secretary of State. The Secretary of State will, based on the information given to him, be subsequently required to confirm the compulsory purchase order made in relation to the area. Judicial scrutiny of the role of the Secretary of State will be limited to ensuring that he has not exceeded his statutory powers.

An example of a case where the courts have intervened is provided by *Eckersley v. Secretary of State for the Environment and Southwark LBC 1977.* Here a clearance area was declared which included the plaintiff's house. The subsequent compulsory purchase order on the area was confirmed by the Secretary of State. An action was brought to quash the order on the grounds that the Secretary of State had failed to consider certain material considerations in reaching his decision including whether the financial resources of the local authority were sufficient to put into effect the clearance and redevelopment. This matter the court held was not within the Secretary of State's jurisdiction and one for the local authority alone to determine in good faith. The plaintiff was more successful when he pointed to the failure of the Secretary of State to ensure that the local authority had adequately examined the relative cost of clearance as opposed to rehabilitation. This matter, the court held, was one for the Secretary of State's consideration, and as there was no evidence that it had been considered properly, a major issue had therefore been ignored. The CPO was ultra vires and accordingly quashed.

17.2 Land Acquisition

Once a clearance area has been declared the next step is for the local authority to proceed to acquire the land and carry out the demolition. One way of achieving this was by the authority making a **clearance order** which effectively made the owners of the property within the area carry out the demolition work themselves. This procedure has been discontinued for clearance areas declared on or after 31st August, 1974. Now the method of dealing with a clearance area is contained in **s.43(1)(b) Housing Act 1957,** which provides that so soon as may be after a local authority have declared any area to be a clearance area they shall . . . proceed to secure the clearance of the area by purchasing the land comprised in the area or otherwise securing the demolition of the building on that land. Various options are thus open to the authority to either, agree with the owners that they should demolish, or acquire the land by agreement, or compulsory purchase and then demolish. The local authority has wide powers to purchase any land within the clearance area or surrounded by the clearance area which is necessary for securing a cleared area of convenient shape or dimensions, or any adjoining land which is reasonably necessary for the satisfactory development or use of the cleared area. Authorities have power to acquire fit property where necessary therefore, but they may be called on to justify its inclusion. Failure to produce evidence as to the need to acquire **'added land'** in such circumstances may lead to a 'CPO' being quashed.

In *Coleen Properties v. Minister of Housing and Local Government 1971* the local authority included modern property in a clearance area and put it into a CPO as added land under **s.43.** At the public local inquiry the authority submitted no evidence that the property was reasonably required and accordingly the Inspector recommended its exclusion from the CPO. Nevertheless the Minister rejected the Inspector's recommendation and confirmed the CPO. The Court of Appeal held that since the Minister's decision was based upon no evidence, it was ultra vires and void. To justify the inclusion of added land it was necessary for the council to prove a real need for it.

Where compulsory purchase powers are exercised, the procedure contained in the third schedule of the **Housing Act 1957** must be adhered to, the Order itself being in the form prescribed by the **Housing (Prescribed Forms) Regulations 1972.** This involves publishing notice of the order in the local press and serving express notice of it, with the right to object, on all interested parties. Any objectors must be heard by holding a hearing or more usually a **local public inquiry** where they can put their case to the Secretary of State's inspector. An inquiry is held where there are objections to the declaration of the area or the inclusion of properties within it, rather than related solely to the compensation payable for compulsory purchase. Having heard the evidence the inspector will then recommend a course of action to the Secretary of State who has a wider discretion to confirm, vary or reject the CPO. Right of appeal against its confirmation must be exercised within six weeks otherwise the CPO confirmation may not be questioned in any legal proceedings. Following confirmation the process of land acquisition is governed by the **Compulsory Purchase Act 1965.** This involves the service of a **notice to treat** on the owner or any person with a leasehold interest to be purchased. This enables any negotiations relating to compensation to take place and in the event of stalemate the matter will be referred to the **Lands Tribunal** for determination. Only then can the conveyance, costs for which are borne by the authority, be carried out and completion take place. The alternative to individual conveyances is provided by **s.30 Town and Country Planning Act 1968.** The procedure here is restricted to large scale CPO's and provides for the issue of a **'general vesting declaration'** which conveys the land affected by the scheme to the local authority on a specified date, without the need for a separate conveyance for each owner. It is achieved by serving notice of intention on owners and fixing a date for final vesting not earlier than two months from its publication. After the vesting date the authority may exercise all the powers of a legal owner and take possession.

17.3 Compensation

The payment of compensation to displaced owners as a result of compulsory purchase is a complex area of law and it is intended here to consider only the general principles. Under **s.59 Housing Act 1959** where a compulsory purchase order follows the declaration of a clearance area the compensation payable is to be assessed in accordance with **Land Compensation Act 1961.** The level of compensation payable by the local authority is often the total of a number of separate items of payment. The rules applicable depend on how the property in question is classified.

A. **Fit property acquired for the satisfactory development of the area (added land).**

By service of notice to treat on the owners, (i.e. notice that the authority has been authorised to acquire the land) **'interested parties'** are given the opportunity to submit particulars of claims for compensation. Such claims may be settled by agreement of course, and usually are, but if the parties fail to agree then the matter will be determined by the Lands Tribunal in accordance with the **Land Compensation Acts 1961** and **1973.** The three elements of compensation are:—

a. the value of the land acquired;

b. if only part of the land is taken, compensation related to the loss in value of the land retained;

c. compensation for disturbance.

The total sum payable should be sufficient to put the owner in the position he would have been had the land not been acquired. In assessing the first element of compensation (a), the Lands Tribunal makes no allowance for the fact that the acquisition is compulsory, and values the land at its **open market valuation.** In addition no account is taken of any increase or decrease in the value of the land which is attributable to development or the prospect of development. Compensation under the second element (b) is applicable where the owner holds other land with the land acquired, and the retained land is depreciated in value. The third element (c) covers all the expenditure which an owner may incur in having to move from the land taken and re-establish himself elsewhere. This includes all monetary expenses in the case of a residential occupier and in the case of a business occupier the costs of re-location of the business and consequent loss of profits, goodwill, etc.

The **Land Compensation Act 1973** provides for special statutory payments to individuals whether or not they have a sufficient interest in the land to entitle them to compensation previously mentioned. These payments include:—

1. **Home loss payments.** This is due to a person displaced from his home in consequence of a compulsory acquisition of the property or the making of a closing or demolition order by the authority. The applicant must have occupied the dwelling as his main residence throughout the previous five years, the amount of the payment being three times the rateable value of the premises with a maximum of £1,500 and a minimum of £150.

2. **Farm loss payment.** This is due to a farmer displaced from the whole of his land by compulsory acquisition provided that he is the owner or holds a term of years with not less than three years to run and he begins to farm elsewhere within three years of displacement. The amount due is a sum equivalent to the average annual profit from the land acquired for a three-year period after deducting a notional rent.

3. **Disturbance payment.** A person displaced from land because of compulsory acquisition, demolition order, etc. with no interest in the land for which compensation is due is entitled to a disturbance payment, e.g. a lodger. This payment consists of removal expenses and where appropriate loss sustained by reason of disturbance of trade or business consequent upon the claimant having to quit the land.

4. **Rehousing.** A housing authority is under a general duty to secure suitable alternative accommodation for persons displaced from residential accommodation as a result of compulsory purchase, etc.

B. Unfit property acquired compulsorily

On the compulsory acquisition of an unfit property, either within a clearance area or as an individually unfit house, the compensation payable is the **cleared site value.** This sum however must not exceed the market value of the site with the property on it (i.e. costs of demolition may exceed the value of a useless property). **'Further payments'** may be available in the following circumstances:—

1. **A house is used partly for business purposes and acquired at site value.** Here the person entitled to the business profits may have a claim for compensation if he held an interest in the house for the two years preceding the compulsory purchase order.

2. If following an inspection of the property an officer of the Secretary of State confirms that it has been **well maintained** over the previous five years. The person responsible for maintenance is entitled to a payment equivalent to four times the rateable value (or such other multiplier substituted by the Secretary of State) but the amount must not exceed the difference between the full market value of the property and the site value. Provision is also made for **partial well maintained** payments where either the exterior or interior has been well maintained.

3. **Full compensation** (i.e. equal to the sum payable for fit property compulsorily acquired) is payable in the case of a dwelling in owner occupation if either it has been occupied by the owner or a member of his family continuously since 23rd April, 1968

or if acquired for occupation after that date but has been in owner occupation for two years prior to the declaration of the clearance area. Even if neither criterion is satisfied the authority has a discretion to make a payment of full compensation to an owner-occupier who satisfies the authority that before purchasing the property he made all reasonable inquiries and had no reason to believe that slum clearance would commence within two years.

4.   The **Land Compensation Act 1961** provides for a **guaranteed minimum payment** of up to the **'gross value'** of the house. This is payable if the compensation which an owner occupier would receive, including the 'owner occupier' payment and the 'well maintained' payment, is less than the gross value of the house. The compensation is then made up to the gross value.

5.   The rights to **home loss** and **disturbance payments** and **rehousing** are equally applicable to the situation where unfit property is compulsorily acquired.

C.   Unfit property not compulsorily purchased

If the authority proceeds by way of closing or demolition there is no entitlement to compensation for either the owner or occupier. All of the above **'further payments'** may be made by the authority however, except the guaranteed minimum of the gross value.

Part 7 - **Employment Law**

CHAPTER 18   The Creation of the Contract of Employment

18.1 The Employment Relationship

The nature of a contract has already been considered in depth in Chapter 3. It is simply an agreement which is legally enforceable. The relationship which exists between an employer (e.g. a housing authority or housing association) and its workforce is based upon a specialist form of contract, the **contract of employment.** Generally the law recognises the existence of two types of employment relationship. Firstly, and most usually, the **contract of service,** which applies to **employed persons** and governs the relationship which exists between the employer and employee. Here the employer will wish to exercise a large degree of control over his workers continuously, on a long term basis. Alternatively there exists the **contract for services** which applies to **self employed persons** and governs the relationship which exists between the employer and independent contractor. Here the employer is primarily concerned about the carrying out of a specific task for a limited period or intermittently, and does not require to exercise a large degree of control over its performance. The classification of the two types of contract is crucial since there are a mass of legal and financial responsibilities which apply to any employment relationship but differ depending on whether the contract is one of service or for services. A comparison of some of the main rights and responsibilities under the two types of contract is shown below.

By comparing the major characteristics of the two types of contract as shown below it can be seen that the status enjoyed by both the employed and self employed has benefits and detriments for employer and worker. The major advantage of self employed status is an economic one for both the contractor, in tax advantages and less national insurance contributions, and the employer, in reduced costs of administration. This benefit of course must be weighed against the detriment to the worker of less job security and the employer, of less control. Certainly a local authority which requires the performance of a specialist task either once, or only intermittently, could be advised to employ a contractor rather than engage a full-time employee. It should be stressed however that it is not possible to create

CONTRACTS OF SERVICE (EMPLOYED PERSONS)	CONTRACTS FOR SERVICES (SELF EMPLOYED PERSONS)

EMPLOYER'S LIABILITY

1. An employer may be made liable under the law for TORTS committed by his employees during the course of their employment.

1. As a general rule an employer is not liable for TORTS committed by independent contractors during the course of their employment.

2. The law imposes a high standard of care on an employer with regard to the health and safety of his employees both under Statute and common law.

2. Generally a lesser standard of care is owed by an employer towards his contractors with regard to health and safety both under the common law and Statute.

ECONOMIC IMPLICATIONS

3. An employee's income tax is deduced by his employer from his wages under the pay as you earn scheme, i.e. PAYE (Schedule E).

3. A self employed person is responsible for his own tax liability and pays tax under Schedule D on a preceeding year basis. This can prove to be a more advantageous method for the taxpayer.

4. Under the **Social Security Act, 1975,** both employer and employee must contribute to the payment of Class 1 National Insurance contributions.

4. Under the **Social Security Act, 1975,** a self employed person is individually responsible for the payment of lower Class 2 National Insurance contributions.

5. As a result of making Class 1 contributions, an employee is entitled to claim all the available welfare benefits, e.g. unemployment, sickness, industrial injuries benefit.

5. A self employed person who makes Class 2 contributions has no entitlement to certain welfare benefits, e.g. unemployment, industrial injuries, but may claim others (sickness benefit).

OTHER STATUTORY RIGHTS

6. Employment legislation, (**Employment Protection (Consolidation) Act, 1978**), has conferred a number of rights and benefits on employed persons, e.g.

    a. the right to a written notice of the details of employment within the first 13 weeks of employment;

    b. the right to receive certain minimum periods of notice on dismissal;

    c. the right to redundancy payment in appropriate circumstances;

    d. the right to protection against unfair dismissal;

    e. the right to be a member of a Trade Union and engage in Trade Union activities;

    f. the right to protection against the employer's insolvency.

6. The majority of statutory rights under the **Employment Protection (Consolidation) Act, 1978,** are not available for self employed persons.

a particular employment relationship by pinning a label on it. Thus an employer could not rid himself of the numerous statutory duties he has in relation to his employees by simply renaming them contractors. It is the **substance** of any employment relationship which will determine its status.

18.2 Distinguishing between the Contracts

The task of distinguishing between a contract of service and a contract for services has been left to the courts. Over the years various tests have been formulated to determine a worker's status. Originally, the courts would only consider the level of control over a worker by an employer. In *Performing Right Society Ltd. v. Mitchell and Booker 1924,* McCardie J. said that "the test to be generally applied, lies in the nature and degree of detailed control over the person alleged to be an employee". Therefore, if an employee could tell his workers not only what to do, but also how and when to do it, then the worker was regarded as an employee, employed under a contract of service. Today, the courts adopt a much wider approach and, while conceding that the degree of control is an important factor, they also take into account all other circumstances to determine a worker's status.

> In *Ready Mixed Concrete Ltd. v. Ministry of Pensions 1968,* the court had to decide the status of a driver for the plaintiff company. His written contract of employment (30 pages long) stated that he was not an employee but this, the court said, was not decisive. It was merely a factor to be taken into account. All aspects of his job were considered, e.g. he purchased the lorry from the company, he had to maintain it himself, his pay was calculated on the basis of concrete carried, he could in some circumstances delegate the driving. These factors pointed to him being a contractor, while others pointed to his status as an employee e.g. he had to paint the lorry in the company colours, he had to use it exclusively on company business, he was required to obey reasonable orders. The facts have been outlined in some detail to show you the difficulty often facing the judges. Here, the court held that the majority of the provisions were consistent with there being a contract for services. McKenna J. stated that there is a contract of service if:—

a. An individual agrees to provide his own work, and

b. The individual submits to his employer's control; and

c.   The majority of the contractual provisions are consistent with it being a contract of service.

Certainly, the status of self employed cannot be achieved simply by including an express provision in a contract. The courts will look to the substance of any employment relationship to decide a worker's status.

> In *Ferguson v. John Dawson Ltd. 1976,* a builder's labourer agreed to work on what was known as 'the lump' and described as a 'self employed labour only sub-contractor'. Having suffered injuries as a result of the employer's breach of a statutory duty, the labourer could only succeed in an action for damages if he could show that he was an 'employee' and therefore protected under the Statute. The court held that the 'lump' was no more than a device to attempt to gain tax advantages and in reality taking all the circumstances into account, the relationship was one of employer and employee and a contract of service.

18.3 Formation of the Contract of Employment

The general contractual rules governing offer and acceptance are relevant to determine when a contract of employment has been entered into. Thus the advertisement of a job is a mere **invitation to treat.** Usually following an interview the employer will make an express offer of a job to the successful applicant on specific terms which may differ with the advertisement. A counter offer by the applicant will extinguish the original offer. The contract is concluded on the communication of the applicant's acceptance and, if the postal rules of acceptance apply, the acceptance is complete on posting. Of course this whole process may take place over a long period involving conversations, letters and interviews. Power to employ staff, vested in a local authority, is normally delegated to a particular committee or sub-committee by virtue of standing orders. If this is the case and the committee acts under **'delegated powers'** as opposed to **'referred powers'** (where confirmation by the full council is necessary), then the acts of the committee are in all respects those of the local authority.

> In *Battelley v. Finsbury BC 1958* a works committee was appointed by the local authority which by virtue of standing orders was responsible for "... appointment and management of the staff of the borough engineer's department". Following an application for the post of assistant road superintendent the plaintiff was interviewed

by the works committee which resolved to appoint him. A letter to the plaintiff informed him of this decision 'subject to confirmation'. When someone else was appointed in his place the plaintiff sued for breach of contract. The court agreed that damages for breach should be awarded as the function of appointing the plaintiff had been delegated to the committee by standing orders and the committee had entered into a contract of employment with him.

There is no requirement that a contract of employment be in a written form, however it is usual practice in many industries and certainly in local government, for the employer to provide the employee with a formal written contract which the employee signs to show his agreement. Also the **Employment Protection (Consolidation) Act 1978** (which contains most of the employee's statutory rights) requires an employer to provide his employee with written particulars of employment within thirteen weeks of starting work. These written particulars should include reference to the main terms of the contract including:—

a. reference to the parties;
b. remuneration;
c. hours of· work;
d. holidays and holiday pay;
e. sickness and sick pay;
f. pension and pension scheme;
g. disciplinary regulations;
h. rights on termination of the contract.

This requirement is one of the numerous statutory provisions relating to employee's rights, the remainder of which are considered in the next section on the contents of the contract of employment.

18.4 Contents of the Contract of Employment

A contract of employment is like any other contract composed of terms which confer rights and impose obligations on the parties to it. Such terms may be **expressly agreed** by the parties or **implied** into the contract from another source. As far as contracts of employment are concerned, other sources could be either a **collective agreement** made between the employer and a Trade Union, **work rules and custom,** or **the law** in the form of statutory provisions or the common law.

299

Express Terms

These are the terms expressly agreed by the employer and employee and may be in writing or may be purely verbal. The **Employment Protection (Consolidation) Act 1978** requires express terms to satisfy the **test of reasonableness** so that if a term is seen to be oppressive it could be regarded as void, e.g. if the employer reserved the right to dismiss the employee for a trivial breach of contract. The express terms of the contract usually relate to matters such as wages, hours, holidays, sick pay, job description, restraints, etc. Local authority contracts of employment are usually in standard form dependent on the type of employment e.g. office or manual worker. Of course, what has expressly been agreed by the parties may often require interpretation in the courts and industrial tribunals. Many employment disputes are first heard in industrial tribunals with the possibility of appeal to the Employment Appeals Tribunal and from there in certain circumstances to the ordinary courts (see Chapter 1).

> In *Cole v. Midland Display Ltd. 1973* the tribunal was faced with the problem of determining the meaning of the term "employed on a staff basis" when it was applied to a manager. The Tribunal held that the phrase meant that the employee was entitled to wages during periods of sickness or no work, but in return the employee could be required to work overtime without pay.

As a general rule the express terms cannot be varied by either party without the others's consent unless an express term confers this right on one of the parties. Any attempt by the employer to impose an **unreasonable variation** of the contractual terms on the employee will amount to a breach, e.g. require the employee to attend a place of work outside travelling distance from home. Of course a requirement to move may be expressly included or even implied from the contract of employment in which case there would be no breach. In *McCaffrey v. A. E. Jeavons & Co. Ltd. 1967,* an employee expressly employed as a "travelling man" in the building trade was held to be bound to move anywhere in the country. It is a question of fact in each case whether a change of job will amount to a breach of the contract of employment. If the contract expressly provides that the nature of the employee's job may be changed then even a variation which would constitute a demotion may be within the contractual terms. To constitute a **consensual variation** of the contract of employment the courts must be satisfied that the employee gives a clear indication that he voluntarily accepts the new terms of his employment.

In *Marriott v. Oxford & District Co-op Soc. Ltd. 1970* the Court of Appeal was required to determine whether there had been a consensual variation of the contractual terms in the following case. A foreman supervisor was told by his employer that the position of foreman was no longer required and that his wages were to be reduced by £1 to reflect his loss of status. The employee continued to work under protest for three weeks before terminating his employment by notice, claiming redundancy. The Court of Appeal held, reversing the Divisional Court's decision, that there had been no free consent to the contractual variation and the change in terms amounted to a repudiation of the contract of employment.

Implied Terms

Terms may be implied into a contract of employment from various sources:—

    a.   Collective agreements;

    b.   Work Rules or Trade Custom;

    c.   The Law.

a.   **Collective Agreements** A collective agreement is an agreement between an employer or Employers' Association and a Trade Union providing for the terms and conditions of employment of those covered by the agreement. The importance of such agreements is illustrated by the fact that an estimated 14 million employees in this country are covered by them. However they are not legally enforceable. They will nevertheless be legally binding on the employer and employee if incorporated into an individual's contract of employment.

    To be part of an individual's contract of employment, the general rule is that express reference must be made to it, e.g. 'Union conditions', 'subject to National agreement'. Often, the statutory notice of the particulars of employment which the employer must serve, will make express reference to a collective agreement and thereby incorporate it into the individual's contract of employment.

b.   **Work Rules or Trade Custom** It is common practice in many spheres of employment for the employer to issue work rules by printing notices or handing out booklets. Such work rules often contain instructions as to time-keeping, meal breaks, disciplinary offences, disciplinary and grievance procedure, sickness and pension rights,

301

and the employer's safety policy. Although there is still doubt as to their legal significance, it seems at present that such documents are unlikely to contain contractual terms.

In *The Secretary of State for Employment v. Associated Society of Locomotive Engineers and Firemen 1972* Ld Denning held that the rule book issued to railwaymen by their employer did not contain contractual terms but rather instructions to an employee on how he was to do his work.

At the present time, it is unlikely that a trade custom or practice will be incorporated into a contract of employment by implication. Certainly a trade custom would have to satisfy the tests of being certain, reasonable and notorious (notable) before it would be regarded as legally enforceable. This was the case in *Sagar v. Ridehalgh 1931* where a custom that deductions could be made from the wages of a weaver for bad work was held to be legally binding.

c.   **Terms Implied by the Law** In every contract of employment, certain terms are implied by the operation of the common law and statute. These terms are the source of many of the rights and duties of both the employer and employee.

Statutory Terms The Employment Protection (Consolidation) Act 1978 contains extensive rights for employees which are inserted by implication into their individual contracts of employment. An employee's remedy for infringement of these rights lies by way of complaint to an industrial tribunal. The rights, which are examined in detail throughout this section, relate to redundancy payments, payment of wages, health and safety, and trade union activities. Statutory rights relating to termination of employment are considered in Chapter 19.

At this point it is convenient to consider an employee's rights in relation to **trade union membership.** The 1978 Act specifically states that an employee has the right to be a member of a trade union and take part in trade union activities. In addition an employer must permit an employee, who is an official of an independent trade union recognised by that employer, to take time off during working hours to carry out official duties or undergo relevant training, **ss.27 and 29,** or carry out public duties, **s.29.** It is only **"independent"** trade unions which enjoy most of the legal benefits and so it is necessary to consider their definition as contained in the **Trade**

Union and Labour Relations Act 1974. Under **s.28** a trade union is an organisation which either:—

    a.   consists wholly of mainly of workers of one or more descriptions and is an organisation whose principal purposes include the regulation of relations between workers of that description and employers or employers' associations; or which

    b.   consists wholly of mainly of constituent or affiliated organisations which fulfil (a) above or their representatives.

The principal purpose of such organisations must include the regulation of relations between workers and employers or its constituent organisations. Trade unions then are **workers' organisations which are designed to regulate industrial relations** but to qualify as 'independent' they must also under **s.30** not be under the control of an employer or employers' association or be liable to interference by any such group. The 1974 Act provides machinery under which a trade union may apply to a **Certification Officer** to establish itself as independent.

While independence carries with it a degree of legal protection for trade union officials, further rights and privileges can be achieved when a trade union is **recognised.** These rights include disclosure of information, consultation concerning redundancies and appointment of safety committees. Recognition involves either **formal recognition** by the employer, or a clear and unequivocal act which demonstrates that both parties intend particular **conduct to constitute recognition.** The entire recognition procedures formerly regulated by the Advisory, Conciliation and Arbitration Service and the Central Arbitration Committee were repealed by the **Employment Act 1980.** An employer can no longer be required to recognise a trade union following the recommendation of ACAS and the CAC.

It would be wrong to leave the subject of trade unions without some mention of the present position in relation to the **'closed shop'** or **union membership agreements.** Such agreements, entered into by employers and trade unions, provide that only members of an appropriate trade union or unions will be employed at a particular work place. If the agreement provides that new employees must be members of a particular trade union then it is a **'pre entry' closed shop.** A **'post entry' closed shop** exists where the agreement is that every employee must be a member of a particular trade union. The **Employment Act 1980** did not affect the validity of existing union membership agreements but made the creation of new approved agreements less likely. Approval now requires a secret ballot and 80% of all those entitled to vote voting in favour of the closed shop. In addition the 1980 Act provides that the right of an employee to contract out of a closed shop is no longer to be tied to religious belief but rather if he **"genuinely objects on grounds of conscience or other deeply held personal conviction"** to being a member of any trade union whatsoever or of a particular trade union. This extended right to contract out applies to existing as well as future union membership agreements so that as we shall see later the dismissal of an employee in these circumstances would be statutorily unfair.

Common Law Terms

Terms are implied into a contract of employment by the common law imposing duties on both the employer and employee.

Common Law Terms

Duties of the Employer	Duties of the Employee
1. To pay wages.	1. To discharge contractual duties with good faith.
2. To provide the opportunity to earn the expected wage, indemnify, and provide a reference.	2. To account for money received on his employer's behalf.
3. To provide a safe system of work.	3. To respect trade secrets.
	4. To obey lawful instructions and take reasonable care.

Employer's Duties

1. **To pay wages.** The common law implies a term into the contract of employment imposing a duty on the employer to pay a reasonable wage for the work done. In the majority of cases, of course, the parties to the contract of employment (i.e. the employer and employee) will have expressly agreed a rate of pay or referred to a rate of pay contained in a collective agreement. However, if no wage is expressly agreed, in the event of a dispute the courts will value the service provided and imply a reasonable wage. In addition to the common law, there are a number of statutory provisions surrounding the payment of wages. Under the **Employment Consolidation (Protection) Act 1978** every employee is entitled to receive a written itemised statement of his pay (including deductions). This statement should include the gross amount, deductions and their purpose, the

304

net amount and if the net amount is paid in different ways, the amount and methods of payment. Also since the mid-nineteenth century statute has regulated how wages may be paid in order to prevent abuse by employers. The **Truck Act 1831** provided that wages of workers must be paid in current coin of the realm only. This was to prevent employers paying wages in kind (goods) or tokens. The Act also provides that deductions can be made from a workers wages only for certain purposes acknowledged in a signed agreement.

In *Daley v. Radnor 1973* an oral agreement between an employer and employee provided that the employer would let premises to the employee at £10 per week rent, such a sum to be deducted from the employee's weekly wage. The employee claimed £1570 which had been deducted from his wages for this purpose. The court held that the sum was recoverable on the ground that the deduction was unlawful.

In order to permit the payment of wages in forms other than cash, the **Payment of Wages Act 1960** was passed. The Act provides that by written agreement employees may be paid by cheque, bank giro, direct bank account debit, etc. To prevent discrimination in the remuneration paid to both sexes engaged in similar work, the **Equal Pay Act 1970** (as amended by the **Sex Discrimination Act 1975**) was passed to attempt to ensure equal treatment. The requirement of equal treatment only applies where the sexes are engaged in similar work for higher rates of pay can be justified where greater skill or responsibility is demanded. Any differences based on physical strength and the time when work is to be done are to be disregarded.

In *Electrolux v. Hutchinson 1977* female workers engaged in broadly similar work to their male counterparts were held to be entitled to equal pay, despite the condition that the men could exclusively be required to work overtime, at weekends, or at night. The fact that the men were rarely called on to do this was a major consideration.

The decision as to whether similar work is being carried on demands a comparison not between the contractual obligations of the parties, but rather a consideration of the things actually done and the frequency with which they are done.

In *Coombes (Holdings) Ltd. v. Shield 1978* the female counter clerks in bookmaker shops were paid a lesser rate of pay than their male counterparts. The employers sought to justify the differences on the grounds that the male employees had extra duties acting as a deterrent to unruly customers and transporting cash between branches. The Court of Appeal held that in deciding the question as to **'like work'** it was necessary to:—

i.   Consider the differences between the things the men and women were required to do;

ii.   Consider the frequency with which such differences occur in practice;

iii.   Consider whether the differences are of any practical importance. This approach should enable the court to place a value on each job in terms of demands placed upon the worker and if the value of the man's job is higher he should be paid an increased rate for the job. In this case the differences were not of sufficient importance to justify a different rate of pay.

One of the main effects of the **Sex Discrimination Act 1975** in amending the **Equal Pay Act 1970** was to provide that every contract of employment is **deemed** to include an equality clause. This clause automatically:—

a.   modifies a term of a woman's contract which is less favourable than a term of a similar kind in a man's contract where he is employed on similar work; and

b.   includes in a woman's contract any term benefiting a man employed on like work.

The equality clause will not operate however if the employer can show that the differences between the contracts is **'genuinely due to a material difference'** other than one of sex. In cases where there are differences involving benefits and detriments the disadvantages of one term may be complemented by the advantages of another.

2.   **To provide work, indemnify and provide a reference.** Generally there is no duty on an employer to provide work for his employees as long as their contractual remuneration is paid. If however an employee's pay depends upon the performance of work (piece-work) then the employer is under an obligation to provide sufficient work to enable a reasonable wage to be earned. A further exception is where the employee's occupation is such that the opportunity to work is an essential part of the contract because of the possibility of loss of reputation, e.g. an actor, entertainer or journalist.

Under the common law, an employee is entitled to be indemnified for loss or expense incurred in the course of employment. In most cases, of course, expenses are provided for expressly in the contract of employment.

There is however, no legal duty to provide employees with a reference on the termination of their employment. If a reference is given however, the tort of **defamation** will provide a remedy for an employee if the employer has maliciously included false statements which damage the employee's character. Also an employer could be sued under the tort of **deceit** or **negligent mis-statement** by another employer who suffers loss as a result of employing someone following an unwarrantable good reference.

3. **To provide a safe system of work.** The present law relating to an employer's duties in relation to the safety of his workforce is embodied within the common law and statute. The common law duty arises under the tort of negligence and involves providing employees with a safe system of work. Statutory duties are imposed under various Acts, e.g. the **Factories Act 1961,** the **Office Shops and Railway Premises Act 1963** (the contents of which are being incorporated by regulation into the **Health and Safety at Work Act 1974).**

An employer must under the common law exercise reasonable care with regard to the safety of employees by providing a safe system of work. It should be emphasised therefore that the duty imposed on an employer is not a strict one and may be fulfilled by the exercise of reasonable care. The basic elements of the tort of negligence (examined in Chapter 9) are relevant to determine liability.

> In *Latimer v. AEC 1953* after a factory was flooded the employer asked his workforce to return, warning them of the dangerous state of the factory floor. Sawdust had been used to cover most of the damp areas but not enough was available and the plaintiff slipped and was injured. To determine whether the employer had broken the common law duty of care he owed to his employees the court weighed the cost of avoiding the injury against the extra risk of injury and held that the employer had acted reasonably in the circumstances.

The common law duty can be broken down as follows:—

a.   **Provide safe fellow workers.** An employer is vicariously responsible under the law for the actions of his employees during the course of their employment (see Chapter 9). If these actions turn out to be negligent and someone (e.g. a fellow employee or third party) has suffered harm as a result, then the employer could be sued and made liable. An employer must therefore take reasonable care to ensure that he provides his workers with safe fellow workers. If the employer is aware of an employee who may create a dangerous situation at work by incompetence or practical jokes, he should discipline the employee, and if the practice continues, if necessary dismiss him. We shall see later in Chapter 19 that this would be regarded as a justifiable ground for dismissal.

> In *Coddington v. International Harvester Co. 1969* an employee negligently pushed a tin of burning paint towards a fellow employee and injury resulted. The court held that the employer was not liable as he could not have foreseen the danger. There was no record of the employee in question being guilty of dangerous behaviour in the past.

b.   **Provide safe plant and appliances.** If an employer is aware that machinery or tools are not reasonably safe and an employee is injured as a result, the employer will be in breach of this duty.

> In *Bradford v. Robinson Rentals 1967* the employer provided an unheated van for the employee to make a 400 mile journey during the winter. The court held that the employer was liable for the employee's frost bite which was reasonably foreseeable.

In the past an employer could satisfy this duty by showing that he purchased equipment from a reputable supplier and had no knowledge of any defect in them. Now, however, following the **Employer's Liability (Defective Equipment) Act 1969** injury occuring to an employee under those circumstances may be attributed to the deemed negligence of the employer. If damages are awarded against the employer, then it is up to him to seek a remedy from the supplier of the defective equipment. At this stage, mention can also be made of the **Employer's Liability (Compulsory Insurance) Act 1969** which requires all employers to insure against the risk of causing personal injury to their employees as a result of their fault.

c.   **Provide safe working methods.** To determine whether an employer is providing safe working methods, it is necessary to consider a number of factors including the layout, training and supervision, warnings, protective clothing. It should be stressed that the common law duty on an employer is to take reasonable care, and if an employer gives proper instructions which the employee fails to observe then the employer will not be liable if the employee is then injured.

> In *Charlton v. Forrest Printing Ink Co. Ltd. 1978* the employer gave proper instructions to an employee who was given the job of collecting the firm's wages. The instructions required the employee to vary his collecting arrangements to prevent robbery. The employee failed to do this and suffered severe injury when he was robbed. The Court of Appeal held that the employer was not liable as he had taken reasonable steps to cut down the risk.

As far as safety equipment is concerned, the common law requires an employer to provide it where necessary, and make it available for use. In some cases, particularly where there is a serious risk of injury, the employer's duty extends to ensuring that workers make use of the safety equipment provided.

> In *Nolan v. Dental Manufacturing Co. 1958* it was held that an employer was liable in negligence when he failed to ensure that safety goggles were worn by a toolsetter who was injured while working on a grinding wheel.

In addition, the standard of care owed by an employer will vary with regard to each individual employee. A young apprentice should be provided with effective supervision while this may not be required for an experienced employee.

> In *Paris v. Stepney BC 1951* the plaintiff, a one-eyed motor mechanic, lost the sight of his good eye while working at chipping rust from under a bus. Despite there being no usual practice to provide mechanics with safety goggles, the court decided that they should have been provided to the plaintiff. The defendants were liable as they could foresee serious consequences for the plaintiff if he suffered eye injury.

d.   **Provide safe working premises.** The requirement of an employer to provide safe working premises for his employees or visitors can be said to be part of the overall duty to provide a safe system of work.

Parliament has recognised that stringent safeguards are necessary in particular working environments. The **Factories Act 1961** and the **Offices, Shops and Railway Premises Act 1963** contain detailed regulations to attempt to secure the health and safety of employees. These Acts often impose onerous duties on an employer with regard to health and safety, e.g. an employer may be made strictly liable if he fails to securely fence a machine which is a source of danger. In 1974 Parliament passed the **Health and Safety at Work Act** which is designed to provide a comprehensive system of law to govern health and safety at work. The Act lays down general duties on employers, employees, suppliers of plant and equipment, those who control premises, etc. The principal general duty is that an employer must ensure, in so far as is reasonably practicable, the health and safety of his workers. This general duty involves:—

i.   providing and maintaining safe plant and a safe work system;

ii.   making arrangements for the use, handling, storage and transport of articles and substances;

iii.   providing any necessary information, instruction, training and supervision;

iv.   maintaining a safe place of work and a safe access to an exit from it;

v.   maintaining a safe working environment.

In addition, a body called the **Health and Safety Commission** has been created, which has been given the function of providing **detailed regulations** on health and safety applying to the various industries. In this way, the previous legislation on health and safety (e.g. the **Factories Act, 1961)** will gradually be replaced. The Commission also produce **codes of practice** which although not regarded as law, give guidance as to how the regulations (i.e. the law) may be fulfilled. Enforcement of the Act is in the hands of the **Health and Safety Executive** which have a number of powers at their disposal. It should be stressed that an employer or employee who breaks the Health and Safety at Work Act is in breach of the **criminal law** and may be prosecuted in a criminal court and fined or even imprisoned for a serious offence. Of course, the inspectors employed by the Executive will normally only prosecute after warnings have not been taken account of. One of the major innovations of the Act is the introduction of **constructive sanctions** which can be used by an inspector employed by the Executive. If an inspector believes that a person is contravening one of the statutory provisions the inspector may serve on that person an **improvement notice** requiring that the contravention be remedied within a specified period. In cases where the contravention involves a risk of serious injury the inspector may serve a **prohibition notice** which will direct that the particular activity is terminated until the contravention is rectified.

Employee's Duties

1. **The duty of good faith.** The duty includes the most fundamental obligation of an employee and involves serving his employer faithfully. Faithful service involves working competently, respecting the employer's property, and not taking industrial action such as strikes, go-slows, work to rule, etc. which would disrupt the employer's business.

   In *The Secretary of State for Employment v. ASLEF 1972* (mentioned previously) the Court of Appeal held that wilful disruption of the employer's undertaking would amount to a breach of this implied duty of good faith. Here the railwaymen were disrupting railway services by working to the letter of the British Rail rule book.

2. **To account for money received.** There is an implied duty on an employee not to accept any bribes, commissions or fees in respect of his work other than from his employer.

   In *Boston Deep-Sea Fishing & Ice Co. v. Ansell 1888* an employee, who received a secret commission from other companies for placing order with them, was treated as being in breach of this duty and his dismissal was justified.

3. **To respect trade secrets.** An employer would be in breach of this duty by working for a competitor in his spare time.

   In *Hivac v. Park Royal Scientific Instruments Co. 1946* an employee was restrained from working for a competitor engaged in work of a similar nature.

311

Certainly, there would be a flagrant breach of contract if an employee were to disclose trade secrets or other confidential information during the course of his employment. Even an ex-employee may be restrained.

> In *Printers & Finishers Ltd. v. Holloway 1965* an ex-employee was restrained from showing secret documents to a competitor and disclosing confidential information he had obtained during his employment.

4. **To obey reasonable orders.** This duty could be included within the general obligation to render faithful service. To be reasonable an order must be lawful, for there is no duty to obey an unlawful order, e.g. to falsify some records. In determining the reasonableness of an order, all the circumstances must be considered including a close examination of the contract of employment.

> In *UK Atomic Energy Authority v. Claydon 1974* the defendant's contract of employment required him to work anywhere in the UK. Accordingly it was held to be a reasonable order to require him to transfer to another base.

> Also, in *Pepper v. Webb 1969* a head gardener, when asked to plant some flowers replied "I couldn't care less about your bloody greenhouse or your sodding garden" and walked away. The court held that the refusal to obey the instructions, rather than the language which accompanied it, amounted to a breach of contract.

CHAPTER 19 Termination of Employment

A contract of employment must inevitably terminate at some time either by the death or retirement of the employee, or death, dissolution or winding up of the employer. Also, as a general rule, contracts of employment for a fixed term will terminate when the contractual period expires, and contracts to do a specific job are automatically terminated on the completion of the project. Otherwise, under the common law, either side to a contract of employment may lawfully terminate it by giving **reasonable notice** or **summarily** (without notice) in some cases where the other party has committed a serious breach of contract. Since the **Industrial Relations Act 1971** employees are given statutory protection against arbitrary dismissal by an employer, the provisions relating to which are included in the **Employment Protection (Consolidation) Act 1978** and the **Employment Act 1980**.

19.1 Termination by Notice

Under the common law either party to a contact of employment may terminate it by notice, the period of which will depend on seniority and length of service.

> In *Hill v. Parsons Ltd. 1972* the Court of Appeal thought that a chartered engineer who has been employed continuously for 35 years was entitled to at least six months notice.

Of course, the express terms of a contract of employment will often stipulate the required periods of notice. Also, the 1978 Act provides for minimum periods (see the table below) but these may be increased by the contract.

Minimum periods of notice

After continuous employment for:	Minimum notice required:
4 weeks up to 2 years	1 week
2 years up to 12 years	1 week for each year
12 years or more	12 weeks

19.2 Wrongful Dismissal

The expression 'wrongful dismissal' refers to a dismissal in a wrongful manner, e.g. by the employer not giving the correct period of notice or payment in lieu of notice. The remedy for wrongful dismissal is an action for damages in the ordinary courts (the County court of the High Court). Of course under the common law summary (instant) dismissal without notice may be justified on certain grounds, e.g. gross misconduct by reason of disobedience, neglect, dishonesty or misbehaviour. Whether the conduct complained of is sufficient to justify summary dismissal without adhering to disciplinary procedures involving warning, etc. is a question of fact for each case.

> In *Pepper v. Webb 1969* (previously mentioned) the action of the head gardener in wilfully disobeying a reasonable order was sufficient to amount to gross misconduct and give grounds for summary dismissal despite the contract of employment providing for three months notice. It should be stressed however that the reaction of the gardener in this case was the culmination of a long period of insolence and the isolated use of choice obscenities by an employee to an employer may not amount to gross misconduct if there is provocation.

> In *Wilson v. Racher 1974* a gardner who proved to have an even wider knowledge of bad language for which he was dismissed instantly was held to be wrongfully dismissed in the circumstances. The employer had provoked the outburst by his own conduct.

> Certainly the action of a betting shop manager in *Sinclair v. Neighbour 1967* of borrowing £15 from the till, and leaving an IOU, was regarded as a sufficient ground to justify summary dismissal.

19.3 Unfair Dismissal

The law relating to unfair dismissal is contained in the **Employment (Consolidation) Act 1978,** the **Employment Protection Act 1980** and their interpretation in many reported cases. A dispute relating to dismissal is first dealt with by an industrial tribunal, with the possibility of appeal to the Employment Appeals tribunal and from their in certain circumstances to the ordinary courts. Every employee to whom the 1978 Act applies has the right not to be unfairly dismissed. The basic qualifying period of continuous employment was raised by Order in 1979 to 52 weeks for an employee to obtain protection except in cases where the dismissal was for refusing to join a trade union or on grounds of sex or race discrimination. Under the 1980 Act, the period is two years for employees of small firms (less than 20). However, the compensation has also been increased by the 1980 Act to a possible £17,060 comprising of £6,250 compensation, £4,050 basic award and £6,760 additional award (if an employer unreasonably refused to carry out an order of reinstatement or re-engagement). It should be pointed out that sometimes a successful applicant may be awarded reduced compensation because of his own contributory conduct.

Dismissal

Once an employee brings a complaint of unfair dismissal against the employer within three months of dismissal, a conciliation officer will visit both parties in an attempt to resolve the conflict and reach a settlement. It should be stressed that in many cases an amicable agreement is reached at this stage because of the conciliation officer's intervention. If the employee wishes to proceed with the claim before a tribunal however then to succeed it is necessary to show there has been a dismissal. There is no dismissal of course if the employee:—

a.   **Resigns.** This may occur by the employee expressly terminating the contract by notice or constructively where the employee by his conduct is taken to have brought the contract to an end, e.g. refused to work.

b.   **Is a party to a frustrated contract.** This would occur when performance of the contract has become impossible because of some event, e.g. illness where the employee is unlikely to return to work for a long period.

c.   **Completes a particular project.** If the employee is employed to carry out a particular project and the work is completed.

d.   **Agrees to terminate.** If it can be shown that the employer and employee have expressly agreed that the contract should terminate on the happening or non happening of a specified event then the contract will terminate on its occurrence.

In *British Leyland v. Ashraf 1978* the employee was given five weeks unpaid leave to return to Pakistan and he expressly agreed that if he failed to return to work on a particular date his employment would terminate. The failure of the employee to return to work amounted to a mutual termination of the contract of employment.

e.   **Enters into a fixed term contract of twelve months or more and agrees in writing to exclude his statutory rights on unfair dismissal.** This is the only case where statutory rights on unfair dismissal may be excluded by agreement.

Having identified situations which would not be regarded as dismissal it is necessary to identify those that would. A dismissal will be taken to have occurred if there is either an express termination by the employer, a fixed term contract is not renewed (subject to the exception above), or there is a constructive dismissal.

Express Termination

If an employer expressly informs an employee that the contract is at an end by saying "you're dismissed", "collect your cards" or "you're fired" the dismissal is clear and explicit. Unfortunately, in practice Tribunals are often faced with placing an interpretation on the language used.

In *Futty v. Brekkes 1974* a fish filleter was told by his foreman 'If you do not like the job you can fuck off'. The Tribunal held that the language used had to be interpreted in the light of the work where such expressions were not unusual and so the words did not constitute a dismissal when the employer walked out.

A **fixed term contract** had been defined as a contract which must run for a fixed term and one which cannot be terminated except by a gross breach of a contractual term be either party. The possibility of an employee giving up his statutory rights relating to unfair dismissal in a fixed term contract over one year has already been mentioned. Quite simply therefore the expiration of a fixed term contract which does not come within this category will result in a dismissal if it is not renewed.

Constructive Dismissal occurs where the employee terminates the contract of employment in circumstances where he is entitled to do so because of the employer's conduct. To determine this issue has always proved to be a difficult question but it now seems that the test to be applied is at least certain.

316

In *Western Excavating (EEC) Ltd. v. Sharp 1978* the Court of Appeal held that to decide what constitutes constructive dismissal the **'conduct test'** should be applied, i.e. was the employer guilty of conduct which was a significant breach of the contract of employment showing that he no longer intended to be bound by one of its terms. It now seems therefore that an employee has to show that his employer was in some way in breach of the contract of employment to demonstrate that the employee walking out amounted to a constructive dismissal. This would occur if the employer attempted to change employment terms unilaterally without the employee's consent, e.g. less pay, change of work place, etc. The breach of course is not limited to the express terms of the contract but would also cover breach of the implied terms.

> In *British Aircraft Corp. v. Austin 1978* the employer was held to be in breach of his implied duty of safety when he failed to investigate a complaint relating to the suitability of protective glasses. This conduct would be a sufficient ground to entitle the employee to terminate the contract of employment and seek a remedy for unfair dismissal.

Quite often of course the employee who walks out is aggrieved not at the employer's conduct but at the conduct of a fellow employee for whom the employer is responsible.

> In *Isle of Wight Tourist Board v. Coombes 1976* the applicant secretary walked out following a remark by her superior — 'She is an intolerable bitch on a Monday morning'. This was held to be a fundamental breach of the contract of employment and a constructive dismissal when she walked out.

Having established that a dismissal has taken place the next question is whether the dismissal is fair or unfair. This is determined by considering all the circumsances of each individual case including the grounds for dismissal and the conduct of the parties.

Fair Dismissal

Once the employee has shown that he has been dismissed, the burden of proof then shifts to the employer to justify the dismissal. He can do this by showing that the dismissal comes within one of the five grounds laid down in **s.57 Employment Protection (Consolidaiton) Act 1978.** Having done that, under the **Employment Act 1980** it is then up to the Tribunal to consider all the facts and circumstances and decide whether or not the dismissal was fair.

Statutory grounds:—

a.   **A reason related to the employee's capabilities or qualifications for performing the work he is employed to do.** The Act defines **'capability'** as meaning skill, aptitude, health, physical or mental quality for the job, and **'qualification'** means any degree, diploma or other academic, technical or professional qualification relevant to the job.

In *Blackman v. The Post Office 1974* the employee was recruited for a particular job on an unestablished basis. A collective agreement provided that such employee's employment should only be continued if the employee passed a written aptitude test. Despite showing aptitude for the job, the employee failed the test three times. The Tribunal held that either capability or qualifications could be a ground relied on for dismissal.

b.   **A reason which relates to the employee's conduct.** Misconduct of the employee may occur in numerous forms and may cover such matters as lateness, absenteeism, incompetence, insubordination, breach of safety rules, immorality, etc. Of course, the gravity of the misconduct and its regularity are key factors in determining whether the employer has acted reasonably in treating it as a ground for dismissal.

In *Trust House Forte Hotels Ltd. v. Murphy 1977* a night porter who admitted stealing liquor from his employer was held to be justifiably dismissed.

An important factor is whether the employer has followed the **Code of Practice on Disciplinary Practice and Procedures** drawn up by the Advisory Conciliation and Arbitration Service to determine whether the employer has acted reasonably. This involves, amongst other things giving the employee **fair warning.** For minor infringements an informal oral warning should be given first, then possibly a formal oral warning and if necessary a final written warning. If the misconduct continues a final step could be disciplinary suspension without pay before dismissal. Of course the graver the conduct the less need there would be for a drawn out procedure, and it has already been stated that it is still possible to dismiss summarily for gross misconduct (mentioned previously). If an employer alleges misconduct and the facts show that this is not the true reason relied on then, obviously, it will not be a sufficient ground.

In *Price v. Gourley Bros. 1973* the applicant worked in a cake shop for 7 years and received top wages for her grade. She was dismissed, and when she asked for the reason was told by the manager that it was "just one of those things". At the tribunal the employer alleged incompetence but as he did not show any deterioration in her conduct it seemed unreasonable that it had been 7 years before he took action. The true reason for the dismissal which was unfair, was simply that the employer was attempting to reduce overheads by dismissing a highly paid employee and replacing her with an employee on lower pay.

Examples of misconduct at work sufficient to justify dismissal also include:—

Boychuk v. Symons Holdings Ltd. 1977 where the applicant was carrying on sexual relations during working hours.

Wilcox v. Humphries and Glasgow Ltd. 1975 where the applicant was in breach of safety instructions.

Atkin v. Enfield Group Hospital Management Committee 1975 where the applicant was justifiably dismissed for wearing provocative badges after having had repeated warnings.

In some cases misconduct outside work may justify dismissal, however in *Cassidy v. H. C. Goodman 1975,* the Tribunal held that for an employee to be justifiably dismissed on the grounds of his private conduct it had to be of exceptional gravity and also capable of damaging the employer's business. Here it was not the case, the employer merely being unhappy about the applicant's private life, and requesting him to settle down.

Alternatively, in *Singh v. London County Bus Services Ltd. 1976,* the applicant who drove a one-man operated bus, was convicted of dishonesty committed outside his employment. The Employment Appeals Tribunal held that misconduct does not have to occur in the course of employment to justify dismissal so long as it could affect the employee when he is doing his work. Here the employee's conduct justified dismissal.

The ground of misconduct was relied on in *Bradshaw v. Rugby Portland Cement Co. Ltd. 1972,* the applicant being dismissed following a conviction for incest with his own daughter for which he was on probation. The Tribunal held that the dismissal was unfair as the offence had no bearing on his work as a quarryman, and the relationship that he had with fellow employees had not deteriorated to any grave extent.

One of a dismissed employee's most important rights is to be given within two weeks, written reasons for his dismissal by his employer. Care should be taken when such particulars are supplied for the employer will be bound by them.

c.   **The redundancy of the employee.** A redundancy situation will exist if the employer closes down his business or part of his business and no longer requires the services of the particular employee. It does not follow however that **redundancy situation** will authomatically produce a fair dismissal. the employer must have had consultation with his workforce, observed proper selection procedures and considered possible alternatives. A redundancy situation could be dealt with otherwise than by dismissing employees, e.g. reducing overtime, short-time working, restricting recruitment.

> This point was argued in *Allwood v. William Hill Ltd. 1974* where the employer closed down betting shops and declared the managers redundant without warning or offering alternative employment. The Tribunal held that a redundancy situation existed but the employees did not have to be made redundant and more effort should have been taken to find them alternative work.

d.   **Because the employee could not continue to work in the position which he held without contravention of a restriction or a duty imposed by Statute.** This means simply that an employer could not be expected to employ a worker if the employment was against the law, e.g. a bus driver who is disqualified from driving.

> In *Gill v. Wallis Meat Co. Ltd.* to have continued to employ the applicant who worked on open meat would have infringed **Food Regulations 1970** for he had grown a beard. Having refused alternative employment his dismissal was held to be fair.

320

e. **Some other substantial reason** such as to justify the dismissal of an employee holding the position which he held. This reason provides a ground upon which an employer could rely if the reason relied on is not one of the previous categories.

> It was relied on successfully in *Wilson v. Underhill School Ltd. 1977* where the applicant schoolteacher refused to accept less than a full pay award, as her colleagues had done, recognising the school was in financial difficulties.

> Usually the **'substantial reason'** ground is relied on along with other grounds.

> Thus in *Blackman v. Post Office* (previously mentioned) a further reason relied on was the substantial reason of the need to honour the collective agreement between the Post Office and the Trade Union.

To recap on the basic steps which must be taken when unfair dismissal is alleged before a Tribunal:—

1. The employee shows that he was dismissed.
2. The employer shows a reason for dismissal that falls within the grounds mentioned.
3. The tribunal decides, having looked at all the facts and circumstances, whether or not the dismissal was fair.

It is step (3) that has recently been introduced under the **Employment Act 1980.** Prior to that Act the onus was on the employer to prove before the Tribunal that he had acted reasonably in the circumstances to treat the reason relied on as justifying dismissal. It is suggested that the change will produce little difference, for an employer will still find it necessary to bring to the tribunal's attention evidence to demonstrate the reasonableness of his action. Whether the employer adhered to an agreed disciplinary procedure is a major consideration to determine this question.

Finally some mention should be made that certain reasons for dismissal have been designated by statute as fair or unfair, **Employment protection (Consolidation) Act 1978** as amended by the **Employment Act 1980.** The Act states that if the principal reason for dismissal is that the employee:—

a. was or propsed to become a member of a Trade Union; or

b. had or proposed to take part in Union activites; or

c. had refused or proposed to refuse to become or remain a member of a non independent Trade Union,

then the dismissal is **necessarily unfair.**

On the other hand a dismissal is to be regarded as fair if:—

i. it is the practice for employees of the same class to belong to an independent Trade Union in accordance with a Union membership agreement; and

ii. the reason for the dismissal was that the employee was not a member of the specified Union or had refused or proposed to refuse to remain a member.

Thus if an **approved union membership agreement** is in force an employee who refused to join an independant Trade Union may be dismissed fairly by the employer. The exception is that a dismissal in these circumstances shall be regarded as unfair if either (a) the employee genuinely objects on grounds of conscience or other deeply held personal conviction to being a member of any Trade Union whatsoever, or a particular Trade Union, or (b) the employee in question has been among the class of employees to whom the agreement relates and before the agreement required membership, and has not been a member of a trade union in accordance with it.

Maternity Rights

To complete the picture in relation to security in employment some mention should be made of maternity rights. The right to maternity leave and pay were introduced by the **Employment Protection Act 1975.** The qualifying period for both rights is two years employment as at the beginning of the eleventh week before the date of her expected confinement. It is also necessary to notify the employer of her intention to return to work where reasonably practicable, not less than three weeks before her departure. Failure to do this may result in a loss of security of employment rights. It should also be stressed that reinstatement rights relate to the actual job which has been left or one that is substantially the same. Certain amendments to the procedure were introduced by the **Employment Act 1980.** It is now mandatory that the employee's notice be in writing, and in addition not less than 49 days after the week of confinement the employer may serve written notice on the employee to confirm her intention to return. To protect her rights the employee must serve this confirmation notice within 14 days and additionally serve notice within 21 days before exercising her right to return to work. Finally an employer of five or fewer employees is under no obligation to reinstate an employee after maternity leave where it is not reasonably practicable for him to do so.

19.4 Redundancy Payments

In 1965 a scheme was introduced whereby an employee who is dismissed because there is no longer a demand for his work can claim a **redundancy payment** in respect of the loss suffered. The present provisions are contained in the **Employment Protection (Consolidation) Act 1978.** Basically, redundancy occurs when an employee is dismissed because his employer has discontinued or intends to discontinue the business for which he was employed or because the need for his particular services has diminished. Of course, the right to payment is lost if the employee unreasonably refused to accept an offer of **suitable alternative employment.** The object of redundancy payment is to encourage mobility of labour while at the same time providing security for employees. Under the present scheme every employer makes contributions to the **Redundancy fund** and will receive a rebate from the fund for any payments he makes provided he gives notice to the Department of the Environment.

To come within the scheme it is necessary to have worked as an employee for the same employer for at least sixteen hours a week for an unbroken period of two years after the age of eighteen. Excluded categories include:—

i.   Workers at retirement age.

ii.   Where a more suitable scheme, contained in a collective agreement, has been approved by the Secretary of State.

iii. Registered Dock Workers and Share Fishermen.

iv.   Civil Servants, National Health employees.

v.   Independent Contractors.

Dismissal due to Redundancy

To qualify for a payment the employee must have been dismissed for reason of redundancy. There is a dismissal if the employer expressly terminates the contract, a fixed term contract expires, there is a constructive dismissal or the employer has died or been dissolved. Failure to establish a dismissal may result in a loss of entitlement to a redundancy payment.

> In *Morton Sundour Fabrics v. Shaw 1966* the employee in question having been warned of the possibility of redundancy left to take other employment. The court held that as he had not been dismissed he was therefore not entitled to a payment.

There is a presumption in the 1978 Act that if an employee is dismissed it is for reason of redundancy unless the contrary is proved. The Act specifically specifies that certain reasons for dismissal will contitute redundancy including:—

i.   If the employer stops or intends to stop carrying on the business altogether;

ii. If the employer stops or intends to stop the type of business in which the employee is engaged;

iii. If the employer reduces or intends to reduce the workforce due to a fall in demand;

iv. If the employer stops or intends to stop carrying on business at a particular location;

v.   If the employer reduces or intends to reduce the workers at a particular location.

An employee could also be classified as redundant if the employer attempts to unilaterally vary the contract of employment, e.g. by requiring him to change job or job location. If an express term confers this right on the employer however there will be no redundancy (see Chapter 18, *McCaffrey v. A. E. Jeavons & Co. Ltd. 1967)*. In situations where an employee's skills have become outdated because of new working methods and he is dismissed, the question is whether there is a redundancy situation or a dismissal on grounds of incapability.

> In *Cannon v. William King Ltd. 1966* a french polisher who refused to do painting was held to be redundant.

Also in *Smith & AEK Purdy Trawlers Ltd. 1966* a seaman who could not operate a new diesel driven trawler was similarly held to be redundant.

However, in *Hindle v. Percival Boats 1969* the applicant was highly skilled and built and repaired wooden boats. His employer began to specialise in the production of fibreglass boats and the demands for the applicant's work were greatly reduced. Eventually he was dismissed as unsatisfactory when he refused to take on less skilled work. The court held that this was not a redundancy situation as the type of work on which he was engaged was still in existence. Had there been a genuine rundown and the applicant's job had been totally swallowed up then the court might have been convinced of a redundancy situation.

There can be no redundancy if the employer makes an offer of **suitable alternative employment** which the employee rejects. The offer will be suitable if:—

1. the provisions of the new contract are similar to the previous contract; or

2. the provisions of the new contract do differ but the offer constitutes an offer of suitable alternative employment.

Whether the offer is suitable or not will depend on examining all the circumstances of the particular case, e.g. work, pay, hours, conditions, travelling, fringe benefits, accommodation, social and family links, children's education, etc.

In *Devonald v. J. D. Insulating Co. Ltd. 1972* the applicant was required to move from a factory in Bootle to another at Blackburn. He refused and on his claim for redundancy the tribunal held that suitable alternative employment had been offered as he was already required under his present employment to do outside contract work.

However in *Fuller v. Stephanie Bowman Ltd. 1977* the applicant typist refused to move from Mayfair to a new office in Soho. She found the move distasteful particularly as the new office was above a sex shop. The tribunal found that the refusal to move was unreasonable in the circumstances based upon undue sensitivity and the claim for redundancy must fail.

Procedure and Calculation

The 1978 Act lays down the procedure to be followed in a redundancy situation particularly where an independent trade union is involved. It involves consultation, advance warnings, written notice to the Secretary of State, the Trade Union given certain details surrounding the redundancy and individual employees given time off to seek new employment. Certain details must be disclosed by the employer to trade union representatives including reasons for redundancies, numbers, how selected, etc.

To calculate the amount of a redundancy payment it is necessary to establish the following:—

i. **'the relevant date'**, i.e. the date that the contract of employment terminated;

ii. **'week's pay'**, i.e. the minimum remuneration to which the employee is entitled in the week preceeding the relevant date (maximum of £135);

iii. **'years of continuous employment'**, i.e. the number of years of employment calculated in weeks in which the employee works 16 hours minimum. Certain matters will break the continuity such as long absence through illness and certain periods although not breaking continuity will not count, e.g. periods of absence due to strikes or lock outs after July 1964.

Having established the above matters the calculation of redundancy payment is as follows:—

For each year employed between the ages of:	Amount of Redundancy Payment:
18-21	Half Week's Pay × No. of Years Worked
22-40	One Week's Pay × No. of Years Worked
Men 41-65 Women 41-60	One and a Half Week's Pay × No. of Years Worked

The maximum length of reckonable service is 20 years and the maximum week's pay is £135, e.g. maximum payment under the scheme is for a man over 60, with 20 years continuous service, on a wage of £135 per week.

$$20 \times 1\frac{1}{2} \times £135 = £4,050.$$

When making the payment the employer should give the employee a written statement of how it has been calculated and any lump sum given to a redundant employee. Failure to provide such a statement could lead to the payment being regarded as simply voluntary rather than a redundancy payment. It should be noted however that much larger sums are payable under private schemes for redundancy payments entered into by employers and Trade Unions.

CHAPTER 20 Discrimination

Numerous studies have shown that discriminatory practices are still widespread in Britain and this has lead to the passing of legislation with the aim of introducing protection against discrimination and hopefully re-educating those who are guilty of it. In the housing field there are possibilities of discrimination occurring:—

a. **in employment,** when a person, on the grounds of race or sex, is treated less favourably in either securing a job, working conditions or promotion prospects;

b. **in housing allocation,** when a person on the grounds of race or sex is treated less favourably in either securing accommodation, the standard and situation of accommodation offered, or access to benefits or facilities.

By virtue of **s.71 Race Relations Act 1976** a general duty is imposed on local authorities to work towards the elimination of discrimination and to promote good race relations and equal opportunities for all. In addition to this general duty there are specific provisions in the 1976 Act relating to housing allocation. Before they are considered however the principal features of the legislation relating to discrimination are set out below.

Race Relations Act, 1976	Sex Discrimination Act, 1975
1) Direct Discrimination	
This occurs where one person: Treats another less favourably on racial grounds such as by segregating workers.	This occurs where one person: Treats another less favourably on the grounds of sex such as providing women with different working conditions.

2) Indirect Discrimination

This occurs where one person:
Requires another to meet a condition which as a member of a racial group is less easily satisfied because
a) the proportion of that group who can comply with it is smaller and
b) the condition is to the complainant's detriment and is not justified.
There would therefore be indirect discrimination if an employer required young job applicants to have been educated only in Britain.

This occurs where one person:
Requires another to meet a condition which as a member of particular sex is less easily satisfied because
a) the proportion of that sex who can comply with it is smaller and
b) the condition is to the complainant's detriment and is not justified.
There would therefore be indirect discrimination if an employer advertised for a clerk who is at least six feet tall.

3) Victimisation

This occurs where one person:
Treats another less favourably because the other has given evidence or information in connection with, brought proceedings under, or made allegations under the Act against the discriminator.

This occurs where one person:
Treats another less favourably because the other has given evidence or information in connection with, brought proceedings under, or made allegations under the Act or the Equal pay Act, 1970, against the discriminator.

4) Enforcement

Complaints alleging any of the above may be made to the Commission for Racial Equality which, in an attempt to eliminate discrimination, has investigatory powers and will attempt a settlement or institute proceedings. Complaints are hears before an industrial tribunal and if a settlement cannot be reached the

Complaints alleging any of the above may be made to the Equal Opportunities Commission which, in an attempt to eliminate discrimination, has investigatory powers and can issue a **non-discriminatory notice** which will place a requirement on an employer. Complaints against such a notice or original complaints are heard before

tribunal can, if the complaint is just
(i)   make an order declaring rights
(ii)   award compensation of up to
£5,200 or 104 weeks pay whichever
is smaller
(iii) recommend action to reduce the
adverse effect of the discrimination,
e.g. promotion.

an industrial tribunal and if a
settlement cannot be reached the
tribunal can, if the complaint is
just
(i)   make an order declaring rights
(ii)   award compensation of up to
£5,200
(iii) recommend action to reduce the
adverse effect of the discrimination,
e.g. promotion.

20.1 Race Discrimination

The 1976 Act is concerned with discrimination on racial grounds which is based upon colour, race, nationality or ethnic or national origin. The various categories of race discrimination (direct, indirect and victimisation) are evident in housing allocation and are specifically referred to in **s.21** of the 1976 Act.

a.   **It is unlawful for a person in relation to premises of which he has power to dispose to discriminate against another:—**

1.   in the terms on which the premises are offered; or

2.   by refusing his application for the premises; or

3.   in the treatment of him in relation to any waiting list for accommodation.

b.   **It is unlawful for a person in relation to premises managed by him to discriminate against a person occupying:—**

1.   in the way he affords him access to any benefits or facilities, or by refusing or deliberately omitting to afford him access to them; or

2.   by evicting him or subjecting him to any other detriment.

An example of **direct discrimination** under **s.21** occurring would be to refuse an applicant's name for rehousing because he is an Asian or to allocate him accommodation in a particular area solely because of his race. The tendancy of racial minorities to attempt to group in localities is a well known one but to attempt to off-set this by a policy of dispersal with the aim of maintaining ratios of black/white, etc. would also be discriminatory. An example of **indirect discrimination** in housing allocation would be to allocate housing points for children only living with an applicant as this would be detrimental to the immigrant who has part of his family yet to join him from abroad. Certainly the general aim expressed in **s.71** can only be achieved in housing management by ensuring a knowledge of the racial composition of an area and its particular needs and problems, and demonstrating a willingness to react sensitively to them.

Race discrimination in employment can occur directly, indirectly or by victimisation and at all stages of the employment process, e.g. advertising for employees, terms of employment offered, refusal of employment, access to training and promotion opportunities.

> An example of direct discrimination occurred in *Race Relations Board v. Mecca 1976*. Here an applicant telephoned to apply for a job and when the Mecca employer discovered the applicant was black put the phone down. This act was held to be direct discrimination as the applicant has been denied the opportunity to apply for a job on racial grounds.

> An act of indirect discrimination occurred in *Panesar v. Nestle 1979* where it was held that a prohibition against employees having long hair discriminated indirectly against Sikhs but that the discrimination was justifiable in the circumstances on the grounds of health and safety.

In some cases discrimination is lawful and justifiable on racial grounds. Firstly if the employee is to work in a private household and secondly if the membership of a particular racial group is a **genuine occupational requirement.** Examples may include:—

1. Drama and entertainment, e.g. employing only a black actor to play 'Uncle Tom'.

2. Artist's or photographic models to achieve authenticity, e.g. a photograph depicting a national scene.

3. Bar or restaurant work where the setting requires an employee from a particular race, e.g. Chinese restaurant.

20.2 Sex Discrimination

The **Sex Discrimination Act 1975** is concerned with discrimination on grounds of sex either by males against females, or vice versa, and on grounds of marital status by treating a married person less favourably than an unmarried person either directly or indirectly.

> In *Nemes v. Allen 1977* an employer in an attempt to cope with a redundancy situation dismissed female workers when they married. This was held to be unlawful discrimination on the grounds of sex and marital status.

In relation to employment any discriminatory practice which comes within the three categories (direct, indirect and victimisation) is unlawful. In addition, the publication of an advertisement showing an intention to commit an act of discrimination is also unlawful, such as 'salesman required' or 'barmaids required'.

In some cases discrimination is lawful and justifiable on grounds of sex if a person's sex is a **genuine occupational requirement.** Examples may include:—

1. Where the job requires a man or woman for physiological reasons other than physical strength, e.g. a female stripper or a male model.

2. Where there are considerations of decency or privacy, e.g. male toilet attendant.

3. Where there are statutory restrictions, e.g. women may not work underground in coal mines.

4. Where the work location makes it unreasonable to provide separate facilities for sleeping or sanitation, e.g. an oil rig.

5. Where the service is most effectively provided by a man or woman, e.g. a female social worker dealing with unmarried mothers.

In *Peake v. Automotive Products Ltd. 1978,* Lord Denning in the Court of Appeal held that the ground of safety and good administration was a justifiable reason for discrimination. Previously, the Employment

Appeals Tribunal had held that the practice of allowing women employees to leave work five minutes before the men was unlawful discrimination against the men. This decision was reversed on appeal, Lord Denning maintaining that it was not unlawful discrimination to treat women with the chivalry and courtesy they deserve.

This decision was subject to a great deal of criticism and eventually in 1979, Lord Denning himself cast doubt on its validity by stating that it had been given without reference to certain relevant parts of the Act and in the modern age, chivalry is no longer a consideration.

These statements were made in *Ministry of Defence v. Jeremiah 1980.* Here the employers created a working practice that if men examiners volunteered for overtime they could be required to work it in shops where colour bursting shells were made. Women examiners, working overtime, were never required to work in these shops because the working conditions required protective clothing to be worn and showers to be taken, and there were no facilities for women in that part of the factory. A male examiner complained to a tribunal that despite extra pay for working in these shops, the employer's practice unlawfully discriminated against him by subjecting him to a detriment. Both the Tribunal and Employment Appeals Tribunal agreed. In the Court of Appeal it was held that subjecting a person to a detriment meant no more than putting a person under a disadvantage. This was the case here and the fact of extra payment could not remove the detriment because the employer could not purchase the right to discriminate. The practice amounted to discrimination by the employer against the male examiners and was therefore unlawful.

APPENDICES

THE LAW SOCIETY
LEGAL AID ACT 1974

APPLICATION FOR
LEGAL AID CERTIFICATE

LEGAL AID
ENGLAND and WALES

OFFICIAL
USE
ONLY

If you have difficulty in completing this form you may be eligible for advice and assistance from a solicitor under Section 1 of the Legal Aid Act 1974 (known as the "Green Form" Scheme).

Surname (Block Letters) Mr. Mrs. Miss.	Forenames
Permanent Address	Address for correspondence if different from Permanent Address
Occupation	Date of Birth

The proceedings for which I apply for legal aid are :—

Have the proceedings already begun?   YES   NO

Are you covered by insurance wholly or in part in respect of the claim?   YES   NO

My opponent(s) is (are) :—

Name	Address

The solicitor I wish to act for me is

Has he agreed to act for you?   YES   NO

Firm's name and address

List of papers which accompany this Application Form :—

Any correspondence relating to an attempt to settle the claim **must** be forwarded.

Have you previously applied for a legal aid certificate in this or any other matter?   YES   NO

If you have

—please give the reference number(s) :

or please give as many particulars as you can, including the approximate date on which the application was made, your surname (if it was different from your present surname) and address at the time.

Have you received advice and assistance from a solicitor under the "Green Form" Scheme in respect of the matter for which you now apply for legal aid?   YES   NO

October 1977

NOTES FOR THOSE APPLYING FOR OR RECEIVING LEGAL AID UNDER THE LEGAL AID ACT 1974, AND THE REGULATIONS MADE THEREUNDER

PLEASE READ CAREFULLY

1. A contribution may be payable towards the cost of the case and a person required to make a contribution will have an opportunity to consider the terms upon which legal aid will be granted before deciding whether to accept the offer of a legal aid certificate.

2. If no contribution is required, a legal aid certificate may be issued forthwith.

3. If the means of a person change, either after a legal aid certificate has been issued or after he has accepted the offer of a legal aid certificate, because
   (a) his disposable income increases by more than £156 a year, or decreases by more than £78 a year, or
   (b) his disposable capital increases by more than £120,
   he must immediately inform The Law Society.

4. A person may be required to attend an interview at any time and supply such further evidence of his means as may be requested either before or after obtaining legal aid. Failure to do so may lead to the revocation of any legal aid certificate issued causing him to become liable for the whole of the costs of his case.

5. If a legally aided person recovers damages or property, or preserves property, in the matter to which his legal aid certificate relates, The Law Society may have a first charge upon such damages or property to meet the expense of his case to The Law Society to the extent that such expense is not covered by the total amount of his contribution, together with any costs recovered from another party to the proceedings.

6. The court may make an order for costs against a legally aided person in favour of another party in the proceedings. This is an additional liability which is quite distinct from any contribution which the legally aided person has contracted to pay to The Law Society, but will not exceed the amount (if any) determined by the court as reasonable, having regard to all the circumstances including the means of all the parties to the proceedings and their conduct in connection with the dispute.

7. If money is received from a body of which a legally aided person is a member by way of financial help towards the costs of his case such money must be paid to The Law Society in addition to any contribution already required.

DECLARATION

I, the undersigned, the applicant for a legal aid certificate have carefully read and understand the Special Notice printed below.

I agree that if it is decided that no contribution is required from me towards the costs of my case at the present time and the issue of a legal aid certificate is approved, such certificate may be issued without further reference to me, although, if my means increase, I may have to pay a contribution at a later date.

I authorise The Law Society to take any step deemed necessary to procure an adjournment of proceedings or any forbearance on the part of any opponent to enable this application to be dealt with, but I understand that unless I am expressly informed to the contrary, my case (if proceedings have begun) will continue in accordance with any notice as to hearing or otherwise that I may have received.

Usual Signature : .... Date : ....

SPECIAL NOTICE

The information to be supplied by this form is required in accordance with the current Legal Aid (General) Regulations. Section 23(1) of the Legal Aid Act 1974 provides as follows :—

"If any person seeking or receiving advice or assistance or legal aid :—

(a) wilfully fails to comply with any regulations as to the information to be furnished by him ; or

(b) in furnishing any information required by the regulations knowingly makes any false statement or false representation, he shall be liable on summary conviction to a fine not exceeding £100 or imprisonment for a term not exceeding four months, or to both."

Statement of my case

Give dates where possible. If personal injuries are involved give full details of the accident and of the injuries suffered and forward Police Report when available.

LEGAL AID ACTS 1974 AND 1979
APPLICANTS STATEMENT OF CIRCUMSTANCES

FORM L.1

This form will be sent by the Law Society to the Supplementary Benefits Commission which is responsible for the assessment of your resources.

If you are receiving Supplementary Benefit the assessment may be made without your completing any other form. If you are not receiving Supplementary Benefit the Commission will require details of your financial circumstances and you will be asked to attend for an interview at one of the Commission's offices.

OFFICIAL USE ONLY
C.P. No. ....
Date of Receipt .... Ref. No.

Mr.*
FULL NAME Mrs.* ....
(*Block letters*) Miss *

ADDRESS (*Block letters*) ....

DATE OF BIRTH ....

If you do not wish the Department of Health and Social Security (Supplementary Benefits Commission) to communicate with you at this address, please give an alternative one:—

....

Telephone number, if convenient to telephone during working hours ....

1. STATEMENT OF MEANS

If you are married and living together and your Husband/Wife is not the other party, please give the following information for both of you; otherwise only for yourself.

(a) If in receipt of or claiming Supplementary Benefit please give address of the paying office and your reference number

....

....

(b) Are you in paid employment? | YES/NO |

(c) Are you self employed? | YES/NO |

(d) **TOTAL GROSS INCOME**

(i) Yourself: £ .... Weekly*
                                                                        Monthly*
                                                                        Yearly*

(ii) Your Husband/Wife: £ .... Weekly*
                                                                        Monthly*
                                                                        Yearly*

(e) **TOTAL CAPITAL**

Total amount of capital (excluding your own dwelling) cash at bank, building society investments, shares, premium bonds, cash etc.

(i) Yourself: £ ....

(ii) Your Husband/Wife: £ ....

....

....

Signature .... Date ....

*Delete as appropriate

338

OFFICIAL USE ONLY

From :   *To:* Supplementary Benefits Commission

(Address) ....

....   Date ....

(Complete and delete paragraphs as appropriate,

Proceedings and Status   1.   (a) Nature of proceedings ....

            (b) In the proceedings the applicant is ....

           *(c) The spouse has a contrary interest and his/her name and address are:

            ....

            ....

Degree of Urgency (if any)   2.   (a) An Emergency Certificate has been issued.

               The deadline for the L2 is ....

            (b) This is a defence application and the determination is urgently required.

            (c) ....

Subject matter in dispute   3.   (a) The following is to be treated as a subject matter in dispute under Regulation 3 of the Legal Aid (Assessment of Resources) Regulations:—

Special circumstances   (b) The following special factors apply:—

Previous application   4.   There has been a previous application by this applicant—

            (a) Your L2 reference was ....

            (b) Our reference was ....

            (c) A Certificate was/was not* issued thereunder.

Linked application   5.   (a) The applications are/are not* legally connected.

            (b) The applications are/are not* financially connected and overlapping.

Details of Court Order   6.   The existing Court Order has been produced to The Law Society and the details are as follows:—

            (a) Name of Court ....

            (b) Date of Order ....

            (c) Name of parties ....

            (d) Amount payable ....

*Delete as appropriate   *Secretary*

THE LAW SOCIETY

LEGAL AID

ENGLAND and WALES

SOLICITOR'S REPORT ON LEGAL ADVICE AND ASSISTANCE GIVEN UNDER
THE LEGAL AID ACT 1974

Key Card

PLEASE USE BLOCK CAPITALS			
Surname	Forenames	Male/Female	AREA REF. No.
Address			

NOTE TO SOLICITORS

With effect from 1st April 1977

Where advice and assistance are being given in respect of divorce or judicial separation proceedings and the work to be carried out includes the preparation of a petition, the solicitor will be entitled to ask for his claim for Costs and Disbursements to be assessed up to an amount referred to in a general authority given by the Area Committee to exceed the prescribed basic sum in such cases.

CAPITAL   CLIENT   £

TOTAL SAVINGS and OTHER CAPITAL   SPOUSE   £

TOTAL   £

Ⓐ

INCOME

State whether in receipt of Supplementary Benefit or Family Income Supplement.

YES/NO   If the answer is YES ignore the rest of this Section.

Ⓑ

Total weekly Gross Income

    Client   £

    Spouse   £

    TOTAL   £

Allowances and Deductions from Income

    Income tax   £

    National Health Contributions, etc.   £

    Spouse   £

Ⓒ
Ⓓ
Ⓔ

Dependent children and/or other dependants   Number

    Under 5   £

    5 but under 11   £

    11 ,,   ,,   13   £

    13 ,,   ,,   16   £

    16 ,,   ,,   18   £

    18 and over   £

Ⓕ

LESS TOTAL DEDUCTIONS   ➡   £

TOTAL WEEKLY DISPOSABLE INCOME   £

TO BE COMPLETED AND SIGNED BY CLIENT

I am over the compulsory school-leaving age.

I have/have not previously received help from a solicitor about this matter under the Legal Aid and Advice Schemes.

I am liable to pay a contribution not exceeding ..   ..   £

Ⓖ

I understand that any money or property which is recovered or preserved for me may be subject to a deduction if my contribution (if any) is less than my Solicitor's charges.

The information on this page is to the best of my knowledge correct and complete. I understand that dishonesty in providing such information may lead to a prosecution.

Date ....   Signature ....

CLAIM FOR PAYMENT TO ACCOMPANY FORM LA/ACC/8B

Name of Client

Where appropriate did the Court give approval to assistance under Section 2 (4) of the Legal Aid Act 1974?   Yes/No.

Has a Legal Aid Order been made?   **Yes/No.**

If so, give date...............................

PLEASE ATTACH ANY AUTHORITIES GIVEN BY THE AREA COMMITTEE

TICK THE APPROPRIATE LETTER TO INDICATE THE NATURE OF THE PROBLEM		Has any money or property been recovered? If so, give details.
A. Divorce or judicial separation (see note on page 1)		
B. Other family matters (Specify in Summary)	G. Accident/injuries	
C. Crime	H. Welfare benefits/tribunals	
D. Landlord/tenant/housing	J. Immigration/Nationality	
E. H.P. and Debt	K. Consumer problems	
F. Employment	L. Other matters (Specify in Summary)	

		Summary of work done:
No. of letters written		
No. of telephone calls Made Received		
Time otherwise spent: Specify in Summary		
Has a legal aid certificate or order been granted? Yes/No. If not, is one being applied for? Yes/No. Certificate or Order No. if appropriate:		

PARTICULARS OF COSTS

	£		£
1. Profit costs		Details of disbursements:—	
2. Disbursements (including Counsel's fees)		Counsel's fees (if any)	
3. Add VAT as appropriate		Other disbursements (listed)	
TOTAL CLAIM			
4. Deduct maximum contribution (if any)			
NET CLAIM			

Have you previously made a claim for legal advice and assistance for your client in respect of divorce or judicial separation proceedings or matters connected therewith.   YES/NO   If Yes, how much was allowed £...............

Signed	Solicitor Date	Solicitor's ref.
Firm name (in full)		
Address		

Date ....

NOTICE OF PROVISIONAL ASSESSMENT

The Area Committee have assessed your costs in this matter as set out below. In view of the fact that the sum assessed is less than that claimed, you may make written representations to the Committee in support of your claim as originally submitted or on any item in it, if you wish. These representations must be received within 14 days of the date hereof. I have deleted this matter from the consolidated claim form LA/ACC/8B with which it was sent and I should be obliged if you would do the same. If you accept the provisional assessment, please include this matter on your next consolidated claim form as assessed below AND RE-SUBMIT THIS FORM WITH IT.

Area Secretary.

£

1. Profit costs
2. Disbursements
3. Add VAT as appropriate

TOTAL CLAIM
4. Deduct maximum contribution (if any)

NET CLAIM

NOTE.— You are advised to keep a copy of this page because if in the same matter your client obtains a L.A. Certificate or Order, you may on taxation of your costs and disbursements be required to produce to the Taxing Officer a copy of this form indicating work done and quantum of payment. You may also require a copy of this page if after submitting your claim for payment you apply to the Area Committee for a financial extension to enable you to give further advice and assistance to your Client.

APRIL 1977

 **LEASE** is made the   day of
One thousand nine hundred and eighty two **BETWEEN**
                  and   all of   Hartlepool,
in the County of Cleveland (the present Trustees of the Hartlepool who and
save the Trustees or Trustee for the time being of the said
are hereinafter called 'the Landlords') of the one part and   and
                              his wife both of   ,
Hartlepool in the County of Cleveland (hereinafter called 'the Tenants' which
expression shall where the context so admits include their successors in title
and assigns) of the other part

WITNESSETH as follows:

1.   In consideration of the rent hereinbefore reserved and of the tenants
covenants hereinafter contained the landlords hereby demise unto the tenants
ALL THAT shop and premises situate and being in   Buildings and
numbered   , Hartlepool aforesaid as the
same are now in the occupation of the tenant **TOGETHER WITH** the water
closet and ash pit in the yard behind the said premises and a right of access
thereto across the said yard and other appurtenances (if any) to the said
premises belonging and heretofore used and enjoyed in connection therewith
EXCEPT AND RESERVING to the landlords and to any person or persons
entitled thereto the free passage and running of gas, electricity water and soil
through and along the pipes, walls, channels, drains and water courses already
or hereafter to be built or placed in through over or under the said premises to
and from all or any of the adjoining premises **TO HOLD** the same unto the
tenant for the term of five years from the   day of
                  One thousand nine hundred and eighty two **YIELDING**
AND PAYING therefor
(a)   (i)   during the first three years of the term the yearly rent of £400
       (ii)   during the last two years thereof a yearly rent to be ascertained in
              accordance with the provisions of the Schedule hereto such rents to
              be paid in advance without any reduction in equal quarterly
              payments in advance to be made on the first day of May, the first
              day of August, the first day of November and the first day of
              February in every year

b.   by way of further rent the yearly sum equal to the sums which the
              landlords shall from time to time pay by way of premium for
              keeping the said premises insured in accordance with clause 3(ii)
              hereof to be paid on the   day of
              in every year

2. The tenant hereby covenants with the landlords as follows:

(i) To pay the rents hereby reserved on the dates and in the manner aforesaid without any deduction

(ii) To pay and discharge all rates taxes assessments impositions and outgoings whatsoever which are now or may hereafter become payable in respect of the demised premises except as aforesaid

(iii) At all times during the said term to maintain and keep the interior of the said premises and all the glass in the windows and all shutters locks and fastenings in good and tenantable repair order and condition and (reasonable wear and tear and damage by fire excepted) in such good and tenantable repair order and condition deliver up to the landlords at the expiration or sooner termination of the said term together with the landlords fixtures (and in particular to paint the inside of the said premises in a proper and workmanlike manner with two coats at least of good oil colour in the fifth year of the said term and at the same time to whitewash colour and paint such interior parts of the demised premises as shall have been heretofore whitewashed coloured and painted)

(iv) Not at any time during the said term to make any addition or alteration in the plan or elevation of the said premises or any alteration or apperture in any party wall or in the principal and bearing walls without the previous written consent of the landlords which shall not be unreasonably withheld

(v) To permit the landlords or their agents with or without workmen and others at all reasonable times during the said term at convenient hours of the day and upon a previous appointment made to enter into and upon the demised premises for the purpose of cleaning drains and for repairing any of the adjoining premises as often as occasion shall require the landlords making good all damage occasioned thereby and also to view the premises to ensure that nothing has been done therein that constitutes a breach of any of the covenants herein contained and also to view and examine the state and condition of the said premises and of all such breaches of covenant decays defects and wants of repair as shall be then and there found for which the tenant may be liable hereinafter to give to the tenant notice in writing to remedy repair and maintain the same within three calendar months then next following within which time the tenant will remedy repair and maintain the same accordingly **AND** in case of default by the tenant it shall be lawful for the landlords their agents servants and workmen at any time to enter upon the said premises for the purpose of stopping breaches of covenant and of executing such repairs and the tenant shall immediately repay to the landlords the amount of the outlay and all expenses so incurred

(vi) (a) to use the demised premises only as a shop for the sale of cigarettes and tobacco and smokers requisites or sundries fancy goods and costume jewellery ladies and gentlemen's toilet and hairdressing requisites newspapers periodicals books stationery greeting and view postcards a limited line of pre-packed confectionery and for the sale of any article commonly or usually sold in connection with such user and business as aforesaid

(b) not to permit or suffer the demised premises to be used or occupied other than for the purposes described in sub-clause (a) of this clause.

(vii) Not to commit or permit or suffer to be permitted any waste whether permissive voluntary or ameliorating in or upon the said premises

(viii) (a) to comply with all obligations imposed by and do and execute or cause to be done or executed all such works acts deeds matters and things as under or by virtue of any Act or Acts of Parliament for the time being in force are or shall be properly directed or necessary to be done or executed upon or in respect of the demised premises or any part thereof by the lessee tenant or occupier and in particular but without prejudice to the generality of this clause to comply with all obligations imposed upon the lessee tenants or occupier under or by virtue of the Offices Shops and Railway Premises Act 1963 and the Factories Act 1961 and at all times to keep the landlord indemnified against all claims demands and liability in respect thereof

(b) upon receipt of any notice order or direction or other thing from any competent authority likely to effect the demised premises forthwith to deliver to the landlord a copy of such notice direction order or other thing

(ix) Not at any time during the said term to assign or underlet or part with the possession of the said premises or any part thereof or of this Lease without the consent in writing of the landlords first had and obtained but such consent shall not be unreasonably withheld in the case of a respectable and responsible person being proposed as assignee or underlessee **PROVIDED** that the landlords may require the proposed assignees to enter into direct covenants with the landlords to perform and observe all the covenants and conditions herein contained and on the tenants part to be performed and observed **PROVIDED ALSO** that no portion of the said premises shall be sublet to any person company or firm carrying on a similar business to that at present carried on by the other tenants or the landlords in the   Buildings and particularly the business of millinery and ladies underclothing gentlemens outfitting and sale and repair of umbrellas ladies handbags and rainproof wearing apparel and the sale or business of confectionery.

(x)   For the period of three months immediately preceding the determination of this lease to permit a notice board to be exhibited on some conspicuous part of the premises intimating that the same are to be let and during such period of three months to permit an inspection at any reasonable time in the day by any person desirous of becoming a tenant of the said premises upon an appointment being made for the purpose

(xi) (a)   to pay all expenses including solicitors' costs and surveyors' fees incurred by the landlord incidental to the preparation and service of a notice under Section 146 of the Law Of Property Act 1925 or incurred or in contemplation of proceedings under Sections 146 and 147 of the Act notwithstanding in any such case forfeiture is avoided otherwise than by relief granted by the court.

      (b)   to pay all expenses including solicitors costs and surveyors fees incurred by the landlord and incidental to the service of all notices and schedules relating to wants of repair of the demised premises whether the same be served during or after the expiration of or sooner determination of the term hereby granted (but relating in all cases to such wants of repair that accrued not later than the expiration or sooner determination of the said term as aforesaid)

      (c)   to pay the landlords solicitors costs in connection with the preparation and engrossment of the Lease and Counterpart and any stamp duty thereon

(xii)   Not without the consent in writing of the landlords to effect any insurance of the said premises or any part thereof

3.   The landlords hereby covenant with the tenant as follows:

(i)   That the landlords will during the continuance of the term hereby created maintain the drains roofs main walls and main timbers and exterior of the demised premises and keep the same and all additions and improvements made (with the landlords consent) thereto in a tenantable order repair and condition

(ii)   To keep the demised premises insured against loss or damage by fire in such sum as the landlords may deem to be adequate in the event of the said premises being destroyed or damaged by fire and such other risks as the landlords may consider expedient during the said term forthwith (as soon as the necessary labour materials and permits are obtained) to lay out in or towards repairing and reinstating the same in a good and substantial manner all monies received under or by virtue of any insurance effect thereon

(iii)   That in the event of the said premises being destroyed or so damaged by fire as to be rendered unfit for occupation and use and provided that the insurance effected by the landlords shall not have been vitiated or payment of the insurance money refused in whole or in part in consequence of some act or default on the part of the tenant then the rent hereby reserved or a proportionate part thereof according to the nature and extent of the injury sustained shall immediately from the happening of such event as aforesaid cease to be payable until the premises shall have been restored and reinstated and again rendered fit for occupation and use **AND** in case any dispute shall arise as to the amount of such proportionment part of the period during which such cesser or abatement of rent should be allowed the matter shall be referred to arbitration as hereinafter provided

(iv)   That the tenant paying the rents hereby reserved and observing and performing the tenants covenants hereinbefore contained shall and may peaceably hold and enjoy the demised premises during the term hereby granted without any interruption or disturbance from or by the landlords or any person lawfully claiming through under or in trust for them

4.   IT IS HEREBY AGREED AND DECLARED between the parties hereto that all disputes and differences which may arise touching the provisions hereof or the operation or construction hereof or the rights or liabilities of the parties hereunder or under any statute rules or regulations of the Local or other Authority affecting the demised premises or the interest of either party under the Lease shall be referred to arbitration by a single arbitrator under the provisions of the Arbitration Act 1950 or any Act amending or replacing the same

5.   PROVIDED ALWAYS that if the rents hereby reserved or any part thereof shall at any time be in arrear and unpaid for twenty one days after the same shall have become due (whether legally demanded or not) or if there shall be any breach or non-observance of any of the tenants covenants hereinbefore contained or if the tenant or any permitted Assignee shall commit any act of bankruptcy or shall compound with creditors or being a company shall go into liquidation either voluntary or compulsory otherwise than for the purpose of amalgamation or reconstruction or in case the demised premises shall be vacant and unoccupied for any period of three calendar months then and in any case it shall be lawful for the landlords at any time thereafter to enter into and upon the demised premises or any part thereof in the name of the whole and again re-possess and enjoy as their former state.

IN WITNESS whereof the landlords and tenants have hereunto set their hands and seals the day and year first before written

THE SCHEDULE

1.   At any time during six months before the expiration of the third year of the term hereby granted the landlords may serve on the tenants a notice in writing (hereinafter called a 'Rent Notice') specifying an increase of the rent payable hereunder from the expiration of the third year of the term (hereinafter called 'the review date') to an amount specified in the Rent Notice and thereupon following provisions shall have effect:

(a)   The tenants within twenty eight days after the receipt of the Rent Notice may serve on the landlords a counter notice calling upon the landlords to negotiate with the tenants the amount of rent to be paid hereunder as from the review date

(b)   If the tenants shall fail to serve a counter notice within the period aforesaid they shall be deemed to have agreed to pay the increased rent specified in the rent notice as from the review date

(c)   If the tenants shall serve such a counter notice then the landlords and the tenants shall forthwith consult together and use their best endeavours to reach agreement as to the amount of the rent to be paid hereunder as from the review date but failing agreement within twenty eight days after service of such counter notice (or within such extended period as the landlords and the tenants shall mutually agree) the question of whether any and if so what increased rent should be payable hereunder shall be referred to the arbitration of a single arbitrator (whose costs shall be born in equal shares by the landlords and the tenants) who (failing agreement between the parties hereto) shall be nominated on the joint application of the landlords and the tenants or if either of them shall neglect forthwith to concur in such application on the sole application of the other of them by the president for the time being of the Royal Institution of Chartered Surveyors, and such arbitrator shall determine (as expert and not as arbitrator) the annual rack rental value of the demised premises at the review date that is to say the annual rent or aggregate annual rents at which the demised premises might reasonably be expected to let without premium in the open market as between willing landlord and willing tenant on a Lease for a term of two years and otherwise upon the terms and conditions of this Lease (other than the provision as to rent) but disregarding:

(i)   any effect on rent of the fact that the tenants or their predecessors in title had been in occupation of the demised premises
(ii)   any goodwill attached to the demised premises since the commencement of the term hereby granted by reason of the carrying on thereat, of the business of the tenants, and
(iii)   any effect on rent of any improvement carried out by the tenants otherwise and in pursuance of an obligation to the landlords

347

And such annual rack rent value so determined as aforesaid or the said sum of £400 (whichever shall be the greatest) shall be the annual rent payable hereunder as from the review date

SIGNED SEALED AND DELIVERED by

in the presence of:-

SIGNED SEALED AND DELIVERED by

in the presence of:-

FORM 7 in Appendix I to the Landlord and Tenant (Notices) Regulations 1969, without the paragraphs on Leasehold Reform Act rights prescribed in the Landlord and Tenant (Notices) Regulations 1967.

LANDLORD AND TENANT ACT 1954

LANDLORD'S NOTICE TO TERMINATE BUSINESS TENANCY

To ....,

....

of.., tenant of

premises known as.......................... ....

(Insert full address)

....

1. I, ...,

....

of ....,
landlord (*Note* 7) of the above-mentioned premises, hereby give you notice terminating your
tenancy on the...day of...................................., 19........ (*Note* 1).

2.   You are required within two months after the giving of this notice to notify me in writing whether or not you will be willing to give up possession of the premises on that date (*Note* 2).

3.   [I would not oppose an application to the court (*Note* 3) under Part II of the Act for the grant of a new tenancy (*Note* 6)] *or*

[I would oppose an application to the court (*Note* 3) under Part II of the Act for the

Here state ground or grounds. grant of a new tenancy on the ground (*Note* 4) that*

].

4.   This notice is given under the provisions of section 25 of the Landlord and Tenant Act 1954.

Your attention is called to the Notes overleaf.

Dated this.....................day of................................ .... 19...........

Signed..
(*Landlord*)

Address..

....

[OVER

Oyez Publishing Limited, Norwich House, 11–15 Norwich Street, London EC4A 1AB, a subsidiary of The Solicitors' Law Stationery Society, Limited.
8/79

Landlord and Tenant 25

NOTES

1. Under the Landlord and Tenant Act 1954, a tenancy of premises to which Part II of the Act applies continues until it is brought to an end in accordance with the Act. One of the ways in which it can be brought to an end is by a landlord's notice to terminate the tenancy. As a general rule, that Notice must be given not more than 12 nor less than 6 months before the date specified in it for the termination of the current tenancy of the premises. This date must not be earlier than the date on which apart from Part II of the Act the current tenancy would expire or could be terminated by notice to quit given by the landlord on the date of the Notice.

2. Part II of the Act enables the tenant on being served with a notice in this form, to apply to the court for an order for the grant of a new tenancy. Such an application however, will not be entertained unless the tenant has within 2 months after the giving of the Notice terminating the tenancy notified the landlord in writing that he will not be willing to give up possession of the premises on the date specified in the Notice. The application must be made not less than 2 nor more than 4 months after the giving of the notice.

3. Where the rateable value of the premises (excluding any part which is not occupied by the tenant or by an employee in his business) does not exceed £5,000, an application for an order for the grant of a new tenancy must be made to the County Court and in any other case it must be made to the High Court.

4. The court has no power to make an order for the grant of a new tenancy if the landlord, having stated in his Notice that he will oppose an application to the court on one of the grounds specified in the Act, establishes that ground to the satisfaction of the court. The grounds specified in the Act are—

    (a) where under the current tenancy the tenant has any obligations as respects the repair and maintenance of the premises, that the tenant ought not to be granted a new tenancy in view of the state of repair of the premises which has resulted from the tenant's failure to comply with these obligations;

    (b) that the tenant ought not to be granted a new tenancy in view of his persistent delay in paying rent which has become due;

    (c) that the tenant ought not to be granted a new tenancy in view of other substantial breaches by him of his obligations under the current tenancy, or for any other reason connected with the tenant's use or management of the premises;

    (d) that the landlord has offered and is willing to provide or secure the provision of alternative accommodation for the tenant, that the terms on which the alternative accommodation is available are reasonable having regard to the terms of the current tenancy and to all other relevant circumstances, and that the accommodation and the time at which it will be available are suitable for the tenant's requirements (including the requirement to preserve goodwill) having regard to the nature and class of his business and to the situation and extent of, and facilities afforded by, the premises which he occupies;

    (e) where the current tenancy was created by the subletting of part only of the property comprised in a superior tenancy, that the aggregate of the rents reasonably obtainable on separate lettings of the tenant's premises and the remainder of that property would be substantially less than the rent reasonably obtainable on a letting of that property as a whole, and that on the termination of the current tenancy the landlord requires possession of the tenant's premises for the purpose of letting or otherwise disposing of the said property as a whole and therefore the tenant ought not to be granted a new tenancy;

    (f) that on the termination of the current tenancy the landlord intends to demolish or reconstruct the whole or a substantial part of the premises or to carry out substantial work of construction on the whole or part of them and that he could not reasonably do so without obtaining possession of the premises; but where the landlord opposes the application on this ground the court can still order the grant of a new tenancy, if (i) the tenant agrees to the inclusion in the new tenancy of terms giving the landlord facilities for carrying out the work intended and, given those facilities the landlord could reasonably carry out the work, without obtaining possession of the tenant's premises and without interfering to a substantial extent or for a substantial time with the use of the premises for the tenant's business; or (ii) the tenant is willing to accept a tenancy of a part of the premises, which can be let separately without substantially reducing the rental income obtainable from the entire premises, and either the tenant agrees to give the landlord facilities for carrying out work as under paragraph (i) above, or possession of the remainder of the premises would be reasonably sufficient to enable the landlord to carry out the intended work.

    (g) that on the termination of the current tenancy the landlord intends to occupy the premises for the purposes, or partly for the purposes, of a business to be carried on by him in them or as his residence; but the landlord cannot rely on this ground if his interest was purchased or created less than 5 years before the termination of the current tenancy and at all times since the purchase or creation of the landlord's interest the premises have been let to a tenant occupying them for the purposes of his business.

5. If the only grounds for opposing an application for the grant of a new tenancy stated in paragraph 3 of this notice are grounds set out in (e), (f) and (g) above, the tenant is entitled on leaving the premises to recover compensation from the landlord at the rate specified in the Act. If other grounds are also stated, the tenant is entitled to the compensation if the court on an application for a new tenancy finds that it is precluded from making an order by reason only of any of the grounds set out in (e), (f) and (g).

6. If the landlord states in this Notice that he will not oppose an application to the court for the grant of a new tenancy, it will be open to the tenant and the landlord to negotiate on the terms of the tenancy. If all the terms are agreed between them, an application to the court will not be necessary; if some but not all of the terms are agreed, the agreed terms will be incorporated in any tenancy granted by the court and the other terms will be such as the court may determine. Any new tenancy, if granted by the court, will not include any part of the property comprised in the current tenancy which is occupied neither by the tenant, nor by a person employed by him for the purposes of his business, unless the landlord requires the new tenancy to include the whole of the property.

7. The term "landlord" in this Notice does not necessarily mean the landlord to whom the rent is paid: it means the person who is the landlord for the purposes of Part II of the Act. The term "business" includes a trade, profession or employment and any activity carried on by a body of persons, whether corporate or unincorporate.

350

NOTICE TO QUIT

(BY LANDLORD OF PREMISES LET AS A DWELLING)

To ....

of ....

....

(I) (We) (as) (on behalf of) your landlord(s) ....

of ....

....

give you NOTICE TO QUIT and deliver up possession to ....

of ....

....

on ....198.... or the day on which a complete period
of your tenancy expires next after the end of four weeks from the service of
this notice.

The information prescribed by the Notices to Quit (Prescribed Information)
Regulations 1980 is contained in the Schedule hereto.

Dated ....198....

Signed..

SCHEDULE

PRESCRIBED INFORMATION

1.   If the tenant does not leave the dwelling the landlord must get an order
for possession from the court before the tenant can lawfully be evicted. The
landlord cannot apply for such an order before the notice to quit has run out.

2.   If the tenant does not know if he has any right to remain in possession
after a notice to quit runs out or is otherwise unsure of his rights, he can obtain
advice from a solicitor. Help with all or part of the cost of legal advice and
assistance may be available under the Legal Aid Scheme. He can also seek
information from a citizens' advice bureau, a housing aid centre, a rent officer
or a rent tribunal office.

PROPOSED TENANCY AGREEMENT

The Tenancy

This is a weekly tenancy agreement for the premises at the address below between
The Council of the Borough of North Tyneside (hereinafter referred to as 'The Council')
and

_____

(hereinafter referred to as 'The Tenant')
Both the Council and the Tenant have certain rights and responsibilities which must be observed. This agreement sets out these rights and responsibilities and says what may happen if one side breaks the agreement.

Address

_____
_____

Start of Tenancy

This tenancy will commence on the_____
day of_____One thousand nine hundred and eighty_____; or
This tenancy agreement will come into effect on the _____day of_____
One thousand nine hundred and eighty_____

Joint Tenancies

In the case of joint tenancies the word 'Tenant' refers to both tenants.

Rent and Rates

The rent and rates and all other charges for the premises are written in the rent card and are payable in advance every Monday.

Legislation

Reference to the Housing Act 1957 or 1980 or other Acts shall be construed to include any future legislation of a similar nature and any statutory addition or modification or re-enactment of those Acts for the time being in force and any order instrument regulation or direction made or issued under or deriving validity from these Acts.

Change in Rent and Rates

The Council may increase or decrease the rent and other charges for the premises (except rates) by giving the Tenants as to other ratepayers.

Ending the Tenancy by the Tenant

The Tenant must give four weeks written notice to the Council ending on a Monday to bring the tenancy to an end. This notification should be sent to the address shown on the front of the rent card.

352

Security of Tenure	The Tenant has security of tenure under the provisions of the Housing Act 1980. The Council may only take steps to evict the Tenant in the circumstances set out in the section 'Grounds for Eviction' on page
Death of Tenant	On the death of the Tenant the tenancy will be transferred to the person entitled to succeed under the provision of the Housing Act 1980. Details of this can be obtained from the Council at the address shown at the front of the rent card.

RESPONSIBILITIES OF THE TENANT

Rent	The Tenant must pay the rent and all other charges for the premises regularly and promptly.
Repairs	The Tenant must repair or replace items damaged through neglect or carelessness of the Tenant or members of the Tenant's household if those items form part of the premises or of the common areas of any building which the Tenant is allowed to use under this agreement.
Informing the Council about Defects	The Tenant must inform the Council as soon as is reasonably possible about any fault in the premises which it is the Council's responsibility to repair. This notification should be sent to the Council at the address shown at the front of the rent card.
Decoration	The Tenant should keep the interior of the premises in a reasonable state of decoration.
Use of Premises	The Tenant must not use the premises for business purposes without the written permission of the Chief Housing Officer.
Gardens	The Tenant should maintain all garden space and hedges in a tidy condition.
Drains, Waste and Soil Pipes	The Tenant must keep the drains, waste and soil pipes clean and free from obstruction.
Cleaning of Communal Areas	In dwellings that have communal hallways, stair-cases, landings and other similar areas, the Tenant is to be responsible jointly with those other Tenants who share those common areas for cleaning the same, except in those situations where a cleaning service is provided.

353

Access	The Tenant must allow Officers or Agents of the Council to enter the premises to inspect the premises or to carry out repairs to the premises or to adjoining premises after receiving at least twenty four hours written notice of the morning or afternoon of the visit and on production of a Council identification pass. But, if in the opinion of the Council's Chief Housing Officer there is an emergency from which personal injury or damage to the premises or neighbouring property might result the Tenant will allow Officers or Agents of the Council to enter the premises using such means as necessary without giving notice.
End of Tenancy	The Tenant must at the end of the tenancy leave the premises and the Council's fixtures and fittings in a satisfactory condition.
Nuisance to Neighbours	The Tenant must not and must ensure that members of his household, other residents of the premises and visitors do not cause nuisance or annoyance to neighbours.
Dogs and Other Animals	In any dwelling to which the only means of access is via a communal entrance or landing the Tenant must not and must ensure that members of his household and other residents of the premises do not keep a dog or other animal in the premises. In any other premises the Tenant must not and must ensure that members of his household and other residents of the premises do not keep more than one dog or other domestic animal on the premises.
Pigeons	The Tenant must not and must ensure that members of his household and other residents of the premises do not erect pigeon lofts or keep pigeons in the garden or any other part of the premises.

MATTERS FOR WHICH THE COUNCIL'S WRITTEN PERMISSION MUST BE OBTAINED

If the Tenant requires any written permission then the Tenant should contact the Area Housing Manager at the address shown on the front of the rent card.

Tenant's Improvements	The Tenant shall not make any improvements to the premises without the Council's written permission but with written permission the Tenant may:

(a) decorate the exterior of the premises;
(b) carry out structural alterations or make any addition to the premises;
(c) alter or add to any fixtures and fittings or to any services to the premises.

The Council's written permission shall not be unreasonably withheld. If permission is given the Council may impose reasonable conditions, any breach of which would be breaking the terms of this agreement. If permission is refused the Council must give its reasons in writing. For the avoidance of doubt it is hereby declared that it shall be the duty of the Tenant at his own expense to obtain the permission of the Local Planning Authority under the provisions of the Town and Country Planning Act 1971 and any other approval of plans, permissions or other things which may be necessary for the execution of any structural alterations, improvements or additions under the Building Regulations 1976 or otherwise.

Grants for Improvement Work	In certain cases a Tenant may be eligible for a grant in respect of improvements carried out to the premises by the Tenant. The Tenant should therefore enquire of the Chief Environmental Health Officer, as to whether or not any improvements intended to be carried out by the Tenant to the premises are eligible for a grant.

Reimbursement of Costs of Tenant's Improvements	At the end of a tenancy the Council will consider any application from the Tenant for repayment of money spent on improvements carried out by the Tenant with the Council's consent. Any repayment, which is discretionary would be based on the cost of the improvements less any money received from a grant.

Assignment, Exchange, Sub-Letting and Lodgers	(a)	The Tenant shall not assign (transfer to another person) the tenancy nor sub-let or part with possession of the whole of the premises. However, the tenancy may be assigned to the Tenant's husband or wife in accordance with a Court Order in proceedings for divorce, nullity of marriage or judicial separation;
	(b)	the Tenant must not exchange premises without the written permission of the Council;
	(c)	the Tenant may sub-let or part with possession of part of the premises with the Council's written permission which shall not be unreasonably withheld;
	(d)	the Tenant may allow any person to live in the premises as a lodger without asking the Council's permission but should note that if the premises become over crowded the Council may be able to evict the Tenant. The statutory provision relating to overcrowding are summarised on the Rent Card as well as the permitted number of persons who may occupy the premises.
	(e)	the Tenant must notify the Council of any intention to take in lodgers or sub-let.

If the Tenant is unsure whether a proposed arrangement amounts to sub-letting or not he should consult the Council at the address shown at the front of his rent book or seek legal advice.

If permission to sub-let is refused the Council must give its reasons in writing. If the Tenant feels that permission has been unreasonably refused, he may challenge the refusal in the County Court.

Motor Vehicles and Caravans

The Tenant shall not without the Council's written consent park any motor vehicle or caravan on the premises unless a garage or hardstanding is provided. Parking of commercial vehicles on the premises is prohibited. Motor cycles must not be parked in communal passageways or hallways.

356

RESPONSIBILITIES OF THE COUNCIL

Tenant's Right to Possession

By this agreement the Tenant is given security of tenure and provided that the Tenant shall comply with his obligations under this Agreement the Council shall not interfere with the Tenant's right to possession of the premises except in the circumstances set out below in the section 'Remedies available to the Council if the Tenant fails to Comply with the Agreement.'

Repair of Structure and Exterior

The Council must keep in good repair the structure and exterior of the premises including drains, gutters and external pipes.

The Council will not be liable for the repair of the structure and exterior of the premises if that repair becomes necessary through the fault of the Tenant or his household.

Repair of Installations

The Council must keep in good repair and working order the installations in the premises:

(a) for the supply of water, gas and electricity for sanitation (including basins, sinks, baths and sanitary conveniences) but not except as aforesaid fixtures, fittings and appliances for making use of the supply of water, gas or electricity; and

(b) for space heating or heating water.

The Council will not be liable to repair any installation if the repair becomes necessary through the fault of the Tenant or his household or if the installation was fitted by the present Tenant without the Council's written permission.

Repair of Communal Parts

The Council must keep in reasonable repair and working order any communal entrances, halls, stairways, lifts, passages, rubbish chutes and communal lighting and other common parts or communal amenities or facilities.

External Decoration

The Council must decorate the exterior of the premises as and when necessary or in accordance with a planned maintenance programme unless the Tenant wishes to carry out external decoration himself under the provisions described in the section 'Tenant's Improvements' above.

Decoration of Communal Parts	The Council must decorate any common parts or communal areas as and when necessary.
Access	The Council must give at least twenty four hours written notice of the morning or afternoon of any visit for the purpose of inspecting the premises or carrying out repairs unless:

(a) the Tenant agrees to a shorter period of notice; or
(b) there is an emergency in the circumstances described in the section 'Responsibilities of the Tenant — Access' above.

TENANT'S REMEDIES IF THE COUNCIL FAILS TO COMPLY WITH ITS RESPONSIBILITIES

Appeal to the Area Housing Consultative Committee	If the Tenant believes that there has been an unreasonable delay by the Council in carrying out any obligation for which it is responsible under this agreement, then the Tenant may apply to the Area Housing Consultative Committee to investigate the circumstances and effect a remedy if necessary. Any notice of appeal to the Area Housing Consultative Committee should be addressed by the Tenant to the Area Housing Manager at the address shown on the front of his rent card.
Legal Remedies	If the Council fails to carry out any of its responsibilities under this agreement, the Tenant can take legal action in the County Court as well as use the remedies open to him under this section.
Defects that are Damaging to Health	If the Tenant informs the Council of defects in the premises which are prejudicial to health and which amount to a statutory nuisance and the Council fails to remedy the defect the Tenant may apply to the Magistrates Court under Section 99 of the Public Health Act 1936 for an Order to make the Council remedy the defect.
Outstanding Repairs	Under Section 125 of the Housing Act 1974 the Tenant has the right to ask the County Court for an Order stating that any outstanding repair that is the Council's responsibility be carried out. The Tenant may also be able to claim damages.

Unfit Accommodation	A Tenant has the right to claim to a Justice of the Peace that his house is unfit for human habitation under Section 157(2) and (4) of the Housing Act 1957.
Tenant's Improvements	If the Tenant feels that permission to carry out an improvement has been unreasonably withheld, or that any condition imposed is unreasonable, he may challenge the refusal or condition in the County Court.

COUNCIL'S REMEDIES IF THE TENANT FAILS TO COMPLY WITH THIS AGREEMENT

Tenant's Repairs and Improvements	If the Tenant fails to carry out any repair or maintenance which is his responsibility or fails to carry out any improvement to the satisfaction of the Council the Council may give the Tenant written notice requiring him to carry out the repair or maintenance or complete the improvement to the satisfaction of the Council within a reasonable time which must be given in the notice. If the Tenant fails to comply with the notice within that time the Council may enter the premises to carry out the necessary work and charge the Tenant the costs incurred by the Council (including administrative costs) for the execution of that work.
Recovery of Rent	If the rent and any other charges for the premises are not paid regularly and promptly, the Council may sue the Tenant for the arrears.
Legal Remedies	If the Tenant fails to carry out any of his responsibilities under this agreement the Council can take legal action as well as use the remedies open to it under this section including action to end the tenancy and recover possession of the premises from the Tenant.

ENDING THE TENANCY

Ending the Tenancy

The Council may only take steps to bring the tenancy to an end in the circumstances set out in the Housing Act 1980 the relevant extracts from which are set out below. The Council can only end the tenancy by obtaining a County Court Order for possession. The Council must serve on the Tenant a preliminary notice giving full details of its grounds for seeking an Order for possession. The Notice must specify a date at least four weeks ahead before which the Council may not bring Court proceedings. The Council may not bring Court proceedings more than twelve months after the date given in the preliminary notice.

Grounds for Eviction

As outlined in the Housing Act 1980, in the following circumstances the Tenant may only be evicted if the Court considers that it would be reasonable:

Ground 1
Any rent lawfully due from the Tenant has not been paid or any obligation of the tenancy has been broken or not performed.

Ground 2
The Tenant or any person residing in the dwellinghouse has been guilty of conduct which is a nuisance or annoyance to neighbours or has been convicted of using the dwellinghouse or allowing it to be used for immoral or illegal purposes.

Ground 3
The condition of the dwellinghouse or of any of the common parts has deteriorated owing to acts of waste by, or the neglect or default of, the Tenant or any person residing in the dwellinghouse and, in the case of any act of waste by, or the neglect or default of, a person lodging with the Tenant or sub-tenant of his, the Tenant has not taken such steps as he ought reasonably to have taken for the removal of the lodger or sub-tenant.

In this paragraph 'the common parts' means any part of a building comprising the dwellinghouse, and any other premises which the Tenant is entitled under the terms of the tenancy to use in common with the occupiers of other dwellinghouses let by the Council.

Ground 4

The condition of any relevant furniture has deteriorated owing to ill-treatment by the Tenant or any person residing in the dwellinghouse and in the case of any ill-treatment by a person lodging with the Tenant or sub-tenant of his, the Tenant has not taken such steps as he ought reasonably to have taken for the removal of the lodger or sub-tenant.

In this paragraph 'relevant furniture' means any furniture provided by the Council for use under the tenancy or for use in any of the common parts (within the meaning given in Ground 3).

Ground 5

The Tenant is the person, or one of the persons, to whom the tenancy was granted and the Council was induced to grant the tenancy by a false statement made knowingly or recklessly by the Tenant.

Ground 6

The dwellinghouse was made available for occupation by the Tenant or his predecessor in title while works were carried out on the dwellinghouse which he previously occupied as his only or principal home and:

(a) he (or his predecessor in title) was a secure tenant of that other dwellinghouse at the time when he ceased to occupy it as his home;

(b) he (or his predecessor in title) accepted the tenancy of the dwellinghouse of which possession is sought on the understanding that he would give up occupation when, on completion of the works, the other dwellinghouse was again available for occupation by him under a secure tenancy; and

(c) the works have been completed and the other dwellinghouse is so available.

361

In the following circumstances the Tenant may only be evicted if the Council provides him with other suitable accommodation.

Ground 7
The dwellinghouse is over-crowded within the meaning of the Housing Act 1957, in such circumstances as to render the occupier guilty of an offence.

Ground 8
The Council intends, within a reasonable time of obtaining possession of the dwellinghouse:

(a) to demolish or reconstruct the building or part of the building comprising the dwellinghouse; or

(b) to carry out work on that building or on land let together with, and this treated as part of, the dwellinghouse;

and cannot reasonably do so without obtaining possession of the dwellinghouse.

Ground 9
The dwellinghouse has features which are substantially different from those of ordinary dwellinghouses and which are designed to make it suitable for occupation by a physically disabled person who requires accommodation of a kind provided by the dwellinghouse and:

(a) there is no longer such a person residing in the dwellinghouse; and

(b) the Council requires it for occupation (whether alone or with other members of his family) by such a person.

Ground 10
The dwellinghouse is one of a group of dwellinghouses which it is the practice of the Council to let for occupation by persons with special needs and:

(a) a social service or special facility is provided in close proximity to the group of dwellinghouses in order to assist persons with those special needs;

(b) there is no longer a person with those special needs residing in the dwellinghouse; and

(c)   the landlord requires the dwellinghouse for occupation (whether alone or with other members of his family) by a person who has those special needs.

Ground 11

The accommodation afforded by the dwellinghouse is more extensive than is reasonably required by the Tenant and:

(a)   the tenancy vested in the Tenant, by virtue of Section 30 of the Housing Act 1980, on the death of the previous Tenant;

(b)   the Tenant was qualified to succeed by virtue of Sub-Section (2)(b) of that Section; and

(c)   notice of the proceedings for possession was served under Section 33 of the Housing Act 1980 more than six months but less then twelve months after the date of the previous tenant's death.

Other Suitable Accommodation

Other accommodation is only suitable under this agreement if it consists of premises let under an equivalent agreement to this one and which are reasonably suitable to the needs of the Tenant and his household. In deciding whether premises are reasonably suitable the Council must take into account:

(a)   the type and size of accommodation which the Council normally lets to people with similar needs;

(b)   the distance of the accommodation from the place of work or education of the Tenant or any member of his household;

(c)   the distance of the accommodation from the home of any member of the Tenant's family if living near to that person is important to the wellbeing of that person or of the Tenant or a member of his household;

(d)   the needs (as regards the size of the accommodation) of the Tenant and his family.

CONSULTATION, INFORMATION AND CHANGES IN THE TERMS OF THIS TENANCY

Changes in Terms of Tenancy

The Council may vary the rent or other charges for the premises in accordance with 'Changes in Rent and Rates' above. Otherwise, the Council may only change the terms of this agreement in accordance with the following procedure. The Council must give the Tenant notice in writing of the proposed change and its effect and invite the Tenant to comment upon it within a reasonable specified time. The Council must consider any comments made by the Tenant before making its decision. The Council shall then give the Tenant at least four weeks notice before the change takes place, together with information explaining the new terms and their effect.

Changes in Housing Management

The Council may only make changes in Housing Management that will substantially affect its secure tenants as a whole or a group of them in accordance with the following procedure:

(a) the Council must inform those Tenants who are likely to be substantially affected by a matter of housing management of any proposed change in housing management, inviting those Tenants to comment upon it within a reasonable time; and

(b) the Council must consider any comment made by the Tenant before making its decision.

'Housing Management' means any matter concerning the management, maintenance, improvement or demolition of premises let by the Council to its Tenants or the provision of services or amenities to such premises. It does not include the level of rent or other charges for the premises.

Tenant's Right to Information

(a) the Council must provide the Tenant on request with a regularly up-dated summary of its rules for dealing with transfers and exchanges of homes including rules governing priority between applicants;

(b) the Council must provide the Tenant on request with details of those particulars which the Tenant has given to the Council about himself and his family and which the Council has recorded as being relevant to his application for accommodation.

364

City of Durham

TENANTS CHARTER

**This booklet contains information
about your tenancy, etc.
Please read it carefully NOW**

INTRODUCTION

In the Housing Act 1980 the Government has introduced new legislation which, among other things, gives tenants of Local Authority (Council) houses certain rights which are collectively known as the "Tenants Charter".

This booklet has been produced in order that the Council can briefly inform all existing and prospective tenants as to their rights and obligations.

It does not provide an authoritative interpretation of the Law, only the Courts can do that. If you are in any doubt about your legal rights you would be well advised to consult your own solicitor.

The principal "Rights" contained in the Act are:-

	Council Officer to contact
Right to Buy your Council House	City Solicitor
Security of Tenure	Housing Officer
Succession of Tenancy	Housing Officer
The Right to take in lodgers	Housing Officer
The Right to sub-let part of your home	Housing Officer
The Right to improve your home	City Engineer
The Right to information about the Council's policies and priorities in the allocation of new tenancies and transfers.	Housing Officer
The Right to be consulted about matters affecting your home or your tenancy.	Housing Officer

THE RIGHT TO BUY

As a secure tenant of the Council you have with very few exceptions, the Right to Buy the home in which you live.

The main exclusions from the Right to Buy scheme are:-

(1) "Sheltered" dwellings for people of pensionable age.

(2) Dwellings designed or specifically adapted for people of pensionable age.

(3) Dwellings designed or specially adapted for disabled people.

A separate leaflet entitled "The Right to Buy" is available from the City Solicitor's Office, Byland Lodge, Hawthorn Terrace, Durham.

PROCEDURE FOR BUYING YOUR HOME

If you would like to buy your home you should apply to the CITY SOLICITOR, BYLAND LODGE, HAWTHORN TERRACE, DURHAM, whereupon details of the scheme will be forwarded to you. You should then complete the "Right to Buy" form (RTB.1) and forward it to the above Officer, whereupon you will be notified whether or not you are eligible to purchase.

SECURITY OF TENURE

The majority of Council tenants are secure tenants under the terms of the Housing Act 1980, though there are limited exceptions to this, e.g. Wardens employed by the Council.

As a secure tenant this means that you cannot be required to vacate your home unless the Council obtains an Order from the County Court.

As a first step the Council has to serve on you a notice telling you the grounds on which the Court is going to be asked to give the Council possession of your home; for example, non payment of rent (Ground (1)). The full list of the grounds is as follows:-

1. You have failed to pay your rent or have broken some condition of tenancy.

2. You or someone else living in the dwelling has behaved in a manner which is a nuisance or annoyance to neighbours.

3. You have damaged either the dwelling or the common parts used with other tenants (e.g. staircase in a block of flats).

4. You have damaged furniture provided by the landlord.

5. You have obtained the tenancy by making a false statement.

6. You have refused to leave a dwelling which was let to you temporarily while building work was being done on your original home, and you had promised to go back when the work was finished.

7. The dwelling is overcrowded as defined in the Housing Act 1957.

8. The Council wants to demolish the dwelling or to do works on it or on the land connected with it and cannot do so while you are still in occupation.

9. You are occupying a dwelling which has been specially altered to suit the needs of a physically handicapped person and there is no longer a person with those needs living in the dwelling and the Council requires the dwelling for someone with those needs.

10. You are occupying a dwelling in a group of dwellings let to people with special needs near some special facility for them (e.g. Communal Hall) and there is no longer a person with those needs living in the dwelling and the Council requires the dwelling for someone with those needs.

11. You have succeeded to the tenancy upon the death of the former tenant and the dwelling is larger than you reasonably need. (This clause can only be used between 6 and 12 months from the previous tenant's death).

367

Next, the Council has to apply to the Court for possession. The Court will not give possession unless the Council establishes that the grounds specified in the notice exist. Also, in some cases, the Court will not give the Council possession unless it thinks it is reasonable in all the circumstances, and in certain situations the Council will be obliged to offer suitable alternative accommodation. The following explains very briefly the basis on which the Courts will make a decision.

Grounds	Conditions
1 - 6	The Court considers it reasonable to make the Order.
7 - 8	The Court is satisfied that the Council will make suitable alternative accommodation available when the Order takes effect.
9 - 11	The Court is satisfied that it is reasonable to make the Order, and that the Council will make suitable alternative accommodation available when the Order takes effect.

RIGHTS OF SUCCESSION

If you are a secure tenant, when you die your tenancy will pass to your husband or wife, if living with you in the property, or else to one member of your family* who has been living with you for at least 12 months. He or she will be your "successor" under the Housing Act 1980 provided you yourself did not succeed to the tenancy.

If you have a joint tenancy with another person, it will pass to him or her when you die, but there will be no further succession. This one succession happens automatically under the Housing Act 1980, but the Council might agree to let a further member of your family take over after that.

It must be noted, however, that in the event of the property being specifically designed for the handicapped or the elderly, the Council may exercise its rights to seek possession in accordance with the provisions of paragraphs 9 and 10 under the heading SECURITY OF TENURE, set out earlier.

> * Family means husband, wife, person living with the tenant as husband or wife, parent, grandparent, child, grandchild, brother, sister, uncle, aunt, nephew, niece, including step relations by marriage and illegitimate relations.

THE RIGHT TO TAKE IN LODGERS

Lodgers can be accommodated without the Council's permission provided that this will not result in overcrowding.

368

If you take in lodgers you must remember that,

    (a) Your rebate may be reduced (if applicable),

    (b) He or she will have no permanent security of tenure and the Council will not usually rehouse the lodger if you want them to leave.

    (c) If you want your lodger to leave, the Council cannot act on your behalf.

    (d) The Council must also be informed that you have taken in Lodgers.

THE RIGHT TO SUB-LET PART OF YOUR HOME

You can also sub-let part (but not the whole) of your house or flat, but you need the Council's prior consent in writing for this.

The Council can not refuse to let you sub-let without good reason and if consent is refused the Council will explain why, in writing.

If the Council refused you the sub-letting and you feel it is being unreasonable, you can appeal to the County Court.

THE RIGHT TO IMPROVE YOUR HOME

You can carry out improvements to your home, although application must be made IN WRITING, and you will need the written consent of the Council.

An 'improvement' means an alteration or addition to the house itself or to the fixtures and fittings, such as the electrical wiring or light sockets, or to the services such as the heating system. It also means putting up a T.V. or Radio aerial, decorating the outside of your home, or erecting boundary or other walls, fences or gates.

For some work you may be eligible for a home improvement grant, and for details you should read the Department of the Environment booklet "HOME IMPROVEMENT GRANTS" which is available at the Council Offices, Byland Lodge, Hawthorn Terrace, Durham.

The Council can not refuse you permission to make improvements without good reason. But if permission is given it can be conditional (for instance, that the work is done to a high standard or in a particular way). If you fail to comply with any reasonable condition the Council may seek to obtain possession of the property.

If you think that the Council's refusal to give you permission for your improvements or the conditions they impose are unreasonable, you can appeal to the County Court. The Court will take into account whether your planned improvement is likely to make the premises less safe for occupiers or cause the Council extra expense, and all other circumstances.

You should note that if you move house, the Council is not likely to reimburse you for the cost of any improvements you have carried out.

If you carry out improvements the Council cannot increase the rent solely in respect of these improvements during your tenancy of the property.

Any tenant who carries out improvements without the written consent of the Council may be required to bear all costs incurred in reinstating the dwelling to its former condition.

THE RIGHT TO INFORMATION

As a Council tenant you have the right to information about the procedures the Council uses for determining the priorities for allocating accommodation, and allowing transfers.

In addition, if you have applied for housing you have the right to check that the information you have given the Council has been correctly recorded.

(A) New Tenancies

If you have friends or relatives interested in becoming a Council tenant, refer them to the Housing Officer at the City Treasury, John Street, Meadowfield, for full details of Council House Allocation and an application form.

Very briefly, any person over pensionable age can apply for accommodation, but other persons will generally only be considered if they are inadequately housed, e.g. living-in, overcrowded or occupying sub-standard property. Single person applicants must be over 21 years of age.

An application will also be accepted in certain circumstances from persons living outside the district.

(B) Transfers

Existing tenants can apply for a transfer to another Council property if:-

    (i)   they have lived in their present accommodation for any necessary qualifying period stipulated by the Council, or

    (ii) they live in overcrowded conditions, or

    (iii) the Council agrees.

Transfers will not be allowed where a tenant has a poor rent paying record or the cleanliness and decoration of their existing property is not up to standard.

(C) Exchanges

The Council will usually agree to tenants exchanging into each other's houses by mutual agreement, but all tenants involved must have complied with the conditions of tenancy, particularly regarding rent payments and cleanliness of their existing property.

(D) Mobility Scheme

In accordance with the Housing Act 1980, the City of Durham Council, along with most other Councils, New Town Corporations and some Housing Associations throughout England and Wales, have joined together in a National Mobility Scheme to help people with a pressing need to move to a different area.

Furthermore, this Council is also a participant of the "County Mobility Scheme" which covers the Housing Authorities throughout County Durham.

The scheme is for people who have a definite need to move, either for a job or for social reasons, to somewhere beyond reasonable travelling distance from their present home.

The Council will look at each case individually and tell you if a nomination is to be made to another Housing Authority.

If your application is approved, everyone in your family who normally lives with you will be included in the permanent move, but not normally lodgers or anyone to whom you have sub-let part of your house.

Because the move would be permanent you should be quite sure you wish to move before applying to the Council.

If you do wish to apply for a nomination under this scheme you should apply to the Housing Officer, City Treasury, John Street, Meadowfield, from whom further information is available.

A summary of the Council's conditions, procedures and priorities in respect of new tenancies, transfers and exchanges can be obtained on demand from

THE HOUSING OFFICER, CITY TREASURY,

JOHN STREET, MEADOWFIELD, DURHAM. DH7 8RG.

A more detailed explanatory leaflet will be available on payment of a fee of 50p.

THE RIGHT TO CONSULTATION

Under the Housing Act 1980 the Council is required to consult with its tenants about matters of housing management which substantially affect all tenants, or a category of tenants, or the tenants of a particular estate or group of properties.

The Council must make arrangements for consulting tenants on matters affecting their homes or their tenancies, such as major repairs or improvement programmes, changes in the Wardens Service, or changes in methods of rent collection, though not the rent levels, and must consider their views before reaching a decision.

Where a matter affecting tenants is considered by the Council to be one of housing management, each tenant affected will be written to, informed of the new proposals and changes, and asked to contact the Council within a specified period if he or she feels they have an objection or point of discussion to raise.

Any representations so made will be considered by the Housing Management Working Party, who will report on their findings to the Housing Services Committee.

The Housing Services Committee may then decide to deal with the matter forthwith or hold a meeting with the tenants concerned, who will have an opportunity to discuss the Council's proposals. The outcome of the meeting will be reported back to the Housing Services Committee, which will come to an interim decision.

Affected tenants will be notified of the interim decision and will be given a period of two weeks in which to object, if they so desire.

Any objections will be reported to the Housing Services Committee, who will then make the final decision.

ENVIRONMENTAL HEATLH

Refuse Collection

Tenants are entitled to have their normal household refuse removed once per week. A separate free collection is available on demand for moving refuse such as furniture, pianos, refrigerators, etc., which cannot normally be accepted by the normal refuse collection team. A further free collection is available on demand for limited quantities of garden refuse, such as grass cuttings or hedge clippings. These special collections are discretionary and are subject to the availability of men and vehicles and there is sometimes a waiting list.

Pest Control

A free service exists for tenants for control in their households of all rodent and insect pests such as rats, mice, fleas, bugs, cockroaches, wasps, bees, etc.

Environmental Health Generally

The Council employs Environmental Health Officers to monitor the environment in which we live, and deal with all types of nuisance, e.g. nuisance from unwanted noise, unsound food, etc., and you should contact them if you have any problems of this sort.

Queries and requests should be made to:

THE CITY ENVIRONMENTAL HEALTH OFFICER

BROWNEY HOUSE, BROWNEY, MEADOWFIELD, DURHAM.

TELEPHONE NO. 780571.

INFORMATION REGARDING HOUSING MAINTENANCE
REPAIRS AND DECORATIONS

1. The Council is responsible for the repairs to your home as detailed in the Conditions of Tenancy section.

2. The Council is NOT responsible for:

   (a) Fixtures and fittings such as curtain rails.

   (b) Gas or electric cookers, refrigerators etc. except in certain categories of dwellings.

   (c) Light bulbs and electric plug tops.

   (d) Keys.

   (e) Window, door or other glass breakages which are as a result of misuse or accidental damage. Subject to the absolute discretion of the Council's duly authorised officers, the repairs of such breakages will be carried out free of charge for Senior Citizens.

   (f) Anything that belongs to you, including internal decorations, and your own television/radio aerials.

REPORTING A REPAIR

1. If you want the Council to carry out a repair you can:

   (a) Fill in the postcard - supplies available from the City Engineer or Rent Collectors.

   (b) Write to THE CITY ENGINEER, BYLAND LODGE, HAWTHORN TERRACE, DURHAM.

   (c) Telephone (during office hours) Durham 67131 and ask for Housing Maintenance Repairs Section extension. Tell us your address, what repairs need to be carried out and when you will normally be at home. It is only by obtaining this information that arrangements can be made for staff to call to quantify in detail the necessary remedial work. Instructions can then be passed to the workforce. Please note that the inspection of dwellings is normally carried out between 8.15 a.m. and 4.15 p.m. Any repair work necessary will normally be carried out between the hours of 8.15 a.m. and 4.15 p.m., Monday to Friday (excluding public holidays).

   If it is necessary for you to take time off work so that access to your home can be made to either inspect or carry out the work, please ensure that firm arrangements are made with the HOUSING REPAIR SECTION, CITY ENGINEER'S DEPARTMENT, BYLAND LODGE, HAWTHORN TERRACE, DURHAM. TELEPHONE DURHAM 67131.

GAS LEAKS

To prepare yourself for possible gas leaks you should make sure you know where the main gas tap is situated - usually near the main gas meter. If you have a gas escape at any time, turn off the main gas tap and report immediately to the GAS BOARD, TELEPHONE NO. SUNDERLAND 42321 (Code 0783) AND NOT THE COUNCIL.

EMERGENCY REPAIRS AFTER NORMAL WORKING HOURS

OUTSIDE NORMAL WORKING HOURS THE COUNCIL OPERATES AN ANSAPHONE SYSTEM FOR REPORTING EMERGENCY REPAIRS.
ONLY USE THIS SYSTEM FOR REAL EMERGENCIES. TELEPHONE DURHAM 67131 AND YOUR MESSAGE WILL BE RECORDED AND TRANSMITTED TO THE DUTY FOREMAN.

PIPED T.V. AND COMMUNAL T.V. AERIALS

Certain Council tenants live in properties which are provided with either a piped T.V. system or a communal T.V. aerial. If the system should become faulty, you should contact the HOUSING MAINTENANCE SECTION AT BYLAND LODGE. Before you report that the system is out of order, please check that it is not your T.V. set that is at fault.

EMERGENCY REPAIRS

Emergency repairs are carried out to avoid danger to the health and safety of residents or serious damage to the structure or contents of dwellings. Emergency works include:-

(a) Blocked toilets where the premises contain only one toilet.

(b) Blocked or leaking drains.

(c) Serious storm, accident or flood damage to rooms.

(d) Burst pipes.

(e) Dangerous structures.

(f) Serious electrical faults.

Where there is an emergency your home will be made safe within 24 hours where possible, and the repair will be completed either at that time or, where possible, within five working days, depending on resources being available and weather conditions not constituting a danger, i.e. working from ladders or on roofs.

BURST WATER PIPES

Abnormal weather conditions have indicated that tenants are not fully conversant with simple procedures necessary to avoid the problems resulting from burst pipes. The lagging of all pipework is not always practical, and lagging will not guarantee that pipes will not freeze; it will only reduce this possibility. In particular, ground floor toilets should have some form of heating in severe weather conditions.

If a dwelling is left without heat for any length of time, then the possibility of a freeze-up will increase. To avoid the results of a burst pipe, which only becomes evident after thawing, the following simple precautions should be taken if the property is to be left unoccupied or without heat for any length of time. These precautions also apply during the summer months, since leaks can occur in pipework due to normal wear and tear.

Procedure when leaving the premises unoccupied or when a burst occurs

   (a) PUT OUT FIRE

*(b) Turn off main stop tap.

   (c) Turn on all Hot and Cold taps on sink unit, bath and wash-hand basins.

*(d) Turn off draw-off tap to back-boiler.

*(e) Turn on cylinder draw-off tap.

   (f) Flush W.C.

   (g) REFILL SYSTEM BEFORE APPLYING HEAT, AFTER BURST IS REPAIRED OR ON RETURNING TO THE PREMISES.

*NEW TENANTS, AND EXISTING TENANTS WHO DO NOT KNOW, SHOULD FIND OUT **NOW** WHERE THE VARIOUS STOP COCKS AND DRAW-OFF TAPS ARE SITUATED SO THAT THEY CAN TURN THE WATER OFF QUICKLY IN AN EMERGENCY. USUALLY, THE MAIN STOP TAP CAN BE FOUND UNDER THE KITCHEN SINK, AND IT IS A GOOD IDEA TO TEST IT EVERY SIX MONTHS TO MAKE SURE IT CAN BE TURNED OFF IN AN EMERGENCY.

IF IN DIFFICULTY, TENANTS SHOULD CONTACT THE HOUSING MAINTENANCE SECTION OF THE CITY ENGINEER'S DEPARTMENT, BYLAND LODGE (TELEPHONE DURHAM 67131) FOR FURTHER ADVICE OR ASSISTANCE.

SWEEPING OF CHIMNEYS

Due to the tar type coal now being used, a lot of complaints are being received about soot falls and smoking chimneys, which are invariably caused by blocked flues, which could also create a fire danger. Tenants are reminded that it is their responsibility to have their chimney swept, and twice a year is recommended.

EXTERNAL DECORATIONS

The Council will endeavour to decorate the outside of your home every five years, subject to weather conditions.

If you live in a house or bungalow you may decorate the outside of your home at your own expense. Please apply in writing to do this to THE HOUSING MAINTENANCE SECTION OF THE CITY ENGINEER'S DEPARTMENT AT BYLAND LODGE. Advice will then be given on the method and materials to be used.

INSURANCE OF HOUSE CONTENTS AND DECORATIONS

THE COUNCIL DOES NOT INSURE THE CONTENTS AND INTERNAL DECORATIONS OF THE DWELLING WHICH YOU OCCUPY. YOU ARE THEREFORE ADVISED TO INSURE THE CONTENTS AND INTERNAL DECORATIONS OF YOUR HOME AGAINST FIRE, FLOOD, THEFT AND SUCH OTHER RISKS AS YOU MAY THINK APPROPRIATE.

If you are not insured against such risks ACT NOW and seek the advice of a reputable Company who can give you the appropriate insurance cover.

DETAILS OF YOUR CONDITIONS OF TENANCY

GENERAL

1. Occupation of a dwelling will mean that the tenant accepts all the conditions of tenancy and will abide by them: failure to comply with any condition of tenancy could lead to eviction. The Council allows married and other couples to have their tenancy granted jointly in the names of the two persons concerned and the aforementioned applies equally to the joint tenancy.

   In the event of any dispute arising between Council tenants as to the user of their premises, the matter in dispute will be decided by the Council.

2. The rent is payable in advance on Monday in each week. The tenant should see that all sums paid to the Collector are entered on the rent card. Tenants must produce their card to the Collector or other duly authorised Officer of the Council whenever required to do so. If the rent is in arrear at any time, the Council may at once give the defaulting tenant Notice of Seeking Possession.

How to Pay your Rent

The amount of rent payable is shown on your Rent Card. You can pay this in a number of ways:-

(a) **To your Rent Collector**

   The Rent Collector for your area will call regularly each week to collect your rent. Should you be out when he is due to call, it can be left, if you wish, with a neighbour.

(b) **Paid at the Cashiers Office**

   Please produce your Rent Card so that it can be endorsed. Payment can be made at either of the following addresses:-

   (i) The City Treasury,
   John Street, Meadowfield, Durham.
   Opening Hours: Monday - Thursday 8.30 a.m. to 4.30 p.m.
   Friday 8.30 a.m. to 4.00 p.m.

   (ii) 80 Claypath, Durham.
   Opening Hours: Monday - Thursday 1.00 p.m. to 4.30 p.m.
   Friday 1.00 p.m. to 4.00 p.m.

(c) **Payment by Post**

   You may pay by posting it to:-

   The City Treasury,
   John Street, Meadowfield, Durham. DH7 8RG.

   You are advised to send only cheques, money orders and postal orders through the post, and these should be crossed and made payable to:-

   City of Durham

   If you send cash, the envelope should be registered, for the Council accepts no responsibility for any cash sent through the post.

Rent Arrears

It is not in the Council's, or your own interest for you to get into arrears with your rent. In cases of genuine difficulty the Council adopts a sympathetic attitude and will try and help wherever possible. If you should find yourself in difficulty in meeting your rent bill, please contact the City Treasurer.

Rent Rebates

If you are living on a small income and find difficulty in paying your rent you may be eligible for a rent rebate. Remember, too, that the level of rebate is affected not just by income but also by the amount you pay and your family circumstances. You can, in fact, enjoy quite a high level of income and still be eligible for a rebate.

It is NOT charity to ask for a rent rebate - it is something you are entitled to as of right and it costs nothing to ask. If, therefore, you are in any doubt as to whether you can get a rent rebate, please enquire at the City Treasury.

3. The tenancy is determinable by four weeks' notice to be given in writing by either side before noon on Mondays.

    In addition, the Council may, following consultation with tenants, vary the terms of tenancy or the services provided after giving four weeks' notice in writing to the tenant.

PART I - COUNCIL'S OBLIGATIONS

1. The tenant has security of tenure and the Council shall not interfere with the tenant's right to the premises except in the circumstances set out earlier under the heading of SECURITY OF TENURE.

2. The Council, as landlord, is responsible for:-

    (a) Keeping in repair the structure and exterior of the dwellinghouse (including drains, gutters and external pipes) but excluding window, door or other glass breakages which are a result of misuse or accidental damage.

    (b) Keeping in repair and proper working order the following installations provided by the Council in the dwellinghouse:-

        (i) for the supply of water, gas and electricity, and for sanitation (including basins, sinks, baths and sanitary conveniences, but not, except as aforesaid, fixtures, fittings and appliances for making use of the supply of water, gas or electricity), except in certain categories of dwellings.

        (ii) for space heating or heating water.

378

(c) Keeping in repair and proper working order where applicable:

  (i) communal amenities where these are provided.

  (ii) the common part of the building (e.g. common entrances, halls, stairways, landings, communal areas).

(d) Decorating the exterior of the property and any other communal parts which are used with other tenants.

The Council does not accept liability for the cost of redecoration of a dwelling following repairs carried out by the Council.

Fences, paving or any part of the premises or the fittings therein, damaged by the tenant or through his negligence, will be repaired by the Council at the cost of the tenant.

The Council will carry out its repairs obligations in accordance with the policy adopted by the Council of repair priorities, subject to availability of resources.

These obligations are subject to the tenant's duty to use the premises in a reasonable manner and if any works of maintenance and repair are needed due to the tenant's failure to act reasonably, then the Council will hold the tenant responsible for any costs which have been incurred.

PART II - TENANT'S OBLIGATIONS

1. THE TENANT SHALL

  (a) Pay the rent and all other charges for the premises regularly and promptly.

  (b) Keep the interior and fixtures of the premises in clean condition, decorated to the satisfaction of the Council and in such condition and state of decoration yield up the same at the end of the tenancy.

  (c) Allow the Council, through their agents or workmen, to enter and inspect the state of repair and cleanliness of any dwelling at all reasonable hours of the day, and to execute any repairs therein.

  (d) Immediately notify the City Engineer of the existence of burst water pipes, or damage to the sanitary fittings, or other defects.

  (e) Pay for items damaged through neglect or carelessness and repaired by the Council.

  (f) Properly cultivate the back garden, and shall not permit any tree or shrub to grow to such a height as, in the opinion of the Council, excludes light and air from the rooms or any of the premises on the Council's estate, or adjoining property.

  (g) If occupying a flat, keep it in a clean orderly condition and wash down weekly the communal hall passages or the stairs and landings to the satisfaction of the Council, and shall not keep more than one domestic pet without the permission of the Council. (Brandon House and Oversteads House - no pets).

2. THE TENANT SHALL NOT

(a) Assign or sublet the premises or any part thereof, without the written consent of the Council and if any person other than the tenant, his wife and his unmarried children, reside on the premises the Council must be informed.

(b) Use the premises other than as a private dwelling, i.e. not for trade or business or any commercial purpose whatever without the consent of the Council.

(c) Without the written consent of the Council:-

(i) Store Calor Gas on the premises, or

(ii) Erect a garage, hut or other structures other than a greenhouse, or

(iii) Make any alterations to the premises or remove any fixtures, or

(iv) Keep poultry, pigeons or animals, or more than two domestic pets, (flat tenants one domestic pet) on the premises.

(d) Park a car, trailer or caravan on a grassed area as this can cause damage (for which you may be liable), and is detrimental to the general appearance of the Estate, but the Council is prepared to consider applications from tenants to construct, at their own expense, and to the satisfaction of the City Engineer, hard standing areas adjacent to their respective dwellings.

Housing Act 1980: Section 5(1) Form No 1

RTB 1.

SECURE TENANT'S NOTICE CLAIMING TO EXERCISE
THE RIGHT TO BUY.

Please read this Notice and the Guidance Notes accompanying it before completing it.

THE NUMBERS BELOW
CORRESPOND TO
THE NUMBERS IN
THE GUIDANCE
NOTES

PART A: TENANTS CLAIMING THE RIGHT TO BUY.

(1) To: . . . . *(Insert **name** of
landlord)*

(2) TAKE NOTICE that . . . .

. . . .

. . . . *(Insert full names
of tenant(s))*

(3) being tenant(s) of the house or flat known as . . . .

. . . . *(Insert address)*

hereby claim to exercise the right to buy it.

(4) Does the tenant named above, or where more than one tenant is named above at least one of them, occupy
the house or flat as his or her only or principal home? . . . . *(Write YES or NO).*

PART B: CONSENT OF ANY JOINT TENANT WHO DOES NOT WISH TO CLAIM THE RIGHT TO BUY.
*This Part is only to be completed by any joint tenant who does not wish to exercise the right to buy with the
joint tenant(s) named in Part A of this Notice, but agrees to them doing so. **The tenancy will come to an
end when the purchase is completed.***

(5) I/We, the undersigned, do not wish to claim the right to buy the house or flat described in Part A of this
Notice and agree to the tenant(s) named in Part A exercising the right to buy and the right to a mortgage.

Signature(s)	Full name(s)	Address(es)	Date

DOE 16334

381

PART C: TENANTS SHARING THE RIGHT TO BUY WITH THEIR SPOUSE AND/OR OTHER MEMBERS OF THEIR FAMILY *This Part is only to be completed where the tenant(s) named in Part A of this Notice require(s) that a spouse and/or other member(s) of the family of the tenant(s) should share the right to buy. Up to three members of a family in addition to the tenant(s) may be named in Part C.*

(6) SPOUSE

Each person named below who—

is the spouse of a tenant named in Part A of this Notice; and

occupies the house or flat as his or her only or principal home

is to share the right to buy—

(Insert full name(s))

(7) OTHER MEMBERS OF THE FAMILY (not including the spouse)

Each person named below who—

is a member of the family of the tenant(s) named in Part A of this Notice; and

occupies the house or flat as his or her only or principal home; and

has lived with the tenant(s) named in Part A throughout the 12 months ending with the giving of this Notice or throughout such shorter period to which the landlord may consent

is to share the right to buy—

(Insert full name(s))

PART D: PERIODS OF SECURE TENANCY (OR OCCUPANCY OF ARMED FORCES ACCOMMODATION) FOR ESTABLISHING THE RIGHT TO BUY AND ENTITLEMENT TO DISCOUNT.

(8) The tenant(s) named in Part A of this Notice spent the following period(s) as tenant(s) (or in accommodation provided for a member of the regular armed forces), as set out in Table 1 below:

382

TABLE 1
To be completed in relation to each tenant named in Part A of this Notice.

A Name of tenant(s) in Part A claiming the right to buy	B Period of tenancy (or occupancy of armed forces accommodation*)		C Name of Landlord (or branch of armed forces*)	D Address of House or Flat*
	FROM	TO		

Periods of occupancy of armed forces accommodation can only be included if the tenant was a member of the regular armed forces on or after 21 December 1979. For armed forces accommodation it is not necessary to fill in column D.

---

⑨ The deceased spouse of a tenant named in Part A of this Notice spent the following period(s) as tenant, as set out in Table 2 below:

TABLE 2
To be completed only where a tenant named in Part A of this Notice became the tenant on the death of his or her spouse. Where exact dates are not known approximate dates should be given.

Name of tenant(s) in Part A claiming the right to buy	Name of deceased spouse	Period of tenancy		Name of Landlord	Address of House or Flat
		FROM	TO		

DOE 16334

(10) ADDITIONAL PERIODS RELEVANT FOR DISCOUNT

PLEASE NOTE — There may be additional periods of tenancy (or periods of occupancy of armed forces accommodation) which have not been listed in Tables 1 or 2 above and which may be relevant for establishing the amount of discount. These are described in the Appendix to this Notice.

PART E: TENANTS' IMPROVEMENTS TO BE DISREGARDED FOR THE PURPOSE OF VALUATION

To be completed only if improvements have been made to the house or flat other than by the landlord.

(11) The following improvements to the house or flat have been made by tenants and should be disregarded for the purpose of valuing the house or flat:

Description of improvement	Name of tenant who made improvement*.

*If an improvement is to be disregarded for valuation purposes, it must have been one carried out by —

    (a)   the present tenant(s); and/or

    (b)   a previous tenant who held the same tenancy; and/or

    (c)   any member of the present tenant's family who was the previous tenant of the house or flat under another tenancy immediately before the present tenancy was granted.

PART F: COURT PROCEEDINGS

(12) Is there a court order in existence as a result of which the tenant(s) of the house or flat is/are obliged to give up possession?

. . . .*(Write YES or NO)*

If YES, give the date specified in the order . . . .

. . . .

PART G: BANKRUPTCY ETC.

(13) Has any person named in Part A or Part C of this Notice—

(i) a bankruptcy petition pending or receiving order in force against him or her?

....*(Write YES or NO)*

If YES, give the full name of each person concerned...

....

(ii) made a composition or arrangement with creditors, the terms of which remain to be fulfilled?

....*(Write YES or NO)*

If YES, give the full name of each person concerned...

....

Is any person named in Part A or Part C of this Notice an undischarged bankrupt?

....*(Write YES or NO)*

If YES, give the full name of each person concerned...

....

PART H: PREVIOUS PURCHASES UNDER THE RIGHT TO BUY

(14) Has any person named in Part A or Part C of this Notice previously purchased a house or flat in England, Wales or Scotland under the **right to buy provisions** of Chapter 1 of Part 1 of the Housing Act 1980 or Part 1 of the Tenants' Rights Etc. (Scotland) Act 1980?

....*(Write YES or NO)*

If YES, give the following particulars:

Name of person(s) who purchased previously	Date of completion of the purchase

DOE 16334

385

PART J: SIGNATURES ETC.

The following is to be signed by each person whose name appears in Part A of this Notice.

 I/We, being the person(s) named in Part A of this Notice, hereby state that to the best of my/our knowledge and belief the particulars given in this Notice are correct and I/We require any person(s) named in Part C of this Notice to share the right to buy.

Signature(s)	Full name(s)	Address(es)	Date

A person who knowingly makes a false statement may be liable to prosecution.

The following is to be signed by each person whose name appears in Part C of this Notice.

(16) I/We, being the person(s) named in Part C of this Notice, agree to share the right to buy with the person(s) named in Part A and hereby state that to the best of my/our knowledge and belief the particulars given in this Notice are correct.

Signature(s)	Full name(s)	Address(es)	Date

A person who knowingly makes a false statement may be liable to prosecution.

PART K: ADDRESS FOR CORRESPONDENCE

If correspondence is to be sent to an address different from any address given in Part J (for example to the address of a solicitor or agent), please give the name and address here:

. . . .

. . . .

PART L: SERVICE OF THE NOTICE

(17) **Insert the address** *of the landlord at which the tenant(s) named in Part A of this Notice propose to serve this Notice.*

. . . .

. . . . *(Address)*

(i) To claim the right to buy the tenant(s) must serve this completed Notice on the landlord.

(ii) Service of this Notice may be effected by post. Where the landlord is a local authority this Notice should be left at or sent by post to the principal office of the authority or any other office of the authority specified by it as one at which it will accept service of this Notice.

(iii) Where the landlord is a housing association this Notice may be left at or sent to its principal office or the office with which the tenant(s) usually deals.

(iv) Where the landlord is the Commission for the New Towns or a new town development corporation, the Housing Corporation or the Development Board for Rural Wales, this Notice may be sent by post to its principal office.

(v) If this Notice is served on or before 3rd April 1981 the date for valuation of the house or flat will be 8th August 1980. If this Notice is served after 3rd April 1981 the date for valuation will be the date of service of this Notice.

(vi) The landlord on whom this Notice is served is required within 4 weeks to serve on the tenant(s) a written Notice either admitting their right to buy or stating why in its opinion they do not have the right to buy. This period of 4 weeks is extended to 8 weeks where the claim of the tenant(s) to exercise the right to buy is dependent on any period with any landlord other than the landlord on which this Notice is served.

(vii) Where this Notice has been served on the landlord it may be withdrawn at any time by notice in writing served on the landlord.

DOE 16334

387

APPENDIX TO THE NOTICE

Additional periods of tenancy (or periods of occupancy of armed forces accommodation) which may be relevant to the amount of discount are —

(a) any period(s) during which any person named in Part A or Part C of this Notice or his or her spouse or deceased spouse was either a secure tenant or the spouse of a secure tenant; or

(b) any period(s) during which any person named in Part A or Part C of this Notice occupied accommodation provided for that person as a member of the regular armed forces or that person's spouse occupied accommodation so provided for that spouse, as long as that person or that person's spouse was a member of the regular armed forces on or after 21 December 1979.

If a tenant wishes any such period(s) to be taken into account and that period has not been included already in either Table 1 or Table 2 of Part D the tenant is advised to provide the landlord with details in writing.

RTB 4.

NOTICE CLAIMING THE RIGHT TO A MORTGAGE

Please read this Notice, and the Guidance Notes accompanying it, before completing it. After completing it, you should keep a copy of the Notice for your own use, and make a note on it of the date on which the Notice was served on the lender.

This form is divided into two Sections. **All** *those sharing the Right to Buy should complete and* **sign Section 1.**

However, a **separate** *copy of* **Section 2** *(Particulars of Income) should be completed by* **each person** *signing Section 1 if they have income of their own which they want taken into account in calculating their mortgage entitlement.*

If there is not enough space in any part of the Notice, continue on a separate sheet and attach it to the Notice.

It is the intention of the
—— Council to verify the income
details supplied by you at
items (6), (7) and (8) on the
form RTB4. Please sign
opposite your agreement to the
check being made.

IMPORTANT: There is a time limit for service of this Notice. In most cases this means that you could lose your right to a mortgage if you do not serve this Notice within 3 months of receiving it.

SECTION 1

All those sharing the Right to Buy should complete and sign Section 1.

Address of house or flat ....

being purchased   ....

....

....

Is the house or flat owned by a housing association...................................*(Write YES or NO)*

If you have written 'YES', insert here the name and address of the **housing association**;otherwise leave blank.

Name ....

Address..

....

....

DOE 16337

389

SECTION 1 continued

(1)

If you are a **housing association** tenant, insert here **The Housing Corporation**

If you are a tenant of **any other body** insert here the name of your **landlord.**

To _____ _(lender)_

TAKE NOTICE that the persons whose signatures appear at the end of this section hereby claim to exercise the right to a mortgage.

(2) Do you intend to apply for an option mortgage?.....................................*(Write YES or NO)*

(3) Do you intend to apply for assistance under the
Home Purchase Assistance Scheme?..*(Write YES or NO)*

---

(4) PRINCIPAL INCOME: *To be completed only where there is more than one person sharing the Right to Buy, and more than one of those persons has income of their own:-*

The name of the person whose income the lender is required to treat as the **principal income** for the purposes of calculating the mortgage entitlement is

....*(Insert full name)*

SIGNATURES: *To be completed and signed by each person sharing the Right to Buy*

TABLE A

Signature(s)	Full name(s)	Address(es)	Date

DOE 16337

390

SECTION 2: PARTICULARS OF INCOME

(5) *A separate copy of Section 2 should be completed by* **each person** *signing Section 1 if they have income of their own which they want taken into account in calculating their mortgage entitlement.*

In completing details of your income and commitments you should give actual figures if available. Estimates can, however, be accepted by the lender.

Address of house or flat ....

being purchased ....

....

Name..*(Insert your full name)*

---

(6) PART A: INCOME FROM EMPLOYMENT

Complete this Part if you have income from employment (including part-time employment) which is not either casual or temporary employment.

Name,
and Address ....

of employer ....

....

Position held ....

(i) Give details of your current pay (before tax or other deductions) expressed as an annual amount:-

Basic Earnings

| £ | per year |

Overtime

| £ | per year |

Bonus

| £ | per year |

Commission

| £ | per year |

Tips, gratuities or
allowances (other than
expense allowance).

| £ | per year |

TOTAL AMOUNT

| £ | per year |

(ii) If you consider that the total amount shown above does not fairly represent your current annual pay, please say why and state such amount as does:-

....

....

....

DOE 16337

SECTION 2 continued

(7) PART B: INCOME FROM A BUSINESS

Complete this part if you have income from a business (including any trade, profession or vocation carried on by a self employed person).

Name ....

and Address ....

of Business ....

Type of Business ....

Name and Address of accountant, if any ....

....

Your annual income from the business will be assessed on the basis of the latest available information as to the current annual net profit of the business (or your share of the net profit) before deduction of tax. If later information becomes available to you after you have served this Notice, you may make it available to your lender.

Insert here the amount of your current
annual net profit, or share of the current
annual net profit, before deductions of tax.

£ _____

DOE 16337

8 PART C: OTHER INCOME

Complete this part if you have any other income.

Give the following details in respect of each source of income.

Source of income (for example retirement pension, investments)	Current income (before tax or other deductions) expressed as an annual amount.
	£ per year

9 PART D: COMMITMENTS

Complete this Part if you are liable to make any of the following payments and those payments are likely to continue for more than 18 months.

	Annual amounts currently payable
(a) Maintenance payments to a dependent child under the age of 16	£ per year
(b) Maintenance payments to your husband or wife or your former husband or wife	£ per year
(c) Payments under a loan agreement	£ per year
(d) Payments under a hire purchase agreement	£ per year
(e) Payments under any other credit agreements	£ per year
(f) Payments under a court order	£ per year

DOE 16337

393

(10) PART E: DECLARATION

Date of birth..*(Insert date)*

You are required to give your date of birth because your age at the date of serving your Notice Claiming to Exercise the Right to Buy determines the multiplier for calculating your mortgage entitlement.

I hereby state that to the best of my knowledge and belief the particulars given in this Notice are correct.

Signature ....

Full name...

Date ....

A person who knowingly makes a false statement may be liable to prosecution.

SERVICE OF THE NOTICE

Insert here the address of your lender on whom you will be serving this
Notice ....
....
....

(i)   This Notice may be served by post.

(ii)   Where the **lender** is a **local authority** this Notice should be left at or sent by post to the principal office of the authority or any other office of the authority which it has specified as one at which it will accept service of this Notice.

(iii)   Where the **lender** is the **Housing Corporation** this Notice should be left at or sent by post to:-

        The Housing Corporation
        149 Tottenham Court Road
        LONDON
        W1P OBN

(iv)   Where the **lender** is the **Commission for the New Towns** or a **New Town Development Corporation** or the **Development Board for Rural Wales,** this Notice may be sent by post to its principal office.

The lender is required by Section 12(4) of the Housing Act 1980 to serve as soon as practicable after the service of this Notice a notice stating the amount of the mortgage to which you are entitled, how that amount has been arrived at and the provisions which, in its opinion, should be contained in the mortgage deed.

DOE 16337

394

NOTICE OF A PROTECTED SHORTHOLD TENANCY
— FIRST REVISION

DWELLINGS WITHIN ENGLAND AND WALES
NOT IN GREATER LONDON

(The Landlord must give this to the tenant before a protected shorthold tenancy is granted. It does not commit the tenant to take the tenancy).

To

IMPORTANT — PLEASE READ THIS NOTICE CAREFULLY. IF THERE IS ANYTHING YOU DO NOT UNDERSTAND YOU SHOULD GET ADVICE (FOR EXAMPLE, FROM A SOLICITOR OR A CITIZEN'S ADVICE BUREAU) BEFORE YOU AGREE TO TAKE A SHORTHOLD TENANCY.

N.B. This document is important: keep it in a safe place.

---

1.   You are proposing to take a tenancy of the dwelling known as   , Southwick, Sunderland in the County of Tyne and Wear from the First day of June 1982 to the First day of June 1983.

2.   This notice is to tell you that your tenancy is to be protected shorthold tenancy. Under shorthold, provided you keep the terms of the tenancy, you are entitled to remain in the dwelling for the fixed period agreed at the start of the tenancy. At the end of this period the landlord has the right to repossession if he wants. Full details about shorthold are given in the Department of Environment and Welsh Office booklet 'Shorthold Tenancies First Revision' obtainable free from Rent Officers, Council Offices and housing aid centres. You are advised to read this booklet before you agree to take a shorthold tenancy.

3.   The rent for this tenancy is the rent that we have agreed, and has not been registered by the Rent Officer. But this does not affect your right as tenant or the Company's right as landlord to apply at any time to the Rent Officer for the registration of a fair rent. This is fully explained in the booklet 'Shorthold Tenancies First Revision.'

4.　　This notice is given to you on the   day of
1982

Signed ....

(on behalf of)   .

of   ,

, .

SPECIAL NOTE FOR EXISTING TENANTS

IF YOU ARE ALREADY A PROTECTED OR STATUTORY
TENANT UNDER THE RENT ACT 1977 YOUR PRESENT
TENANCY CANNOT LAWFULLY BE CONVERTED INTO A
SHORTHOLD. BUT SHOULD YOU GIVE IT UP AND TAKE A
SHORTHOLD TENANCY IN SOME OTHER ACCOMMODATION,
INCLUDING ANOTHER FLAT IN THE SAME BUILDING, YOU
WILL ALMOST CERTAINLY HAVE LESS SECURITY UNDER
SHORTHOLD THAN UNDER YOUR EXISTING TENANCY.

APPLICATION FOR REGISTRATION OF FAIR RENT

(for use except in certain special cases set out in Note 1
which should be read carefully before completing this form)

Please read all the notes carefully

To the Rent Officer

I/We † apply for registration of a rent for the premises named in paragraph 1 below, and submit the following particulars of the premises and the tenancy.

THE PARTICULARS — *(Please write in BLOCK LETTERS or type and complete in duplicate ticking boxes as appropriate.*

Where necessary details may be written on a separate sheet and attached to the form)

1   Address of premises

2   Name of tenant (and address if different from 1 above)

3   Name and address of landlord

4   (a) Description of premises — (including the number of rooms and, if part only of a building, on which floor or floors) ....
....

(b) Is a garage or other separate building or land included in the tenancy?   YES ☐   NO ☐

If YES give details ....

(c) Does the tenant share any accommodation —

(i) with the landlord?   YES ☐   NO ☐   (ii) with another tenant?   YES ☐   NO ☐

If YES give details ....   If YES give details: ....
....

5   State the rent which the applicant seeks to have registered (Exclusive of Rates) See Note 2 £........................per..................

6   Are any services provided by the landlord or superior landlord?   YES ☐   NO ☐

If YES give details ....

7   If the rent specified in 5 above includes any sum payable for services, state what amount, if any, the applicant claims to represent their value   £.........................per...

NB Where the application is made by the landlord he must attach details of the expenditure involved in providing such services: see Note 3

8   Is any furniture provided by the landlord or superior landlord?   YES ☐   NO ☐

If YES give details, or if there is an inventory, attach a copy ....

9   Terms of the tenancy. *(If a copy of the agreement is available it should be attached. It will be returned without delay).*

(a) Term and date of commencement: .... from ....

(b) Rent now payable: £........................per ....

(c) Repairing obligations (i) of landlord ....

(ii) of tenant ....

(d) Other terms: ....

10 (a) Are the premises
separately rated?   YES ☐   NO ☐   (b) Are the rates paid by the
landlord or a superior
landlord?   YES ☐   NO ☐

11 Is the landlord a registered housing association, or housing trust, or the Housing Corporation?   YES ☐   NO ☐

* *Form No5 in the Rent Act 1977 (Forms etc) Regulations 1980*
† *Delete the word which does not apply*

12 Has the Rent Officer previously registered or confirmed a fair rent for the premises?   YES ☐   NO ☐

---

13 1. If this application is made within 2 years* of the date on which a previous registration or confirmation took effect and 2 below does not apply, please state the grounds of application: ....

2. The grounds need not be stated if the application is made

    a — jointly by the landlord and tenant at any time; or

    b — by the landlord alone within the last 3 months of the period of 2 years* from the date on which the previous registration or confirmation took effect; or

    c — by the landlord or tenant at any time if the previous rent was registered by a Rent Tribunal.

*Three years if the previous rent was determined or confirmed by the Rent Officer and his determination was registered, or his confirmation was noted in the Register, before 28 November 1980.

---

14 Has any change in the state of the premises occurred during the present tenancy (see note 4) because of —

(a) failure by the tenant (including a former tenant under the present tenancy) to comply with the terms of the tenancy;   YES ☐   NO ☐

If YES give details ....

(b) improvements, including replacement of any fixtures or fittings, carried out by the tenant (including a former tenant under the present tenancy) otherwise than under the terms of the tenancy;   YES ☐   NO ☐

If YES give details ....

(c) improvements by the tenant (including a former tenant under the present tenancy) to any furniture provided for use under the tenancy, or any deterioration in the condition of any such furniture due to ill treatment by the tenant, any person residing or lodging with him or any sub-tenant of his?   YES ☐   NO ☐

If YES give details ....

---

15 The following question is not relevant to rent registration but an answer would be appreciated.

Is the tenancy a protected shorthold tenancy?   YES ☐   NO ☐

Signed ....   Signed ....
   (landlord/landlord's agent) †   (tenant/tenant's agent) †

                               Date .... 19 ......

In a joint application (see note 5) by landlord and tenant, both parties should sign. In an application by joint tenants, they should each sign, unless one signs as an agent for the rest with their agreement, in which case he should state that he is acting as agent.

If signed by agent, name and address of agent.
(For landlord ....
(
(....
(
(For tenant ....
....

NOTES

1. This form should NOT be used for —

(a) a statutory tenancy which will arise, or has arisen, at the end of a long tenancy under Part I of the Landlord and Tenant Act 1954 (use form No 6), or

(b) a statutory tenancy which has arisen under the Rent (Agriculture) Act 1976 (use form No 7) or

(c) an application supported by a certificate of fair rent (use form No 8).

2. The Rent Officer cannot deal with the application unless item 5 has been completed (ie the rent is specified by the applicant).

3. If the rent includes an element for services and the application is made by the landlord, the Rent Officer cannot deal with the application unless details of the expenditure incurred on services are provided.

4. In the case of a tenancy which has been converted from a controlled tenancy to a regulated tenancy, "present tenancy" means the tenancy both while it was controlled and since it became regulated.

5. Where a joint application is made by both landlord and tenant, there is no right to have the matter referred to a Rent Assessment Committee if the Rent Officer determines without further consultation that the rent specified in the application is a fair rent.

---

† Delete the words which do not apply

Printed for HMSO by Gait Bayliss Rotary Ltd. Dd 8221165 1500M 11/80

RENT ACT 1977
Section 45(2)
(as amended)

Notice of Increase of Rent

under Regulated Tenancy where a Fair Rent has been Registered
by the Rent Officer on or after 28 November 1980.
(See Notes 1 to 3)

Please read the Notes carefully and keep this Form.

Date..................................

To ....

tenant of ....

1. A rent of £   per   (exclusive of rates) has been [registered by the Rent Officer] [determined by a Rent Assessment Committee] for the above premises and takes effect from   19

2. Unless —
    (a) a different rent is registered by the Rent Officer, or determined by a Rent Assessment Committee (*see Note 8*), OR
    (b) the Rent Officer agrees to cancel the registration (*see Note 9*), OR
    (c) the Rent is registered as variable (*see Note 4*)

(See Note 5)   the **maximum rent** (exclusive of rates) you can be charged during the first year from the date in paragraph 1 is

£	per

This is calculated as follows:—

New registered rent

£	per

+

(See Note 6)   Previous rent limit

£	per

+

Service element (if any)

£	per

=

£	per

÷ 2

=

£	per

3. After the end of the first year from the date in paragraph 1 the maximum rent (unless 2(a), (b) or (c) apply) is the full registered rent as shown in 1 above of

£	per

4. **I hereby give you notice** that your rent (exclusive of rates) will be increased as follows:—

Present

£	per

New rent from   19   *

£	per

New rent from   19

£	per

If two increases are shown above I am not obliged to remind you when the second increase becomes payable.

(The date at * must not be earlier than the date in paragraph 1 above nor four weeks before the date of service of this notice.)

Cross out words in square brackets if they do not apply.

CONTINUED OVERLEAF

Cat.No. RM 34   SHAW & SONS LTD., Shaws House, London, SE 26 5AE   LS (1112) (5)

[It is noted in the Rent Register that rates in respect of the above premises are borne by me or a superior landlord. I am entitled to add the amount for rates to the rent and to pass on to you future increases in rates without serving a Notice of Increase.] *(Cross out this paragraph if the tenant pays rates)*

Signature of [landlord] [landlord's agent] .... [on behalf of]

[Name of landlord if notice served by agent ....]

Address of landlord ....

[Name and address of agent ....]

NOTES

Use of notice
1. This notice is only for use for increases which are to take effect when the tenancy is a statutory tenancy. A statutory tenancy comes into being when a tenancy agreed between the landlord and tenant (known as a contractual tenancy) has come to an end and the tenant has security of tenure under the Rent Act 1977.

2. The notice can be served while there is still a contractual tenancy. If the contractual tenancy can be terminated before the (earliest) date in paragraph 4, this notice can be used instead of a notice to quit to turn the contractual tenancy into a statutory tenancy from that date.

Explanatory booklet
3. The Department of the Environment booklet 'Regulated Tenancies' explains in more detail than these Notes how the fair rent system works and the rights and duties of landlords and tenants under the Rent Act. It is available free from Rent Officers, and Citizens' Advice Bureaux, and you are advised to obtain a copy.

Limitation of rent increases
4. The rent shown in paragraph 1 of the notice may not be exceeded unless the rent is registered as varaiable. It will only be registered as variable if the terms of the tenancy provide for the rent to be varied according to the cost of services or works of maintenance and repair carried out by the landlord or superior landlord and the Rent Officer considers the terms reasonable. Secondly, the landlord may only increase the rent during the first year from the date in paragraph 1 of the notice to the extent allowed under the provisions for the phasing of increases.

How phasing works
5. During the first year from the date in paragraph 1 of the Notice the landlord is permitted to charge half of the increase, except that where there is a service element he may charge this in full at once. After the end of the first year he can charge the full registered rent shown in paragraph 1.

Previous rent limit
6. The amount of increase permitted has to be worked out by taking as a starting point the previous rent limit. The previous rent limit is the amount the landlord was permitted by the Rent Act to charge immediately before the Rent Officer registered the rent (whether or not there has been an appeal to a Rent Assessment Committee). (Rates are disregarded for this purpose). The landlord may not actually have been charging this amount.

Service element
7. The service element is the increase in the rent permitted on account of services provided by the landlord or a superior landlord. If there is a service element it has to be recorded in the Rent Officer's register.

Re-registration
8. No application for a new registration may be made during the 2 years from the date in paragraph 1 of the notice unless either—
    (a) it is made by the landlord and the tenant acting together, or
    (b) there has been such a change in the circumstances taken into account when the rent was registered (eg the making of an improvement to the premises) as to make the registered rent no longer a fair rent.

But the landlord may apply 3 months in advance for a new registration to take effect after the end of the 2 year period.

Cancellation
9. As long as there is a regulated tenancy an application to the Rent Officer to cancel the registration can only be made jointly by landlord and tenant.

Help with rent and rates
10. If the tenant has difficulty in paying his rent or rates he should apply to the local Council Offices for details of the rent allowance and rate rebate schemes. The Council will also advise if he may be better off receiving Supplementary Benefit from the Department of Health and Social Security.

ORIGINATING APPLICATION TO AN INDUSTRIAL TRIBUNAL

IMPORTANT: DO NOT FILL IN THIS FORM UNTIL YOU
HAVE READ THE NOTES FOR GUIDANCE.
THEN COMPLETE ITEMS 1, 2,4 AND 12
AND ALL OTHER ITEMS RELEVANT TO YOUR CASE,
AND SEND THE FORM TO THE FOLLOWING ADDRESS

For Official Use Only	
Case Number	

To   THE SECRETARY OF THE TRIBUNALS
CENTRAL OFFICE OF THE INDUSTRIAL TRIBUNALS (ENGLAND AND WALES)
93 EBURY BRIDGE ROAD, LONDON SW1W 8RE   Telephone: 01 730 9161

1   I hereby apply for a decision of a Tribunal on the following question.   **(STATE HERE THE QUESTION TO
BE DECIDED BY A TRIBUNAL. EXPLAIN THE GROUNDS OVERLEAF).**

....

2   My name is (Mr/Mrs/Miss   Surname in block capitals first):—

....

My address is:— ....

....

.... Telephone No. ....

My date of birth is ....

3   If a representative has agreed to act for you in this case please give his or her name and address below
and note that further communications will be sent to your representative and not to you   (See Note 4)

Name of Representative:— ....

Address:— ....

.... Telephone No. ....

4   (a) Name of respondent(s) (in block capitals) ie the employer, person or body against whom a decision is
sought (See Note 3)

....

Address(es) ....

.... Telephone No. ....

(b) Respondent's relationship to you for the purpose of the application (eg employer, trade union,

employment agency, employer recognising the union making application, etc). ....

....

5   Place of employment to which this application relates, or
place where act complained about took place.

....

6   My occupation or position held / applied for, or other relationship to the respondent named above (eg user
of a service supplied in relation to employment).

....

7   Dates employment began .... and (if appropriate) ended ....

8   (a) Basic wages / salary ....

(b) Average take home pay ....

9   Other remuneration or benefits ....

10   Normal basic weekly hours of work ....

11   (In an application under the Sex Discrimination Act or the Race Relations Act)
Date on which action complained of took place or first came to my knowledge ....

IT 1 (Revised September 1979)   *Please continue overleaf*

12   You are required to set out the grounds for your application below, giving full particulars of them.

13   If you wish to state what in your opinion was the reason for your dismissal, please do so here.

14   If the Tribunal decides that you were unfairly dismissed, please state which of the following you would prefer: reinstatement, re-engagement or compensation. (Before answering this question please consult the leaflet "Dismissal — Employees Rights", or, "Unfairly Dismissed?".

Signature .... Date ....

FOR OFFICIAL USE ONLY	Received at COIT	Code	ROIT	Inits

402

NORTH TYNESIDE METROPOLITAN BOROUGH COUNCIL

LOCAL DISCIPLINARY PROCEDURE FOR OFFICERS

1. The Chief Officer of each department shall be responsible for the management and discipline of his department. This responsibility may, if the circumstances demand, be delegated to other officers in the department who may issue verbal warnings to the officers concerned depending on the circumstances. Offences warranting more serious consideration shall be referred to the Chief Officer.

2. Where an officer's work, conduct or omission are such as to warrant disciplinary action, the Chief Officer will give a warning to the officer concerned.

3. Warnings given by Chief Officers shall be given or confirmed in writing, and will give the nature of the complaint and any implication therefrom, and the fact that the officer has been notified of the warning.

4. The further commission of a similar act, or of a subsequent but different offence, may result in a further written warning, which may be a final warning according to the circumstances. The officer's attention must be drawn to the issue of a final warning, and he will be informed that he may ask his trade union/association official to be formally notified. Any final warning will be immediately confirmed in writing as such and a copy shall be sent to the Chief Personnel Officer.

5. Certain types of gross misconduct may lead to instant dismissal, and in each case the provisions of paragraphs 8 and 9 will apply.

6. Should any disciplinary decision be reconsidered and effectively withdrawn any written reference will be expunged from the officer's file and the officer notified accordingly.

7. The Chief Personnel Officer and any of the Chief Officers in consultation may suspend any member of staff for gross misconduct and such action shall be reported to the Personnel Sub-Committee at an appropriate time.

8. Where on grounds related to discipline or efficiency, it is proposed either:

    (i) by an appropriate committee of the employing authority, or
    (ii) by the Chief Personnel Officer and a Chief Officer acting under delegated powers

    to relegate or dismiss an officer then such proposal when formulated shall be conveyed to the officer concerned by letter over the signature of the Chief Personnel Officer stating the grounds on which the proposed action is based.

9. Upon receipt of such a communication, the officer concerned may appeal within ten working days, either individually or through his association or trade union, to the appropriate Committee of the Council.

10. He shall have the right of appearing before such a Committee (with or without a representative of his association or trade union or other representative of his choice).

11. This procedure does not apply to the notice given:

    (i) on termination of employment for which an employee has been specifically engaged;
    (ii) in the event of redundancy;
    (iii) where less than six months probationary service has been completed and dismissal arises from unsuitability for confirmation of appointment.

APPEALS COMMITTEE PROCEDURE

12. The Appeals Committee shall be constituted from members of the Council who are not members of the Committee which decided the matter in the first place, in accordance with Minute 78 of the Personnel Sub-Committee of 3rd June, 1974.

13. The officer shall be given notice in writing at least seven days in advance of the time and place of the hearing, and shall be allowed to be represented by his Trade Union representative or some other person of his choice and shall be enabled to call witnesses and produce documents relevant to his defence at the hearing.

14. The Council's representative(s) will put their case in the presence of the appellant and his representative and may call witnesses.

15. The appellant (or his representative) will have the opportunity to ask questions of the Council's representative on the evidence given by him and any witnesses whom he may call.

16. The members of the Appeals Committee will have the opportunity to ask questions of the Council's representative on the evidence given by him and any witnesses whom he may call.

17. The appellant (or his representative) will put his case in the presence of the Council's representative and call such witnesses as he wishes.

18. The Council's representative will have the opportunity to ask questions of the appellant and his witnesses.

19. The Committee will have the opportunity to ask questions of the appellant and his witnesses.

20. The Council's representative and the appellant (or his representative) will have the opportunity to sum up their case if they so wish. If they both opt to sum up, the appellant or his representative shall speak last.

21. The Council's representative and the appellant and his representative and witnesses shall withdraw.

22. The Committee with the officer appointed as Secretary to the Committee shall deliberate in private only recalling the Council's representative, the appellant, or any of the witnesses, to clear points of uncertainty on evidence already given. If recall is necessary both parties are to return.

23. The Appeals Committee has delegated powers to confirm, amend or reject the disciplinary action. The decision of the Appeals Committee shall be reported to the Council.

24. The above provisions do not exclude the present right of an officer's Union/Association making representation to the Authority at any stage in these proceedings.

This procedure has been agreed between representatives of the Council on the one hand, and of the Staff on the other. Both parties accept that this agreement is not intended to constitute a legally enforceable agreement between them. It is further agreed that the parties to the agreement will use their best endeavours to ensure that the spirit and intention of this agreement is honoured at all times.

NORTH TYNESIDE METROPOLITAN BOROUGH COUNCIL

LOCAL DISCIPLINARY PROCEDURE FOR MANUAL WORKERS

1. Where an employee's work, conduct or omission are such as to warrant disciplinary action, the appropriate supervisor or officer shall give a warning to the employee.

2. This may be done orally or in writing depending on the circumstances. A written warning will give the nature of the complaint and any implication therefrom, and the fact that the employee has been notified of the warning. A record will be kept of all warnings, and the fact that a warning has been given will be notified to the employee's Trade Union representative.

3. The further commission of a similar act, or of a subsequent but different offence, may result in a further warning, which may be a final warning according to the circumstances. The employee's attention must be drawn to the issue of a final warning, and he must be informed that he may ask his Trade Union official to be formally notified. Any final warning must be confirmed in writing as soon as possible and a copy shall be sent to the Chief Personnel Officer.

4. Certain types of gross misconduct may lead to instant dismissal.

5. Should any disciplinary action be reconsidered and effectively withdrawn, any written reference shall be expunged from the employee's file and the employee notified accordingly.

6. The Chief Personnel Officer and any of the several Chief Officers, (or other senior nominated officer) in consultation may dismiss an employee in cases where previous warnings have been ineffective, or for gross misconduct. Where the possibility of serious disciplinary action arises (including dismissal), the employee shall be interviewed by the Officer concerned and told why his services are considered unsatisfactory. The employee shall be given adequate opportunity to explain or defend himself. In particular he has the right to be accompanied during the interview by his Trade Union or other representative. This interview shall be arranged after consultation with the Chief Personnel Officer.

7. Dismissal or other serious disciplinary action shall be confirmed by letter (using recorded delivery when otherwise unavoidable) under the signature of the Chief Personnel Officer. This letter shall state the grounds for the action taken and confirm that the employee may appeal in the appropriate way to the Appeals Committee where he may appear in person and/or with a representative.

8. The Contract of Employment may be suspended either to enable investigations to be made where the possibility of dismissal may arise or where there are grounds for doubt as to the suitability of the employee to continue at work pending criminal investigations or procedure or as an alternative to dismissal. The procedure recommended in the event of dismissal shall also apply to an employee thus suspended. During a period of suspension the employee shall be paid an allowance of not less than half pay. Except where suspension has been used as an alternative to dismissal.

   (a)   in the event of it being adjudged that the employee was not blameworthy, the suspension shall be terminated and the employee shall receive all monies to which he would have been entitled but for the suspension;

   (b)   if the employee is adjudged blameworthy, but is allowed to continue in employment there is discretion as to whether to make up the suspension allowance to equal the whole or part of wages withheld during the period of suspension;

   (c)   if the employee is dismissed, he shall not be entitled to wages other than the sum (if any) due up to the date of suspension, but he shall be allowed to retain any sum already paid to him as suspension allowance during the period of suspension.

9. If at any time in this procedure the employee wishes to exercise his right of appeal against any form of disciplinary action taken against him, he must do so within ten working days of receipt of the warning or notification of termination of employment on disciplinary grounds, or written advice of other disciplinary action.

10. Normally, no disciplinary action shall be taken against a shop steward until the circumstances of the case have been discussed with a full-time official of the union concerned.

11. This procedure does not apply to notice given:

   (i)   on termination of employment for which an employee has been specifically engaged;
   (ii)   in the event of redundancy;
   (iii)   where less than six months probationary service has been completed and dismissal arises from unsuitability for confirmation of appointment.

APPEALS AGAINST DISCIPLINARY ACTION

12. The Appeals Committee shall be constituted from among members who are not members of the employing committee which may have decided the issue in the first place in accordance with Minute 78 of the proceedings of the Personnel Sub-Committee of 3rd June 1974.

13. The employee shall be given notice in writing at least seven days in advance of the time and place of the hearing and shall be allowed to be represented by his Trade Union representative, or some other persons of his choice and shall be enabled to call witnesses and produce documents relevant to his defence at the hearing.

14. The Local Authority's representative(s) shall put the case in the presence of the appellant and his representative and may call witnesses.

15. The appellant (or his representative) shall have the opportunity to ask questions of the Local Authority's representative on the evidence given by him and any witnesses he may call.

16. The members of the Appeals Committee shall have the opportunity to ask questions of the Local Authority's representative and witnesses.

17. The appellant (or his representative) shall put his case in the presence of the Local Authority's representative and shall call such witnesses as he wishes.

18. The Local Authority's representative shall have the opportunity to ask questions of the appellant and his witnesses.

19. The Committee shall have the opportunity to ask questions of the appellant and his witnesses.

20. The Local Authority's representative and the appellant (or his representative) shall have the opportunity to sum up their case if they so wish. If they both opt to sum up, the appellant or his representative shall speak last.

21. The Local Authority's representative and the appellant and his representative and witnesses shall withdraw.

22. The Committee with the officer appointed as Secretary to the Committee shall deliberate in private only recalling the Local Authority's representative and the appellant to clear points of uncertainty on evidence already given. If recall is necessary both parties are to return notwithstanding only one is concerned with the point giving rise to doubt.

23. The Committee shall announce the decision to the parties personally or in writing as they may determine.

24. The Appeals Committee has delegated powers to confirm, amend or reject the disciplinary action. The decision of the Appeals Committee shall be reported to the Council.

This procedure has been agreed between representatives of the Council on the one hand, and of employees on the other. Both parties accept that this agreement is not intended to constitute a legally enforceable agreement between them. It is further agreed that the parties to the agreement will use their best endeavours to ensure that the spirit and intention of this agreement is honoured at all times.

NORTH TYNESIDE METROPOLITAN BOROUGH COUNCIL
LOCAL GRIEVANCE PROCEDURE
FOR MANUAL WORKERS

1. Each employee shall be informed that a grievance on relevant subjects must be discussed with his foreman/supervisor.

2. The foreman/supervisor shall reply orally as soon as possible and in any case within three working days.

3. If the complainant is dissatisfied with the reply he shall be allowed to see his shop steward/trade union representative, who may then take up the matter with the foreman/supervisor.

4. Both initial steps shall be kept at the foreman/supervisor level or where this is impracticable another officer should be specified in the agreement by name or by reference to his post.

5. If the employee continues to be aggrieved he or his representative shall submit the grievance to the foreman/supervisor for transmission to the head of department (or other senior nominated officer). The grievance shall be put in writing on a form to be provided and available for the purpose. The employee or his representative, should keep at least one copy.

6. The head of department (or other senior nominated officer) shall within seven working days, arrange a meeting with the interested parties, and if desired, with a full time union official. This meeting shall be arranged after consultation with the Chief Personnel Officer.

7. As soon as possible after this meeting, the head of department shall confirm the decision in writing with a copy to the Chief Personnel Officer.

8. If the complaint is not satisfactorily resolved at this stage, either side **may** refer the matter to the Joint Consultative Committee for further consideration and recommendation to the Personnel Sub-Committee.

9. Thereafter further procedure where appropriate shall lie with the existing conciliation machinery, of which the Personnel Sub-Committee shall be the first stage.

10. This procedure does not exclude the following possibilities:

    (i) that a man and his representative approach the foreman in the first instance.
    (ii) that a man be represented or be without representation.
    (iii) that a group of employees be represented by a trade union official or by a committee; or that the procedure shall be available to a group of employees sharing a grievance.

The parties referred to may on occasion and by mutual agreement modify the time limit referred to in this grievance procedure.

This procedure has been agreed between representatives of the Council on the one hand, and of employees on the other. Both parties accept that this agreement is not intended to constitute a legally enforceable agreement between them. It is further agreed that the parties to the agreement will use their best endeavours to ensure that the spirit and intention of this agreement is honoured at all times.

413

416